CHILDREN'S LANGUAGE
AND THE LANGUAGE ARTS

McGRAW-HILL BOOK COMPANY

New York St. Louis San Francisco Auckland Bogotá Hamburg
Johannesburg London Madrid Mexico Montreal New Delhi
Panama Paris São Paulo Singapore Sydney Tokyo Toronto

CAROL J. FISHER
University of Georgia

C. ANN TERRY
University of Houston
Clear Lake City

Children's Language and the Language Arts

SECOND EDITION

Library of Congress Cataloging in Publication Data

Fisher, Carol J.
    Children's language and the language arts.

    Includes bibliographical references and index.
    1. Language arts (Elementary) 2. Children—
Language. I. Terry, C. Ann. II. Title.
LB1576.F44   1982   372.6   81-14302
ISBN 0-07-021108-6   AACR2

CHILDREN'S LANGUAGE
AND THE LANGUAGE ARTS

1234567890 DODO 898765432

ISBN 0-07-021108-6

See Acknowledgments on pages 353–355.
Copyrights included on this page by reference.

This book was set in Primer by University Graphics, Inc.
The editors were Phillip A. Butcher and Susan Gamer;
the designer was Anne Canevari Green;
the production supervisor was Diane Renda.
New drawings were done by ECL Art Associates, Inc.
R. R. Donnelley & Sons Company was printer and binder.

Contents

Preface

The language arts program that is presented in *Children's Language and the Language Arts* is based directly on two theories: Piaget's views of learning and the psycholinguistic view of language acquisition and development. Throughout this text, language and intellectual development are related to learning activities. The more knowledgeable teachers are about how children learn and how language develops, the more able they are to use experiences that offer extensive learning opportunities to develop a stronger language arts program. The teacher becomes a decision maker in curriculum planning rather than a dispenser of knowledge and isolated activities which may be meaningless. Selected experiences, based on an understanding of children's abilities and needs at particular stages of development, are given as examples of appropriate language arts activities in both elementary and middle schools. Instead of presenting extensive lists of activities that are often ends in themselves instead of means to an end, this text suggests those which can be extended and molded into a progression that ultimately leads to established learning objectives.

Actual samples of students' oral and written language are included—not only for illustrative purposes, but to develop proficiency in diagnosing and evaluating the learning needs of children. For example, stories written by students of different ages are included for practice in writing comments focused on their positive qualities or for analyzing various mechanical aspects. Samples of children's manuscript and cursive handwriting are shown for practice in diagnosis of their strengths and weaknesses. This text, then, incorporates students' work for practice activities as well as for illustration.

There are three principal parts to *Children's Language and the Language Arts*. Part One, Perspectives: Language Arts, Language, and Learning, presents the theoretical background for the rest of the book. The introductory chapter, Chapter 1, illustrates in words and pictures the rich classroom environment and the types of activities that should be the core of the language arts program. This overview is followed by a chapter on learning theory (Chapter 2), a descriptive chapter on the English language and linguistic variations (Chapter 3), and a chapter on the acquisition of language (Chapter 4).

Part Two, Language Skills: Substance and Strategies, includes chapters on all the oral and written skills of communication. Chapter 5 discusses the development of vocabulary; various approaches to grammar are presented in Chapter 6. Listening, oral discussion, and dramatization receive special attention in Chapters 7, 8, and 9 respectively. An extensive exploration of children's writing is given in Chapter 10. The discussion of children's writing ranges from the recording of direct observations and experiences to writing imaginative stories and poetry. Chapter 11, the final chapter in Part Two, suggests methods of teaching the various supportive writing skills—capitalization, punctuation, spelling, and handwriting.

Part Three, Components: A Comprehensive Language Arts Program, explains the interrelationship of children's literature and reading to the other parts of the language arts. Chapter 12 shows the integration of language and literature; Chapter 13 suggests the importance of using children's language to teach reading. Chapter 14, the last chapter, describes a fully integrated language arts program and discusses how parental involvement can help promote children's learning.

Children's Language and the Language Arts is intended for use as a textbook in a basic course in language arts methods or as a guide for in-service teachers who wish to have a classroom more like the one envisioned in the text. As mentioned earlier, the text contains information for developing a language arts program that considers children's linguistic and cognitive abilities. The opening chapters on learning theory, linguistic variation, and language acquisition each have a concluding section entitled "Understanding through Involvement," which has activities designed to enhance understanding of the theoretical material.

Many preservice teacher-education programs provide field-based experience giving access to students in a classroom situation. In-service teachers have a similar opportunity to try out new ways of working. For these reasons, and because we believe that adults, like children, learn best when they are active participants in their learning, we have included two groups of activities at the end of each of the chapters in Part Two. The first group of activities is called "Preliminary Learning Activities" and does not require a classroom setting or a group of students. It is intended to give the student appropriate experiences that are preliminary to working with children. The second group of activities is called "Participation Activities." It contains activities to be done with children in class or as a result of classroom experience.

The authors wish to thank and acknowledge the many special people who have helped to make *Children's Language and the Language Arts* a published reality. Unfortunately, space limits us to mentioning only a few names. Several of our students have contributed "webs" that appear in Chapters 12 and 14, and we would like to acknowledge their contribution: Sibley Veal, Debbie Swofford, Nila Adair, and Linda Shippey.

A number of people and schools were most helpful in providing photographs to illustrate our text; we particularly want to thank Charles Jones, Elaine

King, Juanita Skelton, Barbara Friedburg, Nikki Ann Spretnak, Marlene Harbert, and Marilyn Reed. Special thanks are also due to the staff and children at the Martin Luther King, Jr., Laboratory School, Evanston, Illinois; the preschool of the University of Houston at Clear Lake City, Texas; Barrington Elementary School of Upper Arlington, Ohio, and the public schools of Clarke County, Georgia.

Finally, but certainly not least, we are grateful to our families, friends, and colleagues who have given us help and encouragement through both the writing and the revising of this book. And we are especially appreciative to Charlotte S. Huck and Martha L. King, the two persons who inspired us to write a text for the language arts and from whom we still draw both insight and inspiration.

Carol J. Fisher
C. Ann Terry

CHILDREN'S LANGUAGE
AND THE LANGUAGE ARTS

PART ONE

Perspectives: Language Arts, Language, and Learning

There are many theories that deal with how children learn and how language is acquired and developed. Each theory has its own implications for specific instructional practices in the classroom. Behaviorist theory, closely associated with B. F. Skinner, regards learning as a conditioning process. Students are assigned a task and they are rewarded in some way when it is successfully completed. If children are unsuccessful, they may be given a negative reward. Behavior modification and language programs, such as Bereiter-Engelmann, are founded on these learning principles. However, because we firmly believe that developmental theory best explains children's linguistic and cognitive growth, we have chosen to present a language arts program that is based on the work of Jean Piaget and current psycholinguistic theory. The two go hand in hand, suggesting a definite sequence to children's development that can be facilitated by a rich and active learning environment.

Part One concentrates on the language arts and learning theory and consists of four chapters. The discussion in Chapter 1 focuses on a classroom setting where all the language arts are integrated, instruction is individualized, and students are actively involved in their learning. Listening, speaking, writing, and reading are shown to be interrelated language processes that occur naturally throughout the school day. The total language arts program reflects a teacher's awareness and understanding of developmental theory.

Chapter 2 provides the learning theory on which the classroom environment in Chapter 1 is based. According to Piaget, children learn best when they themselves are actively involved in their own learning. This suggests that students be given direct experiences and concrete objects that can be seen, handled, and touched. They also need to talk and write about their activities. Thinking skills may be developed through activities that involve sorting, observing, comparing, classifying, and summarizing. Critical thinking skills are vital to today's students.

Chapter 3 describes how the English language has developed both historically and linguistically. Knowledge of language development provides us with important insights into the uniqueness of our language. It also serves as a basis for understanding the many kinds of variations that exist in English: dialects, registers, and usage variations.

The final chapter in Part One, Chapter 4, presents a detailed discussion of how children acquire and develop language. The emphasis is on the children's ability to process from their linguistic environment the language around them, and to develop, test, and revise "rules" about how language operates. Linguistic research is cited to show a developmental sequence in children's language acquisition, and major implications for teaching are discussed.

CHAPTER ONE

The Language Arts Defined

PREVIEW QUESTIONS

1 What topics or subjects are included in the language arts?
2 What are the key characteristics of a language arts program in operation?
3 What might a classroom conducive to such a program be like?
4 What role does the teacher play in the language arts program?
5 What directions might we expect for the 1980s?

If you are not exactly sure what a language arts course includes, it may be because when you were in elementary school the term *language arts* was not used. You might remember, instead, English, reading, handwriting, and spelling. Today, with a renewed emphasis on using language to communicate accurately with others and to express ideas and feelings creatively, the term *language arts* has come into use to describe all the language-related activities in the elementary school program.

To understand more thoroughly what is involved in teaching the language arts today, let's look at an elementary school classroom where children are actively involved in listening, speaking, reading, and writing.

AN OVERVIEW OF A LANGUAGE ARTS PROGRAM

The students in this classroom are not all doing the same thing at the same time. The language arts experiences have been planned around their interests and needs. Not only are the children pictured on these pages engaged in listening, reading, writing, and meaningful conversations; they are active participants in their own learning—choosing and selecting their own books, listening while another child reads a story aloud, and asking friends for help when they need it.

Three of the most important aspects of a language arts program are based on current theory about how children learn and how they acquire and develop their language. Such a program is characterized by (1) *individualization* of the experiences children encounter, (2) active *involvement* in their learning activities, and (3) *integration* of communicative or creative language arts skills with one another as well as other areas of the curriculum.

Individualization

When you observe children in the classroom, you notice almost immediately that some excel in one area and others are better in another. Some children have a background of experience or temperament that makes learning easier for them. Some children develop more slowly than others and are not yet ready for increasingly more complex tasks. If an entire class is given a single assignment, some children will quickly complete it, while others work methodically along, and still others may not be able to do it at all. Teachers who are concerned about developing each child to the fullest need to vary children's assignments, and thus individualize children's learning.

Involvement

We find that children in the elementary school learn best when they are actively involved in each learning situation. What they are doing must seem important to them in a very personal way. Active involvement means working with specific, concrete materials and experiences instead of abstract ideas or materials from a textbook or some other secondary source. Children need things to touch and examine, build and construct, collect, observe, and categorize before they move into reading about more distant ideas or places. As fantasy must be grounded in reality, abstractions must touch experience.

These two groups of students are actively engaged in writing and art projects based on books they have enjoyed. Acting as a facilitator of students' learning, the teacher moves from group to group— asking questions, offering suggestions, and helping *individual* children with their learning needs.

Integration

Instead of setting up a whole series of small blocks of time for each of the curricular areas—8 to 8:10 A.M. for handwriting, 8:10 to 9 A.M. for reading groups, 9 to 9:15 A.M. for spelling, 9:15 to 10 A.M. for library on Monday, creative writing on Tuesday and Friday, and so on—the various areas of the language arts need to be integrated with each other and with other content areas such as science, mathematics, and social studies. Reporting on a science experiment or enacting various occupations develops language arts skills and at the same time promotes basic understanding in other content areas. This type of integrated study provides for large blocks of time and allows the teacher to capitalize on teachable moments instead of letting the clock dictate when a learning experience is to end.

These are the characteristics of the language arts program you will find described in this book. The basis for such a program is found in current linguistic theory which describes how children acquire and develop language and in cognitive psychology which describes a developmental learning process. It values both communicative and creative language and recommends a classroom environment in which (1) learning is individualized, (2) children are actively involved in what they are doing, and (3) content and skills are integrated. It emphasizes both written and oral aspects of the language arts, allowing time for discussions, listening experiences, dramatizations of stories and situations, and

Making strawberry yogurt pie can be a learning experience. After discussing the cooking activity with their teacher, these three students are *involved* in reading and following the recipe for one of their favorite desserts.

an oral sharing of ideas and experiences as well as the development of skill in reading, spelling, handwriting, conventional punctuation, and capitalization. There are skills to be learned and imaginative ideas to be shared. Perhaps most important of all, each child feels good about what he or she can do and about attempting new things.

LANGUAGE ARTS CLASSROOMS

To illustrate, let's look at a self-contained elementary school class where a variety of learning experiences are occurring simultaneously. The drawing of the physical classroom arrangement in Figure 1-1 (page 9) may help you visualize the setting as you read.

When we glance around the room, we see a small group of children seated in the listening area. They have chosen to listen to some Curious George[1] stories and afterward write their own stories about him. Across the room, six children are seated in pairs reading to one another. One child reads several pages while the other listens—then it is time for the other to read. The writing area is a busy place today, too. A small group of students are dictating an experience story to

Meaningful learning experiences can occur when the language arts are *integrated*. After rereading a favorite book, these two students decided to plan a puppet dramatization as a way of sharing the story with others in the class.

their teacher. They listen as one student reads the story from the large sheet of chart paper. A discussion follows and results in a unanimous decision to change the ending of their story.

Leaving the writing area, we pass a science table filled with plants that the children are growing. A cassette tape player has been placed on the table, and a sign reads: *Play me and learn about our plant collection.* We next see four students standing at the art tables, conversing occasionally as they paint with large swooping strokes. Their pictures, rich and colorful, will soon be added to the display space in the art area. Finally, we walk to the drama area where two children have decided to dramatize the Yugoslavian folktale "Nail Soup."[2] Both have searched through the costume trunk and selected some appropriate clothing and props. The girl, taking the role of the old woman, is dressed in a long apron with a scarf tied around her head. Slowly she begins to hobble around the make-believe kitchen. The boy, wearing a soldier's cap, knocks on the old woman's kitchen door. The drama then begins to unfold as the hungry soldier starts his trickery—convincing the woman that her hidden vegetables would make delicious nail soup.

In the middle school, or where there is departmentalized teaching, the classroom is arranged to facilitate active involvement in learning, but the physical equipment and materials are designed for older students' needs (see Figure 1-2).

The classroom library area, or reading area, is a comfortable place for students to read and share books. These children chose this space to read and research information about their special interest topics.

For example, some students are meeting in the conference area with the teacher. They are engaged in sharing and editing individual research reports that will be presented to the class later in the week. A small group of students are quietly involved in the listening area. Before writing their own radio play, they are studying and listening to a number of commercially produced radio dramas. The reference area, containing encyclopedias, dictionaries, and a wide variety of informational books, is busy with students who are planning a display for the classroom. After reading about the lives of several national leaders, they decided to research interesting facts about the lives of United States presidents and then share them with other class members.

As the day continues in both classrooms, students are actively involved in their own learning, language arts skills and content are integrated, and the teacher provides for individual learning needs. Each student feels successful and leaves at the end of the day feeling good about school.

THE TEACHER AND THE LANGUAGE ARTS PROGRAM

Planning an individualized language arts program which integrates language-related activities and assumes that growth occurs when students are actively involved requires a special kind of teacher. A program such as this is administered by a facilitator of learning, not a dictator. The desks, traditionally placed in straight rows, are now grouped together in order to facilitate talk. Students

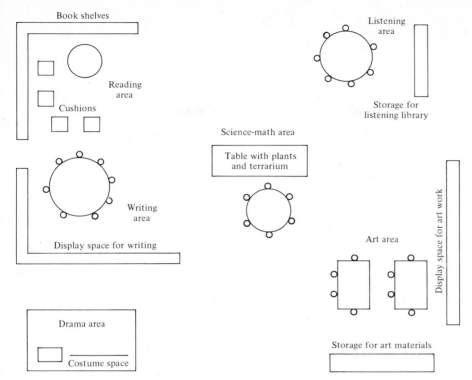

Figure 1-1 Self-contained classroom plan.

Figure 1-2 Departmentalized classroom plan.

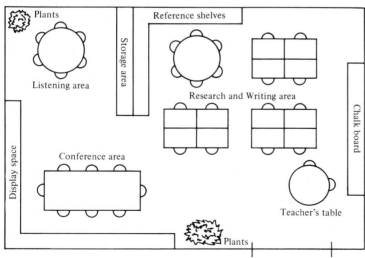

move freely about the room working on projects, choosing books to read, and writing stories or recording observations. The teacher also moves about the room working with groups of children or individual students. The teacher's desk which at one time appeared in front of the room, has been moved to the side and serves as a base from which to operate.

The bulletin boards and even the walls spill over with students' work—stories, poems, paintings, charts of observations, and displays of things they have collected and mounted. Each piece of work is carefully prepared for display, and the collection reflects the students' varying abilities and interests. In classrooms for younger children, there are large cushions or perhaps a rocking chair or a sofa to curl up on while listening to a story. There are easels and paints ready to use and a bin full of clay for modeling. There is a box of fabric remnants, yarns, laces and trims, buttons, sequins, aluminum foil, magazines, pieces of cork, and many other things to use for collages or costumes. Middle-grade classrooms have a reference area and a listening area complete with tapes of stories and matching print material. There is a place for conferring about writing or group projects. There is an area for writing that has a variety of pens and papers to use, and it is a quiet area where students may work undisturbed. There may not be a chair and desk for everyone, but there are chairs at the writing center, at a large table used for making projects, or in the area used for group work. There is also a large carpeted area where everyone can sit and share written compositions or meet for a planning session. Each student has a private storage area for those things traditionally stored in desks.

Teachers who work in this kind of classroom need to structure learning situations just as traditional teachers do; they simply do it in a different way. Structure comes from the questions asked, from the materials made available in the classroom, and from the teacher's knowledge of the subject matter and of each person's interests and abilities. It is not a matter of just doing anything at all and having students learn; it is allowing them to meet challenging and purposeful situations from which they learn best.

The teacher keeps careful records of each person's progress. Through careful observations and individual conferences, the learning needs of each student are monitored. Evaluation and subsequent guidance by the teacher are part of the daily routine; and students are frequently engaged in evaluating their own work and establishing their own learning goals.

Students are constantly involved in activities that reflect an understanding of their learning needs and abilities. Work on skills is balanced with more imaginative activities. Oral experiences are part of the classroom, as are writing and reading. Students have experiences with productive language as well as with receptive language. In essence, the environment is one in which students participate actively in their own learning, and school is an enjoyable place to be.

A good teacher may intuitively provide such a learning environment. The qualities that make a good or successful teacher are cited in a recent teacher competency report from the American Association of School Administrators.[3] The findings were compiled from more than 400 related studies over the last 25 years. In the report, Marvin Roth identified specific characteristics of good teachers. His guidelines appear below, adapted in the form of a checklist. Read each statement carefully and decide how you would rank as a teacher.

Characteristics of Good Teachers

Yes   No

____ ____   You believe not only that children can learn and want to learn, but also that you can help them.

____ ____   You believe that teaching children is more important than teaching subjects.

____ ____   You have empathy, and not only do you understand how the student feels but you let the student know you understand.

____ ____   You listen to get information and listen to help the student.

____ ____   You listen to both sides and get information from those who will be affected before making a decision.

____ ____   You see people as individuals and not as blacks, Indians, or the kids who live in trailers.

____ ____   You have the drive to share your knowledge with students.

____ ____   You read and collect things—on vacation, for example—to bring to class.

____ ____   You use specific teaching techniques which you can describe.

____ ____   You derive satisfaction from your investment in your work—not from what you do as a teacher, but from what you see children learn.

____ ____   You have characteristics that activate learning and have a drive to build rapport.

____ ____   You balance organization with flexibility.

____ ____   You have high expectations for children, coupled with an acceptance of children as they are.

____ ____   You are innovative—for example, you have twenty years of experience, not one year of experience twenty times.

NEEDED DIRECTIONS IN THE LANGUAGE ARTS FOR THE 1980s

Trends or educational movements seem to fade in and out of vogue. To cite one of many examples, numerous schools were built in the 1960s and 1970s around an open-space concept—one large area without walls to separate classes. This physical plan was designed to facilitate team planning and teaching and grouping for skills across grade levels. Now, educators are espousing the virtues of the self-contained classroom—the fashionable classroom of the 1940s and 1950s. And many are exploring ways to convert schools without walls to schools with walls where one teacher is responsible for children's learning needs.

Rather than dwell on issues, trends, or educational movements—which are usually short-lived—it seems appropriate to discuss needed directions in the language arts for the 1980s on the basis of what we know currently about how children learn and what teaching methods promote learning.

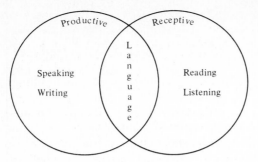

Figure 1-3   The language arts.

Valuing Language in the Classroom

Humans developed language in order to communicate more effectively with others. Essentially then, the purpose of language may be viewed as one of communication. Besides enabling you to converse with a friend or read a long-awaited letter or the day's newspaper, language has a creative side. Creative language may be observed in novels, plays, musical lyrics, and your own speech and writing.

If we look at language from a technical point of view, there are two phases: productive and receptive. The model in Figure 1-3 illustrates the relationship between productive and receptive language.

When we produce an idea or thought, we use primarily speaking or writing as the means of communication. These represent the *productive* phases of language. In turn, if we receive an idea or thought from someone, we are usually involved in reading or listening. These, then, are the *receptive* phases of language. In order to become adept at producing or receiving ideas and information from others, an individual must be able to understand and use language effectively. It is for this reason that a good language arts program includes many opportunities for students to hear, read, and produce language. And helping students become flexible users of language, able to adjust their language to the situation, is an equally valid goal within such a program. The quiet classroom, once thought to be the good classroom, is transformed in the 1980s into one which demonstrates the statement: *Children's language is valued here.*

Emphasis on Teaching Composition

The ability of students to write well is declining. Graves, in reporting the results of a year's study on the status of writing, says, "The problem with writing is no writing."[4] His research substantiates what many have suspected for some time. Children in today's classrooms spend little time writing, especially after they leave the primary grades; rather, they are engaged in filling in blanks, circling multiple-choice items, completing workbook pages that require one- or two-word answers, and finishing one dittoed worksheet after another. To underscore this point, Graves notes in his findings that orders for ditto paper, used most for short written responses, are double or triple what they were ten years ago in our schools, whereas orders for lined paper are on a definite decline.

Because elementary school and middle school curricula today adhere to schedules and because a myriad of subjects vie for time slots within these daily schedules, the teaching of writing in many schools has been reduced—according to Graves—to fifteen- and twenty-minute intervals on a once-a-week basis. The provision of more than thirty minutes per week for writing was an above-average accommodation for children's writing.

If children are to become more capable writers, then the teaching of writing must be viewed as a priority—worthy of the time that it takes to learn worthwhile composition skills. The composing process—(1) think and talk about it; (2) write, think, and write about it; (3) evaluate and edit it—should be an inherent component in any writing program. And teachers must make a concerted effort to know their students' interests, provide audiences other than themselves for students' written work, and create a community writing climate where the composition process is seen as an enjoyable experience rather than as a punishment—a practice that has occurred for too long in many classrooms, as in: *Write 100 times, "I will not chew gum."*

Bringing Reading and Writing Together

Most children attempt writing at a very early age. They scribble, make marks that resemble letters and words and then read this back to a parent. They label their drawings and, at a certain stage, demonstrate some knowledge of how sounds and letters are related. For example, a five-year-old looking at her completed picture wrote the following at the top:

mi prty hous

This young child is bringing an inherent ability to school that a teacher can capitalize on; she is already applying rudiments of phonics. "Reading and writing," says Frank Smith, "are often regarded primarily as school activities but their roots must lie outside the school, and to the extent that school makes something different or unique of reading and writing, the more it will interfere with children's attempts to understand them."[5]

We must begin to make use of the knowledge that children bring to school with them. Given the opportunity to apply new information to that which is already known, students' understanding of concepts and related content will be increased.

In the middle school, the teaching of literature, grammar, and composition should be integrated. Too often they are taught as separate units of study, with the result that students are denied the opportunity to apply related knowledge and skills to meaningful writing situations.

Recognition of Listening as a Basic Skill

The movement in the 1970s, "back to the basics," has given impetus to more and more competency testing in our schools. Unfortunately, such tests usually measure only that which can be easily tested: reading skills, competencies in mathematics, the ability to spell words correctly, and certain language conventions. As a result, these skill areas are perceived as the "basics" to be taught, whereas other skills in the language arts receive much less attention because they do not lend themselves to testing.

The one area of the language arts most frequently ignored and neglected is listening. Many still do not understand that listening can be taught; it is viewed instead as something a person does naturally without learned skills being involved. This viewpoint is erroneous, and children can acquire listening skills if teachers help students learn from oral sources.

We live in a society today that requires everyone to listen more and more. Television is a prime source of information for large numbers of people in this country; and the media, which at one time concentrated on reporting information, now provide running commentaries on a variety of subjects. How are persons able to separate fact from opinion, determine authority, or decide significance if they do not possess critical listening skills?

Children are a major market for consumer products. Turn on the television set any Saturday morning and watch the commercials that are directed to this young audience. How can children be helped to make judgments about what they are being told if they do not understand the propaganda devices that are being used to persuade them?

Listening leads to learning, and critical listening leads to intelligent judgments and understandings. The teaching of listening skills is essential and should begin early in the primary grades.

Recognition of the Relationship between Writing and Spelling

How were you taught to spell? Did you learn—or memorize—a new list of words each week? Was there a pretest? Did you have a final spelling test on Friday?

Spelling instruction, unfortunately, has changed very little over the years. Spelling books are more colorful and attractive today, but they still present weekly word lists that are totally divorced from children's writing. A student can learn the spellings for a Friday test, make an A, and then later in the day hand the teacher a story that is filled with misspelled words. Or students can spell the words for the week correctly, but then do poorly on a sentence dictation test because they cannot spell such basic writing words as *there, because,* and *they.*

A challenge for the next decade is to provide classroom instructional programs that recognize the relationship between writing and spelling. The words that students misspell consistently in their written compositions form the basis for spelling instruction. After all, it is only when we write that we have a need to spell words correctly.

Using a Wider Range of Materials

Because many classrooms operate primarily around a commercially produced series of books, teachers often ignore the wide variety of current materials available to broaden and stimulate students' interests. Curriculum planning, for instance, should include the use of videotapes, films, audio tapes, and special television programs. Helpful resources for using nonprint media in the classroom are readily available to teachers. To give one of many possible examples, Prime Time School study guides are distributed by mail (Prime Time School Television, 120 South La Salle Street, Chicago, Illinois 60603). These study guides make available educational information about high-quality programs ahead of time so that teachers can use the television programs in their classes.

The range of materials is endless once a teacher begins to look. Newspapers and magazines offer current information regarding content that is being studied in the classroom. And guest speakers provide students with firsthand information, while field experiences allow students to see things for themselves. Studying adolescent fiction, rather than only the "classics," gives students insights into problems of today.

SUMMARY

The teacher plans the language arts program and classroom around (1) individual needs, (2) students' active involvement in the learning process, and (3) the integration of related content and skills.

Needed directions in the language arts include the following: valuing language in the classroom, putting an emphasis on teaching composition, teaching reading and writing together, recognizing the importance of listening as a basic skill, teaching spelling in relationship to writing, and using a wider range of materials in classes.

REFERENCE NOTES

[1]Hans A. Rey. *Curious George*. Boston: Houghton Mifflin, 1941.
[2]Harve Zemach. *Nail Soup*. Chicago: Follett, 1964.
[3]Marvin J. Roth. *Teacher Competency Report*. American Association of School Administration, 1980.
[4]Donald H. Graves. "Research Update: We Won't Let Them Write," *Language Arts*, vol. 55, no. 5, May 1978, pp. 635–640.
[5]Frank Smith. "The Language Arts and the Learner's Mind," *Language Arts*, vol. 56, no. 2, February 1979, pp. 118–125.

CHAPTER TWO

Learning through Active Participation

PREVIEW QUESTIONS

1 What stages of development do elementary and middle school students go through, and what behavior is typical of these stages?

2 What kinds of activities and learning environments foster development?

3 What kinds of activities extend students' thinking skills beyond the cognitive-memory level?

4 What critical thinking skills and activities are appropriate for students in the elementary and middle grades?

Throughout the history of education various theories have been advanced to explain how children learn, and these have been interpreted in many ways in actual classroom practices. A major theorist in developmental cognitive learning is Jean Piaget, a Swiss psychologist, whose interest in how children's thought processes develop has led to the view of learning on which the language arts program presented in this text is based.

Piaget became interested in intellectual development through observations of his own two children. He was intrigued with their comments, questions, and errors—seeing them all as clues to their thinking. He began to give them tasks to determine how well they were able to reason and think logically. His research, first with his own children and later with other children at different age levels, has long been known. Many educators are now applying his theories, realizing that they have something important to say about how children learn.

An earlier practitioner who made a lasting contribution to education in this country is John Dewey, an educator whose philosophy of education is being rediscovered in some educational circles. Dewey sought to reform traditional education of the 1930s. He and his followers began the progressive education movement (founded on the belief that children learn by doing) because they were dissatisfied with what they saw happening in the schools of that day. Dewey interpreted the traditional educator's view of learning as the "acquisition of what is incorporated in books and in the heads of elders."[1] Drill, memorization of factual material, and the teacher as an authoritarian figure characterized the traditional school in Dewey's mind; whereas freedom of activity, learning through experience, and the teacher as a director of children's learning were typical of the progressive school.

As one looks at Piaget's investigations and what Dewey was saying in the 1930s, it seems that Piaget's findings support Dewey's educational philosophy. That is, the research Piaget has done concerning children's cognitive or intellectual development substantiates Dewey's theory that children learn by doing. Learning is an active process, not a passive one. Workbooks, ditto sheets, and "pencil-and-paper curricula" are not effective means for stimulating children's learning and thinking; yet they persist and live on in many of today's elementary school classrooms.

To gain a better understanding of a learning environment that incorporates everything that we know about children and learning, let's look more closely at Piaget's research on cognitive development. A review of some of his theories may be helpful in seeing how they can be applied to the elementary school classroom and language arts program.

COGNITIVE ORGANIZATION AND ADAPTATION

According to Piaget, mental development occurs through a process of organization and adaptation. To explain this process more clearly, let's use an example.

Mark is 2½ years old and very interested in learning about the world around him. He is busy tasting, touching, hearing, and observing all things in his immediate environment. As he is doing this, he is mentally processing a variety of stimuli. Mark does this by developing categories, or schemata, for organizing the stimuli. What he takes in through his various senses is mentally organized into newly developed or already established categories. These categories essentially become his frames of reference. For instance, Mark has observed and petted his dog Charley. When he plays in the yard, he frequently sees the neighbor's dog Ralph. From his observations and experiences with Charley and Ralph, Mark develops a "dog" schema, or category. A dog to Mark may mean something having a head, four legs, and a tail, and whatever external stimuli fit in his schema must be a dog. When driving out in the country one day with his parents, Mark sees an animal that has a head, four legs, and a tail. To Mark, it is a large dog. Thus, he calls the pony a dog as he assimilates this new animal into his dog schema because it has all the proper characteristics. Piaget refers to this last cognitive process as *assimilation*. This means Mark took the new stimulus, the pony, and related it to his existing "dog" schema. As Mark has more experiences with ponies, cows, and various kinds of dogs, he will refine his "dog" schema and will develop new categories for animals that are not dogs.

Leo Lionni's book for children, *Fish Is Fish*,[2] illustrates this process in a very meaningful but humorous way. A frog and fish become friends. The frog leaves the pond one day to explore the world. He returns much later to visit his friend and tell him about the "extraordinary things" he has seen. He explains to the fish that he has seen cows. "They have four legs, horns, eat grass, and carry pink bags of milk." The fish pictures a cow in his mind, and sees a fishlike creature with four legs, horns, and a pink bag. The fish has assimilated what the frog has told him about cows into his own existing schema. Until the fish has more experience outside his marine environment, he cannot refine his categories.

To illustrate further, let's take the story on beyond the book. Suppose the fish were caught one day and placed in a glass tank where it could see the world as the frog did. Its schemata would change. It would take in new information and stimuli that would alter or modify its existing ones; or certain external stimuli might cause the fish to create entirely new schemata. When this process occurs, Piaget refers to it as *accommodation*.

In differentiating between the cognitive processes of assimilation and accommodation, Wadsworth explains that in assimilation the stimuli are forced to fit the person's existing structure, while in accommodation the reverse is true. The person changes the schema to fit the new stimuli.[3]

How can we apply this to children's learning? Essentially it means that children need many experiences in order to develop new schemata and refine others. Good preschool or primary programs are conceived and organized around this concept. In them, children become a part of a learning environment that is rich in new and varied experiences. A school week might include a visit to a neighborhood shopping center, a morning at the children's zoo where animals can be petted, a walk through a large grocery store, lunch in a park, and a tour of a nearby tree farm or nursery. When in the classroom, the children have a wealth of materials at their reach—blocks for building, concrete objects to manipulate, puzzles to put together, clothes for dressing up, small animals to feed and observe, and books for browsing and reading. There is time to paint or dramatize highlights of their experiences and time to talk about them.

For older children whose learning is still grounded in concrete experiences, the learning environment involves firsthand observations and direct participation in ongoing classroom activities. The school week might include a visit by someone from the local police department to explain and demonstrate fingerprinting and voiceprinting, a trip to a local florist for a display of traditional flower arrangements, time to build and use a greenhouse to start seeds for early planting, an interview of a local author of children's books, or a hike along a nature trail or nearby river to check on soil or water erosion. The classroom is supplied with an abundance of books—books for recreational reading, books with taped readings, informational books for resources, and homemade books. There are materials to experiment with—jawbones of horses, batteries and wire, light bulbs, electric bells, etc. There are opportunities to work alone, with a partner, or with a large group.

COGNITIVE ORGANIZATION:
IMPLICATIONS FOR TEACHING AND LEARNING

According to Piaget, the processes of assimilation and accommodation continue throughout our lives. The cognitive structures become more numerous and complex as a person grows and develops mentally. However, the same cognitive processes continue to function for the three-year-old, the eight-year-old, and the twenty-five-year-old. The older person is better at differentiating across stimuli and has a more complex network of schemata.

When we consider how a child develops intellectually, the number and quality of the educational experiences become very important. What kind of stimuli are children assimilating and accommodating when they are given worksheet after worksheet to complete? If a child listens to the teacher 75 percent of the school day, what is the quality of the experience? What happens to the intellectual climate when children's curiosities, questions, and conversations do not have as high a value as that of a "quiet" classroom?

If we accept Piaget's theories of cognitive development, then the classroom environment cannot be a passive one. Rather, the child is active in the learning environment, constantly exploring, hypothesizing, experimenting, conversing, and questioning. Convergent experiences limit and stifle children's intellectual development. The teacher is therefore concerned about offering students divergent experiences that extend their thinking and learning processes. Memorization of facts and emphasis on learning content that soon may be out of date do not help children develop new cognitive structures or ways of thinking and discovering.

STAGES OF INTELLECTUAL DEVELOPMENT

As mentioned earlier, the intellectual process is the same for the adult as for the child. Assimilation, accommodation, and a striving for a balance between the two continue throughout one's life, but mental structures become increasingly complex with age. It is the continuing development and change in cognitive structures that have caused Piaget to say there are *stages* of intellectual development. According to Piaget, all children go through identifiable stages, or periods, of cognitive development:

Period of sensorimotor intelligence (birth to approximately two years)
Period of preoperational thought (approximately two to seven years)
Period of concrete operations (approximately seven to eleven years)
Period of formal operations (approximately eleven to fifteen years)

Educators frequently misunderstand what is meant by the cognitive stages and the ages given for each, and thus misinterpret them. This has long been a concern to Piaget, and he warns that they should not be viewed as a set of limitations. As a child moves from one stage to the next, a new potential is reached. The ages represent averages, says Piaget, and cannot be considered static. It is possible for a nine-year-old to be in the preoperational stage of development, whereas a six-year-old may have advanced to concrete operations. However, the development is continuous and children move from one stage to the next, building an increasingly complex network of cognitive structures. One stage grows out of the other, and children become more and more adept at dealing with abstractions. The important point is that children go through these stages in this sequence or order even though there may be differences in their ages when in a given stage.

The child in the period of concrete operations thinks best with something to manipulate, whereas the child who has moved into the period of formal operations may reason logically without the help of tangible or concrete experiences. It seems necessary for teachers to know and understand the changes that occur from one stage to another if they are to plan an appropriate learning environment for children. Piaget suggests, "It is essential for teachers to know why particular operations are difficult for children, and to understand that these difficulties must be surmounted by each child in passing from one level to the next. It is not the stages that are important; it is rather what happens in the transition."[4]

Period of Sensorimotor Intelligence
(Birth to Approximately Two Years)

Why should you be concerned about the first stage described by Piaget? Teachers do not usually work with children of this age. However, when we consider that each new stage incorporates the previous stage, the period of sensorimotor intelligence is significant and cannot be omitted.

This stage of development begins at birth and progresses sequentially through what might be called *substages*. There are six of these.

(1) From birth through about the first month of life, children's behavior and actions are completely reflexive. Children are born with such reflexes as sucking, grasping, crying, and moving various parts of the body. Newborn infants are also totally egocentric: that is, they are aware only of themselves and their basic needs.

(2) From one to four months young children begin to suck their thumbs. Thumb sucking is intentional and demonstrates accommodation to the environment. It is habitual and therefore cannot be considered reflexive action.

(3) Between four and eight months of age children become less egocentric and begin to notice the world around them. They handle objects and move them around, and if they find something of significant interest, they will repeat a

126760

behavior. For example, if children shake a rattle and enjoy the sound, they will shake it again and again.

(4) From eight to twelve months intentional behavior definitely emerges; this involves using specific means to obtain an end. Children may move a stuffed animal aside to reach a favored toy. During this period the children also develop the concept of object constancy. They know an object exists, and when it is taken away or out of sight, they look for it. Before, when an object was moved out of view or hidden, they would make no effort to search for it. Games such as peekaboo and hide-and-seek are good for children this age to play because they help establish the notion of object constancy or permanence. The attainment of object constancy is a major achievement of the sensorimotor period.[5]

(5) The next period, occurring between twelve and eighteen months, is characterized by "experimentation." Instead of simply repeating or practicing interesting behaviors, the infant begins applying behaviors to new situations. Problem solving can be observed as the child finds new means to an end. In essence, the young child is demonstrating a kind of intelligent functioning for the first time.

(6) The sixth and last substage of the sensorimotor period begins at eighteen months and continues through about two years. During this time, mental actions begin to replace physical ones. Problems are solved internally rather than in some physical way. Children arrive at a solution by thinking or reasoning about a situation first. They are not able to visualize something, however, without actually doing it.

Period of Preoperational Thought
(Approximately Two to Seven Years of Age)

Following the sensorimotor period, the child moves into what Piaget calls the *preoperational period*. Children are usually in this stage of cognitive development when they first enter a school setting. Therefore, it is especially important that the changes that occur during this period are understood by people who are interested in working with preschool, kindergarten, or primary school children. Characteristics which children display during this stage of development are egocentrism, lack of conservation, and animism.

Characteristics of preoperational children   *Egocentrism*   During this period the child is very egocentric. The egocentrism demonstrated throughout this stage is unlike that of the newborn infant. Preoperational children are cognizant of others and the world around them, but they experience difficulty in seeing or understanding another's point of view. To them, everyone else sees and thinks just as they do. A teacher will discover that children in the preoperational stage will need and want to be at the center of all activity. As an example, a kindergarten teacher asked if someone would help her five-year-olds learn to work with puppets. She had tried to emphasize the importance of letting the puppet do the actions and talking, but the children insisted on participating, too. "The puppet may begin the story," she said, "but the child inevitably finishes it. They just can't seem to keep themselves out of it!" The response to her request was that little could be done to keep them from taking the part of the puppet; her children's behavior was quite typical. They simply are unable to remove themselves from the situation. This does not mean that puppetry should not be continued in the classroom. Children enjoy puppets, and the experience is certainly worthwhile. Puppetry enables them to use their language creatively and organize their view of reality. Children can identify with the puppets and test out what they know with what others know.

Children's egocentrism is also evidenced through their oral language communication with others. They always think that the other person must know what they already know. If one child is attempting to give information to another, significant parts are often left out and the speaker becomes exasperated when the other person does not understand. To illustrate, Suzanne was asked to build a simple construction with large red and blue blocks. Her friend Juan was placed on the other side of a partition and given an identical set of blocks. When she had completed her block construction, she was asked to tell Juan how to place his blocks to make the same construction. She began, "You put this red block here and this blue block over here and this other block on top of this one." Needless to say, he had difficulty duplicating the construction and began to ask many questions. Finally, becoming frustrated with Juan's apparent lack of understanding, Suzanne put her hands on her hips, looked intensely at her block construction, and said, "Why can't you do it? It's right in front of you!" Elkind suggests that this behavior can "be explained by saying that the child assumes words carry much more information than they actually do, because he believes that even the indefinite 'thing' somehow conveys the properties of the object it is used to represent."[6] Children seem unable to separate the object from the word that refers to it. When Suzanne says, "Put the blue one here," she doesn't understand why Juan cannot do it, because it seems very clear to her. This, in part, is due to her egocentrism; she can visualize only from her point of view.

Teachers of young children can readily observe the egocentrism that exists in their play, conversations, and overt behavior. Rather than becoming annoyed with children because they persist in telling about an experience they have had over the weekend instead of talking about a prescribed topic, the teacher who understands children in this stage of development is interested in what they have to say. Egocentrism can also be observed in children's written compositions. For example, when given a choice between dictating a story about a selection of pictures or their own experiences, a group of kindergarten children unanimously decided to dictate a story about something that had actually happened to them.

Lack of conservation   The ability to conserve involves perceptual constancy, reversibility of thought, and the ability to reason logically. Children's thinking is dominated by their perception; thus, "seeing is believing." For example, a child who is shown the configuration in Figure 2-1 will tell you that there are the same number of blocks in each row. However, if the blocks in row 1 are spread apart as in Figure 2-2, thus making a longer row, the child will say that there are more blocks in row 1. Because the row is longer, the child believes that it contains more blocks. For a child in this stage of development, the rows contain the same number of blocks only as long as there is visual correspondence. The child is not able to reason that there are the same number of blocks in each row when they are just rearranged. Preoperational children have not attained perceptual constancy.

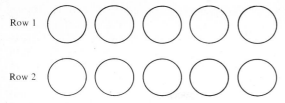

Figure 2-1 **Rows of equal length.**

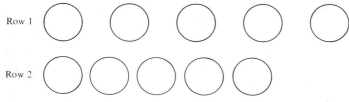

Figure 2-2 **Rows of unequal length.**

Children during this stage of development also have difficulty in doing tasks that require reversibility of thought. It is not until about age seven that a child can reverse operations. Piaget tells about presenting children with three different colored balls—A, B, and C—on a wire. They were told to watch as the three balls were inserted into a tube. The correct expectation was that the balls—A, B, and C—would come out of the other end of the tube in the order in which they were inserted. However, when the tube was rotated 180° before the balls reappeared, the children did not expect the order to be that of C, B, A. They were, in fact, astonished at the outcome.[7]

The preoperational child does not conserve. Bound by their perceptions and lacking reversibility of thought, preoperational children are unable to conceptualize that regardless of any changes in its shape or position, the amount or quantity of matter always remains the same. We observed the child's inability to conserve in the example using blocks. A child who is not conserving can also look at two glasses containing the same amount of water, but because one is taller, believes it contains the most. Such a child is focusing on one aspect, tallness; the child assumes that a tall glass must contain more than a shorter one. It is not until about age seven that children begin to conserve.

Animism The child in the period of preoperational thought believes that inanimate objects have life. The clouds are alive because they move, an automobile is alive because it runs, and a river is alive because it flows. At this age children interpret reality using themselves as models. It is not until later that children can distinguish between reality and fantasy in the way adults do.

Implications for the classroom How can this knowledge about the preoperational child be applied in the classroom? Remember the following when establishing the learning environment for preoperational children.

LEARNING THROUGH ACTIVE PARTICIPATION

1. They are active. Children move about within the classroom setting. Sitting all day is not natural for these children.
2. They are egocentric. They are interested in themselves and will not be interested in their neighbor until later. These children need to be made to feel as though they have something to say and contribute and be allowed to carry out their own ideas.
3. They have their own world of fantasy. Children's imaginative play should be encouraged; they need to listen to both fantasy and realistic books and talk about them.
4. They are beginners. They learn through mistakes, and trial and error is a learning process. The teacher needs to be patient and understanding, giving children time to learn at their own rates.
5. They want stimulation. They have the desire to explore and experiment. Naturally curious, they may ask question after question. The teacher must provide a rich learning environment—things to observe, touch, handle, taste, explore, and so on.
6. They are talkative. They learn by talking and working actively; therefore, conversation is a natural part of the learning environment.
7. They are individuals. All children are different and have neither the same interests nor the same backgrounds of experience. They may be at different levels of development and therefore need choices; they should not be expected to be all together on the same page on the same day.
8. They need to be successful. Encouragement and praise should be continuous within the learning environment.
9. Children are bound by their perceptions. They are unable to conserve until they are in the concrete-operational period of cognitive development. The teacher should assess children's developmental levels and understand their capabilities.

Period of Concrete Operations (Approximately Seven to Eleven Years of Age)

Characteristics of concrete-operational children   This period of intellectual development extends through the elementary school years. During this time the child makes noticeable advances in cognitive organization. In contrast to children in the preoperational stage of development, children in this period are able to reason, and no longer is their thinking dominated by their perceptions. General characteristics of children in this stage of development include the ability to conserve, the continuing need for concrete experiences, and the development of social awareness and interaction.

Concrete-operational children have the ability to reverse their concepts, a reasoning capacity necessary in order to conserve. Children who have attained reversibility of thought, for example, can look at two balls of clay, identical in size, shape, and weight, and when the appearance of one is changed, tell you that the amount is still the same. They are no longer bound by their perceptions. Children are able to reason that the balls of clay contained equal amounts in the beginning and that changing the shape or appearance of one does not alter the quantity.

The concrete-operational child still has difficulty in understanding many verbal and symbolic abstractions. Because of this, students in this stage of development do best when a variety of direct and concrete experiences are provided for them—listening walks, field trips, visiting speakers, and so on. Classroom materials should also be concrete and plentiful—geoboards; measuring cups; cubes and blocks for counting; scrap materials for making puppets, collage pictures, and other art constructions; and models that can be taken apart and put back together.

When children reach the concrete stage of development, they become less egocentric. They are able to take another's point of view and engage in meaningful conversations. It is at this time that assimilation to the peer culture occurs. There is true interaction—children are interested in playing and talking with other children. Games become popular, from checkers to tic-tac-toe, and children have the desire and the ability to follow the rules.

Egocentricity diminishes, and children develop a social awareness not seen in the previous stage. They understand and discuss another's point of view; and it is through interaction with peers that children attempt to validate their own thoughts. Social interaction is important for these children because it promotes cognitive development. Actually, it is through such social exchange that accommodation occurs.

While the children in the concrete stage of development have advanced beyond the thinking of the preoperational period, they have not yet attained the highest level of thought. Therefore, they cannot yet mentally handle verbal abstractions without the help of concrete or tangible experiences. That is, concrete-operational children can solve problems only by using real objects and events. Their thinking is grounded in the concrete. Like preoperational children, they need direct concrete experiences—excursions around the neighborhood, field trips within the community, and conversations about what is observed. There should be materials in the classroom that can be manipulated, touched, and talked about. In reality, this stage may be considered as a transition period between preoperational thought and the last stage of cognitive development, when formal thought finally appears.

Implications for the classroom A knowledge and understanding of the concrete-operational child essentially dictates the type of learning environment that is provided. You will want to remember the following about children who are approximately seven to eleven years of age.

1. They require an abundance of concrete materials and experiences. Children during this period are still partially bound by their perceptions and, according to Piaget, think best with something in their hands. Therefore, the classroom is filled with a wide assortment of materials to manipulate and handle, small animals and plants are available for observation, field trips and environmental excursions are provided, writing grows out of real experiences, and so on.
2. They need a rich language environment. Their oral language is developing throughout the period of concrete operations. The teacher encourages conversation and discussion, makes a wide variety of books available to children, reads stories aloud, and provides a listening center with records and tapes.

3. They are active. Concrete-operational children can sit for longer periods of time than preoperational children; however, they still need opportunities to move about and become actively involved in their learning.
4. They have individual interests. Learning can and should grow out of children's interests. The teacher recognizes this and encourages individual pursuits through reading, constructing models, discussion, record keeping, and so on.
5. They want the approval of adults. Thus, encouragement and praise can stimulate and foster children's learning.
6. They are different from one another. They have different interests and learn at different rates. They will be at different levels of development. Teachers provide for these differences by offering learning choices and experiences that meet personal needs. The children have opportunities to decide about what they learn.
7. They are socially aware of others. Children this age want to communicate and exchange ideas with others. The classroom environment encourages and facilitates children's communication.

**Period of Formal Operations
(Approximately Eleven to Fifteen Years of Age)**

Children during this period develop formal-operational thought. They differ from concrete-operational children in that purely verbal tasks are no longer difficult for them. They can now perform cognitive tasks without the help of manipulative materials or concrete experiences. Therefore, the student is capable of solving all classes of problems. A fifteen-year-old's thinking may not be equivalent to an adult's, but the cognitive structures necessary for such thought have been attained. The development until this time has been qualitative, and any changes in thought hereafter are quantitative. Assimilation and accommodation continue throughout adulthood, altering one's thinking, but the potential for mature thought is reached at the end of the formal-operational period.

**DEVELOPMENTAL STAGES:
IMPLICATIONS FOR TEACHING AND LEARNING**

In talking about education Piaget refers to the *traditional school* and the *active school.* For our purposes let's borrow and use these terms throughout this section to contrast the two types of learning settings.

Considering what has been said about children's cognitive development, the thinking and reasoning abilities of a child of elementary school age are not the same as an adult's. Therefore, we as educators cannot expect a young child to perform as an adult. However, Piaget suggests, "Traditional school theory has always treated the child, in effect, as a small being who reasons and feels just as we do while merely lacking our knowledge and experience."[8] Viewing the child in this manner, some educators have attempted to supply the content or subject matter necessary for children to function on an adult level. Elementary school curricula have been developed stating what content shall be taught but giving little attention to children's developmental levels (this includes physical, social, linguistic, and cognitive development of the child). The teacher dictates what content is to be learned next by the child and how it is to be acquired. Learning is structured according to what the teacher wants, rather than allowing children to use their own organizational patterns. This acquisition of knowledge usually takes the form of completing workbook or ditto pages, answering questions, or doing written exercises assigned from a commercially produced textbook.

In contrasting the traditional with the active school, Piaget indicates that the latter type of learning environment "appeals to real activity, to spontaneous work based upon personal need and interest."[9] This does not imply, however, that children can do whatever they want; it means that learning takes place through a child's inherent interests and natural curiosity. The teacher in the active school considers students' social, physical, cognitive, and linguistic development when structuring the learning environment. The curriculum, rather than being built around content, is built around the child. More specifically, children are active participants in their own learning. Reading, writing, and listening grow out of meaningful experiences. Conversation with peers is regarded as a significant part of a child's mental, social, and linguistic development. Concrete or real objects and events are always present in the learning environment. The children act on their environment, rather than being acted upon, and thus internally organize experiences (assimilation and accommodation). This is the learning climate of the active school.

The teacher is responsible for establishing the learning environment. The physical organization, concrete materials, and experiences are planned by the teacher. It is the teacher who is the knowledgeable source in the active classroom, not the textbook materials spelling out areas of content. The teacher understands how children learn best and is aware of each child's needs, abilities, interests, background of experience, and level of development.

The teacher who forms the classroom curriculum around the child's needs, interests, and abilities becomes a facilitator or director of learning. The teacher in the active school is not in the role of the dispenser of knowledge. Through a teacher's intervention at the appropriate time, a child's learning may be extended or the quality of an experience raised. Questions, comments, words of encouragement, or suggestions can all act as learning stimulants. A question at the right moment may extend a child's thinking or cause that child to study a problem in greater depth.

Trust is important in this type of learning setting. That is, a teacher must learn to trust children with their own learning. Trial and error are integral parts of the learning process. Children need to be given time to work out solutions to problems. As they explore and experiment within their environment, assimilation and accommodation occur. Throughout this process, intervention by the teacher can be significant; however, intervention can become interference if it is not presented appropriately when the child needs the help.

It is important for the teacher to listen to children; their questions, comments, and conversations offer insights into their thinking. Much can be learned about a child's level of development if one listens carefully and knowledgeably. Children's errors also reveal their thinking; in fact, it probably is more beneficial for the teacher to look closely at children's mistakes than at what they say or do correctly. Piaget states, "Above all, teachers should see the reasons behind errors. Very often a child's errors are valuable clues to his thinking."[10]

THE DEVELOPMENT OF THINKING SKILLS

The teacher who listens and plans learning experiences around students' cognitive abilities also considers ways in which to facilitate and broaden their thinking. The classroom curriculum reflects the idea that students who are encouraged to become actively involved in finding out, discovering, solving problems, constructing models, sharing projects, and touching, seeing, and describing the world around them develop language and thinking skills that will serve them for the rest of their lives.

What kind of thinking is required of most students? Are they usually given low-level cognitive-memory tasks that require them to recall facts and predetermined answers? Or do teachers provide activities that will develop a wide range of thinking skills, including the ability to evaluate and make judgments about oral and written material? Are young children given enough opportunities to sort and group objects? Are older students encouraged to make close observations and then write about their findings? These tasks, and others similar to them, extend students' thinking abilities by challenging them to use skills that demand flexibility of thought. These experiences also can be a natural part of the daily classroom curriculum, as is shown in the following discussion of several different types of thinking experiences.

Sorting

Children can participate in a variety of sorting activities as part of their everyday learning. For instance, a group of students went on a neighborhood walk and

Sorting activities can be a natural part of the everyday learning environment.

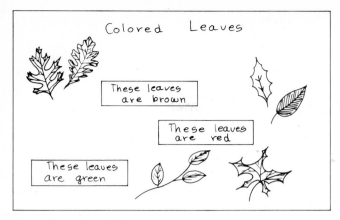

Figure 2-3   Autumn display.

collected a number of interesting items. These were sorted, labeled, and attractively displayed. One group of four children sorted their collections of leaves by placing the green leaves in one pile, the brown leaves in another, and the reddish leaves in still another. They then selected representative leaves from each of the three piles, attached them to a large piece of posterboard, and wrote brief descriptions to identify each of the categories, as in Figure 2-3.

Another class decided they could help the appearance of the school by cleaning up the area around it. They spent part of a morning picking up litter—bottles, cans, gum and candy wrappers, and old pieces of newspaper. When the students returned to the room, they sorted and counted the different items to find out what seemed to be littered most often around the school. They discovered that they had collected more gum and candy wrappers than any other item. This finding led to a discussion about why there were so many gum and candy wrappers and what might be done to correct the litter problem.

Besides offering children a variety of sorting experiences such as these, items for sorting may be available on a special table in the classroom, or sorting boxes can be made with very little effort. Counters, balls, blocks, toothpicks, small toys, straws, pencils, paper clips, and rubber bands are only a few of the items that might be placed in sorting boxes. If you cover the boxes with wrapping paper or contact paper, they will be much more attractive.

Very young children usually will sort objects according to color. For example, given a collection of green, yellow, and red buttons, a child will place all the red ones together, all the green ones together, and so on. Asked if there is another way to sort them, the child may say *no,* even though some buttons are square and others are round. A child whose thinking is more advanced may quickly sort the buttons according to color, size, and shape. The student who is in the concrete-operational stage of cognitive development may be able to sort objects according to a wide variety of attributes, including texture and weight. By asking a few thought-provoking questions, a teacher may also help a child see new ways of sorting objects and thus extend the child's thinking.

LEARNING THROUGH ACTIVE PARTICIPATION

Observing

Opportunities to observe closely are helpful in developing and extending children's thinking. What does it mean to observe closely? We have all admired a beautiful piece of furniture or lovely garment. Without close observation, however, it is difficult to evaluate the quality of the furniture or the garment. What about the workmanship? the design? the quality of the wood or fabric? These are questions that we answer by using and applying critical observations.

We need to help children become better observers. Having students observe details and describe them in writing is one way of doing this. For example, some children were interested in caring for a budding plant that their teacher had brought to school. To extend the learning experience, the teacher suggested that they record their observations of the plant each morning when they checked on it. Over a period of several weeks the students wrote their precise observations of the plant. They described the different stages of blooming and recorded observations about its size, its shape, its color, the number of leaves, the quantities of buds and when each opened, and the amount of water that the plant required. One student wrote her observations in the form of a diary, and another student shared a poem that he had written about the plant. Their final project was to compare their writings and compose a group experience story about their observations.

These students were becoming close observers. A variety of experiences that will develop children's observational skills are close at hand in most elementary school classrooms—observing the birds that come to the window each morning, the weather as it changes from day to day, the goldfish, hamster, or guinea pig, the trees as their leaves change to the autumn colors, or indoor plants that the students have planted.

Comparing

As adults we are required to make comparisons; for instance, when we buy a car, we compare the qualities of one automobile over another on the basis of our individual needs. After comparing and contrasting several makes of cars, we make some type of decision. Children, too, make comparisons when they shop for such things as toys, candy, and gifts.

Experiences that involve comparing one thing with another can be included very easily in the school day. Students can increase their skills at recognizing likenesses and differences as well as making certain kinds of judgments. A teacher's questions can create situations where children are asked to make comparisons: *How are these two shapes different? How is this story like the one we read yesterday? How are these two shells alike? What can you say about their size? Who is taller, Jimmy or Kay?* Questions such as these can be asked during any part of the day.

Students may also enjoy comparing and contrasting books. A number of children's stories have similar themes, plots, characters, or illustrations. Book comparisons can inspire conversations between the teacher and young children; and for older children, they provide opportunities for in-depth discussions. Are the characters Dandelion and Dazzle, in the books titled with their names, alike in some way? How is the book *Deep in the Forest* similar to the book *The Three Bears*? What similarities do you find between the two stories *Island of the Blue Dolphins* and *Julie of the Wolves*? In planning the questions that you ask about books, you will need to consider the children's level of cognitive development. However, there are many picture books that may be used with older children.

The following presents a partial listing of literature that may be compared.

Picture Books to Compare

Lionni, Leo. *Fish Is Fish*. New York: Pantheon, 1970.
Massie, Diane Redfield. *Walter Was a Frog*. New York: Simon & Schuster, 1970.

Galdone, Paul. *The Three Bears*. New York: Seabury, 1972.
Turkle, Brinton. *Deep in the Forest*. New York: Dutton, 1976.

Zemach, Margot. *It Could Always Be Worse*. New York: Farrar, Straus & Giroux, 1976.
Viorst, Judith. *Alexander and the Terrible, Horrible, No Good, Very Bad Day*. New York: Atheneum, 1972.

Keats, Ezra Jack. *The Snowy Day*. New York: Viking, 1962.
Bourne, Miriam. *Emilio's Summer Day* (Ben Shecter, illustr.). New York: Harper & Row, 1966.

Wildsmith, Brian. *The Lion and the Rat*, a fable by La Fontaine. New York: Watts, 1963.
Steig, William. *Amos and Boris*. New York: Farrar, Straus & Giroux, 1970.

Freeman, Don. *Dandelion*. New York: Viking, 1964.
Massie, Diane Redfield. *Dazzle*. New York: Parents Magazine, 1969.
Zion, Gene. *Harry the Dirty Dog* (Margaret Bloy Graham, illustr.). New York: Harper & Row, 1966.

Lionni, Leo. *Swimmy*. New York: Pantheon, 1963.
Valens, Evans G. *Wingfin and Topple* (Clement Hurd, illustr.). Cleveland: World Publishing, 1962.

Shecter, Ben. *Conrad's Castle*. New York: Harper & Row, 1967.
Shulevitz, Uri. *One Monday Morning*. New York: Scribner, 1967.

Raskin, Ellen. *Nothing Ever Happens on My Block*. New York: Atheneum, 1966.
Seuss, Dr., pseud. (Theodore S. Geisel). *And to Think That I Saw It on Mulberry Street*. New York: Vanguard, 1937.

Asbjornsen, P. C., and J. E. Moe. *The Three Billy Goats Gruff* (Susan Blair, illustr.). New York: Holt, 1963.
Asbjornsen, P. C., and J. E. Moe. *The Three Billy Goats Gruff* (Marcia Brown, illustr.). New York: Harcourt, Brace, 1957.

Books and Poetry to Compare

Crews, Donald. *Freight Train*. New York: Greenwillow, 1978.
McCord, David. "Song of the Train," *One At A Time*. Boston: Little, Brown, 1974.

Williams, Barbara. *Albert's Toothache* (Kay Chorao, illustr.). New York: Dutton, 1974.
DeGroat, Diane. *Alligator's Toothache*. New York: Crown, 1977.
Silverstein, Shel. "The Crocodile's Toothache," *Where the Sidewalk Ends*. New York: Harper & Row, 1974.

Emberly, Barbara. *Drummer Hoff* (Ed Emberly, illustr.). Englewood Cliffs, N.J.: Prentice-Hall, 1967.
Silverstein, Shel. "The Generals," *Where the Sidewalk Ends*. New York: Harper & Row, 1974.

Schlein, Miriam. *The Girl Who Would Rather Climb Trees* (Gwyn Brown, illustr.). New York: Harcourt, 1975.
McCord, David. "Everytime I Climb A Tree," *One At A Time*. Boston: Little, Brown, 1974.

Briggs, Raymond. *The Snowman*. New York: Random House, 1978.
Silverstein, Shel. "Snowman," *Where the Sidewalk Ends*. New York: Harper & Row, 1974.

Mayer, Mercer. *There Is a Nightmare in My Closet*. New York: Dial Press, 1968.
Prelutsky, Jack. "The Wozzit" and "It," *The Snopp on the Sidewalk* (Byron Barton, illustr.). New York: Greenwillow, 1977.

Middle-Grade Books to Compare

Wahl, Jan. *Dracula's Cat* (Kay Chorao, illustr.). Englewood Cliffs, N.J.: Prentice-Hall, 1978.
Wahl, Jan. *Frankenstein's Dog* (Kay Chorao, illustr.). Englewood Cliffs, N.J.: Prentice-Hall, 1977.

Mayer, Marianna. *Beauty and the Beast* (Mercer Mayer, illustr.) New York: Four Winds, 1978.
McKinley, Robin. *Beauty*. New York: Harper & Row, 1978.

Smith, Doris Buchanan. *A Taste of Blackberries*. New York: Crowell, 1973.
Paterson, Katherine. *Bridge to Terabithia*. New York: Crowell, 1977.

O'Dell, Scott. *Island of the Blue Dolphins*. Boston: Houghton Mifflin, 1960.
George, Jean. *Julie of the Wolves*. New York: Harper & Row, 1973.
George, Jean. *My Side of the Mountain*. New York: Dutton, 1959.

Kerr, Judith. *When Hitler Stole Pink Rabbit*. New York: Coward-McCann, 1972.
Reiss, Johanna. *The Upstairs Room*. New York: Crowell, 1972.

Fitzhugh, Louise. *Harriet the Spy*. New York: Harper & Row, 1964.
Sachs, Marilyn. *Veronica Ganz*. Garden City, N.Y.: Doubleday, 1968.
Rodgers, Mary. *Freaky Friday*. New York: Harper & Row, 1972

Burch, Robert. *Queenie Peavy*. New York: Viking, 1966.
Gold, Sharlya. *Amelia Quackenbush*. New York: Seabury, 1973.

Estes, Eleanor. *The Hundred Dresses*. New York: Harcourt, 1944.
Blume, Judy. *Blubber*. Scarsdale, N.Y.: Bradbury, 1974.
Greene, Constance C. *The Unmaking of Rabbit*. New York: Viking, 1972.

Classifying

Sorting and classifying are somewhat related activities. Both require a person to group items according to identifiable characteristics, and both involve the same type of thinking. However, classifying is usually a more complex and abstract task than sorting. Whereas sorting involves the manipulation of objects, classifying usually does not; therefore, classification activities are difficult for young children. They require not only abstract thought, but also background knowledge and experience. For example, classify or group the following words: *Mustang, Rabbit, Datsun, Corvette, Honda, Mazda*. One way of classifying the words might be to group them in a class called *automobiles;* or they may be placed in a class called *small cars*. When we classify, we may also have subclasses. For example, some of the cars are made in America and others are made in foreign countries. When we classify objects, places, people, animals, and so on, it is possible to categorize them in a variety of ways.

Classification experiences can occur naturally in the classroom. As students prepare bulletin boards or set up science displays, they can classify and label objects. For example, a collection of leaves, shells, rocks, and pebbles might be classified or grouped according to a number of their attributes (color: dark, light; weight: light, heavy; size: small, medium, large; texture: rough, bumpy, smooth; and so on). A small group of students might work together and plan several classification schemes based on related attributes. After a discussion, they could decide which arrangement they preferred for their display. This type of activity helps students identify regularities and relations of things in their environment.

A popular classification activity, which is certainly not new, is called *animal, vegetable, mineral*. Using these three classes, try grouping the following items: horse, paper, tire, gasoline, lettuce, broccoli, milk, bread, people, mink, pencil, and emerald.

As students progress in their ability to classify, they might be challenged to develop a matrix which graphically illustrates a cross-classification of items. They might begin with a matrix consisting of four squares as shown in Figure 2-4.

A more complicated matrix might include more squares and show a number of related attributes. Look at Figure 2-5 and try completing the matrix.

There are an infinite number of possibilities for developing classification skills. *Thinking Goes to School*[11] is an excellent source for classification games that can be used with various age groups. As students have more experiences

Animals

	Dog	Cat
Large	Saint Bernard	Tiger
Small	Chihuahua	Siamese kitten

Size

Figure 2-4   Simple cross-classification.

Transportation

	Private	Public
Land		
Water		
Air		

Figure 2-5   Classification matrix.

with classifying, they will readily comprehend how things around them may be grouped into classes and subclasses.

Summarizing

Telling or writing a summary requires a different type of thinking from that used in sorting, observing, comparing, and classifying. We must take a body of content and briefly capture its essence. The main points of what we have read or heard need to be summarized in the appropriate and logical sequence. If we summarize a story, we have to decide what content, events, and characters are most important to include. If we summarize a speech that we have heard, we must be able to distinguish between relevant and irrelevant points.

It is very important that children have a purpose for telling or writing a summary. Therefore, the word *summary* is frequently associated with the formal written book report, a traditional assignment that has made more children nonreaders than readers. However, the skill of summarizing can be developed through a variety of purposeful and meaningful activities. Some suggestions follow.

Invite outside speakers into the class. They are valuable resources, and they can provide students with opportunities to practice summarizing skills. Tell the students to listen for main ideas and write them down as they listen to a speaker. Afterward, conduct a discussion of the main ideas and compose a summary together. Write the summary on a chart or the chalkboard. You may want students to copy the group summary as a model to follow.

Have students listen as you read an article from a newspaper or magazine. Discuss the main ideas and list them on the chalkboard. Working in small groups, ask the students to weave them into a summary of the article. Transfer the group summaries to transparencies which in turn can be shared, discussed, and evaluated by the entire class.

Give the students an article along with a summary that requires rewriting. In small groups, have them find and discuss the problems with the summary before evaluating it as a whole class.

Pupils can tape-record or write summaries of books which they have enjoyed reading. Summaries recorded on cassette tapes may be placed in a listening center, or they may accompany a bulletin board that is developed around a favorite book. Written summaries may take the form of book reviews or blurbs on book jackets that students design and make.

DEVELOPING SKILLS OF CRITICAL THINKING

Critical thinking is related to critical reading and listening. There are activities in listening that you will want to refer to in Chapter 7 that relate to critical thinking. In this section we will limit the discussion to what is meant by the term *critical thinking* and ways one might critically analyze oral and written statements.

What is critical thinking? Ennis defines critical thinking as the correct assessment of statements based on certain judgments.[12] How are these judgments made? Appropriate questions are asked and answers applied to the material that is being evaluated. Following is a representative selection of questions that may be considered depending on the type of material under scrutiny.

Is the problem identified and addressed?
Is there ambiguity in a line of reasoning?
Do statements contradict one another?
Is the statement specific enough?
Is a definition adequate?
Is an observational statement reliable?
Is something merely an assumption, or is it supported by facts?
On the basis of preceding statements, does the conclusion follow logically?

Students in the upper elementary and middle grades can critically evaluate newspaper and magazine articles, statements made on television or radio, and reading material available in the classroom. Certain questions may be asked regarding statements in textbooks, basal readers, or library books.

If we are to develop good thinkers—people who can make wise decisions and objective judgments—then we need to be concerned about teaching a variety of thinking skills beginning in the elementary school. Teachers need to evaluate the activities and experiences that are provided for their students. If they are primarily pencil-and-paper tasks requiring rote recall or a limited response, then children are involved in low-level thinking tasks. However, if they are developing classifications, writing detailed observations, comparing and talking about books, making critical judgments concerning written and oral statements, then they are participating in stimulating and higher-order thinking activities.

SUMMARY

Piaget's theory of intellectual development suggests that all children go through identifiable stages of cognitive development. A teacher who understands the characteristics of these stages plans a learning environment that considers the children's level of development. And experiences to develop and extend students' thinking and reasoning abilities are an inherent part of such an environment.

UNDERSTANDING THROUGH INVOLVEMENT

1. Collect a variety of items to be sorted. Have kindergarten children sort the items. Next, have fourth-grade children sort the same items. Compare how the young children sorted the items with how the older students sorted them.
2. Select a five- or six-year-old child and a seven- or eight-year-old child. Conduct the following activity *separately* with the two children, assessing each child's ability to take another's point of view.

   If the children do not remember the story *Goldilocks and the Three Bears,* you will want to read it aloud to them. Ask them to first retell the story from the bears' point of view. Afterward, have the children retell the story from Goldilocks' point of view.

   The story is written from the point of view of the bears; therefore, retelling the story from Goldilocks' standpoint requires reversibility of thought and the ability to take another's point of view.
3. Read two books aloud that may be compared. Prepare several questions that will stimulate a discussion of their likenesses and differences. After the discussion, encourage the children to make a chart or construct a bulletin board to illustrate the similarities between the two books.
4. Plan a classifying experience. Try it with both young and older elementary school students. Compare their responses.
5. Children's questions are clues to their thinking. Record, either in writing or on tape, young children's questions and analyze them using your present knowledge of developmental theory. This may be done in a school setting or with young children you know.

   Answers to questions will also provide insights to children's thinking. To illustrate, try asking the following questions and record young preoperational children's responses. Conduct the same activity with concrete-operational children and then compare the two sets of responses. *Where does the sun go at night? During the day, where does the moon go? Are trees alive?—flowers?— rocks? Why does the rain fall?*
6. Develop two or three classification matrices and try them out with middle-grade children. Then see if the students can make another classification matrix of their own.

REFERENCE NOTES

[1]John Dewey. *Experience and Education.* New York: Collier, 1939, p. 19.

[2]Leo Lionni. *Fish Is Fish.* New York: Pantheon, 1970.

[3]Barry J. Wadsworth. *Piaget's Theory of Cognitive Development.* New York: McKay, 1971, p. 16.

[4]Eleanor Duckworth. "Piaget Takes a Teacher's Look," *Learning,* October 1973, p. 25.

[5]Mary Ann Spencer Pulaski. *Understanding Piaget.* New York: Harper & Row, 1971, pp. 19–20.

[6]David Elkind. *Children and Adolescents: Interpretive Essays on Jean Piaget.* New York: Oxford University Press, 1970, p. 52.

[7]Jean Piaget. *Six Psychological Studies.* New York: Vintage Books, 1967, p. 31.

[8]Jean Piaget. *Science of Education and the Psychology of the Child.* New York: Viking, 1970, p. 159.

[9]Ibid., p. 152.

[10]Duckworth. "Piaget Takes a Teacher's Look," p. 24.

[11]Hans G. Furth and Harry Wachs. *Thinking Goes to School.* New York: Oxford University Press, 1975.

[12]Robert H. Ennis. "A Concept of Critical Thinking," *Educational Leadership,* vol. 21, October 1963, pp. 17–20, 39.

CHAPTER THREE

Describing Linguistic Variations

PREVIEW QUESTIONS

1   How does the English language change, and what kinds of events trigger such changes?
2   What functions does language serve?
3   What kinds of communication are nonverbal?
4   How do dialects differ, and what features of dialects are important for teachers to know?
5   What is language usage as a variation of language, and what are appropriate ways to handle differences in usage?

English, like other languages, varies in many different ways. It has changed across time, so that the English spoken today is somewhat different from that of Shakespeare and very different from that of Chaucer. There are also geographic variations, particularly in how English is spoken. These variations include distinctions between American and British English; they also include differences among New Englanders, midwesterners, southerners, and so forth. There are social variations in our use of language; we do not talk the same way to our close friends or family as we do to our minister or school superintendent. We vary what we say and what we write. The words we use when we talk with others in our own field are somewhat different from those we use with outsiders. We also use language for different purposes—sometimes talk is a way of acquiring information; other times it is simply a way of maintaining social relationships. Language usually suggests words and sentences, but we communicate a great deal without words. A teacher puts an index finger across the lips to ask for silence; a shrug of the shoulders says *Who knows?* Nonverbal communication, intentional or not, conveys a great deal of meaning. For some students in our schools, English is a foreign language. A good language arts program must consider all these variations.

A BRIEF HISTORY OF ENGLISH

English was not the native language in the British Isles. When Julius Caesar explored the island in 55 and 54 B.C. it was inhabited by Celts. About one hundred years later the Roman legions came and conquered the southern two-thirds of the island and remained there until the early 400s. There were raids from the northern Germanic tribes, who settled in what is now England. When the legionnaires withdrew, the Celts were unable to stop the invaders, and so the Germanic peoples were able to make permanent settlements. These three tribes all spoke Low West German dialects, which became fused into what we call Old English. Since there are very few Celtic words which were borrowed or retained in Old English, the Angles, Saxons, and Jutes probably had little contact with the Celts. The latter retreated to what is now Scotland, Wales, Ireland, and Cornwall.

There was a means of writing at this time—the Runic alphabet—but it was used only for magic spells and inscriptions; there were no written histories, and the literature was transmitted in oral form. Extended writing was introduced by the Roman missionaries who came to convert England to Christianity beginning in A.D. 597. The development of written literature and history was slowed down by the Viking raids and invasions from 787 until 886 when King Alfred the Great of West Saxony made a treaty which gave the Vikings the northeastern part of the island. It was also King Alfred the Great who had many books translated into English, and the Anglo-Saxon Chronicle was begun during his reign.

The next major influences on written English take place in the 1400s. At this time education was extended to the middle classes, and both men and women learned to read and write. These skills were no longer the province of just the nobility, the religious orders, and clerks. Then in 1476 Caxton set up a printing press in London, and books became available to many more people. The existence of printing established certain conventions of writing—especially spelling—and also established the English of the London area as a standard.

In the 1700s there were several important influences on the written language. In 1706 the Kersey edition of *The New World of English Words* was published, the first dictionary to include basic words as well as more unusual ones. Samuel Johnson's dictionary was published in 1755. It derived its words from the language actually used and included word meanings and dated references indicating when particular words appeared. The 1762 publication of Lowth's *Short Introduction to English Grammar* had a significant influence on written language. In contrast to Priestly's grammar published the year before, Lowth was more concerned with regularity than actual usage; and his grammar, based on the concept of a universal and Latinate grammar, reflected how he thought English *should* be spoken and written.

One of the interesting features of the English language is the astounding number of non-Germanic-based words, or borrowed words, in our language. These are primarily Latin, Greek, French, and Scandinavian in origin. Scandinavian words entered the language at the time of the Viking raids and were easily absorbed by the Anglo-Saxons who had come from neighboring areas. Latin words entered English primarily at two time periods. Many were brought by the Roman missionaries who by A.D. 700 had made England a center of learning and scholarship in which most writing was in Latin. Another period of borrowing occurred in the 1500s at the time of the English Renaissance. At this time another group of Latin words was borrowed in addition to many Greek ones. The borrowings from French also occurred at two main times. Many French words came into the language at the time of the Norman conquest in 1066. Frenchmen were put in the important secular and religious positions; they saw no reason to change their language, and so the English were almost forced to learn some French to get along. Many of these words became an integral part of the language. Then in 1216 Henry III became king of England and again imported many French people. Thus a new group of French words entered the English language along with this new ruling group.

Words are still being borrowed from other languages, but the vocabulary of a language changes in other ways, too. New inventions, places, and phenomena have to be named (*space shuttle, astronaut,* and *cosmonaut*). This may be done by making compound words from other words or word parts, or by blending two words together as in *smog* or *brunch.* Proper names and brand names may become generally used. Word meanings may also shift by becoming specialized or generalized, elevated or degenerated. Thus *hūswif* became contracted to *hussy* and was so uncomplimentary that the original elements were later recombined to *housewife.* Some usages become common and accepted, and others drop out of ordinary usage.

The development of the English language has not been just a series of borrowings from other languages along with the development of a written language. A third series of changes has taken place in the pronunciation and syntax of English. Since English was a blend of three German dialects, it originally had many of the characteristics of German. There were word endings or inflections to indicate gender, tense, case, and so on. These inflectional endings began to disappear as an established word order developed in the 1300s and 1400s. More recent changes in syntax are the development of the past and progressive verb tenses such as *have been being treated* and an increase in verb-adverb combinations such as *put down, put off,* and so on.

The most significant of the sound changes occurred between about 1450 and 1650 and is called either the great vowel shift or the fifteenth-century vowel shift. Before the shift the pairs of short and long vowels had about the same general sound; the difference was simply the length of time they were held. The vowels were similar to those in modern Spanish or Italian. After the vowel shift occurred, the sound /a/ as in *papa* changed to /e/ as in *place;* the /e/ changed to /i/ as in *feet;* the /i/ became dipthongized to /ai/ as in *bite;* the /ɔ/ of *off* changed to /o/ as in *stone;* the /o/ changed to /u/ as in *fool;* and the /u/ became dipthongized to /au/ as in *mouse* (slash marks indicate sounds or phonemes). The vowel shift occurred after many of the spelling conventions had been established, and so today we often use the same letters to represent phonetically unrelated sounds. In fact, the sound shift accounts for most of our inconsistency in spelling vowel sounds.

The chart which follows indicates the major historical events which affected the English language and the progression of changes in the language. Information for the chart comes primarily from L. M. Myer's *Roots of Modern English.*[1] The samples of Old English from *Beowulf,* of Middle English from Chaucer, and of Early Modern English from Shakespeare illustrate the changes which have taken place in the language throughout the last twelve centuries.

DATES	HISTORICAL EVENTS	INFLUENCE ON LANGUAGE
55–54 B.C.	Britain inhabited by Celts Julius Caesar invades Britain	No English language Celtic languages and Latin spoken
43 A.D.	Roman conquest of Britain	in geographic area of Britain
409	Roman legions withdrawn Celtic inhabitants must resist Pict raids from the north and Germanic raids along east coast	
450–650	Anglo-Saxon invasion Angles from Denmark occupy the northern two-thirds of what is now England; the Saxons from northern Germany occupy most of the southern third; a third group (Jutes?) occupies the southwest corner	OLD ENGLISH PERIOD (400–1100) All three Germanic tribes speak Low West German dialects that are mutually understandable; these fuse into what we call Old English; very little borrowing or use of Celtic Probably no written histories of this period; Runic alphabet used for magic spells and inscriptions; literature transmitted orally
597	Roman missionaries begin converting England; St. Augustine of Canterbury sent by Gregory the Great with 40 companions	Although people illiterate, the missionaries introduce extended writing; within one hundred years England becomes one of the centers of learning and scholarship; much of writing in Latin as Bede's (ca. 731) *Ecclesiastical History of the English People,* but from 650 on some poetry in English, especially in Anglian dialect

DATES	HISTORICAL EVENTS	INFLUENCE ON LANGUAGE
787–886	Danish Viking raids begin in northern England; from 850 or so Danes begin to make permanent settlements. In 886 King Alfred the Great, king of Wessex (West Saxony) stops them and by a treaty gives them the northeastern part of England leaving the southern part free. The Danes are gradually absorbed into the English population. More Danish raids in 900s and early 1000s	The Vikings destroy books which are useless to them and which they fear might contain magic spells their enemies could use against them King Alfred the Great has many books translated into English; there is an English translation of Bede's *Ecclesiastical History* and *The Anglo-Saxon Chronicle* is begun

---

SAMPLE OF OLD ENGLISH

"þu eart endelaf   usses cynnes, Wægmund inga;   ealle wyrd
thou art last remnant of our kin   of-Waegumundings; all   fate

forsweop   mine magas   to metodsceafte, eorlas   on elne;
swept away my   kinsmen to destiny   earls   in valor

ic him   æfter sceal."
I them after must."

c. 700 A.D. *Beowulf*, lines 2813–2816

DATES	HISTORICAL EVENTS	INFLUENCE ON LANGUAGE
1066	Norman conquest of England by William the Conqueror who defeats King Harold at the Battle of Hastings; William gains control of all of England and organizes it into one country instead of numerous semi-independent earldoms; redivides land holdings and puts Normans and other Frenchmen in most of the important positions, both secular and religious	Norman rulers speak French and see no reason to change; some English learn French as a way to get ahead; a great many more learn at least some French words and these become a part of English
1100s	Kings and nobles consider themselves Frenchmen who have lands in England	
1204	Normandy lost to the English crown; nobles must choose between English and French holdings	**MIDDLE ENGLISH PERIOD** (1100–1500)

DATES	HISTORICAL EVENTS	INFLUENCE ON LANGUAGE
1216–1272	Henry III is King of England and imports Frenchmen from areas outside Normandy whose speech is more like Central French and unlike Norman French, especially that spoken at that time in England	The Norman English begin to feel quite English in contrast to the new French in power; more and different French words enter the language By the late 1200s French begins to disappear as the primary language, even with the nobility
1250s	Oxford and Cambridge well established	
1350	English is used in schools	
1362	English required to be used in all lawsuits	English of this period is not a unified language, but a variety of dialects which must be translated to be understood; there is no book of grammar, no dictionary, no spelling book, and not even agreement on the alphabet Many sound changes take place; perhaps more important is the beginning of the loss of inflectional endings (to indicate gender, tense, case . . .) and the development of a standard word order
1387–1400	Chaucer's *Canterbury Tales*	Tremendous number of French words added to English vocabulary from 1200–1400; some are Norman French and some Central French

---

SAMPLE OF MIDDLE ENGLISH

At nyght was come into that hostelrye
Wel nyne and twenty in a compaignye
Of Sondry folk, by aventure yfalle   (*aventure = chance*)
In felaweshipe, and pilgrimes were they alle,
That toward Caunterbury wolden ryde.

c. 1390 A.D. Chaucer, *Prologue to the Canterbury Tales,* lines 23–27

1400–1500	Extension of education and more secular education; by 1500 many middle-class men and women learn to read and write English	MODERN ENGLISH PERIOD (1500–Present)
1476	William Caxton sets up first printing press, and London becomes the center of printing	Careers as authors encouraged Establishment of conventions of writing, especially spelling

DATES	HISTORICAL EVENTS	INFLUENCE ON LANGUAGE
1476		London English established as the standard, except for Scottish dialect
1500–1660	English Renaissance	
1642–1660	First Civil War Restoration	Many changes in pronunciation (the Great Vowel Shift) although spelling set
		Tremendous increase in vocabulary; borrowings from Latin, borrowings from other modern languages, revivals from middle English. This gives English many synonyms to express exact shades of meaning and words that express an idea that might take four or more "native" words to express (e.g., *conflagration:* a number of fires burning at the same time and adding to each other)

SAMPLE OF MODERN ENGLISH—ENGLISH RENAISSANCE PERIOD

But that the dread of something after death—
The undiscovered country from whose bourn
No traveller returns—puzzles the will,
And makes us rather bear those ills we have
Than fly to others that we know not of?

c. 1600 A.D. Shakespeare, *Hamlet,* Act III

DATES	HISTORICAL EVENTS	INFLUENCE ON LANGUAGE
1660–1800	The authoritarian period	Throughout this period in America new vocabulary from borrowed Indian words and new things (*squash, bluff*)
		Development of the great difference between how people actually speak and school theory of how they should speak based on concept of a universal grammar
1670–1713	Unsuccessful attempt by Dryden and Swift to set up something in England comparable to the French Academy	
1706	Kersey edition of *The New World of English Words*	First dictionary to include basic vocabulary as well as "hard" words
1714	George I succeeds Queen Anne; he is German and does not even learn to speak English	Movement to set up an English Academy dies

DATES	HISTORICAL EVENTS	INFLUENCE ON LANGUAGE
1747–1755	Samuel Johnson's Dictionary	Derived from language actually used and includes meaning, dated references, and a grammatical introduction
1762	Lowth writes *Short Introduction to English Grammar*	Becomes *the* authority on what is correct; authoritarian attitude and concern for regularity rather than actual usage
1800s	Trade with the world and the establishment of the British Empire	Only about two-thirds of the population of the British Isles speak English; others are the Irish, Scottish, and Welsh Vocabulary is growing from 50,000 words in Johnson's dictionary to 450,000 in *Webster's Third New International Dictionary*
1840	Population of U.S.A. surpasses that of England and its individual characteristics affect the English language	Borrowed words from other settlers (*cookie* and *sleigh* from the Dutch) as well as from Indians
1900s	Industrial Revolution	Modern technology adds new words; compound words; acronyms like NATO; brand names like Kodak or Stetson Great changes in the meaning of older words such as *nice* which once meant *silly* and *deer* which once meant any *wild animal* The main structural changes in English since the 1700s are: simplification of inflections stopped, further development of the past and progressive verbs, and an increase in verb-adverb combinations such as *put down, put off, put out*
1932	*Current English Usage* by Leonard completed by National Council of Teachers of English	Revival of interest and acceptability in basing grammar on usage (a theory advanced by Priestly in 1761 but not accepted then); usage classified as literary, colloquial, or popular/illiterate
1952	Fries's *Structure of English*	Grammars developed which *describe* how English operates instead of *prescribing* what is correct or incorrect Structural grammar
1957–1965	Chomsky's *Syntactic Structures* and *Aspects of the Theory of Syntax*	Transformational Generative grammar
1970s		Emphasis on sociolinguistics

Many children in the upper elementary grades enjoy working with the history of words. They may like collecting words based on new inventions or other newly invented words. They may even enjoy inventing some of their own by compounding or combining other word parts. They might interview older people to find out what the slang words were when they were young and make up a list of new and old slang expressions. They can also write to children in another part of the country to find out what words they use for certain things.

Older students might like to trace the origins of words connected with particular sports, foods, or fashions. This can be one activity as a part of a larger unit of study. In working with modern historical events, students might make a list of words new to our language between 1900 and 1940 and another list containing new words from 1941 until the present. These would be words related to events which took place during those time periods. Exact dating can be checked in *Webster's Third New International Dictionary* (Springfield, Massachusetts, 1966).

CONCEPTS OF LANGUAGE

Some aspects of the nature of language are apparent when we examine its historical development. Others need to be examined in terms of how language is used. The qualities of language affect both what we understand about variations and changes in language and how we feel about those variations and changes.

Language is *systematic*. The changes that have occurred over time are not haphazard; they occur in recognizable patterns. Although many people complain about irregularities in the phoneme-grapheme correspondences, or sound-letter relationships, actually English is very systematic. In fact, changing the spellings of words to reflect their pronunciations more closely would actually proliferate problems for speakers of all dialects other than the dialect chosen. Would you want everything spelled the way it would be pronounced in Great Britain?

Language is *evolving*. We are constantly adding new words for new things, making new blends like *beefalo*, and revising our sense of whether a word usage is "generally acceptable" or not. We borrow words from other languages—the *chic* look, a *chaise longue*, the *patio*, a *waffle*, *dopè*, and *poppycock*. They borrow from us too. If you listened to a German sportscast, you might hear *dribbeln*, *kicken*, *skoren*, *knockouter*, or *sprinten*. *Charm*, which used to mean only a magic spell, is now complimentary. A *villain* was simply a farm worker; now the term is derogatory. The fact that our language changes enables us to adapt to new things and express ourselves very precisely.

Language is *conventional*. We can communicate with each other because we agree on what words mean and what word order signifies. If we agreed that the pet that barks bow-wow is called a gleep, that would be fine as long as everyone called it a gleep. We all interpret *Mary Ann beat Tom* as meaning that Mary Ann did the beating and Tom was the one beaten. Because there are rules about how language works and what words mean, we can talk or write to each other and to people we have never met.

Language is *arbitrary*. There are a few words whose meaning is reflected in the word itself. These are onomatopoetic words like *swoosh* or *ping*. Most words, however, are purely arbitrary; their meaning has nothing to do with them. There is nothing "cardlike" about the word *card*.

Language is *symbolic*. We use a word or a group of words to stand for an idea. The word is not the thing, person, idea, and so forth; it only represents the item.

Language is *redundant*. There are many ways to express a concept in language. English, in particular, uses multiple indicators of certain relationships which enable us to grasp quite easily the speaker or writer's idea, even if we do not notice each inflection. For example, in *Jim and Paul go to their jobs right after school*, there are four indications of plurality—the *and*, *their* instead of *his*, *go* instead of *goes*, and *jobs* instead of *job*. This redundancy enables us to read more quickly and listen more effectively.

These characteristics of language—that it is systematic, evolving, conventional, arbitrary, symbolic, and rendundant—should help us see its nature more clearly and view more accurately the variations and changes we encounter in it when we communicate.

FUNCTIONS OF LANGUAGE

Children's experiences with language, even from the very early stages of acquisition, help determine their view of how language is used and what it is for. A child's view of the uses of language may be quite different from that of the teacher, who sees language primarily as a means of conveying information. For the child sees many uses for language: it may create a new world through make-believe and sound and rhythm play, it may be highly personal as it helps to develop personality, or it may be used to control behavior.

In discussing the functions of language, Halliday[2] suggests that language is defined for the child by its uses and summarizes the models of language in terms of the child's intentions. The *instrumental function* occurs when children use language to get something they want—to satisfy material needs. In its *regulatory function* language is used to control behavior, as the child hears, *Do as I tell you*. Language also has an *interactional function* when it is used to mediate and maintain personal relationships, to define who is *one of us* and who is not. A fourth model of language is the *personal function*, in which language is a facet of the child's individuality. Here language is a means of making public the self—the self as a speaker. The *heuristic function* of language includes language as a way of finding out about things by asking questions. Children also use language to find out about language, so that by school age they know what a *question* is, what an *answer* is, and what *knowing* and *understanding* mean. In its *imaginative function*, language can be used to create a whole new world, a linguistically created environment focused on sounds. The final model is the *representational function* that adults are so aware of. Here, language is a means of communicating information or ideas; it is *I've got something to tell you* in use.

Let's examine a bit of conversation between two three-year-olds playing with some cars in a preschool.

Tom: That's my gold car, Bob.
Bob: No, I want it. You take the red one.
Tom: OK. Watch me. Brrr-brr. It's going to crash.
Bob: Mine's going fast too. It's fast like a rocket. Jet power.
Tom: Look out—there's a big turn up ahead. Better slow down.
Bob: Ohhhh, I'm going to crash, too. Call the ambulance.
Tom: Breaker, breaker. We need an ambulance.
Bob: Get a fire engine. We got a fire.
Tom: Ten-four. We can start to put it out. You and me, Bobby, we can put water on it. All race cars have a fire extinguisher.
Bob: I can do it. I can do like Superman. I am strong.
Tom: You hold it; I'll squirt water there.

In this rather brief conversation, a number of things are revealed. Both children exhibit some of their knowledge of the world. Bob knows about rockets and that they may have jet power. Tom knows about CB radios and fire extinguishers. They both use language in a variety of ways to serve different functions. Bob uses it as an instrument to get what he wants, "No, I want it" and later "Get a fire engine. We got a fire." They use it to regulate each other's behavior, "You take the red one." The interactional function is revealed with "We can start to put it out. You and me, Bobby, we can. . . ." Bob uses language in its personal function as he says, "I can do it. I can do like Superman. I am strong."

The children shift into full fantasy part way through their conversation. At first the cars represent real ones. They "rev" the engines and drive fast. Then, with the crash, the boys go into a full role-playing situation and call for the fire engine and ambulance on their CB and put the fire out. Here language serves an imaginative function. Tom also uses language in a representational way as he explains, "All race cars have a fire extinguisher." Within a short conversation, nearly all the functions of language are used.

Children's image of language is very broad in terms of the possible functions it serves. Teachers need to be aware of the multiple functions of language, for they are all equally real to the child. Teachers who fail to recognize that the imaginative function is as valid for children as the representational function may fail to see the needs and opportunities inherent in a given experience. Some children may not meet the demands that school makes, because they are not meeting the demands of school language. The teacher must help children develop their language in all its models or functions, not just concentrate on the representational function. For we always encounter language in use—language functioning.

Talking is one way of learning and of refining one's knowledge. Tough discusses this relationship as follows:

Characteristic of the young child's learning is the need for the actual experience, the information that comes to him through senses. Talk alongside this experience may draw his attention to the important aspects of this experience, will demonstrate a relationship, perhaps, or will help him to structure the whole into something which is coherent and meaningful. Talking that is relevant to his experience may then provide the child with a meaning for the experience different from that which it would have had if it had happened without the accompanying talk.[3]

Although we refer constantly to the need for rich experience, this does not necessarily mean highly unusual experiences. Taking a walk to a nearby store or shopping area, having a room mother demonstrate candle making, or making popcorn can provide rich experiences for children if the talk is right. Talking is one of the major ways that we learn about all kinds of things, not just language.

NONVERBAL LANGUAGE

Communication involves both being understood and understanding others. Verbal language is part of this, but nonverbal language also communicates. In fact, nonverbal cues are most often accepted as the "real thing" when they contradict verbal language.

Nonverbal language consists of virtually everything that communicates meaning except for verbal language. It may involve the tone of voice, facial expressions, body stance or posture, gestures, the expressions of the eyes, physical distance, dress, or even the omission of words or deeds. A brief aversion of the eyes or body shift can indicate disagreement or boredom. A lift of the chin and opening of the eyes may show a spark of interest. Some nonverbal language—a gesture of the finger meaning *come* or a narrowing of the eyes to say *no*—is used intentionally. Other nonverbal cues are given without our awareness. This often happens as we try to mask our real feelings with verbal language. Our unawareness of the cue is no indication at all, however, that the cue is not being noticed and responded to.

Relationship of Verbal and Nonverbal Behavior

Nonverbal behavior can add to verbal communication, supplement it, or substitute for it. Knapp[4] lists six ways in which verbal and nonverbal behavior interrelate: (1) *Repeating*. Nonverbal behavior simply repeats what is communicated orally. Pointing to an area while saying *It's there* is an example of this. (2) *Contradicting*. What one says may be contradicted by one's nonverbal communication. Saying *That's good* in an automatic fashion without the corresponding nonverbal enthusiasm reflects this contradiction. (3) *Substituting*. Often a nonverbal message can be used in place of a verbal one. A pat on the back, a smile, and a wink all tell a child that he or she has done well. (4) *Complementing*. Nonverbal messages can elaborate or modify the verbal message. Children's anger can be reflected in the distance from the teacher they take and in the stiffness of their bodies. (5) *Accenting*. The nonverbal message may accent the verbal in much the same way we may underline a word in a letter we're writing. Often this is done with gestures and head movements. (6) *Regulating*. Nonverbal behaviors help to regulate conversation, indicating who is to speak next and so forth.

While the functions of nonverbal behavior are separated here into six categories, they are often inseparable, and one nonverbal behavior may serve more than one function. Pointing to the door while saying *You are excused* repeats the verbal behavior while accenting it. Maintaining honesty and giving complementary rather than contradictory verbal and nonverbal messages is an important aspect of teaching.

Areas of Nonverbal Communication

There are many different ways that we communicate nonverbally. Wiemann and Wiemann[5] suggest four areas of nonverbal communication: the environment and personal space, body movement and orientation, the face and eyes, and nonlanguage behavior. All these relate to aspects of classroom instruction.

The environment and personal space In school, the environmental factors that are important are the room arrangement and placement of furniture. By altering the room arrangement, the teacher can alter the likelihood that students will participate. A circle or semicircle may encourage children to talk to one another. Sitting in rows facing the teacher focuses attention on the teacher as director. Personal space has to do with how close you want to get to others. Americans generally converse at about arm's length—1½ to 4 feet. Children tend to sit closest to each other and adolescents moderately close; adults are more comfortable at the farthest distances. Any number of factors may alter the distances with which people are comfortable, such as the topic of conversation, physical elements like the amount of noise or light, and the relationship between the speakers.

Body movement and orientation Much nonverbal communication is conveyed through gestures and through body movement and orientation. Gestures may substitute for verbal language as when a crook of the finger motions someone to go to the person gesturing or a shake of the head sharply signals *No!* They may add to our meaning as we motion appropriately while saying, *Left to right*. Body movement—the way we lean toward someone, for example, or how we sit—conveys messages about tension and liking.

The face and eyes There are certain cues that we transmit with our face or eyes that are somewhat constant and convey an impression. These are things like hair style and grooming. Most nonverbal communication related to the face and eyes, however, is related to the emotions we express. Researchers in this area have identified six basic emotions—disgust, fear, sadness, happiness, anger, and surprise—and contend that other emotions are combinations of the display features of these six. [Display features in the face are (1) cheeks and mouth, (2) brows and forehead, and (3) eyes and eyelids.] Some of these basic emotions appear to be cross-cultural; that is, the same facial expression conveys the same emotion to peoples from widely divergent cultures.

Eye signals are very important in communicating interest, showing attention, signaling a desire to talk, avoiding interaction, and making a statement about a relationship. Teachers can signal students that they should talk by a look, and children often avoid being called on by not looking directly at the teacher. Students who look directly at the teacher while he or she is explaining something are assumed to be "paying attention."

Nonlanguage vocal behavior   The vocal cues which accompany language but which do not have specific content are often called *paralanguage*. They include such things as pitch and tempo, clearing the throat or whispering, yelling, moaning, the intensity of speech, and fillers such as *ummm, uhh,* or *er.* Some nonlanguage vocal behavior—such as using the fillers noted above, changing a sentence in midpoint, repeating words, and stuttering—indicate anxiety. Using fillers such as *ah* may provide time for thinking and serve as a way to keep the floor.

An understanding of nonverbal language is extremely important because teachers often work with children whose nonverbal language system may differ from the teacher's. Where the systems differ there may be a serious lack of communication. Teachers who are aware of nonverbal cues may use these cues to change the personal interrelationships in the classroom and encourage communication from children.

Teachers who work with children of various cultural groups need to understand what meanings their own nonverbal cues project and how to interpret the nonverbal messages they receive from their students. An obvious illustration of this is eye contact. Suburban children habitually maintain eye contact with the teacher to project attention and respect. In Southwestern Indian cultures, however, children lower their heads and eyes to show deference and respect. Nonverbal behavior of children in inner-city schools may be interpreted as "smarty" or insolent when it is not intended that way at all. The more aware a teacher is of the nonverbal behavior of students, the more effective the communication between teacher and students.

Teachers may use their knowledge of nonverbal communication to enhance the communication and interaction in their classrooms. To illustrate, let's consider space and distance—two areas of obvious importance in the classroom. In the traditional classroom the teacher's desk is at the front of the class with the students' desks in rows facing it. The teacher's territory is that area around the desk and from the desk to the board and to the first row of pupils. Galloway comments, "More imaginative, fluid arrangements of desks and furniture influence the potential meaning of a learning context."[6] Distance is often maintained by staying in one's own territory or by setting up a table or some other object as a divider. Intentionally removing these can establish closeness, rapport, and more interaction. Physical arrangement of the room, therefore, reveals how a teacher feels about interaction and communication in the classroom. There are a number of other nonverbal cues which will encourage communication: a smile or nod to show enjoyment or agreement, a warm greeting or praise, vocal intonation and inflection patterns which indicate approval and support, a spontaneous attempt to help a pupil, the maintaining of eye contact when listening, and a stance of alert attention. All these are suggestive of interest and enthusiasm on the part of the teacher and tend to motivate. They set up the situation for success.

Nonverbal language is not something to be taken lightly. Because it is so subtle, it is very difficult to fake. Perhaps the most important factor in nonverbal communication is that it must be congruent with verbal behavior and with other aspects of nonverbal communication. Just saying *Good!* or *That's fine* is not communicating success unless the voice and the facial expression are saying the same thing.

DIALECTS OF ENGLISH

Dialects are variations of a language. Speaking a dialect other than the one most frequently used in a particular place or situation means differences in language—but only differences, not deficiencies. The English language is composed of a group of dialects which overlap, and so the dialect spoken in one area is understandable to speakers of a neighboring dialect. Speakers of dialects several regions apart, however, may experience some difficulty in understanding each other. Ashley and Malmstrom suggest that a language is a composite structure of overlapping idiolects, or speech patterns of an individual at a particular time of life.[7]

Dialects are usually determined by geographic regions or areas, although social factors also affect dialects. This is particularly evident when a group of people from one region come to live within a different geographic area but continue to associate mostly with each other for various social or economic reasons.

We tend to think that the way we ourselves speak is the right way, and that others are either "affected" or "ignorant." This is partly because we don't really have a clear understanding of dialect variation and partly because the way we speak is such an intrinsic part of ourselves. Somehow we just wouldn't be the same people if we spoke quite differently. Would you be you if you didn't sound like yourself?

In discussing whether one dialect is better than another, we have to define *better*. Better in what way? For the general purposes of communication, no one dialect is better than another. Each dialect is capable of expressing the thoughts of the speaker as well as another. Each particular dialect is also the best way of communicating with other speakers of that dialect. There are, however, some dialects which have greater social acceptability than others. Right or wrong, this is the situation today; and many who wish to become accepted by a different group must alter their language to be accepted. Eliza Doolittle of *My Fair Lady* must change her language to be accepted as a duchess instead of being marked as a flower girl. Perhaps this will change; perhaps it is already changing. Certainly we had several distinct dialects reflected in the language of three consecutive presidents during the 1950s and 1960s: Presidents Eisenhower, Kennedy, and Johnson. There is also a trend in radio and television to drop the single-style national network English for more individualistic language in announcers and performers.

Before discussing the teacher's role in working with children who speak less socially acceptable dialects, let's examine some of the causes for dialect variation in the United States and the kinds of variation which exist in dialects. There are five major dialect regions in this country: the coastal New England region, the northern region, the north midland region, the south midland region, and the southern region. The dialect regions do not follow state boundaries, since those boundaries do not reflect two of the basic reasons for dialect divergence—patterns of original settlement and patterns of migration. Examine the map in Figure 3-1, which illustrates the major dialect regions.

The dialect regions indicate that a person from northern Georgia or Alabama has a dialect more similar to someone from southern Ohio or Indiana than to someone from Florida. Someone from upper New York State would sound more like someone from Wisconsin than someone from southern New Jersey.

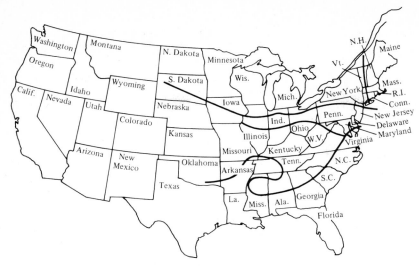

Figure 3-1 The five major dialect regions of the United States.

In today's highly mobile society, however, many individuals have a unique dialect which is the result of having lived in several areas or having participated in several social contexts. If you examine a map that shows physical features, the division of regions begins to look quite sensible. If you add to it the original settlement areas and trace the migrations westward, the dialect regions actually look reasonable. Another great influence on dialect patterns has been the impact of major cities on the surrounding area. Cities such as New York, Philadelphia, Charleston, Chicago, St. Louis, New Orleans, and San Francisco were important cultural centers as well as the focus of later immigrations.

How Dialects Differ

Just as there are three major areas of contrast in describing a language, the same contrasts are used in describing dialects. There may be *phonological* differences, or differences in pronunciation; *lexical* or *semantic* differences, which involve specific vocabulary; and *syntactic* differences, which involve the addition or omission of words or inflections and changes in the order of words.

The most frequent differences are phonological ones. These differences in pronunciation are very obvious even to a casual listener. They seldom cause real difficulty in understanding, but they may cause difficulties in reading—particularly in the area of phonics instruction. Two words that are pronounced differently in one dialect may be homonyms in another dialect. *Pin* and *pen* may be pronounced the same or distinctly differently; *merry, Mary,* and *marry* can be homonyms, or only the first two may be pronounced the same, or none of the three may sound alike.

The next most frequent dialect difference occurs in the lexical items used. A carbonated beverage is called many different things: in Rochester, New

York—*pop;* in Queens, New York—*soda;* in Boston—*tonic;* in Georgia—*Coke.* A small river may be called any of the following: *creek, stream, brook, run, branch, fork, prong, gulf, binnekill, binacle, rivulet, gutter, kill, bayou,* or *burn.*[8] These differences in words used for particular things will not usually cause difficulties in understanding.

The least frequent difference is in the syntactic area. When syntactic differences do occur, though, they usually cause real difficulty in comprehension. In Spanish-influenced English, *no* is used before a verb if the verb is followed by a negative word as in *Sarah no talk to no one.* In Afro-American English the inverted word order is used for indirect as well as direct questions as in *I want to know is he going somewhere.* The apparent absence of the possessive *-'s* in this same dialect as in *My aunt house* may be a syntactic difference, or it may be, as some linguists suggest, simply a difference in pronunciation. The addition of words is exemplified in some dialects by *I might could give you that* in the South or by *The Mr. Smith is here* or *on the Grand Avenue* in Spanish-influenced English.[9]

Features of Black English and Spanish-Influenced English

Teachers in the United States often have students in their classes who speak a black English dialect or whose dialect reflects Spanish. Understanding how one dialect is different from another is important especially in helping children to read and spell, and also in developing good attitudes toward children who speak differently from their teacher. Since lexical items change so much from place to place and from child to child, these will not be listed. They are relatively easy for a teacher to identify. The phonological and syntactic differences—at least the major ones—are described below.[10] (Arrows point to the change made.)

Features of black dialect

Phonological

Vowels:

1. Omission of glide with long vowels and diphthongs

    ride → *rod*   *oil* → *all*

2. Addition of glide with short vowels

    sit → /*siyat*/

Consonants:

3. Absence of *r* and *l*

    Paris → *pass*

4. Absence of final /t/ and /d/

   band → *ban*   *He played ball* → *He play ball*

5. Use of substitutes for *th*

   then → *den*   *nothing* → *nufin*

6. Use of substitutes for nasals, /n/ for /ŋ/

   going → *goin*

Syntactic

Verb constructions:

1. Nonstandard verb forms

   said → *say*   *were* → *was*   *gave* → *give*

2. Perfect construction inflections

   I have walked → *I have walk* (see also item 4 under "Phonological")

3. Overcorrection of present tense to first and second persons

   -s added: *I walks, you walks*, etc.

4. Expression of future by *gonna* or *goin'* and contracted *will*

   I gonna, he goin', and *I'll go* → *I go*

5. Use of invariant *be* for habitual actions

   He is busy → *He be busy*

Other constructions:

6. Inverted word order for indirect questions

   I wonder if he is going → *I wonder is he going*

7. Negation: use of double negatives and *ain't* as a negative

   He ain't going nowhere   *He didn't do no work*

Features of Spanish-influenced English

Phonological

Vowels:

1. Use of long vowel sounds for both long and short English vowels

*sit → seat   bet → bait   bat → bait   nut → not
caught → coat   full → fool*

Consonants:

2. Use of substitutes for nine English consonants that do not occur in Spanish

v *(very)*   j *(judge)*   z *(zoo)*   sh *(ship)*   ng *(song)*
zh *(measure)*   th *(with)*   th *(then)*   r *(real)*

3. Omission of certain consonant sounds at ends of words

All consonants except *d, s, l, r, n,* and *y*

4. Pronounciation of *s* in consonant clusters as a separate syllable

spot → es-pot, and so forth
*sp-   st-   sk-   sl-   sm-   sn-   sw-   spl-
spr-   str-   skr-   skw-*

Lexical

Although many words are similar in both Spanish and English (cognates like *segundo-second* and *especial-special*), there are many Spanish words that look like English words but mean something quite different (false cognates like *pan: bread,* or *fabrica: factory*)

Syntactic

1. Omission of verb endings, third person singular and past tense, and omission of auxiliaries and related inflections

*He plays ball
He played ball   → He play ball
He does play ball*

2. Omission of some subject pronouns since Spanish verbs have pronounlike endings

Is it red? → Is red?   He is the one → Is the one.

3. Use of double negatives (Spanish places *no* before the verb when a negative follows)

They went nowhere → They no went nowhere

4. Omission or inappropriate use of contractions

I'm going → I going   Yes, I am → Yes, I'm

5. Omission of possessive and plural *-s*

dogs → dog   girl's coat → girl coat

6. Incorrect use of gender references (Spanish gender agrees with the noun modified)

the table . . . she

7. Use of the definite article with person and place names

the Miss Watson   It is on the Prince Avenue

8. Use of the wrong preposition (In Spanish *en* could be on, in, at, into, to, for, and about)

The book is at the table

Considerations for the Classroom

There is no problem in dealing with children who speak a dialect divergent from the teacher's own if the dialect they speak is equally socially acceptable. Thus, a teacher from the midwest who teaches in suburban Boston or Providence does not feel any need to alter the dialect patterns of children in the class even though their dialect is quite different. The problem arises when the teacher is faced with children who speak a different dialect which is not as socially acceptable.

Three factors must be considered in deciding what to do with dialect differences in such a situation. First, teachers need to remember that for purposes of communication no dialect is better than any other, and that each is best for communicating with its own speakers. Second, the way one speaks and the dialect one uses is an integral part of each person. This is particularly true of young children who do not have much knowledge and understanding of the world outside their own family and neighborhood. Teachers who try to change the language used by elementary school children are in essence saying that the way they talk is right and the way the children and their parents talk is wrong. Finally, although some dialects are less acceptable universally in business or social contexts, a person can add a second dialect or change a present dialect as a result of a rational and conscious effort to do so. When children or young adults indicate that they want to change their dialect or learn another dialect, then the teacher can be of help.

This does not mean that a teacher doesn't need to know about dialects or doesn't have to deal with dialect differences. The teacher needs to be able to determine exactly what differences exist and how these differences will affect the child's understanding of reading instruction or instruction in writing. Just as most of us have learned to write the *k* in *knot* that we don't pronounce, some children will have to learn to write the *'s* on *my aunt's house*. Phonic programs for reading instruction based on one dialect may not fit the pronunciation patterns of another dialect. Most important of all, teachers need to accept the idea at both the intellectual and the action level that differences in dialect are only that—differences—and not ignorant or immature or defective speech.

LANGUAGE USAGE

Language usage has to do with the choices we make among the options available. It involves variations that are primarily social in nature, the etiquette of language. Do you say, *can hardly see* or *can't hardly see*? Would you write, *I only wanted one, but I received three* or *I wanted only one, but I received three.* Would you correct (or want to correct) someone who said, *The four reporters settled the question between them.* What if a child said, *He did it good* or *I'll play if he don't want to.* What you choose to say will depend to some extent on your audience, and on whether you are speaking or writing. (Can you imagine saying, *I'm sorry I shall be unable to attend?*) It will also depend on how formal, how "proper," you want your language to be. What do you say when you answer the telephone and the caller asks for you? (1) *This is she (he) speaking.* (2) *This is (name).* (3) *This is her.* (4) *Yes?* Somehow saying *This is she* seems artificial, strange. Yet saying *This is her* doesn't sound right either. Probably your mother and some of your teachers made you say *May I* when asking for permission rather than *Can I.* Do you still do that? Always? Most people adapt their language to the situation, changing some usage forms as language changes.

Traditional school grammar attempted to say what was "correct" usage by tying usage choices to grammatical constructions. Thus, usage becomes very prescriptive. Originally good usage was the language used by people who were well-educated and politically, socially, or economically powerful. Starting in the seventeenth century, grammarians set the rules that are often taught today even though they do not reflect actual practice. For example, traditional grammar teaches that *like* is a preposition, not a conjunction ("Nobody will miss her like I shall"—Dickens), and it is used often in advertising and common speech ("tastes good like a cigarette should," "tell it like it is," or "they ask questions much like I do"). Today, we appear to be returning to the earlier concept of usage and accepting the language of well-educated and politically, socially, or economically powerful individuals as a guide to appropriate usage. In recent writing the terms applied to usage more often relate to appropriateness rather than to correct and incorrect usage. In fact, there is often not a simple two-part division, no right and wrong. Usage is now "better in this situation" or "less appropriate here."

For most children, usage choices are a reflection of the language used in their home and immediate environment. There are also regional differences in preferred usage, as well as socioeconomic differences. The amount of formal education of the adults in a child's surroundings helps to determine the choices that an individual child makes. If a family is bilingual, the other language will influence the child's patterns of English usage. The purpose of instruction should be to help children make usage choices which are appropriate for a particular situation.

Teaching More Appropriate Usage Patterns

When working with students on more standard or more formal usage, several principles are important. Pooley suggests that the teacher must size up each class, noting which usage patterns might need to be worked on. Children must be stimulated to become observers of language—their own and others'—and motivated to add to their repertoire more formal usage patterns. Instruction must be part of the natural uses of language, not exercises which divorce language usage from communication for a purpose. Finally, since students learn usage from hearing language, oral practice is preferable. This may be accomplished through storytelling, language games, creative dramatics and role playing, oral reports, and so forth.

Teachers in elementary grades often hear hundreds of "nonstandard" usages, but to be successful can correct only a few. Which ones should teachers concentrate on? Pooley suggests the following:

Speech forms subject to intensive teaching in elementary grades[11]

Verb Forms

ain't or *hain't*
I *don't* have *no*
learn me a song
leave me go
have ate, *have* did, etc.
he *begun*, he *seen*, he *run*, he *drunk*, he *come*, etc.
I *says*
he *brung*, he *clumb*
we, you, they *was*
was *broke* (broken), was *froze*
knowed, growed, etc.

Pronoun Forms

my brother, *he* (and other double subjects)
him and *me* went, Mary and *me* saw, etc.
hisself, theirselves, etc.
them books, *this here* book, *that there* book
it's *yourn, hern, hisn, ourn*

Similar suggestions are made for the junior high school. Teachers should choose items for instruction that are widely used in the class and that they believe will cause students to pay the most severe penalty. An abbreviated list of Pooley's suggestions is included below.

Speech forms for the junior high school[12]

Pronouns

Will you wait for John and *I*? Let him and *I* do the work.
Us boys want to go.
This is the man *which* did it.

Double Negatives

He *don't have none* . . .
Haven't you never been . . .
Jane don't have no pen.
I *haven't nothing* to do.

Verb Forms

Irregular past tense forms like *begun, brung, done, drunk, give, run, says, seen, have ate, has began, have broke, have drank,* etc.

Agreement with subject:

One of the books *are* lost.
Each of them *are* interesting.
He *don't* play chess.

Other:

You *had ought* to do that.
He *set* in the chair.

Adjectives and Adverbs

a apple
them boys
these kind, *those* kind

Miscellaneous

If he'd *of* come, would *of* come, should *of* come (a spelling error for *have* or *'ve*)

Junior high school or middle school teachers should also use any items from the elementary school list that students persist in using in more formal situations (in school talk).

Opportunities for Usage Experiences in Oral Language

There are several ways that children can become familiar with varying choices in usage. Very young children can be given the chance to become involved in dramatic play. As they play the father, mother, or police officer, they assume the language that is appropriate to that person's situation. Teachers may raise the quality of the dramatic play by adding props such as hats and costumes to the play area or by intervening with questions will extend children's thinking about the role or situation. At this stage the children are involved in exploring situations, and it is not a time for the teacher to give instruction about what they should say or how it should be said.

Older students can work with role playing. As they are active in taking on various roles, the teacher can discuss what kinds of talk a doctor uses, what a teenager would say, or how a musician or judge would express an idea. Role playing can also put the same person in a variety of situations that would call for changes in language. What would a parent say about their child's misbehavior to their best friend, to the school principal, to the child? How would someone tell about a bad test grade to parents, to friends, or to the teacher? How would you report an accident you had seen to the police officer; how would it be reported on the evening television news; how would you tell it to friends? Using role-playing situations and language changes and various usage patterns to help create believability in a particular character is both an interesting and an effective way to deal with various usage patterns.

There are also opportunities for working with usage patterns within the framework of classroom discussions and presentations. This is particularly true for those children who have been exposed to very little formal usage. In informal classroom discussions or conversation, the usage choices reflect this informality. As you move into presentational discussions such as round-table or panel discussions, there is a call for a somewhat more formal language. By helping children make distinctions between the formality of the situation and the kind of group involved in the discussion and the appropriateness of particular usage items, you are helping children grow in their ability to select appropriate usage for particular situations. Making distinctions between home talk and school talk or between talk with friends and talk with others can help children become more flexible in their choices. Asking *How would you say that in "school talk"?* will often elicit the form you prefer.

Opportunities for Usage Experiences in Written Language

There are several kinds of work in written language that provide children with opportunities to select among options in usage. These activities are more appropriate for older children for several reasons. Younger children are more involved in simply getting their ideas into written language, and making fine distinctions in written usage becomes too much of a task. Working with the teacher on group stories or recordings of events does help younger children make distinctions between the oral and written modes of expression. Written language is not merely talk written down; there are conventions in writing that do not exist in oral expression, and there are ways of expressing ideas orally that have no parallel in writing.

The teacher can help older students take into account whether the audience is known or unknown, and what the purpose of the writing is, and then determine suitable usage selections. A teacher can structure opportunities for writing that call for various registers of language to be used. Instead of isolated practice that has little meaning, there are real writing situations that call for realistic choices.

Students can assume roles in writing much as they might take roles in oral dramatizing. An event from a story or from real life may be described from several viewpoints. Children who have read *A Taste of Blackberries*[13] might describe Jamie's accident as it would have been reported in the newspaper, as a diary entry by one of his friends, or as Mrs. Houser would have written about it to her daughter. The dedication or improvement of a nature trail or of some new playground equipment for the school might be described by children in a thank-you letter to the parent's group who had developed it, in an article for the school system's monthly newsletter, or in letters to their pen pals in another part of the country.

Letter writing offers an opportunity for variations in language usage. A few examples are letters to various business concerns ordering free or inexpensive materials for their classroom and letters to a favorite author or to pen pals. Some may want to write to former classmates who have moved away. Although teachers would not necessarily proofread or correct *personal* letters, they can give guidance before the writing period about the kinds of language that might be appropriate. In writing business letters the teacher may want to go over the draft of the letter before it is recopied and sent. Guidance in the prewriting period can be extremely helpful to students when doing this type of letter writing.

Students in the upper grades would be doing some written reporting. At times this may involve describing some firsthand observations or the results of a survey or experiment. They might also collect recipes or directions for making something as part of a unit of study. All these reporting situations call for variations in usage.

As children participate in the usage area in either oral or written formats, there are several important principles to remember. Children's language reflects their strong emotional and linguistic ties to family and close friends. There is rarely a way to change language patterns without saying or implying that the teacher is right and family and friends are wrong. The initial goal of the teacher is to develop security in expressing ideas. It is the content of the talk or writing that is important. If children want to change their language at a later time, for whatever reason, they may. In the elementary and middle school, though, the objective is more *fluent* and *flexible* use of language to express ideas. Viewing usage as a range of choices dependent upon the situation leads children to accept their familiar language and that of other children and adults as variations instead of levels of correctness. We are building in choices based on knowledge of how people use language in various situations.

REGISTERS OF LANGUAGE

Three dimensions of variations occur in language: (1) geographical variations—dialect; (2) social variations—usage; and (3) individual variations—registers. Registers overlap to some degree with the other two kinds of variations since each speaker speaks a dialect and reacts to social considerations and education in the usage patterns preferred. Registers of language are patterns of language the individual speaker chooses to use. Register involves considerations of the mode of discourse—oral or written—and of the style or degree of formality. It takes into account the field of discourse (politics or shopping or whatever) and the interaction of the individual's dialect with the mode, style, and field of discourse.

Reflected in the concept of register is the fact that speaking a particular dialect will affect the span of choices available within a particular situational context. This is especially important for teachers to recognize because it explains many of the language differences among children who speak different dialects in the classroom. It accounts for some of the observations that researchers not familiar with register variations have made about particular dialect groups. For example, many of the comparative studies of the language of white and black children did not take into account the situation in which the black children were speaking and what kind of language would be appropriate for them to use in this particular register in their dialect. The same physical situation is no guarantee of equality in both groups, because what is appropriate language behavior for one dialect-speaking group in a given situation is not necessarily appropriate behavior for speakers of another dialect.

Children are aware of the need to make differences in their language depending on particular situations. Even very young children take on different vocabulary, intonations, and sentence structures when playing adult roles. Listen to some preschoolers playing house or some primary school children playing school. Their language reflects their knowledge about how adults act in those roles. Older children are more adept at making changes in their language. In talking with each other they may say *bugs and stuff* and then change that wording to *insects and other things* when reporting their group's discussion to the teacher and the rest of the class. Adults, too, make similar changes in their language depending on the situation. A teacher may report to the principal or parent that a child *has very little self-control.* This same teacher may say to peers or friends that the child *is driving me crazy with all the pushing and hitting.*

Many teachers are startled at some of the language used by children in their class who speak a dialect significantly different from their own. This is especially true of younger children who are less aware of appropriate changes to make from the intimate family and friends situation to the more formal classroom situation. Their intent is not to shock or to be unruly; they simply have selected language inappropriate for use in the classroom because of their immaturity and lack of experience. If the teacher can remain calm and suggest that the language they have used is fine in certain situations, but is not appropriate in this situation, the incident becomes useful instruction instead of rejection.

ENGLISH AS A FOREIGN LANGUAGE

In many parts of the United States there are children in our schools whose native language is not English and whose cultural traditions are not American. They must be helped to live in an English-speaking society, but not at the price of alienation from their family and native culture. These children need many of the experiences with language that all children need—opportunities to do or see or hear something and talk about it. They need an environment rich in English language structures and vocabulary and opportunities to use language in various ways.

Education for children who are bilingual—those who have some language abilities in two languages—usually necessitates recognizing biculturalism. A bicultural component[14] would involve a teacher knowledgeable in the history and culture of the pupil's home language, recognition of the contributions of the child's home culture in all subject areas, and material dealing with that culture and history included in the curriculum.

In elementary schools, children who are not yet proficient in English language skills should be taught within their native language to attain literacy while instruction in English oral skills is begun. The final goal of the program is literacy in English. Such an approach values the child's home language and culture while developing the skills to progress in the English language community also. (See Chapter 4 for further discussion.)

SUMMARY

The history of English has a rich and long tradition of change and variation. That same pattern of language change continues today as new words are added to our language and as we accept more individualistic kinds of expression. We are becoming more interested in preserving children's abilities to speak other languages and other dialects without restricting them from also being accepted within the framework of the American culture and English language. We are viewing usage not in terms of a right-wrong dichotomy, but in terms of appropriateness. The role and the influence of nonverbal communication are recognized. The main objective in elementary and middle schools is developing students' confidence in expressing their ideas in both oral and written language.

UNDERSTANDING THROUGH INVOLVEMENT

1. Ask several people who come from different areas of the United States to read several paragraphs aloud and try to pinpoint both similarities and differences in pronunciation.
2. One of the most interesting aspects of dialectical differences lies in the words we select to express a particular idea. Following is a checklist that may be used to survey people about the words they use for particular things.
   (a) To be absent from school: *lay out, lie out, play hookey, play truant, skip, skip school, ditch, flick, flake school, blow school, absent*
   (b) End of school day: *school lets out, turns out, breaks up, breaks, leaves out, goes out, is out, is over, closes*
   (c) Teacher writes with chalk on the: *board, blackboard, chalkboard, writing board, eraser board.*
   (d) Missed the school bus: *got bus-left, got left, missed the bus*
   (e) Said when promoted in school: *passed, got promoted, made my grade, made my pass, was moved up, was put up*
   (f) Got ahead of you in line: *cut line, jumped line, broke in line, broke up, scrounged, pulled up, butted in line, ditched*
   (g) General name for a carbonated drink: *Coke, soda, soda pop, pop, drink, soft drink, tonic, dope*
   (h) Sleeveless undershirt worn by men: *undershirt, gall shift, T-shirt*
   (i) A boy who is aggressive toward girls: *forward, getting fresh, being mannish, fast*

(j) Paper container for groceries: *bag, poke, sack, toot*

(k) Others related by blood: *family, folks, kind, kinfolks, people, relation, relatives, relations, kin*

(l) Dog of no special kind: *common dog, cur, cur dog, face, feist, mongrel, nocount, heinz, sooner, mixed dog, mutt*

Additional items may be found in the two sources from which these were selected.[8,15]

3. Since it is often hard to recognize dialect variations with which we are in constant contact, one person may tape-record short interviews with each member of your class and then play back these interviews for analysis.

4. Divide into groups of three to seven people and assign some new names for ordinary objects (a pencil, chalk, notebook, book, and chalkboard). Practice talking about the classroom using these new names your group has invented. Compare the names your group chose with those chosen by other groups. Are any of the names better than the other? Are they better than the name we ordinarily use for the object? Why is it important to have the same name for any given object?

5. Look through advertisements for newly coined words. These may be found in newspapers, in magazines, on television, or on billboards.

6. Tape-record a native Spanish speaker speaking English on television and list the pronunciation and syntactic features you find that are different from your own dialect.

7. Listen to a tape recording of someone speaking a black English dialect and mark every time you don't understand something. Now listen to the same tape again and tally in a different column every pronunciation or syntactic difference you note. Compare the two.

8. If you have a chance to observe or work with children speaking a dialect distinctly different from your own, make a list of all the lexical items they use that are new to you.

9. Have older students categorize the dialects of the comic characters in televised situation comedies. How do the dialects they speak compare with dialects used by characters in leading roles?

10. Authors sometimes try to suggest dialect by special spellings, called *eye dialect*. Rawling's *The Yearling* uses eye dialect to reflect the Florida "cracker" speech:

Hit ain't for us ignorant mortals to say what's right and what's wrong. Was ary one of us to be a-doin of it, we'd not of brung this pore boy into the world a cripple, and his mind teched. We'd of brung him in straight and tall like his brothers, fitten to live and work and do.

(a) Ask older students to find examples of eye dialect in the books they're reading.

(b) Younger students could do the same, searching for eye dialect in the comic strips.

(c) Middle-grade students could tape-record someone speaking a distinctive dialect (or use a tape provided by the teacher) and then try to write a different passage using eye dialect.

11. Sixth-grade or older students might check several grammar books or usage

references for what they say about a given usage item. Do the different sources agree? Items like the following are revealing:

(1) *shall* and *will*, (2) *dived* and *dove*, (3) *real* and *sure*, (4) *like* and *as*, (5) *feel bad* and *feel badly*, (6) *reason is because*, (7) *lie* and *lay*, (8) *than* as a preposition like *than me*, (9) *farther* and *further*, (10) *may* and *can*

Books to check might include:

Bryant, M. M. *Current American Usage: How Americans Say It and Write It.* New York: Funk & Wagnalls, 1962.

Bernstein, T. M. *The Careful Writer.* New York: Atheneum, 1965.

Copperud, R. H. *American Usage: The Consensus.* New York: Van Nostrand Reinhold, 1970.

Lamberts, J. J. *A Short Introduction to English Usage.* New York: McGraw-Hill, 1967.

The American Heritage Dictionary of the English Language. New York: American Heritage Publishing Co., 1969.

Webster's Third New International Dictionary. Springfield, Mass: Merriam, 1966.

12. Have students make a list of the slang words they use, perhaps in brainstorming groups. Have them survey their parents about what words they used in their place.
13. Search for word blends and make a class list. Have students invent some of their own blends (like *brunch* from *breakfast* and *lunch,* or *fantabulous* from *fantastic* and *fabulous*).
14. Currently a major change in language is taking place as writers and speakers try to avoid sexist language. Students might make a class collection of new words replacing sex-linked ones. (What is used for chair*man*, police*man*, post*man* or mail*man*, paper *boy*, and so forth?) How do people avoid the masculine referents *he, him,* and *his* for a singular undetermined word? (Like *The student should do* HIS *best;* or *The child spells it; then* HE *corrects* HIS *own paper.*)
15. Try some role-playing experiences with others and with some observers to record differences in register or usage from situation to situation. The observers should look for differences in pronunciation, lexical items or vocabulary, and syntax. Some possible situations are:
    (a) You receive a D in a course in which you were expecting at least a B. What do you say to (1) friends, (2) your teacher, and (3) an appeals board headed by the dean of your college?
    (b) You are involved in an automobile accident because the person ahead of you turns right from the center lane of a four lane road just in front of you. What do you say to (1) the police officer, (2) your parents or spouse, and (3) your close friends?
    (c) You order something from a mail-order catalog and when it arrives it is not the color, or size, or brand you paid for. (1) What do you write to your friend about it, and (2) what do you write to the company? Be your own observer in this one.

Now try to think of some situations that would relate to children's experiences that they could act out to discover differences in their own language in different situations.

REFERENCE NOTES

[1]L. M. Myers. *The Roots of Modern English*. Boston: Little, Brown, 1966.

[2]M. A. K. Halliday. *Explorations in the Functions of Language*. London: Edward Arnold, 1973.

[3]Joan Tough. *Talking, Thinking, Growing*. New York: Schocken Books, 1974, p. 112.

[4]M. L. Knapp. *Nonverbal Communication in Human Interaction*. New York: Holt, 1972.

[5]Mary O. Wiemann and John M. Wiemann. *Nonverbal Communication in the Elementary Classroom*. Falls Church, Va.: Speech Communication Association, 1975.

[6]Charles M. Galloway. "Nonverbal Language in the Classroom" (mimeographed). Columbus: Ohio State University, 1967, p. 14.

[7]Annabel Ashely and Jean Malmstrom. *Dialects USA*. Champaign, Ill.: National Council of Teachers of English, 1967.

[8]Roger W. Shuy. *Discovering American Dialects*. Champaign, Ill.: National Council of Teachers of English, 1967, pp. 17–24.

[9]Jean Malmstrom and Constance Weaver. *Transgrammar*. Glenview, Ill.: Scott, Foresman, 1973, pp. 355–378.

[10]Ibid. (adapted).

[11]Robert C. Pooley. *The Teaching of English Usage*. Urbana, Ill.: National Council of Teachers of English, 1974, p. 18.

[12]Ibid., pp. 188–190.

[13]Doris B. Smith. *A Taste of Blackberries*. New York: Thomas Y. Crowell, 1973.

[14]Protase E. Woodford. "Bilingual/Bicultural Education: A Need for Understanding," in *The Challenge of Communication* (Gilbert A. Jarvis, ed.). Skokie, Ill.: National Textbook, 1974, p. 401.

[15]Hugh Agee. "The Analysis of Student Talk: Classroom Possibilities for Dialect Study," *The English Journal*, September 1972, pp. 878–882.

CHAPTER FOUR

Acquiring Language

PREVIEW QUESTIONS

1 How do children learn to speak their native language?
2 What influence do adults—parents and teachers—have on children's language?
3 Why do children vary in their ability to use language?
4 What can teachers do to help children develop linguistic maturity?

Children's first words bring joy and amazement to their parents. What a thrill and delight—they can talk! At first they may just say, *Mama* or *Dada,* but very soon they can express an entire idea. Telegraphic sentences like *me cookie* or *all-gone doggie* become longer as they begin to speak more like the adults with whom they are in contact. Learning to talk seems so natural and children learn so quickly that most adults simply take it for granted. How do such young children do it? Are they born knowing how to speak? Do children imitate what they hear? Is it taught? Children move from saying a two- or three-word sentence to full adult speech. What explains this?

An understanding of how children acquire language is critical to any language arts program. It is especially crucial to a program like the one suggested in this text that aims to build upon each child's ability to use language both communicatively and creatively. The teacher needs to know what factors have been important in the child's development of language because they have implications for classroom practices.

The psycholinguistic view of language acquisition presented here comes from cognitive psychology and linguistics. This view of acquisition suggests that children draw language from their linguistic environment, which is then internally processed to develop the common sets of rules used by adult speakers. Thus, language acquisition is similar to the scientific method in which observations are made, hypotheses are formulated, and the hypotheses are then tested against the data collected. As they learn to talk, children progressively amend their language until it becomes more and more like that spoken by adults with whom they are in contact. Smith says that "a child learning to talk is systematically trying out alternative rules to see which ones apply—that he is 'testing hypotheses,' literally conducting linguistic experiments, to discover specifically what kind of language is talked around him."[1]

Basic to this view of how language is acquired is a consideration of the child's capacity for language, how language is processed, what sequence of development may be expected, and what variations may be involved.

THE BASES OF LANGUAGE ACQUISITION

The source of language acquisition includes both the human capacity for language and the particular linguistic environment of the child. Language acquisition results from a complex combination of biological and environmental factors.

Biological Factors

Linguists do not agree on exactly how biological factors affect language learning, but they do agree that human beings inherit some capacity or facility for a spoken language. One view of the biological factors important to language development is that of Lenneberg, who has explored those biological endowments that make language as we know it uniquely possible for human beings. His research suggests that language is a species-specific trait of humans.[2] Lenneberg also suggests that language might be expected from the evolutionary processes themselves and that the basis for language capacity might be transmitted genetically.

McNeill agrees that there is a biological basis for language, although his view is quite different from Lenneberg's. He suggests that human beings inherit the notion of a sentence as a way of organizing language. He states that virtually everything that occurs in language acquisition depends on prior knowledge of the basic aspects of sentence structure. Thus the concept of a sentence may be part of the human being's innate mental capacity. McNeill's argument is as follows:

> The facts of language acquisition could not be as they are unless the concept of a sentence is available to children at the start of their learning. The concept of a sentence is the main guiding principle in a child's attempts to organize and interpret the linguistic evidence that fluent speakers make available to him. What outside observers see as distorted or 'telegraphic' speech is actually a consistent effort by a child to discover how a more or less fixed concept of a sentence is expressed in the language to which he has, by accident, been exposed.[3]

Others would argue that what the child inherits biologically is the ability to organize the surrounding language and figure out what substitutions can be made, how to indicate plurality or past time, how indeed language works to communicate ideas. There are not sufficient data at present to judge which view of biological factors is correct. There do, however, appear to be adequate data to support the idea that biological factors are involved in language acquisition in some way.

Environmental Factors

In addition to the biological capacity of humans for language, an important factor in language acquisition is the environmental or experiential factor. Central to language acquisition is verbal contact with adult speakers of the language. Two very early studies (those of McCarthy and Davis) have established the importance of such contacts. A more recent investigation by Cazden indicates that within the adult-child interaction a particular kind of verbal stimulation may be important.

McCarthy and Davis, in two separate studies in the 1930s, examined differences in language development among twins, children with brothers or sisters (not twins), and only children.[4] Both researchers found that only children are superior in linguistic skill to the other two groups, and that children with siblings other than twins are superior to twins. The studies thus indicate that children who associate more with adults and with adult language are more linguistically mature than children who spend more time with other children.

The importance of the adult input in children's linguistic development was evident in another experimental study by Cazden.[5] One group received forty minutes a day of extensive and deliberate expansions of their telegraphic sentences. In this treatment the adult repeated in full-sentence form what the child had said in telegraphic form. For example, *all-gone milk* might be expanded by the adult as *Yes, your milk is all gone*. A second group was exposed to an equal amount of time spent in focusing attention on the children's ideas; but instead of repeating what they said, the adult continued the conversation with a related sentence. In this group, *all-gone milk* might be extended to *Do you want some more?* or perhaps *Then let's clean up and go outside.* The third group received no special treatment. Contrary to expectations, the second group—who had received responses to their sentences, with the adult extending ideas and introducing different grammatical elements, word meanings, and relationships among ideas—performed better on all the measures of language development than the first group, who had received only the simple expansions of their sentences into full-sentence form. Cazden comments that "semantic extension proved to be slightly more helpful than grammatical expansion" for several reasons that may have a bearing on language development programs for children.[6] In the extension treatment there was a richness of verbal stimulation and the focus was on the child's ideas instead of on grammatical structures. McNeill has also suggested that attempts to expand children's telegraphic sentences into full sentence form may be inaccurate at least part of the time and thus may mislead or interfere with development. Cazden's research seems to indicate that the kind of adult contact that is particularly important involves using mature rather than simplified language to extend children's sentences and ideas.

Psychological Structures

Language is an intellectual response, and in Piaget's view, particular intellectual responses are not inherited. Instead, children inherit a tendency to organize their intellectual processes and to adapt to their environment.[7] The theoretical framework suggested by Piaget indicates that biological factors affect intelligence in three ways: there are inherited physical structures that set broad limits on intellectual functioning; there are inherited behavioral reactions that influence the first few days of human life; and there are two basic inherited tendencies—organization and adaptation.

Organization Organization is "the tendency common to all forms of life to integrate structures, which may be physical or psychological, into higher-order systems or structure."[8] The process of organization may be clearly seen in language acquisition as children apply their own organization to linguistic rules. In the early stages of language, important content words are employed in the child's speech and only the nonessential words (as far as meaning) are left out. In later stages of acquisition, rule development or organization appears when rules are applied too generally to words which do not follow the overall pattern. This is quite obvious as the child says *catched, runned,* or *holded,* or says *mines* instead of *mine,* adding the /z/ sound used on *his, hers, yours,* or *theirs.*

Adaptation Adaptation to the environment takes place through the two complementary processes of assimilation and accommodation. "Broadly speaking, *assimilation* describes the capability of the organism to handle new situations and new problems with its present stock of mechanisms; *accommodation* describes the process of change through which the organism becomes able to manage situations that are at first too difficult for it."[9] After accommodation the individual is able to assimilate increasingly novel situations; these are then accommodated, and an increasingly complex and more mature system evolves. Adaptation through these two processes as described by Piaget may account for the way new linguistic structures in the adult language children hear are incorporated into the existing language and how their linguistic rules are revised to fit the new evidence children get from trying out their language.

Piaget's description of how intellectual functioning operates within the child suggests that this functioning is an interaction of inherited abilities and personal experiences. Thus, the psycholinguists who describe the inherited capacity for learning language and the researchers who have found important influences in the child's linguistic environment agree when we consider language to be an intellectual function as described by Piagetian theory.

PROCESSING LANGUAGE FROM THE ENVIRONMENT

How children use the adult language in their environment is a key issue in language acquisition. It has strong implications for what teachers should do to help children develop their language, what methods are most effective, and even what content is appropriate.

Most children sound very much like their parents; they pronounce words the same way their parents do, and they use many of the same lexical items or vocabulary as well as many of the same grammatical or syntactic structures. From this, one could easily assume that children learn their language from their parents or other adults with whom they are in close contact. They do, but not merely by imitating the adult language they hear; instead, children incorporate the language surrounding them into their own rules system. If you examine the speech of two-year-olds, you find consistent patterns unlike those used by adults. Parents do not say, *I holded* or *Ask me if I no make mistake*. Imitation or copying of adult speech does not account for differences such as these. Processing and rule development does account for the similarities between children's speech and that of their parents and also for the differences between the two.

How Adults Modify Language for Very Young Children

When children first begin to talk, adults typically change their language in a variety of ways. Thus, children are presented with language that is especially adapted for them—language that is adjusted to what they appear to understand. Clark and Clark[10] suggest that how adults talk to very young children is influenced by three things: (1) making sure that children realize an utterance is addressed to them, (2) choosing the right words and sentences so that the child can understand, and (3) saying what they have to say in many different ways.

Getting attention Adults often use attention getters or attention holders to keep children involved and participating, such as using the child's name or exclaiming *Look!* before a statement. Adults also use a higher pitch when talking to very young children and sometimes whisper directly into their ears. Typically adults use a greater range of pitch with children, and so there is an exaggerated up-and-down quality to the talk. Touching the child, using gestures, and pointing also help to get and hold the child's attenton.

Selecting what to say Adults make what they say to the child relevant by talking about what is going on in the child's world, often making a running commentary on the child's activities. They adjust the words they use to those they perceive as easier for children to pronounce, or words that are more useful, and those that are most easily understood. Instead of naming the breed, adults say, *There's a dog (or doggie)*. They use fewer pronouns, saying, *Daddy's going to wash Linda's hair now* instead of *I'm going to wash your hair now*. Adults also encourage children to take turns by responding to their yawns or gestures as if they were part of the conversation and later by using question-and-answer formats or prompting-type questions like *You saw* WHAT? Adults seldom correct the form of what children say; instead, they correct the content. *That a birdie house* would get a smile and *Umm-hmmm*, while *That's a birdnest* might be answered by *No, that's a squirrel's nest*. This emphasis on meaning or content rather than on form is a significant aspect of parents' talk that is too often missing in a school situation.

Altering language Adults change their language by slowing down their speech, using shorter, simple sentences, and repeating parts of what they say. By speaking slowly and pausing at the end of their utterances, adults separate one phrase from another and one sentence from another—perhaps making it easier for children to understand. One reason for a great deal of the repetition in children's language is the use of "sentence frames"[11] like:

Where's _____.
Let's play with _____.
Look at _____.
Here's _____.
That's a _____.
Here comes _____.

These are completed with a name of a person or thing, and the frame serves to mark off the beginning of the new word as it is put in the familiar place in the frame. Repetitions are frequently used by adults. (*Pick up the* RED ONE. *Find the* RED ONE. *Not the green one. I want the* RED ONE. *Can you find the* RED ONE?) These repetitions may give children information about the structures in language and also help children understand longer sentences because they can concentrate only on the repeated part.

It is not completely clear whether all these adaptations are either necessary or even helpful. Experiments to determine this without risking a child's development have not been conducted. Some evidence from children of deaf parents who only use sign language or children exposed to a second language only on television suggests that it is at least helpful and perhaps even necessary for adults to talk to children using language intended specifically for them. Oversimplification is not helpful, but some adjustment of adult language when speaking to very young children seems to be valuable.

How Children Incorporate Adult Language

The psycholinguistic thesis is that children draw language from their linguistic environment and then process this language to discover regularities and induce generalizations or "rules" about its phonology and semantic and syntactic structures. The "errors" that children make are evidence of the rules they have developed. As they gain more experience with language and with mature language, their rules more closely approximate that of the adults'.

Do children imitate adult language?   An interesting insight into this processing of language comes from a study that asked children to imitate sentences[12]; their inability to do so is most revealing about what language rules they have, and at the same time reveals the ineffectiveness of direct copying or imitation in learning a language. The elicited imitation involved specific sentences in order to see what constructions the children would repeat accurately and which they would change or be unable to repeat at all. One such sentence given to a 2½-year-old was, *This one is the giant, but this one is little.* It was repeated as, *Dis one little, annat one big.* The researchers comment that evidently the child has comprehended the underlying meaning of the sentence, and is then using that meaning in a new form when imitating. They point out that this process of filtering a sentence through one's own productive system is a process that would be described in Piaget's terminology as, "a sentence, when recognized, is assimilated to an internal schema, and when reproduced, is constructed in terms of that schema."[13] This sort of recasting of sentences to fit one's productive patterns is especially obvious in repetitions such as *Mozart who cried came to my party,* which was repeated as *Mozart cried and he came to my party,* or *The owl who eats candy runs fast* repeated as *Owl eat a candy and he run fast.* Evidently *who* clauses were not part of this child's productive system, and so they were changed as the child tried to repeat them.

Two other studies examined imitations in children's speech as a part of investigating the process of language acquisition. In these studies—unlike Slobin and Welsh's work, in which children were specifically asked to imitate sentences—a whole body of the children's language was examined. Ervin studied grammatical differences between imitated and free utterances of one- and two-year-olds and concluded that there is no evidence that the child's progress toward adult grammar is greatly affected by imitation of adult sentences.[14] This same general conclusion may be drawn from a longitudinal study of two children, called Adam and Eve. A part of this study examined the children's imitations of their mother's speech. The researchers found that the children's utterances were not really imitative, and that "grammatical mistakes" the children made revealed their search for regularities in the language.[15]

What children actually do in using the adult language that surrounds them is to try to discover regularities in it, to organize it into patterns or rules. A child who hears *today* and *tonight* and then says *tomorning* is not imitating adult language, but is instead processing the language heard to discover how it works and then developing a rule to use. When the rule the child has developed is not actually used (as in this example), it becomes very obvious what type of thinking, organizing, and processing is occurring.

Should children's language be corrected?   Just as children learn to behave in ways deemed acceptable to their parents by a process of being "corrected" when they do not act properly and being "reinforced" or praised when they do, it would seem that parents can and should use this same way to shape their children's language. Think of all the times, though, a parent says, *Say, Thank you* or *Please*. Language develops very rapidly, and "so far no evidence exists to show that either correction or reinforcement of the learning of grammar occurs with sufficient frequency to be a potent force."[16] Cazden cites a conversation between an adult and a four-year-old to show how impervious to correction a child's rule system can be.

Child: My teacher holded the baby rabbits and we patted them.
Adult: Did you say your teacher held the baby rabbits?
Child: Yes.
Adult: What did you say she did?
Child: She holded the baby rabbits and we patted them.
Adult: Did you say she held them tightly?
Child: No, she holded them loosely.[17]

Another such conversation is quoted in McNeill about a parent who is deliberately trying to teach a child a form not within the child's own system.

Child: Nobody don't like me.
Parent: No, say "Nobody likes me."
Child: Nobody don't like me.
Parent: No, nobody likes me.
Child: Nobody don't like me.
         (Seven more repetitions of this)
Parent: No! Now listen carefully. Say "Nobody likes me."
Child: Oh! Nobody don't likes me.[18]

An explanation for this resistance to correction is part of the principle of assimilation. In order for something to be assimilated, there must be a degree of only moderate novelty. Anything that is too new, too novel, is not assimilated, because it does not correspond to anything in the child's schemata or existing internal organization.

Children receive sufficient information from their environment if they are exposed to mature adult language to use in the process of adaptation without needing specific correction or reinforcement. When they are mature enough linguistically to make these changes, they will restructure their existing linguistic rules and incorporate the new items.

What strategies do children use?   In using the language environment to discover how language works, the child appears to use certain operating principles or strategies. Foss and Hakes[19] point out that children learn to apply an increasingly complex and sophisticated set of strategies to the utterances they hear. Some are strategies governing which aspects of the surface forms of talk children pay attention to, and some are related to the interpretations that children associate with the utterances. The strategies used in language acquisition may be similar to the general strategies children use with nonlanguage aspects of learning.

Slobin describes seven such strategies that seem to show how children operate. These "self-instructions" for language acquisition are:

1. Pay attention to the ends of words.
2. The phonological forms of words can be systematically modified.
3. Pay attention to the order of words and morphemes.
4. Avoid interruption or rearrangement of linguistic units.
5. Underlying semantic relations should be marked overtly and clearly.
6. Avoid exceptions.
7. The use of grammatical markers should make semantic sense.[20]

Children appear to attend to the language they hear within the framework of the situation they are in. The strategies that are first used appear to relate to very general, regular, aspects of language. Later, children deal with the more narrow, exceptional parts of language.

THE SEQUENCE OF LANGUAGE ACQUISITION

The preceding section has indicated that the process of language acquisition involves systematic and progressive rule development and then verification or revision of these rules using evidence given by other speakers of the language. This systematic and progressive development is evident in the predictable order of acquisition of linguistic items. Although there may be relatively wide variations in the rate of acquisition or in the age at which particular items are acquired, the order of acquisition of these items is strikingly similar.

Early Language and Motor Development

The following chart of motor and language development is adapted from Lenneberg.[21] The approximate ages corresponding to each section have been omitted in order to focus on the developmental trends involved. The chart covers the period from six months of age to about four years of age.

MOTOR AND LANGUAGE DEVELOPMENT: SELECTED MILESTONES

Motor Development	Language Development
Supports head when in prone position; then plays with a rattle when placed in hand; then sits with props	Makes gurgling sounds usually called cooing; then responds to human sounds; then the vowel-like sounds begin to be interspersed with more consonant sounds
When sitting bends forward and uses hands for support; then stands up holding on and grasps with thumb apposition; then creeps efficiently and pulls to a standing position	Cooing changes to babbling; then vocalizations are mixed with sound play; differentiates between words heard; appears to try imitating sounds, but isn't successful
Walks when held by one hand; walks on feet and hands with knees in air	Identical sound sequences are replicated and words (*mama, dada*) emerge; shows understanding of some words and simple consonants

Motor Development	Language Development
Grasp, prehension, and release fully developed; gait stiff and propulsive; sits on child's chair with only fair aim	Has a repertoire of 3 to 50 words; still babbling but with several syllables and intricate intonation patterns; may say *thank you* or *come here,* but can't join items into spontaneous two-item phrases
Runs, but falls in sudden turns; can quickly alternate between sitting and standing; walks stairs up or down with only one foot forward	Vocabulary of more than 50 items; "telegraphic speech" as tries to join vocabulary into two-word phrases; increase in communicative behavior and more interest in language
Jumps into air with both feet; takes a few steps on tiptoe; good hand and finger coordination	Fast increase in vocabulary; frustrated if not understood; utterances have two to five words; characteristic "child grammar"
Runs smoothly with acceleration and deceleration; makes sharp and fast curves; walks stairs by alternating feet; can operate tricycle	Vocabulary of some 100 words; 80 percent of utterances intelligible even to strangers; grammatical complexity roughly that of adult usage
Jumps rope, catches ball, and walks a line	Language well established; deviations more in style than in grammar

Acquisition of Syntactic Structures

Numerous studies have been conducted to establish the sequence of acquisition of syntactic structures. Three such studies will be briefly discussed here as they deal with children at different age levels.

In the study of syntactic acquisition of two young children called Adam and Eve, Bellugi and Brown found the identical order of appearance of certain inflections in both children's language although there was a considerable difference—from 8½ to 15 months—in the ages of the children when the inflectional forms first appeared.[22] The inflections were items such as -s for plurals and -ed for past tense of verbs. Moreover, the order of appearance of these inflections did not match with the frequency of the forms found in the language of the children's mothers.

Stages of acquisition of syntactic structures were also identified by Menyuk in a study of nursery school and kindergarten children.[23] The language of the children was recorded in family role playing, in answering questions, and in talking about pictures. She found that certain transformations were used by significantly more first-grade children than kingergarten children, showing maturation between nursery school and first grade.

The third study which showed evidence of stages in the acquisition of syntactic structures was Chomsky's study of children between five and ten years of age.[24] Chomsky examined four particular constructions—not usually present in the grammar of five-year-olds but normally acquired by age ten—in an effort to determine the order of acquisition and the approximate age of acquisition. She found that one construction involving understanding of pronoun reference was quite rapidly and uniformly acquired at 5½. Two of the other constructions appeared to be under control from age nine on, and the fourth construction was not completely controlled by all the ten-year-olds.

These studies, and others which have examined the acquisition of various syntactic structures, have found that individual structures are acquired in a particular order although the age of acquisition may vary from one individual to another. There is then a sequence of acquisition that is quite regular. It seems independent of experiential factors except in the rate of acquisition.

Acquisition of Semantics

The acquisition of semantics, or word meaning, is less clear than that of syntax. Early studies dealt mostly with vocabulary frequencies and derivations of words, and linguistic investigations until recently concentrated on phonology and syntax. Although the details of the acquisition of semantics are not clear, there are many similarities between syntactic and semantic acquisition. There seem to be stages in semantic acquisition as children progressively amend their early language until word meanings approximate those of adults.

One view of semantic acquisition is that word meanings are learned by adding "features" or meaning components to the lexical meaning of words. Clark suggests that:

> When a child first begins to use identifiable words, he does not know their full (adult) meaning; he only has partial entries for them in his lexicon. The acquisition of semantic knowledge, then, will consist of adding more features of meaning to the lexical entry of the word until the child's combination of features in the entry for the word corresponds to the adults.[25]

Thus, very young children may call anything on four wheels a car—including trucks and moving vans. As they have more experience with different vehicles, they refine *car* in various ways until what they call a *car* is just what an adult would. In the process of refining the meaning of words, children both particularize (*car* to *Chevy, Ford, station wagon,* etc.) and generalize (*car* to *pickup, van,* etc.).

With older children an indication of this same process of refining meanings until they approximate the adult meaning may be seen in words that are closely related by having many overlapping features. In word pairs such as *boy-brother* or *girl-sister,* one word of each pair may refer to a subset within the other word and yet have additional features. All brothers, for example, are boys, but not all boys are brothers. *Brother* is a subset of *boy* with the additional feature of family relationship. Many middle-graders still have difficulty with this distinction, and when asked how many brothers or sisters they have, will include themselves.

The semantic features theory is that there are combinations of the presence or absence of particular features that make up the lexical meaning of the word. The chart below illustrates the features of *before* and *after.*

Before	After
+time	+time
−simultaneous	−simultaneous
+prior	−prior

This approach to semantics, that of semantic features, is still controversial. Brown and McNeill have explored semantic acquisition using the notion of semantic features and have looked for developmental trends. This theory, if not generally accepted, does represent a major line of thinking in the area of semantics.

Another view of the role of semantics in the language of young children is expressed by Bloom.[26] She examined the telegraphic speech of a number of children and found that grammatical explanations of sentences such as *Mommy sock* neglected to include the connection with cognitive-perceptual development and the inherent semantic relations that underlie the juxtaposition of words in these early sentences. *Mommy sock* meant different things at different times. Once it meant the child was picking up her mother's sock, and another time it described the mother putting on the child's sock. In Bloom's view of semantics, language has a surface structure and an underlying semantic (not grammatical) structure.

Another researcher has explored the context within which a particular word or lexical item is used and suggests that until the child is quite mature, somewhat after age ten, lexical items do not have a meaning separate from the sentence context used by the child.[27] Menyuk points out that even when a word is understood and used in one sentence structure, the same word may not be understood in a different sentence structure. This would indicate, as Bloom has suggested, that somehow there are underlying semantic relationships reflected in the particular grammatical context.

In the acquisition of semantics, we may see the two principles of development suggested by Piaget in the development of mental structures: organization and adaptation. The sentence context serves as an organization for semantic properties, and adaptation seems to be the process through which the child acquires increasingly more mature lexical references through experiences with the linguistic community.

Even though we do not have definitive data on the process of semantic acquisition, we do know some of the factors which enable children to increase their vocabulary—increase both the number of words and word meanings they can use and also increase the precision of the meanings of these words. One factor which aids development is contact in a meaningful situation with a wide variety of words, both in speech and in written materials. Another is feedback from adults about word meanings as the words come up in the context of the situation. A discussion of vocabulary development is included in Chapter 5.

Development of Complexity

Complexity in language involves compressing two or more simple structures into a single sentence through compounding, subordinating, and embedding. For example, the following sentences may be combined several ways.

I had a baseball.
It was new.
I took it to school.
I lost it.

They may be made into compound sentences: *I had a baseball, and it was new. I took it to school, and I lost it.* They may be made into complex sentences by subordination: *My ball that was new was a baseball. When I took it to school, I lost it.* Or they may be combined with some embedding into a single sentence: *I lost the new baseball I took to school.* In the latter case, *It was new* becomes embedded as a single adjective.

As children mature, there is a developmental increase in the number and kinds of structures they use. This should not imply that young children use only simple sentences, for children at kindergarten age do use compounding, subordination, and embedding. However, there is an increase in the number of transformations used as age and ability with language increase. This is true of both oral and written language. A major study examining the development of children's oral language was conducted by Loban over a period of years. In 1952 a group of over three hundred children was selected and oral language samples were obtained annually throughout their school years. This study found that students showed an increase in complexity of language throughout the years with a noticeable rise about the time of fifth grade. The primary difference in grammatical complexity between the less mature and more mature children was in the dexterity of substitutions within patterns and not in the number of different patterns used.[28]

A key study in examining differences in syntactic maturity in written language used students in grades 4, 6, 8, 10, and 12 as well as two groups of adults. They were all given a passage containing very short simple sentences and were asked to rewrite it in a better way without omitting any information. Their rewriting was then checked on five syntactic measures. Hunt[29] found that as schoolchildren mature, they tend to embed more of their elementary sentences or kernel strings, and that this embedding is done in different ways at different age levels. As with oral language, older students tended to write significantly longer clauses and T units. A *T unit* is a minimal terminable unit, an independent clause with its modifiers. It is a more accurate measure of complexity than sentence length since it prevents run-on sentences from increasing length artificially.

These studies, along with others which have examined complexity in children's language, indicate a pattern of increasing complexity in both spoken and written language throughout the elementary grades. Although a variety of means to combine structures is used at all grade levels, it is at first done mostly through coordination and later through subordination and embedding. One may expect a great many run-on sentences throughout the early elementary grades, but these should decrease as children's language matures.

PATTERNS AND VARIATIONS IN LANGUAGE ACQUISITION

While there is great variation in certain aspects of language and in the age at which certain structures or meanings are acquired, there are overriding patterns in the acquisition process which apply to all aspects of language.

Patterns in Acquisition

The process of language acquisition, like any cognitive process, exhibits patterns that may help us understand certain things that children say or do. Taylor[30] points out that children everywhere master linguistic rules, forms, and functions in the following pattern:

Essential before less essential
Simple and short before long and complex
Few before many
Gross and distinct before subtle and finer
Salient before less salient
Concrete before abstract
Isolated items individually before items in relation
Regular before irregular (unless irregular items are common and simple)
Forms with more general application before forms with restricted application
Basic functions before particular details of forms to express the functions

It is within this sort of framework that the acquisition of language takes place. The variations in language are primarily differences in the structures acquired at a particular time by a child or differences in the acquisition of a particular structure by children of the same age.

Variability in Acquisition

Individual variability   A very clear picture of the differences between children in the acquisition of particular structures occurs in a study discussed earlier in the chapter. In this study, the researchers were investigating the appearance of various syntactic or morphological inflections in "Adam" and "Eve's" language.[31] Of the five inflections reported, the one acquired when the children were closest in age was the *-ing* on present progressives. Eve used this inflection at 19½ months and Adam used it at 28 months, 8½ months' difference. On the other hand, the third person ending *-s* on present tense verbs was reported for Eve at 26 months, but not for Adam until 41 months, a 15-month difference. In spite of such tremendous variations in the age at which these children used the inflections, the order or sequence of use was the same.

This kind of individual variability may be found for other syntactic or semantic structures as well as for various elements of motor development. There simply is a great deal of variability in individual children's rates of development. In language acquisition, particularly, the factor that appears to be most important is the individual linguistic environment of the child.

The individual linguistic experiences of children serve as the source from which children process their language. The words they hear, their pronunciations, and the structures which are used by people around them serve as a basis for developing linguistic rules. The particular linguistic environment of the child may also be important in the kinds of interaction opportunities provided—opportunities for the child to test and revise particular linguistic rules.

Social variability   In addition to the factors mentioned previously which cause people to vary in their language, there are also variations used within a particular social context. Within any dialect of English there are varieties or *registers* of that dialect appropriate for use in particular situations. People vary their language depending upon their current situation and what they believe to be correct within their dialect for that situation.

Even children use registers of language. Just ask a seven-year-old to enact an adult and you will observe different inflections, different vocabulary, and different gestures. The use of different language in written modes of discourse is also easily observed in children. By the time they are in the upper elementary grades and have been exposed to a considerable amount of written material, children write quite differently from the way they talk—showing an understanding of a register of written language. (See Chapter 3 for further discussion of language variation.)

There is, then, variability in language due to the particular situation in which language is used as well as variability due to differing linguistic environments. It is this variability within language which the teacher observes so clearly in the classroom and which necessitates varying assignments or experiences for different children.

THE ACQUISITION OF TWO LANGUAGES: BILINGUALISM

Bilingual people—those who speak two or more languages that involve differences in sound, vocabulary, and syntax—acquire their languages in one of several ways. Some children learn the two languages almost simultaneously at the time when they are first learning to talk. Other children learn one language at home and another when they go to school some time after they are five or so. Still others acquire a second language as a school subject during the elementary or secondary school years. The effectiveness of second-language learning and, indeed, the process of learning differ among these three kinds of bilingualism.

Children who are exposed to two languages simultaneously "during the critical acquisition period while the brain is still 'plastic' (brain organization is not completed), . . . become bilinguals as easily and naturally as others become monolinguals."[32] Some early studies of bilingual children showed them to be at a disadvantage; however, recent studies show that bilingual education is successful in the sense that children have mastered two languages adequately, and their academic achievement has not suffered because of bilingual education.[33]

When learning a second language at school later in childhood, there are differences depending on whether the language being learned is primarily for enrichment, with English as the native language, or the language being learned is English for children who speak another language natively.

For enrichment purposes, the most effective way of learning a second language at school is through an immersion program in which the new language is used as a medium of teaching. Programs using an immersion method have been frequent in the United States and Canada where French is used to teach predominantly English-speaking children. Even programs in which a second language is taught as a school subject are preferable to delaying learning a second language until adulthood. Children learn the pronunciation and intonations of the new language more easily and are less self-conscious about making errors in the new language than adolescents or adults.

For children living in the United States whose first language is not English, the case is significantly more complicated. The *Lau v. Nichols* case mandates that non-English-speaking children have a *meaningful opportunity to participate in the public educational program*. Three approaches have been used to meet federal requirements. Some children are simply given ESL (English as a second language) instruction. They leave their regular classroom for English class and then return to the regular classroom. In these programs, typically the children fall further and further behind, since they spend most of their day in a class where they can neither comprehend nor respond. A second approach is using immersion in English. While this method has had the greatest success of any of the attempts to promote bilingualism, some specialists hold that it doesn't work in the absence of equal status for both languages. "With respect to the Chicano, Latin American, or any child living in a highly ethnically homogeneous neighborhood, the technique has little chance for success. The primary reason is that the children are simply not afforded language models outside of the school's which are really any different from themselves."[34] The third approach is full-time instruction in the native language with simultaneous instruction in ESL. In this approach the children learn all their regular school subjects in their native language while having special classes in English. DeAvila and Duncan contend that the dominant English language of the environment ensures that children become proficient in English.

What to do to best help children from non-English-speaking backgrounds is an important question. The 1980 report from the National Center for Education Statistics found that 3 million Hispanic children are enrolled in elementary and secondary schools. In addition, we have children from many other language backgrounds.

Since language cannot be separated from aspects of culture, we urge teachers who have children who speak another language to spend time in understanding the cultural heritage represented, and not to regard these children as deficient. There is some evidence of advantages in being bilingual. Bilinguals score higher in creativity, perhaps because they have two language systems representing two cultures and therefore look at common things in more ways than monolinguals. There is also some evidence of greater flexibility in bilingual children and of superiority in verbal intelligence.

LANGUAGE ACQUISITION OF HANDICAPPED CHILDREN

Certain children have special problems that relate to their acquisition of language. Since so much of the source for language development lies in oral conversation—in those special interactions of the young child with adults—deaf children have some difficulty acquiring language. Mentally retarded children, who must process the language they hear, find organizing patterns within it, and fit new aspects of language into their existing structures, also have special problems in the acquisition of language. Although speech handicaps such as voice problems, articulation problems, and stuttering are somewhat different in their relationship to the acquisition of language, they are of concern to elementary and middle school teachers. In fact, some of these are often confused with normal stages in acquisition or have their roots in early language development.

Deafness

Children who are deaf are not exposed to oral language, and although they begin to babble at about the same age as hearing children, they "stop babbling early and later experience great difficulty in learning to talk intelligibly unless hearing aids correct their hearing loss."[35] Even with a great deal of training, deaf children often cannot master natural intonations and rhythm in speech. They tend to have a higher-than-average pitch, speak more slowly, and pause for breath more often. They also have difficulty articulating consonants and vowels, particularly with voiced and unvoiced consonants (like /p/ and /b/) and with nasals and diphthongs. Early intervention, like that in the Nuffield Hearing and Speech Center in England which used the very small amounts of hearing the children have to help them develop oral speech, shows great promise for deaf children.

Mental Retardation

Mentally retarded children go through the same stages in the acquisition of language as all children, and "their language is almost exactly like that of a normal child of the same *mental age*, where this is assessed by comparing their motor skills, memory, and so forth. The same limited set of meanings is expressed in their first sentences, though the rate of development is much slower."[36] A severely retarded child may take a year to make the progress a normal child would make in one month. There is also some evidence that retarded children use many more set patterns, "prefabricated routines," apparently relying more on rote memory than on creating their own sentences.

Speech Handicaps

Almost half of speech handicaps involve some sort of articulation problem, and about 10 percent involve stuttering. Many of the problems in articulation are outgrown by age seven or eight. The sound substitution errors that children make are highly systematic and are most often initial consonant sounds. Consonant sounds which cause the most difficulty are /l/ or /r/ (child substitutes /w/); /ð/, the voiced *th-* (child substitutes /d/); /θ/, the unvoiced *th-* (child substitutes /f/ or /t/); /dʒ/ as in judge (child substitutes /d/); /ʃ / as in *sh-* (child substitutes /s/); /t/ (child substitutes /s/ or /ʃ /); and /ɑ/; /j/; /s/; /v/; and /z/. The articulation errors that children make are in the consonants and consonant clusters that require more complex articulation and fine auditory discrimination and are generally mastered later by all children. Parents and teachers should not become unduly concerned about such articulation differences or try too hard to correct them. Many will simply disappear with maturity.

The other speech handicap that seems particularly important to discuss is stuttering. The fluency of speech in the stutterer is disturbed by blocking, repeating, or prolonging sounds, syllables, words, or phrases. There is some evidence of an inherited basis for stuttering, but environmental factors play a significant role. Children who stutter are typically made to pay attention to the way they talk because of their parents' (or teachers') high standards of fluency. All children and adults repeat words or sounds, hesitate, and do everything the stutterer does; it is just less frequent. Over 80 percent of all stutterers recover sponta-neously, according to Sheehan. Their recovery is attributed to role acceptance as a stutterer, growing self-esteem, development of adequacy and self-confi-dence, relaxation, and greater understanding of the problem.[37] It is especially important to provide an atmosphere as free from pressure as possible, not to overreact to stuttering or articulatory problems, and to show as little anxiety as possible to the speaker.

While it is important to understand the special problems of handicapped children, the most significant aspect of teaching such children is that what is good for children is good for *all* children. Emphasis on the content of the mes-sage, a relaxed atmosphere, and lots of opportunities to interact with adult lan-guage in meaningful contexts help special children develop language skills.

IMPLICATIONS FOR TEACHING

There appear to be two distinct implications for classroom practice stemming from the theoretical view presented of how children acquire language. If the basic process of acquisition involves using the language environment as a source for language "data," then it is important for the teacher to provide a rich lan-guage environment in the classroom. If the rules developed by children about how their language operates are then tested and revised in terms of the feedback they receive as they use language, then there must be many opportunities to use language in various ways.

Need for a Rich Language Source

Providing a classroom environment full of opportunities to hear rich and varied language involves selecting and reading literature that has a variety of sentence structures and a wealth of words as well as real literary qualities. It also implies that the teacher should not simplify sentence structures or vocabulary unless the children indicate a lack of understanding. Rich language could also be intro-duced by using various media such as films, audiotapes, and recordings and by inviting guest speakers. This kind of language environment should present lan-guage in a meaningful context and offer a variety of experiences from which children can draw language data.

Literature for children   Literature is a particularly rich source because so many books and poems for children contain imaginative language and children enjoy hearing them.

Look at the language used in the following selections from literature and poetry written for children of various ages. Examine the complexity of the sen-tences and the choice of words used. To get a feeling for complexity in mature language, examine sentence length and the use of clauses. Rich vocabulary is apparent in words which are precise and those which create a vivid picture in the mind of the reader.

In the highly popular *Miss Nelson is Missing*, the children lose their sweet Miss Nelson and get Miss Swamp, who is a real witch. The children finally go looking for Miss Nelson.

Children enjoy hearing and repeating the creative language that appears in so many of today's books for children.

Other kids went to Miss Nelson's house.

The shades were tightly drawn, and no one answered the door.

In fact, the only person they *did* see was the wicked Miss Viola Swamp, coming up the street.

"If she sees us, she'll give us more homework."

They got away just in time.[38]

H. M. Hoover's *Return to Earth* presents the middle school reader with a fascinating look at earth in 3307 with glimpses into fanaticism that might be today.

Long after the house had fallen silent, Samara lay curled up in the yielding blue softness of the blue windowseat, wide-awake, taking comfort from the darkness. She was aware of being very tired. It almost frightened her. She had never felt that way before. The long Dolmen ritual and her anger at the monk's arrest had started it. Her mother's anger with her had heightened it. And then to see the old villa burning. That was like watching her only real friend die.

She kept thinking of Galen Innes sitting there by his pool house, his face lighted by the flames. "Do we have any home, people like us?" Like *us*? The only answer was no.[39]

Poetry, too, is a rich source of language. Its rhythm and rhyme appeal to children; its words are strange and intriguing.

BEDTIME STORIES

"Tell me a story,"
Says Witch's Child.

"About the Beast
So fierce and wild.

About a Ghost
That shrieks and groans.

A Skeleton
That rattles bones.

About a Monster
Crawly-creepy.

Something nice
To make me sleepy."

Lilian Moore[40]

Poetry for older children can also present rich language and imagery.

THE OWL ON THE AERIAL

Just at dusk
As the full moon rose
And filled his canyon.
Out of his crevice
Floated the owl.
His down edged wings
Silent as moonlight

With three-foot wingspread.
Claws that could paralyze
Rabbit or squirrel.
He battened on beetles
Drawn to the manlight.
And just for a little
He lit on the aerial,
His curved claws clutching
The shining metal.

Softly the moonlight
Sheened on his feathers
While under his feet,
Unfelt by him,
The moon lay still
And men like those
In the house below
Floated upon it.

Clarice Short[41]

Through literature for children the teacher can introduce a variety of language patterns and vocabulary in meaningful ways. There is a rich context for understanding, and concrete imagery to delight and capture the child's imagination.

There is research evidence to show that using literature has some effect on children's language ability. Studies such as those by Cohen, Fodor, and Cullinan et al.[42] have found literature to be effective in facilitating some aspect of language acquisition or development. All these studies used an activity program or oral discussion as a follow-up to the stories read to children in the experimental groups.

Language of the teacher   Another source of language input for the classroom is the language of the teacher. Too often teachers working with children in the primary grades attempt to simplify their language so that they will be easily understood. There are, of course, times when this might be necessary for the safety of the children. Other than those few rare times, the teacher can facilitate language development more by speaking in a normal adult way. The context within which language is used helps to clarify much that may not yet be under control of less mature speakers. If the teacher is sensitive to the responses—both verbal and nonverbal—of children, further explanations can make clear any lack of understanding while developing vocabulary at the same time.

Another facet of the teacher's language is the kind of response elicited from children. Teachers must create a need for children to respond to their experiences in a variety of ways. This may occur in individual discussions or as part of a group experience.

Nonprint media   Another source of a rich language environment which may be provided within the classroom setting is the variety of films, audiotapes, and recordings available. These media also provide a context for language that is meaningful. They should be selected for their inherent interest as well as for their language possibilities.

The content of the nonprint media may involve another subject area such as mathematics, science, or social studies. Recordings, tapes, films, and filmstrips of both poetry and prose are also available. If the teacher can set up a listening area for independent use, children can select what appeals to them and work individually or in small groups with the materials.

The creation in the classroom of a rich and varied language environment is important for all children. It is crucial for children whose home environment does not provide experiences for children to respond to through language. The need to use language to communicate ideas and feelings in an original and creative way is to some extent culturally determined. For teachers working with children who have not been exposed to this need to use language, the richness of and response to language in the classroom are vital.

Opportunities to Engage in Language

A major feature of the process of language acquisition and development is the testing and revision of the internalized rules of how language operates. This applies to the acquisition of specific syntactic constructions and also to the acquisition or refinement of semantics or word meanings.

Communicating and explaining   The teacher needs to set up situations that give children opportunities to talk with others. Children need experiences in sharing ideas and explaining things. This may be done with the whole class, with small groups of children, or between individual children. Children should be allowed to talk freely with each other when it will not interrupt classroom activities and as long as that talk is not rowdy or purposeless. In group discussions and in sharing activities, children should be encouraged to describe and explain and interact with each other. The teacher can accomplish this by asking a variety of questions and by encouraging children to ask questions or add their own experiences. Activities which require joint cooperation, effort, and thinking also prompt meaningful talk among children.

Imagining and creating   Through the various avenues provided in oral composition, the teacher can encourage imaginative and creative uses of language. Dramatic activities and storytelling lend themselves to this kind of language use. Inventing new words and using familiar ones in new ways, rhyming and discovering "found" poetry, and telling real and invented stories all lead to imaginative and creative uses of language.

In classrooms we provide opportunities for children to respond to their experiences creatively in various artistic media. This kind of response should be encouraged in creative language activities also. Children, even at the early age levels, should have an opportunity to tell or write stories and poems. If the task of writing is difficult for them, provision should be made for dictating to others. Children should share orally as well as in written form the stories and poems they have written.

Playing with words and sounds is natural for children. Rhyming words and making up new words are not unusual at all. It is typical to see this in young children who have not been "disciplined" so much that their creative response has been squelched. If teachers want to foster creative responses by children to their environment, then they must cherish creativity and imagination in children. Students need to be encouraged and given opportunities to work creatively with language in both oral and written forms. They need to hear imaginative language used in both stories and poetry.

A More Natural Learning Environment

An integral part of early language acquisition is the kind of environment in the home that fosters learning. This environment is characterized by some qualities that also make a good learning situation at school. Some aspects of the home environment are not possible in a school setting, at least not in their entirety; but a classroom more like home would be beneficial to all learning, and certainly to language learning.

Emphasis on meaning, not form   In the language learning that takes place before children are of school age, parents and other adults respond to children in terms of what they mean. Little attention is paid to "correct form." While children do need to develop skill in using conventional aspects of language, this is a gradual process and comes with a real purpose. We want to help the listener or reader understand what we are saying or writing. We learn to write good letters when someone we like very much is away, not when the teacher decides it's time for a unit on writing letters. Handwriting becomes important when we find others can't make sense of our story because they can't read the writing (or printing). Saying *he doesn't* instead of *he don't* becomes important when we realize that someone we want to impress cares which phrasing is used.

One of the major purposes of language arts instruction is to develop fluency in using language, both oral and written language. We want adults who can speak easily, describing or explaining their ideas fully. We hope for the same qualities in written expression. We seek both the ability to produce a large quantity and an easy flow of language. If teachers insist on correctness—on form—too soon, children never really develop fluency of expression. They become too concerned with punctuation or spelling to get their ideas down. They worry about whether to use *lie* or *lay* and about being corrected if they pick the wrong one, and so they don't answer the question or tell the story that comes to mind. Too much pressure too soon to use adult forms interferes with language development.

Reduction of stress   There is little stress on the young child learning language at home. Parents are confident that their children will learn to talk, and indeed very few children fail to learn. Not so with learning to read and write. Cramer points out that "the circumstances accompanying the teaching of reading and writing are often stressful and frequently produce anxiety in the learner. Stress interferes with learning and produces anxiety when it is excessive."[43] While most parents realize that children begin to talk at different ages and continue at different rates, they worry if their child doesn't make at least "one year's progress" during each school year. Some children may fail to learn to read and write because of the school situation. A bad start, too much stress, not being ready—all may build a barrier to learning both then and later:

> Excessive competition, ability grouping, lack of patience, rigid grade levels, parental and teacher ignorance of developmental processes, and inappropriate instructional materials and techniques are among the major factors that lead to failure in reading and writing. Each of these factors is an environmental condition and, hence, can be changed by teachers, schools, and society.[44]

Emphasis on interrelated skills   Although, as we have discussed, adults do adjust their language when speaking to very young children, this adjustment is not a matter of deciding which language skills are needed for speech and then setting them up into a sequence of activities. Oral language is acquired rather naturally, with the child figuring out how language works and then trying it out. Although writing and reading are not completely analogous, some aspects of learning to talk have parallels in reading and writing. Children need to be read to often, and they need to see their ideas put into printed form as they observe. They need opportunities to look through books and other reading materials. There are times when they see how important information can be put into print and read by others. A great deal of exposure to written language and encouragement to try it—without any insistence on adultlike form—help children enter the world of print. Writing and reading have parallel oral forms in speaking and listening. Just as listening and speaking interact with each other, so do writing and reading. There is every evidence that they should be taught at the same time to reinforce each other.

Individualization   While adults typically interact on a one-to-one basis with preschoolers, this is not possible in our public schools. At least it is not possible all day long for every student. It certainly is feasible for teachers in a public school setting to have some time each day to listen to a child read, to look at and respond to a story or painting, to listen to something a child has experienced, or to say something special to each child. For many children, five minutes of the teacher's full attention is worth an hour's attention to the group. Oral language typically gets an immediate response, while writing and reading receive a delayed response. A more immediate reaction to children's reading and writing may help them learn.

SUMMARY

There are some specific classroom practices that may be drawn from the theory of language acquisition presented here. There is a need for the teacher to provide a classroom environment that has rich language experiences for children. There is a need for children to have many varied opportunities to engage in both communicative and creative uses of language. A classroom setting that permits and encourages these activities not only helps students develop their language potential but also facilitates growth in all the language arts.

UNDERSTANDING THROUGH INVOLVEMENT

1. Tape-record several children at different ages telling a story based on the same wordless book (see the list of these in Chapter 13). Then examine the stories for differences in complexity of the sentence structures used, the number of words per sentence or per main clause, and the fluency with which the children told the story (no long pauses, fillers like *and-uh,* or completely garbled language).
2. Another interesting activity with different age levels is to see what words children associate with the ones you give. Generally the less mature children will give a word that follows the one you say, somewhat more mature children will give a word that begins with the same letter or sound, and the fully mature children will give a word that will substitute for the one you give because it is the same part of speech or in the same word class. You might try:

Hat	*Tall*	*Monday*	*Eagle*
Walk	*Come*	*Knife*	*Spoon*
Red	*Hot*	*Pen*	*With*
Mother	*Book*	*Brother*	*Glass*

3. This activity involves asking small groups of first- or second-graders and fifth- or sixth-graders to put two short sentences together into one sentence. They may add words or leave words out or change them around. Look for differences in the ease with which they combine the sentences and the variety of ways they can do it. They should see the sentence pairs, hear you read them, and then give their answers orally. Some sentence pairs you could use are:[45]

   (a) The cat is black.
       The cat likes hot milk.
   (b) Sam watched the clowns.
       The clowns blew up balloons.
   (c) My hat is blue.
       My hat has flowers on it.
   (d) My sister is going to camp this summer.
       She will learn to swim at camp.
   (e) My sister likes to play with her dolls.
       Her dolls all talk.

4. There are differences between what a child understands and what that child can say. This may be seen clearly by asking children between 2½ and 3½ years of age to look at some pictures of various animals. You first point to certain ones asking, *What is this animal called?* After a while, switch and ask the child to point to the wolf (or elephant, giraffe, etc.). There should be a noticeable difference between what the child can name and what that same child can point to when hearing the name.

5. Examine some children's trade books or library books that would be appropriate for primary school or preschool children. In these picture books, look for vocabulary that is interesting and different and also for sentence complexity. Although sentence length is not as accurate a measure as some others in determining complexity, it does work fairly well in professionally written material and is simple to do. Use the first ten or fifteen sentences in five or ten books to get a feel for the kind of linguistic complexity that is used in well-written picture books for children.

REFERENCE NOTES

[1]Frank Smith. *Understanding Reading—A Psycholinguistic Analysis of Reading and Learning to Read.* New York: Holt, 1971, p. 50.

[2]E. H. Lenneberg. "A Biological Perspective of Language," in *Language* (R. C. Oldfield and J. C. Marshall, eds.). Baltimore: Penguin, 1968, pp. 32–33.

[3]David McNeill. *The Acquisition of Language.* New York: Harper & Row, 1970, pp. 2–3.

[4]D. McCarthy. "Language Development of the Preschool Child," in *Child Behavior and Development* (Roger C. Barker et al., eds.). New York: McGraw-Hill, 1943, pp. 107–128. E. A. Davis. *The Development of Linguistic Skill in Twins, Singletons with Siblings, and Only Children from Age Five to Ten Years.* Minneapolis: The University of Minnesota Press, 1937.

[5]Courtney B. Cazden. *Child Language and Education.* New York: Holt, 1972, pp. 121–125.

[6]Ibid.

[7]H. Ginsburg and S. Opper. *Piaget's Theory of Intellectual Development.* Englewood Cliffs, N.J.: Prentice-Hall, 1969, p. 17.

[8]Ibid., p. 18.

[9]A. L. Baldwin. *Theories of Child Development*. New York: Wiley, 1967, p. 176.

[10]Herbert H. Clark and Eve V. Clark. *Psychology and Language*. New York: Harcourt Brace Jovanovich, 1977, p. 320.

[11]Ibid., p. 327.

[12]Dan Isaac Slobin and Charles A. Welsh. "Elicited Imitation as a Research Tool in Developmental Psycholinguistics," in *Studies of Child Language Development* (Charles A. Ferguson and Dan Isaac Slobin, eds.). New York: Holt, 1973, pp. 485–497.

[13]Ibid., p. 490.

[14]Susan M. Ervin. "Imitation and Structural Change in Children's Language," in *New Directions in the Study of Language* (E. H. Lenneberg, ed.). Cambridge, Mass.: MIT Press, 1964, pp. 163–189.

[15]Roger Brown and Ursula Bellugi. "Three Processes in the Child's Acquisition of Syntax," in *New Directions in the Study of Language* (E. H. Lenneberg, ed.). Cambridge, Mass.: MIT Press, 1964, pp. 131–161.

[16]Courtney B. Cazden. "Suggestions from Studies of Early Language Acquisition," *Childhood Education*, vol. 46, December 1969, p. 129.

[17]Ibid., p. 128

[18]David McNeill. "Developmental Psycholinguistics," in *The Genesis of Language* (F. Smith and G. Miller, eds.). Cambridge, Mass.: MIT Press, 1966, p. 69.

[19]Donald J. Foss and David T. Hakes. *Psycholinguistics*. Englewood Cliffs, N.J.: Prentice-Hall, 1978, p. 286.

[20]Dan I. Slobin, "Cognitive Prerequisites for the Development of Grammar," in *Studies of Child Language Development* (Charles A. Ferguson and Dan Isaac Slobin, eds.). New York: Holt, 1973, pp. 191–206.

[21]E. H. Lenneberg. *Biological Functions of Language*. New York: Wiley, 1967.

[22]Ursula B. Bellugi and Roger Brown. "The Acquisition of Language," *Monograph Social Research in Child Development*, vol. XXIX, no. 1, 1964.

[23]Paula Menyuk. "Syntactic Structures in the Language of Children," *Child Development*, vol. XXXIV, June 1963, pp. 407–422.

[24]Carol S. Chomsky. *The Acquisition of Syntax in Children from 5 to 10*. Cambridge, Mass.: MIT Press, 1969.

[25]E. V. Clark. "What's in a Word? On the Child's Acquisition of Semantics in His First Language" (unpublished paper). August 1971, p. 12. For further discussion of this theory, see E. V. Clark. "On the Acquisition of the Meaning of Before and After," *Journal of Verbal Learning and Verbal Behavior*, vol. 10, 1971, pp. 266–275; and H. H. Clark and E. V. Clark. "Semantic Distinctions and Memory for Complex Sentences," *Quarterly Journal of Experimental Psychology*, vol. 20, 1968, pp. 129–138.

[26]Lois Bloom. "Why Not Pivot Grammar?" in *Studies of Child Language Development* (Charles A. Ferguson and Dan Isaac Slobin, eds.). New York: Holt, 1973, pp. 430–440. Also see L. Bloom. *Language Development: Form and Function in Emerging Grammars*. Cambridge, Mass.: MIT Press, 1970.

[27]Paula Menyuk. *The Acquisition and Development of Language*. Englewood Cliffs, N.J.: Prentice-Hall, 1971, p. 182.

[28]Walter D. Loban. *The Language of Elementary School Children*. Champaign, Ill.: National Council of Teachers of English, 1963.

[29]Kellog W. Hunt. "Syntactic Maturity in School-Children and Adults." *Society for Research in Child Development Monograph*, vol. XXV, no. 1, February 1970.

[30]Insup Taylor. *Introduction to Psycholinguistics*. New York: Holt, 1976, p. 235.

[31]Ursula Bellugi. "The Emergence of Inflections and Negations Systems in the Speech of Two Children," in *The Acquisition of Language* (D. McNeill, ed.). New York: Harper & Row, 1970, p. 83.

[32]Ibid., p. 239.

[33]Ibid., p. 246.

[34]Ed DeAvila and Sharon Duncan. "A Few Thoughts about Language Assessment and a Sociolinguistic Alternative to the Lau Remedies," in *Bilingual Education* (LaFontaine et al., eds.). Wayne, N.J.: Avery Publishing Group, 1978, p. 141.

[35]Peter A. de Villiers and Jill G. de Villiers. *Early Language.* Cambridge, Mass.: Harvard University Press, 1979, p. 125.

[36]Ibid., p. 50.

[37]J. G. Sheehan. "Speech Therapy and Recovery from Stuttering," *The Voice*, vol. 15, 1965, pp. 3–6.

[38]Harry Allard and James Marshall. *Miss Nelson is Missing.* Boston: Houghton Mifflin, 1977, p. 18.

[39]H. M. Hoover. *Return to Earth.* New York: 1980, p. 49.

[40]Lilian Moore. "Bedtime Stories," in *See My Lovely Poison Ivy* and *Other Verses about Witches, Ghosts and Things.* New York: Atheneum, 1975, p. 3.

[41]Clarice Short. "The Owl on the Aerial," in *Zero Makes Me Hungry* (Edward Leuders and Primus St. John, eds.). Glenview, Ill.: Scott Foresman, 1976, p. 22.

[42]Dorothy Cohen. "The Effect of Literature on Vocabulary and Reading," *Elementary English*, vol. XLV, February 1968, pp. 207–217. Eugene M. Fodor. "The Effect of the Systematic Reading of Stories on the Language Development of Culturally Deprived Children," *Dissertation Abstracts*, vol. XXVII, no. 4, October 1966, p. 952-A. Bernice E. Cullinan, Angela Jaggar, and Dorothy Strickland. "Language Expansion for Black Children in the Primary Grades: A Research Report," *Young Children*, vol. 29, January 1974, pp. 98–112.

[43]Ronald L. Cramer. *Children's Writing and Language Growth.* Columbus, O.: Merrill, 1978, p. 19.

[44]Ibid., p. 20.

[45]Frank Zidonas et al. "Sentence Combining," *Protocol Materials in English Education, Language Development.* Tampa: University of South Florida, 1975.

PART TWO

Language Skills: Substance and Strategies

This portion of the text presents strategies for teaching children essential language skills on the basis of developmental learning theory. This theory suggests that content and basic skills are best learned within the context of meaningful and concrete experiences.

Chapter 5 is devoted to teaching vocabulary skills. Because experience is necessary for vocabulary development, it forms the basis for the instructional program. The goal is to extend students' vocabulary through experiences which include wide reading, discussion, listening, field trips, and neighborhood excursions as well as direct teaching activities.

The teaching of grammar is presented in Chapter 6. Various kinds of grammars found in textbooks are described and discussed for informational purposes. Activities for children are suggested to help them become more flexible and more fluent in using English in oral and written forms.

Chapter 7 presents a framework for listening instruction, suggesting that listening is part of an interchange system. The impact of television on listening behavior is also explored, and instructional activities using children's television viewing are included in the discussion.

Four major types of oral composition are discussed in Chapter 8: sharing, discussing, reporting, and storytelling. Sharing is viewed as a means of facilitating children's language and concept development. The various kinds of discussions are divided into those that are primarily for planning and those used for presentation. Specific ideas for oral reporting and storytelling are included.

Although drama is certainly a form of oral composition, it is discussed in a separate chapter because it is quite different in nature and purpose from the other forms of oral language activities. The kinds of drama discussed in Chapter 9 range from dramatic play and movement to pantomime, role playing, and improvisational drama.

A personal letter, report, or invitation can be a creative endeavor just as can the writing of an imaginative story or poem. Therefore, the discussion in Chapter 10 combines instructional approaches for a wide variety of writing experiences.

The final chapter in this section, Chapter 11, focuses on teaching the supportive writing skills—punctuation, capitalization, spelling, and handwriting. Instruction is accomplished within a meaningful context and does not interfere with the spontaneous flow of children's thoughts as they write.

CHAPTER FIVE

Extending Vocabulary

PREVIEW QUESTIONS

1 Why is it important to develop students' word-meaning vocabulary?
2 What is meant by "levels of word knowledge"?
3 How do we learn the meanings of words?
4 What activities are useful in teaching vocabulary?

Language uses words to communicate as art uses line and color or as dance uses movement and rhythm. The better a child's vocabulary is, the more effectively he or she can understand others and communicate ideas.

ASPECTS OF DEVELOPING VOCABULARY

Words help us organize our ideas and experiences; they are a part of thinking.

> Words are the units of speech, of language. Words are experience-namers, and our stock of words influences our view, our perception and conception of the world.... Vocabulary development is a matter of seeing conceptual relationships, putting handles on objects and ideas so we can manipulate them effectively. Our ability to *name* things sharply influences the extent of our cognitive skills.[1]

When we tell others about an experience we've had, we need to choose the precise words that will convey that event as accurately as possible. Writing, too, is highly dependent on selecting the words that will communicate our vision to others. When there is no voice and only the words are on the paper, those words must be just right or much meaning is lost.

Vocabulary and Reading

Vocabulary development is a crucial aspect of learning to read. The number of different words a person knows and the number of different meanings for these words both affect reading ability. Here we are not talking about "word-recognition vocabulary" or the number of words students can identify in print. We are talking about associating meaning with a word. The more words you know, the more easily you can recognize a word in print. Knowing just one meaning of a word will help you use word analysis to decode it. If you know *bank* as the place where Mom or Dad go to cash a check or the small piggy you put pennies in, then when you see *b-a-n-k* you can sound it out and immediately say *bank*. Reading comprehension is somewhat different. To comprehend well, you must know the precise meaning of the word as it is being used. If you know bank only as a place for money, what meaning can you get from:

The boys sat on the bank and dangled their feet in the water.

or from:

The plane went through the cloud bank at 3,500 feet.

How could boys sit on the First National and put their feet in water? Why do clouds have banks? Who would put money in a cloud? For comprehension, you must know *bank* as "the rising ground bordering a lake, river, or sea" and as "a piled up mass of cloud or fog" as well as "a place of business of a money changer."[2] Children who only know *game* as something we play, like tag or monopoly, would have trouble understanding, *She soaked the game in vinegar and water before cooking it.* Those who know *duck* as the bird that goes quack-

quack would surely have trouble with, *She bought three yards of white duck.* Many children who have well-developed skills in word analysis still have difficulty getting meaning from what they read because they have a limited knowledge of words and their meanings.

Word Meaning

We must help children develop their word knowledge in two ways: first, they need to learn many new words; second, they need to learn multiple meanings for the words they already know. In addition to learning the literal meaning for words, children need to develop some sensitivity to the associated or suggested meanings apart from what the word explicitly means. If you are short, would you rather be called *little, petite,* or *squat?* Were your remarks *brief, curt,* or *succinct?* Which of these is the largest: *massive, huge, enormous, big,* or *mountainous?* Does *massive* suggest anything other than size? Heaviness, perhaps. While it is important to know synonyms, it is equally important to know the shades of meaning by which they differ from each other. These word connotations are a major aspect of vocabulary learning. A thesaurus may give the following synonyms for *hit: batter, touch, smite, strike, knock,* and *smash.* There's a lot of difference between *smashing* people and *touching* them, and *smite* is positively biblical. We teach children in the primary grades the names of the basic colors: *red, blue, green, brown, white, black, yellow, orange, purple,* etc. When do they learn *emerald, jade, chartreuse, olive, mint, celery,* or *avocado?*

Factors in Ease of Learning

Some words are easier to learn than others; *eat* is easier to learn than *true,* and *circle* is easier to learn than *friend.*

At least five factors play a part in the difficulty or ease of learning a particular word. (1) The degree of abstraction involved is one of these factors. The more abstract words or concepts such as *truth* or *friendship* are more difficult than *circle* or *eat.* (2) The complexity of the concept adds increasing difficulty, and so *democracy* or *truth* may be more difficult than *friend.* (3) The frequency with which a word is used is the third factor, and words that are used more frequently are somewhat easier to learn. (4) The amount of context surrounding the word also makes a difference in how easy or difficult a word is to learn. Do you know the word *elute?* No? Now consider it in a "high-context" sentence: *To elute that stain, use carbon tetrachloride.* The amount of context is not just the number of words; the higher the context, the fewer possible alternative responses exist. Here are three sentences with a word missing. It is the same word. Notice how the possible responses narrow with increasing amounts of context.

Low context: *Buy five or six _____ when you get to the store.*
Medium context: *He picked some _____ from the tree.*
High context: *You have to squeeze _____ to make lemonade.*

(5) The fifth factor that affects ease of learning is a person's interest in learning a word. Boys and girls who are fascinated with flight will learn *drag* and *thrust;*

they will talk about the *camber* of the wing, the *fuselage*, the *rudder*, and the *ailerons*. These will seem easy to learn, while the concept of *opposite* and *alternate* may be difficult. Interest as well as experience plays an important role in learning word meanings.

Levels of Word Knowledge

To further complicate the situation, there are different levels of knowing a word. Dale et al. suggest four categories[3] to describe them:

1. *I never saw it before.*
2. *I've heard of it, but I don't know what it means.*
3. *I recognize it in context—it has something to do with. . . .*
4. *I know it.*

Try classifying the following words into these four categories for yourself: *auger, flounce, gambrel, lyre, bizarre, heinous, dinghy.* The words that you do know will depend on your experiences. If you live near the water, you probably will know that a *dinghy* is a small boat, but you may not know that an *auger* is a tool for boring holes in wood. If you are musical, you may know that a *lyre* is a stringed instrument; those interested in architecture will know that *gambrel* is a style of roof. A *flounce* is a ruffle as well as a way of moving; *bizarre* is odd or eccentric, and *heinous* is hatefully or shockingly evil.

Some of the words that we recognize when we read them might not be understood if we heard them. And even some of those we know when we read or listen to them, we never use ourselves in speaking or writing. We may not even know how to say them. Do you know how to say *heinous*? (The first syllable rhymes with *weigh*.) Each of us has a speaking, writing, listening, and reading vocabulary. When children enter school, their speaking vocabulary is much larger than their writing vocabulary or their reading vocabulary. By the time they leave school, their reading vocabulary will far surpass the others. How well we know a word, then, depends on both the level of our knowledge and the mode in which the word is being used.

Special Children's Vocabulary

Because vocabulary depends so much on experience, children who have significantly different backgrounds from each other will know very different words. Some of the words they know will not be useful at school; many beginners know *barbecue* and popular brand names of beer, but not *bunny* and *carrot*. Unfortunately for them, typical beginning school materials are full of bunnies eating carrots, but have no barbecues with beer.

Less able children may need more contacts with a new word to make it a permanent part of their vocabulary. They will need opportunities to use new words in meaningful ways. The more concrete you can make the meaning, the more easily it will be learned. Also, many children know things they can talk about, when they can't write them. Some of your less able readers may be the very best storytellers.

Children who come from different language backgrounds have special needs for vocabulary development. Generally speaking, translation from one language to the other is not desirable. Bilingual children need to develop separate language systems; and while occasional translations to make meaning clear are certainly appropriate, translation as a standard practice is not. Lots of talk in the target language about an object, real experiences, role playing, discussion of uses and shades of meaning, and a wide reading in books in the target language all help the bilingual child add words to his or her vocabulary. In some ways, speaking another language may be an advantage since English has many borrowed words. Children who speak Spanish, Portuguese, French, or Italian may have the special advantage of being able to relate English words derived from Latin, French, etc., to parallel ones in their native language. Pointing out these instances will help them think and use what they already know.

VOCABULARY AND CONCEPT DEVELOPMENT

We cannot divorce vocabulary development from conceptual development. Every word is essentially a concept. By understanding the concept associated with a word, we understand the meaning of the word. For example, the word *water* is meaningful to us because we understand the concept of water. We have had experiences with water—we swim in water, we drink water, we wash dishes in water.

Certain concepts are more concrete than others, and the words associated with them are easier to learn. For instance, if you want children to understand the concept of squareness and the word associated with it *(square)*, you show them pictures of squares, have them cut out squares, and perhaps even draw squares. The concept is very teachable because it can be demonstrated in very concrete and tangible ways. But how do you teach children the concept of honesty? How do they learn the meaning of the word *honest*? Intangible and emotive concepts such as this are learned through experience—either direct experience, vicarious experience, or a combination of both. When children have had plenty of experiences related to the concept of honesty, they will understand the concept and the word *honest*.

Vocabulary develops through experiences and the association of these experiences with words. Intelligence and environmental factors cannot be overlooked when we are assessing the depth and breadth of children's vocabularies, but a learning environment that offers a wide variety of experiences can only promote and extend children's vocabulary development.

METHODS OF TEACHING VOCABULARY

"Vocabulary development in school must be a planned program. . . . Incidental teaching, alone, tends to become accidental teaching."[4] There is no doubt that a teacher needs to provide learning experiences that will incorporate the development and expansion of children's vocabularies. Opportune moments for developing concepts and associated vocabulary are often overlooked in the classroom. As an example, a small group of children came to the word *jostled* in their reading. None of the children knew the meaning of the word, but one child attempted to give a definition using the context of the story. The teacher interrupted the child, gave the definition of the word *jostled*, and then announced it was time for the next reading group. What might this teacher have done instead? The students could have been encouraged to predict the meaning of the word by using contextual clues. They might have demonstrated the meaning of the word by participating in a role-playing situation, such as being jostled on a crowded bus. Other situations in which one might be jostled could have been discussed, and the word itself could have been found in the dictionary to determine if there were other meanings.

All types of learning and communication experiences offer opportunities to develop a child's vocabulary. "All education is vocabulary development, hence conceptual development; we are studying words and symbols all the time."[5] We do know that planned experiences can be used effectively to extend and broaden children's vocabularies, and they can be incorporated easily into the ongoing learning environment.

Direct and Concrete Experiences

Involvement in direct and concrete experiences helps to develop all types of vocabularies. Children need a variety of sensory experiences—touching, listening, tasting, and smelling. Along with direct experiences go conversations and discussions. By talking with children, a teacher can help them understand concepts and word meanings. For example, a child walked into class one morning carrying a lizard. Instead of placing the lizard aside in a nearby box, the teacher gathered the children around to look and talk about the lizard. They discussed the shape and size of the lizard, its color, and the texture of its skin; and one of the children went to the library to get a book about lizards because they wanted more information. They composed stories about the lizard either individually or in a small group with their teacher. That afternoon they built a vivarium for the lizard on the basis of information they had gathered from their reading. Several children pursued their interest in lizards further and recorded new words on a special chart hung above the vivarium. The words on the chart were *habitat, tropical, aquatic* and *terrestrial, camouflage, nocturnal* and *diurnal,* and the names of three kinds of lizards—*gecko, iguana,* and *chameleon.* Several days later when the group had finished their extra research, they shared information with the whole class. During the discussion their teacher helped them relate the new words to other words they knew; thus, they talked about *aquariums* and *terrariums,* and they brainstormed words related to terrariums such as *terrace, terrain,* and *territory.* One child suggested *terrible;* but when they looked it up, they found it came from *terrēre* (to frighten) instead of from *terra* (earth).

In another class, Mrs. Maroni's sixth-graders learned many new words as they worked with a new illustrative medium, *collage.* Working with the art teacher, Mr. Traylor, the class recorded any new words they encountered while experimenting with different types of collage. Their word list included *pattern, texture, dimensional, medium, embossed, contrast, relief, coil, proportion, perspective, unity, vibrant, fabric, material, textile.* Some were completely new words; others like *medium* were new meanings for familiar words. Both Mrs. Maroni and Mr. Traylor made a conscious effort to use the new words appropriately as they discussed the students' projects; and as the words were used by both teachers and students, they became a part of the sixth-graders' own stock of words.

These two examples suggest the potential for learning words during the course of regular classroom events. Almost every activity has such potential, but as a teacher you must recognize it and use the appropriate words yourself and encourage your children to use them too. If you talk about the lizard as a *land animal* instead of *terrestrial* and build a *place* for it instead of a *vivarium*, your students will not learn those new words.

You can also structure vocabulary learning as a part of other content or study areas. Third- or fourth-graders studying energy might study about coal and learn *alloy, coke, elements, fossil fuel, conversion, refining, synthetic* and *natural, fuel, reclaim, by-product,* and perhaps even *bituminous* and *anthracite.* A seventh-grade social studies class might study the construction of the Statue of Liberty and learn *monument, symbol, brow, mammoth, sculptor, pedestal, site, intricate, beacon, immigrant, dismantle,* and *reassemble.* Kindergartners planting some tulips might learn *bulb, fleshy, stem, stalk, soil,* and *cluster.* Older students studying such plants might also learn *cycle, tuber, rhizome,* and *corm.*

At least three important ingredients of learning are present in the situations described: the students were interested in the activity and were involved in it, the words were encountered in a meaningful context, and there was ample opportunity (even need) to use the new vocabulary. Their teachers made a special effort to highlight new words and to find out information about the topic and about the words themselves. These teachers helped the children relate the new words to each other and to other known words.

Direct Teaching of Root Words and Affixes

Learning various affixes—that is, prefixes and suffixes—and the meanings of common roots has been a traditional way to study vocabulary. Some problems are inherent in such a method, but also some real potential exists. One of the difficulties is that many prefixes do not have a single meaning. For example, the prefix *de-* may mean *from,* or it may mean *down,* or it may indicate *reversal* or *undoing.* Sometimes the prefix no longer has any force or meaning, as in *desolate* or *dedicate.* Then, too, many English words begin with the letters *de* when they do not form a prefix, as in *decorate* and *decoy.* The same problems exist with root words and suffixes.[6]

There are some useful combining forms that have clear, invariant meanings. (Combining forms differ technically from affixes; a combining form plus an affix may form a word, but two affixes cannot.) In this category Deighton lists 26 which appear in some 200 current English words and are often employed in newly developed scientific words:

Useful Combining Forms[7]

anthropo- (human being)
auto- (self, same one)
biblio- (book)
bio- (life)
centro- (center) [*centri-*]
cosmo- (world, universe)
heter- (other, different) [*hetero-*]
homo- (same, similar)

hydro- (water, liquid)
iso- (equal, uniform)
lith- (of stone)
micro- (small, short)
mono- (one, single, alone)
neuro- (nerve, sinew)
omni- (all)
pan- (all, completely)

penta- (five)
phil- (loving) [philo-]
phone- (sound, voice, speech)
photo- (light, photograph)
pneumo- (air, lung, respiration)

poly- (many, much)
proto- (first)
psuedo- (false, spurious)
tele- (distant)
uni- (one, single)

He suggests that there are also ten prefixes that have regular, invariant meanings and few words beginning with the same letters where they are not a prefix. These should prove helpful and worth learning. Two others (marked with *) are added to the list although they have more than one meaning because they are so frequently used.

Useful Prefixes[8]

apo- (away from)
circum- (around)
equi- (equal)
extra- (outside, beyond)
intra- (within, during)
intro- (into, inward)

mal- (bad, abnormal, inadequate)
mis- (bad or wrong)
non- (not, reverse of)
syn- (with, along with)
*in- (not or into, or to intensify a word) [ir-, il-, im-, en-]
*un- (not, reverse, remove, completely)

Deighton also recommends two sets of suffixes and combining forms that are worth classroom time. One group is for noun endings, and the other is adjective endings; both lists have invariant meanings.

Noun Endings[9]

-ana (collected items)
-archy (rule, government)
-art (characterized by)
-aster (inferior, worthless)
-bility (capacity)
-chrome (colored)
-cide (killer, killing)
-ee (associated with, small kind of)
-fer (one that bears)
-fication (making)
-gram (drawing, writing, record)
-graph (written or for recording)

-graphy (writing)
-ics (study, characteristic quality)
-itis (disease, inflammation of)
-latry (worship)
-meter (instrument for measuring)
-metry (measuring)
-ology (expression or theory of)
-phore (carrier)
-phobia (fear of)
-ric (having character or nature of)
-scope (means for viewing)
-scopy (viewing, observing)

Adjective Endings[10]

-est (form the superlative of)
-ferous (bearing, producing)
-fic (making, causing)
-fold (multiplied by)
-form (in the shape of)
-genous (producing, yielding)
-scopic (resembling)
-wards (moves or is directed toward)
-wise (in manner of)

-less (without power, unable to)
-able (capable of, liable to) [-ible, -ble]
-most (most)
-like (the same as, resembling)
-ous
-ose
-acious } full of
-ful

These prefixes, suffixes, and combining forms will give students considerable help in dealing with unfamiliar words. Most of them are probably appropriate for study in the upper elementary, middle school, or junior high school years. A few might be discussed with younger children in an appropriate context.

The most effective way to teach such material is through an inductive approach. You might ask your students to tell you all the words they know that begin with *un-* and write them on chart paper or on the board. Suppose they suggest *untidy, unlucky, unable, undone, unhappy, uncovered, unknown, unpaid, unpopular, unwrap, unloved,* and *unpack.* Discuss the collection of words, what each means, or pantomime the actions they represent. Then discuss what the *un-* at the beginning of each means and how it alters the meaning of the base word. Another way to accomplish this inductive kind of approach is for you to present a series of words with the same combining form or affix: *automatic, autograph, autobiography, autocratic, automobile, autonomy, autohypnosis, automat,* and *automation.* Let the students tell you the meanings of as many as they can. Someone can volunteer to look the others up as you discuss them. What then does *auto-* mean?

Once word parts are introduced in such a way, you can provide additional reinforcement and practice through various games. These will be discussed later in the chapter and can provide a good review. Presenting affixes or combining forms in a list on Monday to be looked up, learned, and tested on Friday is ineffective. Children need to be able to interrelate words and have opportunities to use them for real learning to take place. We all need multiple contacts with new words to make them our own.

Word Derivations

Many children can have an enjoyable and profitable time studying the history of words. The study of word origins is intriguing and can entice some students into a lifetime fascination with words. If this study is to be successful, two key points are necessary.

> (1) The children must be personally involved, suggesting, contributing, experimenting in terms of history of etymology (at their level), and thereby seeing the relationship of word history to their everyday lives. This goal can be reached by encouraging the children to use key word studies in discussion and conversation (for example, making adjectives such as *jovial* from *Jove, solar* from *Sol, lunar* from *Luna,* etc.). (2) The teacher must become as expert as he can in words and word origins as they relate to general language development. He must, in effect, become "word-conscious," bringing to the classroom a knowledge of the "new" words to be discussed.[11]

Young children might be interested in such word study through tidbits of information you can include in various activities you do. Making pretzels would involve a whole variety of skills such as following directions, recalling sequence, developing new words (*dissolve, knead, sprinkle, coarse*), reading for a purpose, developing fine-muscle dexterity, classifying, and describing. (The recipe is given as an appendix to this chapter.) While you are making the pretzels or waiting for them to bake, you might want to tell the class about the origin of the pretzel.

Pretzel

A food that got its name from Germany is the PRETZEL. The German word *Prezel* or *Brezel* came from the Latin *brachium* meaning arm. (A *braccialetto*, in Italian, is a bracelet.) Also, *pretium* is Latin for "reward," and in the sixteenth century, monks used to give glazed cakes to children when they learned their prayers. It may be that the twisted shape of the PRETZEL represented the folded arms of the monks. Since these cakes were a reward, they were given the name *pretiola*, or "little rewards." The shape of the PRETZEL stayed the same, but the name changed from *pretiola* to PRETZEL.[12]

Besides pretzels, this same book tells about a lot of other food words such as *potato, cantaloupe, tangerine, hamburger, ketchup, spaghetti, cereal, waffle, coleslaw, delicatessen, coffee, vinegar, lollipop, chocolate, sandwich,* and *desserts.* Other sections deal with words about people, the animal world, things that grow, things we wear, things we enjoy, etc. If you don't have access to equipment for baking, why not make some coleslaw?

There are many ways to interest older students in word study. Middle-graders should enjoy figuring out how things got their names. They could map words like *hamburgers, wieners, gouda cheese, champagne, frankfurters, Persian cats, Great Danes, Dalmatian dogs,* and *Siamese cats.* Or they could compare a map of their region of the country with Europe, looking for similar names. Are some names descriptive of geographical features *(Clearwater, Boulder)?* Are some places named after famous people *(Lincoln, Houston, Columbus)?* Are there Indian names *(Sioux City, Tallahassee)?* Where do their own names come from? There are many books intended for choosing a name for a new baby that tell the meaning of names, or another good reference is *The Tree of Language* by Helene and Charlton Laird (World Publishing, 1975). Hennings suggests many activities to interest older students in word study in *Words, Sounds,* and *Thoughts* (Citation Press/Scholastic, 1977).

Books and Reading

According to research, it is possible to develop and increase a child's vocabulary by reading books aloud frequently.[13] The following story was retold and tape-recorded by a student after a well-known Aesop's fable had been read aloud and discussed. Notice the words and phrases in the child's retelling that have been taken from the original fable—*King of the forest, roars, nibble, paw, trap,* and others.

Once there was a mouse. He forgot where he was going and he ran over a poor lion and the lion said, "What do you mean by this?" And he put his paw over the mouse. He was fixing to eat the mouse. And the mouse said, "Oh, King of the forest, please do not do this to me, for one day I may be able to help you." And then he set the mouse free. And a short while later the lion got caught in a trap and he roars and all the animals heard him. And then, the mouse heard him. And the mouse said, "That was the lion that set me free." And then the mouse woke up and came running and never stopped till he came to the lion and the trap was made of rope and the mouse began to nibble the rope. He made a big hole so the lion could get out. And then the lion said, "I'll always remember this: Little friends can be great friends."

While reading and discussing several books about the Civil War, these students kept a glossary of words that were new to them. They now are dramatizing selected words from their list, and others in the group are attempting to guess the words.

Vocabulary is also increased the more a child reads independently. Therefore, more should be done in a classroom than simply providing a few books for children to read. Make a concerted effort to select a wide variety of books rich in vocabulary that will stretch and extend students' language. Provide time each day to read a book aloud and then place it in the classroom library area. Encourage students to reread it if they are interested, and call attention to other books in the area they may wish to explore and read. Your enthusiasm for and about particular books can have considerable influence on children's reading.

Discussion of particular words after reading a story or poem aloud can extend children's knowledge of words. For example, reading "Wake Up"[14] to children presents such words as *dozing, sodden, creeping,* and *stillness.*

WAKE UP

Dozing in the summer sun,
eyes almost closing,
a bullfrog on a sodden log
appears to be sleeping

. . . a waterbug comes creeping

suddenly frog's leaping
with a jump, clump, thump
to shake the stillness of the lake

urp   blurp   kerchurp!

EXTENDING VOCABULARY

Because the new words are presented in a meaningful context, children have little difficulty understanding their meaning if they are unfamiliar. Calling attention to certain words and briefly discussing them can ensure that they are noticed. After reading the story or poem, talking about the words or dramatizing them and using them in other contexts help children incorporate them into their own vocabularies. *Show me how the frog looked when he was dozing. What words in the first stanza tell you about how he looked?* ("Eyes almost closing," "appears to be sleeping.") *What do you think* SODDEN *might mean? Do you know* SOGGY? *Show me how the water bug moved.*

It is just as important to read books aloud to older children as it is to younger ones. After reading aloud a chapter of an intermediate book, spend some time talking about a few of the special words in the story and how the author used them. What are some synonyms, and how do those synonyms differ in the shade of meaning conveyed? Look at the following passage from *The Eyes of the Amaryllis*, a book with many interesting possibilities because of its rich language.

> Jenny stood hypnotized at the window, watching as the wall of black came onward. Gradually, the room grew dimmer, the dazzling patch of sky was curtained out. And then the clouds engulfed them. Instantly, the wind began again, shrieking louder than ever, and the world outside was lost in new sheets of rain that swept in the opposite direction now, northward toward the town at the other end of the bay.
>
> This shift seemed to catch the house off-guard. There was a crash high over their heads, and a sluice of water spread into the parlor from the fireplace, like blood streaming from a wound. "Why, the chimney's gone!" Gran exclaimed. She sounded shocked, surprised. The sudden breaching of her fortress seemed to jar her own determination; she bent a little in her chair, gripping the wooden head, and her voice had lost a fraction of its metal.[15]

For most middle school or junior high school students, some of the words in the description of the hurricane will be new, perhaps *sluice* and *breaching*. Some will be new meanings for familiar words, like *jar* and *metal*. Here context will be a great help in deciding the meaning of the words.

Well-written books for children at all levels will present new words and new word meanings in context. Children who have developed an interest in words with teachers who encourage them to pursue this interest will quickly develop their vocabulary and their pleasure in reading.

The books listed below are appropriate for reading aloud or for independent reading. They are just a few of the excellent books with rich language suitable for children of various ages.

Books with Rich Vocabulary: Some Special Books with Special Words

Aiken, Conrad. *A Little Who's Zoo of Mild Animals* (John Vernon Lord, illustr.). New York: Atheneum, 1977. (The award-winning author and poet, Conrad Aiken, has composed verses about imaginary animals that intrigue and fascinate older students. "In your lonely luminous palace of Aurora Borealis/ lovely lonely Tiger-mine burn and shine flame and shine.")

Baskin, Hosea, Tobias Baskin, and Lisa Baskin. *Hosie's Alphabet* (Leonard Baskin, illustr.). New York: Viking, 1972. (This illustrated ABC book for older students presents creative language throughout; for example: *F*—"a furious fly"; *S*—"a gangling entangling spider"; *Z*— "a ruminating zebu.")

Emberley, Ed. *Ed Emberley's ABC*. Boston: Little, Brown, 1978. (Students are required to look for animals and objects in the pictures that represent the letters of the alphabet. For example, a jaguar, jug, juggler, jewel, and jack-nife appear on the *J* pages.)

Gallienne, Eva Le, transl. Hans Christian Andersen's *The Nightingale* (Nancy Ekholm Burkert, illustr.). New York: Harper & Row, 1965. (This, as in other tales by Hans Christian Andersen, contains exceptional language. Words are woven ingeniously together to create a beautiful tale.)

Jarrell, Randell, transl. *Snow-White and the Seven Dwarfs* (Nancy Ekholm Burkert, illustr.). New York: Farrar, Straus, 1973. (The language is typically unique to fairy tales; characters and events are described in such a way that the reader instantly feels the good and evil moods of the story. "Then the Queen was horrified, and grew yellow and green with envy.")

Keats, Ezra. *Over in the Meadow*. New York: Four Winds, 1971. (Originally a counting song, *Over in the Meadow* offers delightful verse for young children.)

Mahy, Margaret. *The Dragon of an Ordinary Family* (Helen Oxenbury, illustr.). New York: Franklin Watts, 1969. (The word *ordinary* is well understood after reading this story. The author also uses words such as *glowered, triumphantly, gloomily, mysterious, curiously,* and *nervously* to tell an enchanting story that ends in a surprising manner.)

Tolstoy, Alexei. *The Great Big Enormous Turnip*. (Helen Oxenbury, illustr.). New York: Franklin Watts, 1968. (There is no doubt about young children's understanding of the word *enormous* after reading this story.)

Wildsmith, Brian. *Birds*. New York: Franklin Watts, 1967; *Fishes*. New York: Franklin Watts, n.d.; *Wild Animals*. New York: Franklin Watts, n.d. (The names and labels for groups of creatures have appeal to both children and adults. Whether it is a *corps of giraffes*, a *nye of pheasants*, or a *flock of dolphin*, students will find the illustrations and words intriguing in these three books.)

Games and Practice Activities

Although encounters with new words in a personal situation or within a meaningful context are very important in developing vocabulary because they are so effective, other activities or games structured for practicing new words or learning affixes and combining forms are helpful and do not depend as much on incidental, chance factors.

Charts and lists Classrooms at all levels should have lists of words—color words, words that can substitute for *said*, other ways of saying *good* or *bad*, words that tell how things move, size words, etc. In addition, students may want to keep a list of their own new words for the month or for the year. Perhaps a homemade book (directions in Chapter 13) would be good for this. As an alternative, teachers may provide word lists to start a new unit in science or social studies, or words from these new units can be highlighted as the study goes along.

Working with context Several games can be developed that involve using context to determine the answer. A form of concentration has pairs of cards: one

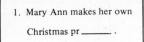
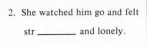

1. Mary Ann makes her own

   Christmas pr _____ .

2. She watched him go and felt

   str _____ and lonely.

Figure 5-1. Sample cards for "what's that word?"
Answers: 1, presents; 2, stranded (or strange).

with a sentence containing a blank for a missing word and the other with that missing word. These are put under slightly larger squares numbered from one to twenty (or in library pockets on a posterboard) and the children guess the two numbers that they think will match. If they are not right, the sentence or word cards are put back and the next player tries. The cards with the words and sentences could be numbered on the back, but this limits the adaptability of the game for adding new pairs and some children just memorize the number pairs that match instead of learning the words.

"What's that word?" is played with numbered index cards that have a sentence with part or all of one word missing; Figure 5-1 gives two examples. The difficulty level can be varied to suit the class, and different groups can have different sets of cards. A master list numbered with the correct words would enable children to play the game independently.

"Buy a clue" starts with the players or teams having the same number of tokens (poker chips, beans, bottle caps, etc.). In turn they draw a card that has a sentence with a word blank. The object is to guess the word. They can get help by buying a letter or letters—1 token per letter. A wrong guess carries a 5-token penalty. The winner is the person or team with the most tokens left.

Working with categories Categorizing words in different ways is important in developing vocabulary. Two different games will illustrate this type of practice. In one of these, shown in Figure 5-2, cards (4 by 6 inches) have five words printed on them, and the student has to tell which word doesn't belong and why. (The same words could have several different correct answers.) Possible answers might be *spatula*, because it's not used to eat with; or *chopsticks*, because there are two of them; or *knife*, because that's not intended to pick up food.

Another category game, shown in Figure 5-3, can be played with the whole class at one time or independently. The teacher or a student sets up a grid with categories of words on one axis and a letter for each column or row on the other axis. Then the children try to fill in each square of the grid with words they think the others won't think of. You get 1 point for each correct response and an additional point if no one else has your word. Having to think of words others won't put down encourages the children to extend their vocabulary.

A.   chopsticks   spoon

knife   fork   spatula

Figure 5-2   Category card: Which word doesn't belong?

	Feelings	Colors	Vegetables
B	*bold*		
L			*lentil*
R		*ruby*	*rutabaga*

Figure 5-3. Another category game: Think of a word in each category, beginning with the letter indicated.

Matching meanings Working with word meanings can be done in a number of different ways at all levels of maturity. There are some basic game formats that involve matching, and some types of matches can be used with any one of the formats.

Game Formats	*Vocabulary Matches*
Card games (like "go fish")	Picture to word
Board games	Word to definition
Concentration	Word to synonym
Tic-tac-toe	Word to antonym
Crosswords	Definition to word
Quiz questions	
Races	
Darts	

For example, you could make up a set of cards (laminating new faces to an old deck of playing cards) with thirteen sets of four synonyms. These would be dealt like rummy, with children "playing" three or four of a kind (the synonyms), or like "go fish," where they ask for the synonym they need. A board game might include a set of pictures and a board with a twenty-step path to the end of the rainbow; the players each draw a picture from the set, and if they can correctly name the picture, they move the number of steps indicated. In darts, the players might throw their darts to determine the number of points they will score for correctly giving the meaning required. A variation would be to throw one dart; and the number hit would indicate the particular set of questions to be answered or words to be defined.

An interesting synonym (or antonym) game is done like a miniature crossword puzzle with the missing word being a synonym or antonym. In addition, this is a good way to introduce students to the concept of a crossword in which the letters must make words both ways. An example of a synonym-antonym game is shown in Figure 5-4, on page 112. Once you get these started in the class, the students should be able to take over and set up their own after you double-check them.

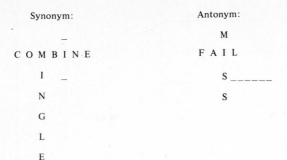

Synonym: Antonym:

                                         M
C O M B I N E   F A I L
    I _   S _ _ _ _ _ _
    N   S
    G
    L
    E

Figure 5-4. Synonym or antonym game.
Answers: mix (synonym); succeed (antonym).

Working with affixes and combining forms Some of the game formats and matching games can be used equally well with affixes and combining forms. One could match an affix to its meaning, an affix to a root word, words having the same root, etc. These could be done in any of the formats listed above. There are some other special activities that work especially well for word parts. Younger children would have posterboard squares with a number of different words on them. Then there would be a set of small cards with affixes on them. The children, one at a time, would draw a small card and find a word on their square to combine it with. (Make your own rules about doubling letters or dropping -e.). An example is shown in Figure 5-5. Each child's individual square would have somewhat different words on it. Each would draw a card and play it by putting it on one of the words. Thus, re- would cover *call* or *pay;* -ly could go on *quick* or *slow;* and -ing would cover *spell.* The object is to cover all words on your individual square.

A variation of this for older children has roots, combining forms, and affixes all on one large card. Two players or pairs use the same card and try to make and write down as many different words as possible from the same set. Figure 5-6 is an example.

Figure 5-5 Affix game.

Individual square:

see	slow	care
quick	pay	sing
spell	tell	call

On cards:

-ing

-ly

re-

-er

-ed

-est

-less . . .

LANGUAGE SKILLS: SUBSTANCE AND STRATEGIES

pass	im	port
ed	trans	form
de	act	able

How many words can you make from these?

Figure 5-6   Another affix game.

Making word extensions   Instead of just matching a word with its meaning or an affix with a word, there is the possibility of seeing *how many*. How many words begin with the same prefix? How many words can you think of with the same base? How many synonyms can you give for _____? Thinking up such extensions can be done in a game format, or it can simply be an ongoing class activity. Instead of boring board work, a prefix or root word could start children scurrying to find answers. A category written on the board in the morning or at the beginning of class to be checked just before lunch might be an interesting and profitable activity.

Word study can be a challenging and enjoyable experience for both teachers and children. The prerequisite for an effective program is a teacher who is interested and enthusiastic about learning new words. If that same teacher looks for ways to motivate an interest in word study and provides experiences that lead to concept and vocabulary development, the program should be very successful.

SUMMARY

Extending one's vocabulary in terms of both the number of words known and the multiple meanings for words is an important aspect of language development. Word knowledge is vital in communication and in thought processes. The more precise our word choice, the better we communicate with others. A rich classroom environment with many opportunities to experiment with words will help students develop their knowledge of words and word meanings.

PRELIMINARY LEARNING ACTIVITIES

1. A study of word origins can be interesting to students. Plan a study that you think a small group of older students might enjoy. Collect the maps, recipes, visuals, and references you would want to use.
2. Select one of the suggestions for a game or activity and actually make up a game that you could use with children the same age as those you teach or plan to teach. Think of ways to adapt your game, ways to make it durable and attractive, and pinpoint the learning that will take place.
3. Make an annotated bibliography of books available in your area that can be used with a study of vocabulary.

4. Plan and develop several direct experiences (field trips, neighborhood walks, or cooking activities) that would be effective in developing concepts and vocabulary words associated with them. Describe the activity and list the words that might be learned.
5. Find a book you'd like to read to children at the grade level you like, and list the words that might be new to the children and any activities or questions or explanations you might use to help them understand and use the new words.

PARTICIPATION ACTIVITIES

1. Take a field trip in the school neighborhood or do some special activity in class. Have the children collect words that they want to discuss later. These should be written on large sheets of paper or on the board and later discussed, categorized, or analyzed.
2. Read a book you've found or one from the list included in this chapter to some students and conduct a follow-up activity that should extend the children's vocabulary and enhance their response to the book.
3. Make and use a vocabulary game with a group of students.

APPENDIX TO CHAPTER 5: RECIPE FOR PRETZELS

Ingredients

2 ½ cups warm water	2 eggs
2 yeast cakes	1 tbsp. water
2 tsp. salt	coarse salt
2 tbsp. sugar	vegetable oil spray
8 cups flour	

Utensils

Large mixing bowl or two	Pastry brush
Wooden spoons	Spatula
Measuring cups, measuring spoons	Pastry cloth or board
Cookie sheets	

Directions

Dissolve the yeast in warm water.
Add the salt and sugar.
Gradually add the flour.
Knead the dough.
Divide it into 40 to 60 pieces.
Shape each piece into a traditional pretzel shape or a letter.
Mix the eggs and water together.
Brush each piece with egg and water mixture and sprinkle with coarse salt.
Spray cookie sheets with vegetable oil spray and put pretzels on sheets.
Bake 15 to 25 minutes at 425°.

REFERENCE NOTES

[1]Joseph P. O'Rourke. *Toward a Science of Vocabulary Development*. The Hague: Mouton, 1974, p. 18.

[2]*Webster's Seventh New Collegiate Dictionary*. Springfield, Mass.: Merriam, 1970, p. 68.

[3]Edgar Dale, Joseph O'Rourke, and Henry A. Bamman. *Techniques of Teaching Vocabulary*. Palo Alto, Calif.: Field, 1971, p. 3.

[4]Ibid., p. 5.

[5]Ibid.

[6]Lee C. Deighton. *Vocabulary Development in the Classroom*. New York: Teacher's College, 1959, pp. 17–23.

[7]Ibid., p. 26.

[8]Ibid., pp. 26–28.

[9]Ibid., pp. 26–28.

[10]Ibid., p. 31.

[11]Dale, O'Rourke, and Bamman. *Techniques of Teaching Vocabulary*, p. 247.

[12]Arthur Steckler. *101 Words and How They Began* (James Flora, illustr.). Garden City, N.Y.: Doubleday, 1979, unpaged.

[13]Dorothy H. Cohen. "The Effect of Literature on Vocabulary and Reading Achievement," *Elementary English*, vol. XLV, February 1968, pp. 209–213, 217.

[14]Eve Merriam. "Wake Up," in *The Birthday Cow* (Guy Michel, illustr.). New York: Knopf, 1978, unpaged.

[15]Natalie Babbitt. *The Eyes of the Amaryllis*. New York: Farrar, Straus & Giroux, 1977, p. 111.

CHAPTER SIX
Considering Grammar

PREVIEW QUESTIONS

1 What is the difference between grammar and usage?

2 What are the research findings regarding sentence diagramming and the improvement of writing?

3 What kinds of grammar appear in language arts textbooks for students?

4 What does research reveal about sentence-building and sentence-combining exercises?

5 Can you describe several grammar-based activities that influence students' writing performance?

The very word *grammar* produces a variety of responses. Historically grammar became associated and almost synonymous with the teaching of English in our public and private schools. Even today some teachers and some parents feel that the schools should teach more grammar, while others are vehemently opposed to any grammar instruction. Part of this wide range of opinion is due to the fact that the term *grammar* is used in several different ways to mean many different things.

Traditional grammars or "school grammars" are *prescriptive* in nature. They prescribe or decree what is correct to say or write, basing their prescription on written material by well-known classic authors; and this material, of course, follows the traditional rules of Latin. They include such typical practices as underlining the subjects and predicates of sentences or even diagramming them. Even though it is contrary to research findings, many feel that studying grammar makes one a better writer and a more "correct" speaker. Thus, in one sense of the word, grammar is a set of rules which tells how language should be used.

Newer grammars which have appeared in school textbooks are built upon a completely different basis. Grammar is used to mean a theory of language or a description of how English operates. Instead of prescribing what should or should not be, these more recent grammars have attempted to describe how native speakers of the language actually use that language. The two major kinds of descriptive grammars are structural and transformational generative. Both have attempted to look at language in a scientific, analytical way and describe how language is actually used, rather than decreeing how it should be used.

There are still choices of language forms which the speaker or writer must make since English has a number of options. The choice that an individual makes within a particular situation is called *usage*. We recognize, for instance, that *The cat gray here isn't* is not a sentence a native English speaker would say. It is not grammatical, even though we can probably understand what the speaker is trying to communicate. It is a matter of usage, however, when deciding to say, *The gray cat isn't here* or *The gray cat ain't here*. In discussing grammar in this chapter and usage in Chapter 3, we use the term *grammar* to describe how language works and the term *usage* to describe the choices or options within the language that one makes. Pooley compares this distinction between grammar and usage to the difference between behavior and etiquette.[1] Grammar, like behavior, is what happens without any judgments being made; usage is like etiquette, and varies because of social and situational forces.

We feel that the abstract and rather theoretical study of grammar is not appropriate subject matter for children of elementary school age. The focus on language in the elementary school years should be on helping children become more able to use language to express their ideas and to communicate with others. We should be able to help children put their ideas into words and sentences in a variety of ways. Therefore, grammar-based activities, such as sentence combining, are advocated and discussed later in this chapter.

KINDS OF GRAMMARS

Although we consider the abstract and theoretical study of grammar inappropriate for elementary school children, we think it is necessary for teachers to become familiar with and understand different grammars. At least three major kinds of grammar are found in school textbooks today: traditional grammar, structural grammar, and transformational generative grammar. The most recent work in linguistics has centered on the relationship between meaning and structure. Newer grammars such as case grammar[2] and generative semantics[3] have delved into semantics rather than syntax as a prime component of our system of language. This chapter, however, will examine the grammars used with children.

Traditional Grammar

Traditional grammar, mainly based on Latin, classifies words into various parts of speech such as nouns, verbs, adjectives, prepositions, and conjunctions. These parts of speech are defined primarily in terms of meaning or content, as in "A noun is the name of a person, place, or thing." This can present problems to students when using such words as *blue* and *walk*. What parts of speech are they? Blue describes so it must be an adjective, as in *My blue shirt is dirty*. But what part of speech is *blue* in the next sentence? *Blue is the best color*. The word *blue* is now a noun. Let's use one other example. *Walk* is quite obviously a verb in *I walk to school,* but it becomes a noun in the sentence *The walk is icy*.

Traditionally, sentences are classified as simple, compound, complex, or in some cases compound-complex. Sentences can also be described as declarative, interrogative, exclamatory, or imperative. One of the practices most closely associated with traditional grammar is the diagramming of sentences developed by Reed and Kellogg.[4] The most important sentence elements are put on a horizontal line and separated by shorter vertical or diagonal lines. Minor elements of the sentence are placed below the main line in a way that shows their relationship to the other elements of the sentence. An example of this is:

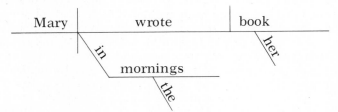

The above diagram indicates that *Mary* is the subject, *wrote* is the verb, *book* is a direct object modified by *her*, and *in the mornings* is a prepositional phrase modifying *wrote*.

The most important elements of this grammar are the word and the sentence. Little attention is paid to paragraphs or other larger units of writing. Also, there is little emphasis on word order although English, an analytic language, is based on this. The sentence diagrammed above might have been *In the mornings, Mary wrote her book* or *Mary wrote her book in the mornings*. There is no way to determine from the diagram how to reconstruct the original sentence.

Recognizing that usage varies, authors of traditional grammars accept the practices of only the best speakers and writers of English as a standard. This implies a prescriptive "best," and therefore traditional grammar in the classroom usually operates in a highly structured fashion. *Do this* and *Don't do that* or *This is right* and *This is wrong* become the daily instructional routine for the English teacher.

Structural Grammar

Structural grammar is descriptive; it attempts to describe how people use language rather than prescribing how language should be used. An early and exhaustive explication of structural linguistics was made by Charles Carpenter Fries with the publication in 1952 of *The Structure of English*. One of the most important principles of structural grammar is that grammatical function is independent of word meaning. In order to make this point, many structuralists used sentences made up of nonsense words. In *Sligy bobbles wugged ziches*, *bobbles* is a noun modified by *sligy*, *wugged* is a verb, and *ziches* is another noun. The fact that we don't know what action *wugging* represents or what a *zich* looks like does not interfere with our identification of what parts of speech they are. Fries stated that the grammatical function or structural meaning is signaled by particular devices (such as word endings, articles, and so on).

Fries rejected the traditional parts of speech and defined or categorized words into four major form classes and fifteen groups of function words. Since these do not all correspond to the traditional parts of speech, he gave each of them different names such as *Class 1* and *Class 2* or *Group A*. He also used the terms *determiner* for words such as *the*, *a*, and *an* and *intensifier* for words such as *very* and *much*. Sometimes structural grammar is called "slot-and-filler" grammar because of the pattern substitution concept used to establish the parts of speech in these new categories without referring to the meaning of the words. Class 1, for example, includes all the words that fit in the following blank:

The _____ is / are good.

Similar "test frames" help describe the nature of the other classes of words.

Structural grammarians also use the stimulus-response (S-R) model in psychology to explain not only how language functions as a means of communication, but also how children acquire language. This theory emphasizes the view that behavior is learned through reinforcement. Fries felt that children learn language by associating certain language forms with the situations that called them forth. In dealing with novel sentences, he contended people use analogy to sentences already known. They are able to do this, Fries thought, by using structural signals and sentence patterns.[5]

The emphasis in Fries's *Structure of English* is on sentence structure, and it was a radical departure from traditional grammar. It became known as the "new" grammar or "linguistics" although it represented only part of the linguistic community at that time and today represents an even smaller part.

Transformational Generative Grammar

Transformational generative grammar also represents a descriptive approach. It attempts to describe not only how language is used, but also how related sentences are changed from one form to another (transformed) and how new sentences can be formulated (generated) from our unconscious or conscious knowledge of how our language operates. The person most closely associated with transformational generative grammar is Noam Chomsky, who first published this theory in 1957 in *Syntatic Structures* and further delineated it in his 1965 *Aspects of the Theory of Syntax.*

One of the characteristics of transformational generative grammar is the distinction made between the surface structure and the deep structure of language. Linguists have noticed that many sentences which appear to be parallel are actually very different. Malmstrom and Weaver give the following example of three sentences which appear on the surface to be formed identically:

Jon wanted the guest to eat.
Jon wanted the baby to eat.
Jon wanted the hamburger to eat.[6]

In the first two, both the surface structures and deep structures (or underlying structures) are similar; the noun preceding *to eat* is to do the eating. The third, although it resembles the other two in its surface structure, is very different. The noun preceding *to eat*, the *hamburger*, is not to do the eating; Jon is. Therefore, the underlying structure of the latter is different from the other two.

Another type of problem sentence that interested transformationalists was the ambiguous sentence that might have more than one underlying structure. An example of this is: *Visiting relatives can be a nuisance.*[7] This might mean that it is a nuisance to visit relatives or that having relatives visit you is a nuisance.

The final problem leading to the concept of deep and surface structures is shown by pairs of sentences which do not look similar on the surface but are closely related at the deep structure level since they are nearly synonymous:

A new student painted the picture.
The picture was painted by a new student.[8]

These parallel sentences occur because of the different transformations that have been made in the deep structures before they appear in the surface structures.

Transformational generative grammar has rejected the stimulus-response model as an inadequate explanation of how children acquire their native language. Transformational generative linguists do not believe that children understand a sentence simply by recalling a prior experience with the sentence. Instead they propose that children attempt to organize a system of language rules subject to their cognitive capabilities and language environment. Transformational generative grammar, therefore, attempts to duplicate the rule system that adult speakers of the language employ.

Transformational generative grammar describes two sets of rules. The first set is called *phrase-structure rules* and represents the grammatical relationships indicating meaning between the words in the deep structure of the sentence. The second set of rules, *transformational rules*, accounts for changing the deep structure form into the surface structure form of the sentence.

The phrase-structure rules are written like an algebraic formula and are often represented by tree diagrams.

This phrase-structure rule and its matching diagram indicate that a sentence (S) may be rewritten as a noun phrase (NP) and a verb phrase (VP):

PS1　　S ⟶ NP + VP

$$
\begin{array}{c}
S \\
\diagup\ \diagdown \\
NP \qquad VP
\end{array}
$$

A second phrase structure rule is:

PS2　　NP ⟶ DET + N

$$
\begin{array}{c}
S \\
\diagup\ \diagdown \\
NP \qquad VP \\
\diagup\ \diagdown \\
DET \qquad N
\end{array}
$$

This states that the noun phrase may be rewritten as a determiner (DET) plus a noun (N). As you might imagine, when the sentences become more complex, the rewrite rules and tree diagrams also become more complex.

Transformational rules are also written like a formula, but are labeled T instead of PS and use the double arrow instead of the single arrow to indicate what may be transformed into what. The transformational rules are applied in order, although some may not be used if they aren't relevant to a given sentence.

T1 accounts for changing subject pronouns into object pronouns after a transitive verb. It is written as:

$$
T1 \quad V_t + \begin{bmatrix} I \\ we \\ he \\ she \\ they \end{bmatrix} \Rightarrow V_t + \begin{bmatrix} me \\ us \\ him \\ her \\ them \end{bmatrix}
$$

Rule T2 applies when the pronoun *I* is used with a form of *be* in the present tense. Following this transformational rule we would say *I am watching* instead of *I are watching*.

$$
T2 \quad I + PRES + BE \Rightarrow I = PRES_1 + BE
$$

These rules appear quite complex and are certainly inappropriate for elementary school students; they do, however, illustrate the kind of thought process that native English speakers unconsciously use in producing sentences. This is the process that children have under basic control by the time they enter school.

Studying grammar brings to a conscious level what we do subconsciously with language. However, there is little need for elementary school children to study formal grammar. Research indicates that such instruction rarely improves a student's facility with oral and written language. However, grammar-related activities such as combining or expanding sentences may improve both oral and written communication.

GRAMMATICAL KNOWLEDGE

Although most adults have some instruction in grammar by the time they finish school, most of the rules which they apply in their everyday language have not been learned. Some of these relate to phonemics or pronunciation. For example, the *-ed* suffix on past tense verbs may be pronounced /d/ or /t/ or /əd/. Teachers do not teach children the rules for this, and yet both children and adults can pronounce *-ed* properly whether it appears in real or nonsense words. Try the following:

walked	*prepared*	*waited*
backed	*ignored*	*adopted*
priced	*hurried*	*disconcerted*
chopped	*behaved*	*headed*
zitched	*wugged*	*regicated*

The words in the first column, including the final nonsense word, all end with the /t/; those in the middle column all have the /d/ ending; those in the third column all end with the /əd/ phoneme.

Adults unconsciously adhere to rules of syntax or word order. We were not taught the rules for the proper order of multiple adjectives preceding a noun. Even so, if given some examples of possible combinations of these adjectives, we will all come up with the same order or orders. Try the following and see if you agree with others:

1.	*small*	*green*	*two*	(Martians)
2.	*enormous*	*red*	*one*	(geranium)
3.	*purple*	*big*	*four*	(monsters)

The regular order of these adjectives of size, color, and number is (first) number, (second) size, and (third) color. For emphasis, however, the second and third may be reversed. Other "rules" for other combinations of adjectives exist, and all native speakers use them without any formal instruction. Young children operate with these same rules—usually by the time they are four or five years old. Some of the rules are used in all the dialects of English, and others may vary with particular dialects.

The kinds of rules which have traditionally been the job of the English teacher are those for formal or proper usage. *Don't end a sentence with a preposition* or *Don't use a double negative.* These maxims actually deal with options or choices which a speaker may make depending on dialect, social situation, and mode of communication (whether oral or written). Teachers need to recognize the extensive amount of knowledge about language that children possess and use by the time they enter school, instead of focusing on the knowledge they may lack.

GRAMMAR IN THE CLASSROOM

The primary aim of the language arts program is to help children become more able to use language to express their ideas both orally and in writing. The formal study of grammar does not help them meet this goal. Two of the more recent research studies, one conducted by Roland Harris[9] and the other reported by W. B. Elley,[10] are cited to substantiate this statement. In Harris's study, students adhered to the regular curriculum during the first four days of each week, but on the fifth day, half of the students received grammar instruction while the other half wrote stories. At the end of two years, students who had been instructed in grammar wrote less complex sentences and made more errors in writing than those who had written stories. The second investigation, sometimes referred to as the New Zealand study, involved three groups of students and compared three curricula: (1) the study of transformational grammar, (2) the study of traditional grammar, and (3) free reading and creative writing. In summarizing the results of the three-year study, Elley claims there were no significant differences between the performances of the three groups. In the report he says, "It is difficult to escape the conclusion that English grammar, whether traditional or transformational, has virtually no influence on the language growth of typical secondary school students."[11]

While findings of these two studies agree about the ineffectiveness of grammar instruction, they indicate differences with regard to writing and its influence on students' performance. We know that the mere act of frequent writing does not improve a person's ability to write better sentences or sentences with fewer errors. Therefore, one should ask if instruction accompanied the writing, and if so, what form of instruction occurred along with it.

A substantial amount of evidence exists to show that certain kinds of grammar-based writing experiences can improve students' writing abilities. Research studies indicate that the manipulation of syntax, or sentence-building activities such as sentence combining, can influence writing performance. Frank O'Hare[12] reports in a now classic study that seventh-grade students who were exposed to both oral and written sentence-combining practice over an eight-month period "wrote compositions that were judged to be significantly better in overall quality than those written by students who did not have the practice." He also generalized from the results of the research:

> Although the findings of the present study relate specifically to seventh graders, there is no obvious reason for assuming that sentence combining practice should not be used in elementary and senior high school, as well as junior high school.[13]

Other less formal studies support O'Hare's generalization. Their findings have shown sentence combining to be a valuable activity with students at least as early as fourth grade. Younger children can participate in sentence-combining and sentence-expanding activities using an experience story as a base before they can profit from prestructured combining exercises. Considering what we know about young children's cognitive abilities, these findings appear to make sense. Because of the level of reasoning involved, young primary-school students who are in the preoperational stage of intellectual development will experience some difficulty, and perhaps even frustration, when asked to do sentence-combining exercises.

Because the evidence in favor of using sentence-building activities to improve students' writing is more than convincing, the following section of this chapter is devoted to a variety of exercises that a teacher might incorporate into the composition program. It is best that oral discussion precede any written practice, since the emphasis is on total language growth. The primary aim, stated once again, is to help students become better able to use language to express their ideas *both orally and in writing*.

Expanding Basic Patterns

One of the activities that can help children be more effective in their use of language is expanding simple sentence patterns in various ways. This activity should be done within the language and the experiences of the child. A format that is particularly useful with this kind of expansion work is the group experience story. Suppose that the children had visited a nearby doughnut shop and were now writing about this trip. The teacher could first ask for ideas about what to write. One child might say: *We saw a man cut out the doughnuts.* Another might mention: *I like doughnuts.* The teacher would then write these ideas on the chalkboard or a large sheet of chart paper. The children would then find various ways to add ideas to the original sentence.

For: *We saw a man cut out the doughnuts.*
    What could we add about the man?
        a man in a white jacket
        a man in the back room
        a man with a chef's hat
        a young man
    What did he do besides cut them out?
        roll and cut out
        cut out and twist
        cut out and fill
    How did he cut them out?
        carefully
        real fast
        with a knife
        with a special cutter

For: *I like doughnuts.*
    Why do you like them?
        because they're sweet
        because they're good
    Which doughnuts do you like best?
        chocolate ones with frosting
        twisted ones with cinnamon

The children could talk about ways to add to the original sentence before writing it on a chart.

We saw a man in a white jacket cut out and twist the doughnuts.
I like twisted doughnuts with cinnamon because they're sweet.

Another method of expanding sentences is designed around an exercise format, rather than an experience story. Begin with a kernel or simple sentence, such as *Jan ran.* Then ask the students to tell as many different ways that Jan ran. Their ideas should be written on the chalkboard or recorded on a large chart. For example,

Jan ran.
Jan ran slowly.
Jan ran rapidly.
Jan ran fast.
Jan ran backward.

After a number of suggestions are written, ask the students to tell *why* Jan ran in this manner. Some possibilities are mentioned here.

Jan ran slowly because of his sore ankle.
Jan ran rapidly because he was late.
Jan ran fast because he was in a hurry.
Jan ran backward because he thought it was funny.

Next, ask the students to add words that will tell *who* Jan is. For example, looking at the sentence *Jan ran slowly because of his sore ankle,* they might say:

Jan, my brother, ran slowly because of his sore ankle.
My friend Jan ran slowly because of his sore ankle.
Jan, the boy who came in last, ran slowly because of his sore ankle.

Following the telling and recording of various ideas, students may be given an opportunity to complete similar exercises independently or in small groups. Once these are completed, however, some sharing and discussion of the exercises should occur.

Combining Sentences

As research studies have shown, students become more effective in their use of oral and written language if they have meaningful practice with various ways of combining sentences. Group experience stories or charts can be excellent sources of material for sentence combining. For example, suppose a group of students experiment with water erosion and then dictate the following sentences about the experience.

We poured water down a hill.
Part of the hill was grassy.
Another part was just dirt.

The teacher would then ask how these could be combined to make one sentence. The same ideas must be kept, but words can be added or dropped, or the order of words can be changed. To illustrate, look at the following sentence.

We poured water down a hill that was partially grassy and partially plain dirt.

Students can work together to combine and expand their sentences.

If there are alternative ways to combine sentences, students should be encouraged to think of all the possibilities. For instance, consider the possible ways to combine these three sentences.

The dog is black.
The dog ran fast.
The dog's name is Skipper.

Some possible combinations:

Skipper, the black dog, ran fast.
The black dog, Skipper, ran fast.
The black dog named Skipper ran fast.
The black dog, whose name is Skipper, ran fast.

How might you combine these three sentences?

Rachel owns a horse.
The horse is brown and white.
Rachel rides her horse every day.

Some possible combinations:

Rachel rides her brown and white horse every day.
Rachel's horse is brown and white, and she rides him every day.
Rachel owns a horse that is brown and white, and she rides him every day.
Every day, Rachel rides her brown and white horse.

The purpose of sentence-combining exercises is to enable students to progress from writing a series of simple sentences to writing longer or more complex sentences. Since "sentence maturity" is related to a writer's ability to use subordination, to vary sentence length, and to vary syntactic structure, the process of combining and building sentences seems to give students the necessary skills that lead to writing mature, well-constructed sentences.

A variation on the same theme is combining sentence parts. This type of activity should be presented after students have had some practice with combining complete sentences. Look at the following sentence parts and think about how they might be combined into one sentence.

Her cat climbed a tree
Because of the large dog
In a heavy rainstorm

Some possible combinations:

Because of the large dog, her cat climbed a tree in a heavy rainstorm.
In a heavy rainstorm, her cat climbed a tree because of the large dog.
Her cat, in a heavy rainstorm, climbed a tree because of the large dog.

In order for sentence-building activities to be most effective, exercises such as the ones mentioned here should be discussed first, then followed with practice and more discussion. Merely giving students a ditto page of sentence-combining exercises will not bring about the anticipated change in their oral and written language.

Finding Movables and Selecting Words

Certain words or phrases may be placed in different parts of a sentence. For example, the sentence *I knew he had to be my pet when I saw him* can be changed to read *When I saw him, I knew he had to be my pet.* Changes such as this sometimes subtly alter the emphasis or effect of a sentence.

There are several ways to use sentences from a reading text, a weekly children's news magazine, or a collection of sentences reproduced on a transparency or ditto sheet. Children may want to use their own writing—moving words, phrases, or clauses around and then comparing the new version with the original piece of writing.

Some of the words or phrases that may be used as movables within a sentence are:

Adverbs *(Eventually he moved/ he moved eventually)*
Adjectives *(gigantic orange balloon/ orange gigantic balloon)*
Prepositional phrases *(he walked in the house/ in the house he walked)*
Clauses *(Since he came early, we . . ./ we . . . since he came early)*

The selection of specific words to convey a particular meaning—or words that are appropriate for a particular kind of writing—is very helpful for the older child. This is the area of field of discourse (discussed in the section on register in Chapter 3) that determines some of the vocabulary or lexical items that one chooses to use in a particular piece of writing. Scientists, for example, make a distinction between *soil* and *dirt*. In the earlier discussion of combining sentences about erosion, *soil* would be preferable to *dirt*.

Other words are chosen for the particular shade of meaning they convey. Children in the upper elementary grades may examine a thesaurus which lists synonyms and antonyms. In *Roget's College Thesaurus* the listing for *walk* as a verb is *ramble, stroll, promenade, saunter, travel (on foot), march, parade, tramp, hike, tread, pace, step.* Although these are synonyms for *walk*, there is a great deal of difference between *strolling* and *tramping* or between *sauntering* and *pacing.* If you do not want to use a thesaurus, you can have the children list words that have almost the same meaning and conduct a follow-up discussion on the connotations. What are a few synonyms for the word *thin? Slender, skinny, underweight, bony.* If you are not talking about a person, but about material, what words might describe it? *Sheer, fine, delicate, filmy.*

Developing an awareness of what effect a particular word has or what moving a word, phrase, or clause to a different part of a sentence does is important in developing writing skills. The function of language in a particular and meaningful situation is the most appropriate way of working with grammar in the elementary school. In contrast to teaching a formal grammatical description of English through traditional, structural, or transformational theory, working with language in this way offers potential for improving the quality of children's writing.

Writing Imitations

In *Teaching Writing K-8,* Jack Hailey[14] summarizes numerous presentations made over several years by teachers and consultants working with the Bay Area Writing Project in California. A variety of sentence-building activities are recommended in the book, and among them is an exercise—"writing imitations"—that is closely aligned to literary structures and sentence combining. "Writing imitations" is a "paridigm designed to assist children in building vocabulary power for specific units of writing, such as verbs or descriptors or nouns."

Hailey describes one form of "writing imitations" as a fill-in-the-blanks game:

> Take a paragraph or selected sentences from a piece of children's literature. Delete the action verbs or the adjectives or the prepositional phrases, and have children fill in the blanks. This activity need not be done individually; pairs or groups of children can work together. . . . Children's internal grammar will lead them to pick a word that fits, and their ears will judge the result.[15]

The following example demonstrates this first form of "writing imitations."

The hut was as the Prince had told them. A _____ layer of dust covered the _____ tables and benches. A spider had spun an _____ web in one corner, but even the web was _____. On a hearthstone lay the _____ remnants of a

LANGUAGE SKILLS: SUBSTANCE AND STRATEGIES

_____ *fire. Near the hearth, a number of* _____ *crockpots,* _____ *and* _____ *now, had been overturned.* _____ *bowls and* _____ *jars, shattered into fragments, were strewn about the floor.*

The hut was _____*; the noises of the forest did not enter.*

Lloyd Alexander, *The Castle of Llyr* (New York: Holt, 1966)

The second form of imitation exercise is related to sentence combining. Students are given sentences from good literature and then asked to write sentences that have the same structure but different content. For instance, consider the following example:

She glided away on the skates of Uncle Richard, taller and taller, and taller, never once falling down.

Carol Fenner, *The Skates of Uncle Richard* (New York: Random House, 1978)

Student imitations:

I rode away on my new bicycle, straighter and straighter and straighter, never once falling off. (Sara)

I dove off the high board at the pool, faster and faster and faster, never once closing my eyes. (Nicky)

I rolled down the hill on my skateboard, faster and faster and faster, never once falling down. (Natalie)

These imitation exercises are most appropriate for older students; however, younger children should be hearing stories that contain repetition, refrain, and complex sentence structure. And whenever possible, they should be asked to participate in stories by repeating refrains, verses, and creative sentences.

Teaching Parts of Speech

The research on the relationship between studying traditional grammar (parts of speech) and speaking or writing is clear. Knowing traditional grammar does not make one a better writer or speaker. Being able to use the terminology of parts of speech to discuss aspects of style or sentence construction may be useful for older students. Younger children would profit more from experiences that develop their capacity to explain, compare, summarize, sequence, or evaluate. Grammar is very abstract and does not coincide with the abilities of children in preoperational or concrete-operational stages of development.

When you do begin to teach students parts of speech, it is important to provide them with many examples for drawing inferences. Just saying that an adjective is a word which modifies (or describes) a noun or pronoun and then asking students to identify adjectives in a selected passage does not teach adjectives effectively. A more workable way would be to show your class one or more interesting objects and ask for words that describe them. Write down the adjectives the students give as a list on chart paper or on the board. If they give a phrase or some other part of speech, convert it to adjective form if possible or list it off to one side. When you have a long, long list of adjectives set up, then you label them as such.

We can also borrow from the structural grammarians with their "slot-and-filler" approach. What words would fit in the blank below?

The _____ object came from another planet.

"Writing imitations"—described earlier in this chapter—could also be used with only one part of speech (the one being studied) removed. In any case, students should start with their own words, with language itself, and learn the label *after* setting up the category of words.

Once you have identified a class of words and labeled it, students should have many opportunities to work with that part of speech before moving on to another. Some activities might involve finding sentences with interesting adjectives in magazines, newspapers, or literary works. Small groups of students could set up lists of adjectives with similar denotations and varying connotations *(hard: rigid, stiff, firm, stubborn, stark, inflexible, adamant, concrete, difficult, unyielding)*. They could study how adjectives can be used in writing, separating those that label *(nice, good, pretty, bad)* from those that detail *(blonde, misty, gilded, lumbering)*. They might practice using adjectives in sentences of their own devising. Abundant experiences with one part of speech before starting another will lead to real learning.

SUMMARY

Three kinds of grammars are discussed in the chapter: (1) traditional grammar, (2) structural grammar, and (3) transformational generative grammar. Teachers should know and understand the different grammars because they will be confronted with one or more of them in school textbooks.

Findings from research studies suggest that the formal study of any grammar has little, if any, influence on students' oral or written performance. However, sentence-building activities, such as sentence combining, have proved to be effective in improving a student's writing ability.

PRELIMINARY LEARNING ACTIVITIES

1. Examine the following four samples of exercises like those in textbooks for children. Then label them traditional grammar, structural grammar, or transformational generative grammar.

Sample 1

Write the following sentences, putting in the correct word for each blank:
(a) One girl _____ (is, are) absent today.
(b) Many books _____ (is, are) in our room.

Sample 2

Combine each of the following pairs of sentences by joining the noun phrases with either *and* or *both . . . and.*
(a) An orange is on the counter. An apple is on the counter.
(b) The girls were on the bus. The boys were on the bus.

Sample 3

Write four sentences using two of the words below in each sentence.
Use *a, an, the,* or a number as a determiner before each: *park, ball, lake, boats, birds, trees*

Sample 4

Transform the affirmative sentences below to negative ones by adding a form of *do* and *not* and changing verb forms when needed.
(a) Jane caught the ball bunted toward first base.
(b) The jockey carried a good luck charm.
(c) The buses stop in front of the grocery.

2. Find a literature selection that is appropriate for "writing imitations." Identify and then delete either the action verbs or adjectives from the sentences. Give the altered selection to a fellow classmate to complete. Afterward, ask the classmate to evaluate the selection for its appropriateness.
3. Select several sentences that could be used for an imitation exercise in which students write their own sentences using the structure of the sentence from the piece of literature. Take your selections from one or more books, choosing sentences appropriate to students the age you plan to teach.

PARTICIPATION ACTIVITIES

1. Take a trip with a group of children—to a nearby store, florist or nursery, to an area of the playground or neighborhood—or have someone bring something interesting to school (a motorcycle, electric car, show dog, antique, and so on). Then work on an experience story with the group doing some expansion of basic sentences or sentence combining.
2. Test whether children can accurately describe the order of adjectives preceding a noun. Give them sets of cards on which the adjectives and the noun have been written and ask them to arrange the cards in order. Another alternative is to see if children will pronounce accurately the *-ed* suffix on verbs that they may not know. You can do this by using words from the lists in the section "Grammatical Knowledge" or other words that you make up. The words should be printed or written on separate cards.
3. Develop a game that would involve sentence expansion or sentence combining and try it with a group of children.
4. Find several appropriate sentence selections from children's books and then ask a group of older students to write sentences that have the same structure. Have them share their writing.

REFERENCE NOTES

[1]Robert C. Pooley. *Teaching English Grammar*. New York: Appleton-Century-Crofts, 1957, p. 106.

[2]Jean Malmstrom and Constance Weaver. *Transgrammar*. Glenview, Ill.: Scott, Foresman, 1973, p. 259.

[3]Ibid., p. 273.

[4]Alonzo Reed and Brainerd Kellogg. *Work on English Grammar and Composition*, 1877, in H. A. Gleason, Jr., *Linguistics and English Grammar*. New York: Holt, 1965.

[5]Mark Lester. *Introductory Transformational Grammar of English*. New York: Holt, 1971, pp. 16–20.

[6]Malmstrom and Weaver. *Transgrammar*, p. 61.

[7]Ibid., p. 62.

[8]Ibid., p. 63.

[9]Richard Braddock et al. *Research in Written Composition*. Urbana, Ill.: National Council of Teachers of English, 1963, pp. 70–83.

[10]W. B. Elley et al. "The Role of Grammar in a Secondary English Curriculum," *Research in the Teaching of English*, vol. 10, no. 1, Spring 1976, pp. 5–21.

[11]Ibid.

[12]Frank O'Hare. *Sentence Combining: Improving Student Writing without Formal Grammar Instruction*, Research Report no. 15. Urbana, Ill.: National Council of Teachers of English, 1973.

[13]Ibid., p. 70.

[14]Jack Hailey. *Teaching Writing K through 8*. Berkeley, Calif.: Instructional Laboratory, University of California, 1978.

[15]Ibid., p. 80.

CHAPTER SEVEN

Listening and Language

PREVIEW QUESTIONS

1 Why is listening an important language skill?
2 How can listening be taught?
3 What are the possibilities of using television to develop listening skills?
4 What critical listening activities are appropriate for elementary school children?

Almost everything a child learns before about age six comes from listening. And much of what is learned later in school may come from listening, too, if the studies of the time spent listening are accurate. A study done before the television era showed that three-fourths of a person's communication time is spent in the oral modes—over 40 percent of it in listening.[1] Reports of television viewing of children in 1980 indicate that preschoolers average 31 hours 23 minutes of television per week and that children between six and eleven watch television an average of 27 hours 16 minutes.[2] A great deal of time in school is also spent listening. A classic study by Wilt[3] found that over half of the classroom time in elementary school is spent in listening, the majority of that to the teacher. Furthermore, the findings of Wilt's investigation indicate that teachers were unaware of how much time they required children to listen, and few of them ranked listening as the most important language skill. The tremendous amounts of time children spend in listening (we estimate over 9 hours on a school day) absolutely demand development of skill in this area.

KINDS OF LISTENING

Listening is not a single-dimension skill. Sometimes we enjoy having music in the background or a television going in another room. At some level we are aware of the sound, but we certainly aren't actively listening.

Other times we listen intently to television or radio because we want to know if our school will be closed that day or if we'll need to carry an umbrella or sweater. We listen to a political debate, mentally refuting the opposition's points; we listen to a friend sympathetically, not making any judgments; we listen to a lecture, taking notes on important points; we listen to a new recipe for a dip; we listen to a record or tape to see if we want to buy it; we listen to the swirl of conversation at a big party, one foot tapping to the music's beat. Different levels of listening are used for different purposes.

The classic categorization of listening comes from a committee of the National Council of Teachers of English[4] and includes four kinds of listening:

Marginal: The listener is somewhat aware of sounds in the environment, but is not actively responding to the stimulus.
Appreciative: Here the listener responds to poetry, music, stories, and so forth primarily for enjoyment and the stimulation of creative or expressive thoughts.
Attentive: The listener focuses on the stimulus to get information, to participate actively. This type of listening is involved in following directions, taking part in a discussion, finding the main idea or sequence of events, and so forth.
Analytic: In this kind of listening, one interprets and evaluates the material heard. Determining bias or point of view, evaluating information, and judging accuracy are all aspects of analytic listening.

More recently listening has been classified by purpose into five categories—appreciative, discriminative, comprehensive, therapeutic, and critical.[5] *Appreciative listening* involves listening to enjoy or to gain a sensory impression from the material. *Discriminative listening* refers to the distinguishing of the auditory or visual stimulus and includes sensitivity to nonverbal communication. *Comprehensive listening* is listening for the purpose of understanding a message. *Therapeutic listening* (or empathic listening) is listening in which the listener serves as a "sounding board" to enable the speaker to talk through a problem. *Critical listening* involves the listener in evaluating or judging the message, taking into account the effects of the language, arguments, appeals, and credibility of the speaker. Other writers on the subject select other ways of categorizing listening, but it seems quite clear that listening is not simply hearing what is said, or even understanding what is heard. Instead it appears to be a cluster of complex skills that relies on thought processes, memory, and language reception skills.

FACTORS AFFECTING LISTENING

A number of factors can affect listening ability. Some of these relate to the individual's ability to hear—a necessary first step in listening; others to the various levels of listening. Taylor[6] identifies four factors that can affect hearing. Two of these relate to physical abilities: auditory acuity and binaural considerations (or being able to hear adequately from both ears simultaneously). The other two are environmental: auditory fatigue and masking. After a long period of time spent listening we tend to "turn off." Fatigue sets in and we can no longer concentrate as well and hear as much. Another factor that affects ability to hear is masking, the low-level but continuous sounds that we must disregard in order to hear other things. In schools, typically there are numerous sounds that can mask. There are fans on the air conditioning or blowers on the heating equipment, voices from other rooms or other groups in the same room, sounds from films or filmstrips in the room next door. There is a constant shuffling of feet, a pencil sharpener being used, mowers or airplanes outside, or the hum of traffic on a nearby busy street.

There are also factors that affect listening ability beyond the level of hearing. The amount of attention or concentration spent on listening will affect one's ability to understand. So will the background of experience the listener brings to the situation. When you've been skiing yourself and then listen to someone talking about a new technique in turning or jumping, it's easy to understand. For someone who has only water-skied, it is fairly understandable. For the non-skier, it may not make sense at all. Style of delivery and rate of input can affect how well you listen and understand; and making unrelated associations can lead you astray as a listener. Children listen best when they are truly interested and so pay attention and concentrate, provided that the topic is somewhat within their experiential background and the source or speaker is of good quality.

CULTURAL DIFFERENCES IN LISTENING

We tend to assume that everyone uses the same cues to indicate we are paying attention and understanding the speaker. This is simply not true. Hall vividly describes the contradictory aspects of conversation with Navahos:

> Unlike middle-class whites, the direct open-faced look in the eyes was avoided by Navahos. . . . I ultimately learned that to look directly at a Navaho was to display anger. . . . Another Navaho taboo was to use the name as a form of direct address. Nor were voices ever raised—except in anger.[7]

Imagine the teacher sent to work with Navaho children who had no training in Navaho culture. For typically, the teacher raises his or her voice, calls on a student by name, and looks directly at the student, expecting eye contact. The Navaho child looks down to avoid such contact, interpreting the teacher's behavior as *anger*. The teacher, meanwhile, interprets the child's unwillingness to look back directly and respond as evidence of dishonesty or stupidity.

Similar differences in appropriate listening behavior exist in many other cultures with which we have contact in school. It is true of blacks, Puerto Ricans, Mexican-Americans, Vietnamese, and so forth. Many teachers are distressed that the black children in their room do not give the expected signs of paying attention:

> Basically, the informal rule for black culture goes somewhat as follows: If you are in the room with another person or in a context where he has ready access to you, there are times when there is no need to go through the motions of showing him you are listening because that is automatically implied.[8]

Misunderstandings about what children should do when listening can contribute to unnecessary conflicts when children are behaving correctly within their cultural background, but this behavior is not culturally appropriate in the teacher's background. Teachers need to become familiar with the nonverbal and verbal aspects of the culture of children they teach.

TEACHING LISTENING

We need to view listening as a valuable and legitimate component of the elementary school curriculum as well as an area that can be taught. To support this, there are findings from a number of research studies that indicate instruction can improve children's listening skills. Pratt[9] concluded, after conducting an experimental program designed to develop specific listening skills, that listening instruction can be effective. Working with fifth-grade students, Hollow[10] found that a planned instructional program improved students' listening abilities. She reported that pupils at varying levels of intelligence benefited from the program.

We have talked in earlier chapters about providing a rich language environment for children. In such an environment children are encouraged to converse about topics of interest, share and discuss favorite books, read aloud to book partners, and talk freely with their teacher and peers. This rich language environment is also the rich listening environment. Children are not required to listen to the teacher two-thirds of the time; instead, purposeful listening is continuous throughout the school day. Skills in speaking and listening develop more naturally in this type of learning setting—and rightfully so. *Oracy*, a term originally coined at the Birmingham University School of Education, refers to the skills of listening and speaking, just as *literacy* refers to the skills of reading and writing. The reciprocity between listening and speaking is natural and can occur within classrooms where teachers value language. In such classrooms teachers make opportunities for both speaking and listening because it is through them that language develops. However, we need to differentiate between a qualitative and quantitative language environment. If the classroom is organized and managed in a laissez faire fashion where children merely "chat" with one another and there is no direction given to their conversations and discussions, little learning of any kind can take place. Rather, it is the carefully planned and organized environment that facilitates skills in oracy. It is a setting where learning experiences are continuous and not chopped up in little time segments. Andrew Wilkinson, a British educator, describes an effective classroom learning climate in this way:

> The English teacher has special opportunities for providing a rich variety of speech situations, amongst which discussion is prime. The traditional English time-table assigned different aspects of the subject to different periods. Now we think of the time-table in terms of a central continuing theme or experience out of which emerge opportunities for various aspects of production (writing and speaking) and reception (listening and reading). We start, not with the skill to be taught, but with the central experience upon which the skills may operate. Within this framework many opportunities for speaking and listening occur naturally.[11]

In such a skillfully organized environment children are actively involved in interesting and meaningful experiences. Skills in both oracy and literacy develop naturally within the framework of the experiences themselves. To cite an example, a group of children were particularly interested in making fudge after visiting a candy factory as part of their study of the community. The teacher brought several fudge recipes to school and told the children they could choose the one they liked best. The students gathered on the large area rug and began sorting through the recipes. Throughout their discussion, a number of questions were raised: *How many ingredients will we need for this recipe? Does this fudge have to be cooked? Will this recipe make enough fudge for everyone in the class?* After writing the final two recipes they were considering on chart paper, the students continued the discussion until they reached consensus. These children were speaking and actively listening to one another. No one withdrew from the discussion; they were all involved listeners because they were deeply involved in using their listening skills to make an important choice. The activity also included meaningful practice in reading and handwriting as well as considerable skill in a planning discussion.

A similar cluster of listening activities in a middle-grade classroom centered on the filming of a television pilot for a series about bicycling being made in town. First the students looked at several films of professional bicycle races. Then they interviewed a local bicycle dealer about racing equipment. Finally, they wrote to the technical director of the series, asking him to come to their class for an interview, which he did. The listening situations involved all the students because of their interest in the television pilot; their letter inviting the director to visit was a masterpiece, free from any errors and written in exemplary script. They found their own films using indexing and research skills. Several students voluntarily made displays of the information they found because other classes were so interested.

When teaching listening, the most important factor to remember is *integration*. Listening is not taught as an isolated subject in the elementary school curriculum; it permeates all the language arts and the entire school day.

RAISING THE QUALITY OF CHILDREN'S LISTENING

Within the context of ongoing classroom learning experiences, the teacher can raise the quality of children's listening. The teaching of specific listening skills or good listening habits can occur within this framework, without formally saying, *Today, children, we are having a lesson in listening,* or continually repeating *Children, you are not listening! Let's pay attention!*

What skills should you be concerned with teaching? If you help children improve their listening comprehension, you will subsequently help them in all learning areas. Pratt[12] suggests that the following skills are involved in the comprehension of ideas:

Noting details
Following directions
Organizing into main and subordinate ideas
Selecting information pertinent to a specific topic
Detecting clues that show the speaker's trend of thought

Within the organization of daily classroom learning experiences, children can be taught to note details, determine main ideas, select the most useful and pertinent information about a topic, and follow directions. They can detect clues that point out the speaker's trend of thought or draw inferences from what has been said. If a group of students is listening to a cassette recording of a children's book, the teacher can guide a discussion of the story. A planned series of questions can involve children in identifying significant details. A discussion may center on the main ideas of the story or the author's purpose in writing the story. Reading books aloud provides the teacher with many opportunities to develop skills in listening comprehension.

An excellent example to mention is the Listen-Read Project.[13] This study put listening and books together to improve children's reading, and the findings showed many valuable side benefits to the program. Each day children used a listening center and heard cassette recordings of books. While listening, they each had a paperback book of the story being read. There was a choice of activities that followed the listening sessions: paired reading, writing of group experience stories, role playing of the stories, and discussions in which children were asked inferential and evaluative questions. The outcome is described as follows:

Descriptive data collected from the teacher indicated that the children became more adept at handling books, displayed increased attention spans in reading and far greater facility in oral language. The high level of concentration, made possible through the use of headsets, was still further evidence of the efficacy of the program in developing listening skills. Because of smaller groupings with part of the class administering its own Listen-Read activity, the teachers were less controlling and encouraged more open discussion. As a result, children who had been quiet and shy began to offer their ideas about the books they had enjoyed.[14]

The use of books is not the only means of teaching listening comprehension skills. For instance, children are continually asked to follow directions in order to complete learning tasks. Teachers can correlate the teaching of this listening skill with daily learning activities, keeping in mind the age and cognitive stage of the children. For example, children listen and follow directions when they make books (Chapter 13), prepare certain types of art projects, participate in movement experiences, or role-play scenes from a favorite story.

The evaluation of children's listening skills is an immediate and continuous process if you teach listening within the context of daily classroom learning experiences. You have instant feedback that suggests that John can or cannot follow directions. A group discussion focusing on the significant points made by a visiting speaker will enable you to assess quickly children's listening comprehension abilities.

Intervention by the teacher can raise the quality of listening and thus affect learning. Intervention usually takes the form of asking students questions. The questioning focuses on suggestions, ideas, or information that will extend and

Listening to children is an important aspect of teaching.

further develop the child's learning experience. To illustrate, a small group of children went on a listening walk with the teacher. When they were asked to describe various sounds as they walked through a park, the teacher discovered that the children were listening on a very superficial level. They had not heard the chirping of a cricket, the sound of the wind as it rustled through the trees, or the sound of an annoyed and irritated blue jay. They had only heard the predominant or "big" sounds—the buses and cars as they passed by, a man yelling at his dog, and a baby crying. The teacher's questions encouraged the children to listen and describe all kinds of sounds that they heard around them. Do you hear the birds? What kind of birds are they? Can you imitate the call of the cardinal? How is the cardinal's call different from the blue jay's?

The teacher who listens to what children say and encourages them to talk and ask questions has an accurate guide to children's thinking abilities. You can only intervene in children's conversations and discussions to raise the level or quality of the learning if *you* listen. Evaluating children's listening skills depends upon listening to all that they say. The teacher of listening needs to be a model listener.

LISTENING AS A THINKING SKILL

Listening is not the same as thinking, although it has a strong base in thinking. This is especially evident when we look at the more complex thinking skills

> It may be that all instruction in reading beyond the very first or decoding stage is really training in *how to think*. It may be, too, that the teaching of listening—beyond basic instruction in following directions or paying attention—is actually training in thinking. . . . The terminology used in listening instruction "listening for a speaker's main ideas," "listening for supporting details," or "listening to recognize inferences" describe thinking activities as much as listening. Underlying both listening and reading skills probably are the same or similar mental processes.[15]

This seems to suggest that developing good listening skills involves developing good thinking skills. In addition to simply receiving and comprehending information in an oral mode, we must learn to organize it. This organization may involve applying the new information, analyzing it, or synthesizing it. Organization may also involve evaluation. Sometimes our evaluation is a simple response—*I like it*, or *I hate it*. Other times we judge the information on preestablished criteria, and at the highest level, we value it. Thus good listening involves all of Bloom's cognitive skills (in hierarchical order): knowledge, comprehension, application, analysis, synthesis, and evaluation.[16]

Teachers can structure instruction so that students need to use all these thought levels in listening. The questions that we ask in a discussion, the purposes set for listening, should reflect all aspects of cognition.

TELEVISION: ITS POSSIBILITIES FOR TEACHING LISTENING

Television is a source of pleasure for both children and adults. As mentioned earlier in the chapter, television is a prime consumer of much of the American population's time. Larrick[17] contends that children watch 5,000 hours of television before entering first grade and average 22,000 hours of television by the twelfth grade. That 22,000 hours of television compares to about 11,000 hours in school.

Are students learning and becoming more knowledgeable because they view television to this extent? The research is inconclusive at this time, but present findings tend to lean toward the negative side. Himmelweit[18] compared a group of children who were television viewers with a group who were not and found that the nonviewers were more knowledgeable. In fact, the more intelligent television watchers tended to do less well in school if they were avid viewers of television. Slater[19] working with third-graders, found that school achievement, reading, arithmetic, and intelligence had a negative correlation with television viewing. Another study reported by La Blonde[20] suggests that there is no significant relationship between fifth-grade students' television habits and school achievement. However, the findings did indicate a positive relationship between television viewing and students' performance on Word-Study Skills of the Iowa Tests of Basic Skills. This finding is not too surprising since a number of other studies have conclusively shown that television contributes to vocabulary development. Both Himmelweit[21] and Schramm[22] indicate that television helps to build the vocabulary of children just beginning school. Children who watch and listen to television are from six months to a year ahead of nonviewers in vocabulary development.

Bring Television and the Language Program Together

Why not capitalize on the amount of time children spend watching television? Studies show that students enjoy and learn from instructional television, and the same results can be obtained using commercial television. Savage,[23] in promoting the idea of using children's out-of-school television experiences to build a language program, says: "A common criticism is that television is creating an unthinking generation. The trick for teachers is to get their pupils reacting to what they see and hear on TV." The potential that exists for increasing children's language and listening skills through commercial television is certainly great. If students receive guidance and direction, they will surely become more knowledgeable about the world around them. Television is also an excellent source for teaching students to become critical listeners. When educators talk about beginning where children are, they need to consider commercial television as a potential learning device.

Here are some ideas for using children's television viewing to increase their language and listening abilities. Once you begin using children's television experiences as a viable part of the language arts program, you will probably think of many more useful ideas.

1. Dramatization and television may be used together. After viewing the same television show, children can dramatize a favorite scene or episode.
2. Have the children view a daytime serial. Ask them to predict what will happen tomorrow and then watch it to see how accurate their predictions were.
3. Discuss different endings that could have been written for an episode of a popular series show they watched the night before.

4. Ask children to view an informative show that has been well reviewed and use it as a basis for discussion.

5. Children can compare and contrast television news coverage with newspaper coverage of significant events.

6. Children might produce a news show of their own after interviewing school faculty and students.

7. When a new program premieres on television, ask students to watch. Discuss and evaluate the program the next day with the children. Some students may enjoy writing a review of the new show.

8. Use popular shows to work on listening skills. Have the children practice listening for details and sequence by retelling an episode of a favorite show from the previous afternoon or evening. Ask those listening to add details.

9. For vocabulary development, have children report new words (or phrases) they hear and discuss them. Or have children listen for particular kinds of words—synonyms for *good* or *bad*, words with multiple meanings, slang words, and so forth.

10. Potter[24] suggests taping theme music from programs for children to identify. Older students could tell why the theme music "fits" the show it is from. Students can also be asked to listen for the words to the theme music and put it on charts. (This might make reading more enjoyable for some reluctant readers.)

11. Middle-grade students could practice note-taking skills while watching an informational program. If the teacher records the program, facts can be verified and students can compare their notes.

12. Television also provides opportunities for practicing summarizing skills. Assign students to watch a news-feature show like *60 Minutes* or *PM Magazine* and write a fifty-word summary of one segment. Compare summaries. (To make this a challenge, the summary must be between forty-five and fifty-five words.)

Critical Listening and Television

We live in a society where we are constantly being sold something. Have you watched any commercials recently and said to yourself, "Such ridiculous ads! Who would rush out and buy any of those products after seeing the commercials?" The answer—a lot of American people buy those products! Television executives contend that viewers often complain bitterly about an irritating commercial and then go right out and buy the product advertised.[25] The evidence indicates a certain amount of gullibility on the part of adults, but what about children? Working with students ages eight to ten, Cook[26] found they were willing to accept the propaganda presented in television commercials, regardless of their level of intelligence. One can conclude from the available research that skills in critical listening should be taught in the elementary school and not left until students are in high school or college.

It is difficult to divorce critical listening from critical reading, and critical thinking is basic to both. Research investigations by Devine[27] and Lundsteen[28] show a positive relationship between critical reading and critical listening. Evidence from both studies reveals that the ability to listen critically can be taught. For this reason, Devine recommends that skills in critical reading and critical listening be taught together. The skills are so interrelated that teaching them concurrently will provide reinforcement.

How do you go about teaching critical listening and critical reading? You might begin with teaching children certain propaganda techniques that are widely used by advertisers. Older students can identify the use of these techniques in newspapers, magazines, billboards, radio, and television.

Widely Used Propaganda Techniques[29]

Bandwagon: Everybody is doing it. All members of a group are doing it.
Card stacking: Falsehoods that distract. Illogical statements to give the best or worst possible case for an idea.
Glittering generalities: Virtue words like *truth* and *honor*. Empty yet colorful words.
Name calling: Giving an idea or product a bad label.
Plain folks: Attempts to delude an audience into thinking the speaker is just like them.
Testimonial: A respected or hated person who says that a given idea is good or bad.
Transfer: The authority and prestige of something respected are carried over to something else.

Students can also learn to distinguish fact from opinion. Young children might look at a selection of pictures and discuss statements about them. For Figure 7-1 those statements might be: *The girl is happy. The girl is wearing a sweater and skirt. The dog likes the girl. The dog is small. The dog belongs to the girl.*

Figure 7-1 Critical interpretation of pictures.

Students can choose their own pictures from newspapers or magazines and write their own statements about them. These may be exchanged with a partner or displayed somewhere in the classroom. Small- and large-group discussions can focus on why certain statements are factual and why others are opinion.

Older students can listen to radio or television news reports and analyze what is fact and what is opinion. The same activity can be done with newspaper editorials. After having a number of experiences, some students may want to write and record their own editorials about current topics or events. Reading aloud a biography of a famous person or a book that is historical fiction offers opportunities to determine fact from fiction, too. Questions such as: *Did this really happen? Was the person like the author describes? Is this a true event?* can lead to some interesting and enjoyable research for children in the upper-elementary grades. Authenticity may also be questioned—*What qualifies this author to write about this subject? How much research was necessary in order to write this book? Is the factual information accurate?*

All good fantasy is grounded in reality, and children can learn to distinguish between the two. A picture book such as *Where the Wild Things Are*[30] can be read aloud and discussed, focusing on what parts of the story are reality and what parts are fantasy. Because the illustrations in this book depict both fantastic and realistic situations, they too can be included in the discussion.

In an age when listening is rapidly becoming a primary means of obtaining information as well as a source of enjoyment through radio and television, it seems that it deserves much more attention than it is presently getting in our schools. Given an interesting and meaningful learning environment along with appropriate instruction, students' listening skills can be improved; and children can become critical listeners and thinkers.

SUMMARY

Since so much of our learning and communication time is spent in listening, it is critical for teachers to develop and refine their students' listening skills. Students need to learn how to adjust their level or kind of listening to the particular situation. We must help them become more responsive and more critical listeners rather than passively absorbing all they hear.

PRELIMINARY LEARNING ACTIVITIES

1. Plan a listening library to use later with children. Your library may include:
   (a) Stories recorded on cassette tape—if possible, have paperback copies of the stories for children to look at while listening
   (b) Records that children will enjoy listening to more than once
   (c) Poems recorded on cassette tape that will interest most children
   (d) Tape-recorded instructions that provoke a listening situation (*Listen to the sounds around you for the next five minutes and write about as many as you can*)
   (e) Open-ended stories read on cassette tape—after listening to an open-ended story, children write or tape-record their own original endings

(f) Recordings on cassette tape of a series of television or radio commercials that represent all seven propaganda devices—children can identify each propaganda device as they listen

(g) A recording of two contrasting reports—children can compare the two by listening for similarities and differences

Now it is your turn. How many other listening experiences can you add to your library?

2. The idea of using a sharing basket is discussed in Chapter 8. Sometime each day, children who wish to share (perhaps an imaginative story, poem, painting, and so on) place a note or the project itself in the basket. Make a sharing basket and plan the listening and speaking rules that will guide its use.

3. Children enjoy listening walks, and a number can be planned in and around the school. The purpose for listening is established before taking the walk. For example, children or a teacher may plan a walk around the school grounds to listen for unusual sounds. Or after reading the book *The Tiniest Sound*[31] the walk may focus on listening for "tiny" or "soft" sounds. Plan a variety of listening walks that may be taken in and around most schools.

4. Prepare a sample letter to be sent to parents informing them about upcoming television shows that their children might watch. You may wish to include possible follow-up activities, related books, questions, etc., to promote parental participation.

PARTICIPATION ACTIVITIES

1. Have children write open-ended stories that can be read aloud and then completed by other children. The ending to the stories may be written or verbalized. If you are working with a small group of children, you may ask each child to add a sentence to the story until they reach a logical ending—or the last child in the group may end the story.

2. Develop and use a listening-reading transfer lesson. You will plan two similar lessons: the first lesson will require children to *listen* and demonstrate certain skills; the second lesson will require children to *read* and demonstrate the same skills.

   For more information, read Patricia M. Cunningham's "Transferring Comprehension from Listening to Reading," in *The Reading Teacher*, vol. 29, no. 2 (November 1975), pp. 169–172.

3. Ask your children to view and listen to their favorite television show and write an experience story about it. Children may do their writing at home or even the next day at school. Older students could be asked to write a summary, a critical review, or a prediction of the next week's show if it is a continuing story.

4. There are innumerable activities related to critical listening that children will enjoy. Here are a few:
   (a) Have several students tape-record a number of Saturday morning television commercials and analyze them in class according to the seven propaganda devices mentioned in this chapter. Older students might be asked to record commercials during children's programming time and during adult programming times and compare the two.

(b) Tape-record several television cereal commercials or shampoo and hair coloring commercials—whatever will appeal to your students. Then have them bring in the box or containers for the same products and compare information and discuss the appeal made.

(c) Students can make up their own commercials for a product they "invent." The class may identify the appeal or propaganda device being used, or summarize the factual information given, or both.

5. Take a listening walk. After reading your class *The Listening Walk* by Paul Showers,[32] take them on a similar walk. They could even write their own version of the book when they get back.

REFERENCE NOTES

[1]Paul T. Rankin. "The Measurement of the Ability to Understand Spoken Language." Doctoral dissertation, University of Michigan, Ann Arbor, 1926.

[2]G. E. Delury, ed. *The World Almanac and Book of Facts, 1980*. New York: Newspaper Enterprise Associates, 1980.

[3]Miriam E. Wilt. "A Study of Teacher Awareness of Listening as a Factor in Elementary Education," *Journal of Educational Research*, vol. 43, April 1950, pp. 626–636.

[4]Commission on the English Curriculum of the National Council of Teachers of English. *The English Language Arts*. New York: Appleton-Century-Crofts, 1952.

[5]Andrew D. Wolvin and Carolyn Gwynn Cookley. *Listening Instruction*. Urbana, Ill.: ERIC Clearinghouse on Reading and Communication Skills, 1969, pp. 7–13.

[6]Sam Taylor. *What Research Says to the Teacher: Listening*. Washington, D.C.: National Education Association, 1964.

[7]Edward T. Hall. "Listening Behavior: Some Cultural Differences," *Phi Delta Kappan*, vol. 50, March 1969, pp. 379–380.

[8]Ibid.

[9]Edward Pratt. "Experimental Evaluation of a Program for the Improvement of Listening," *Elementary School Journal*, vol. 56, March 1956, pp. 315–320.

[10]Sister Mary Kevin Hollow. "Listening Comprehension at the Intermediate Grade Level," *Elementary School Journal*, vol. 56, December 1955, pp. 158–161.

[11]Andrew Wilkinson. "Oracy in English Teaching," *Elementary English*, vol. 45, no. 6, October 1968, p. 743.

[12]L. E. Pratt. "The Experimental Evaluation of a Program for the Improvement of Listening in the Elementary School." Doctoral dissertation, State University of Iowa, Iowa City, 1953.

[13]Helen E. Schneeberg and Marciene S. Mattleman. "The Listen-Read Project: Motivating Students through Dual Modalities," *Elementary English*, vol. 50, no. 6, September 1973, pp. 900–904.

[14]Ibid., p. 902.

[15]Thomas G. Devine. "Listening: What Do We Know after Fifty Years of Research and Theorizing?" *Journal of Reading*, January 1978, pp. 302–303.

[16]Benjamin S. Bloom, ed. *Taxonomy of Educational Objectives: The Classification of Educational Goals. Handbook 1: Cognitive Domain*. New York: McKay, 1956.

[17]Nancy Larrick. "Do You Have TV Interference?" *Today's Education*, vol. 67, 1978, pp. 39–40.

[18]Hilde T. Himmelweit, A. N. Oppenheim, and Pamela Vance. *Television and the Child*. London: Oxford University Press, 1958, p. 21.

[19]Betty Rech Slater. "An Analysis and Appraisal of the Amount of Televiewing, General School Achievement, and Socio-Economic Status of Third Grade Students in Selected

Public Schools of Erie County, New York," *Dissertation Abstracts*, vol. 25, April 1965, p. 5651A.

[20]J. A. La Blonde. "A Study of the Relationship between Television Viewing Habits and the Scholastic Achievement of Fifth Grade Children," *Dissertation Abstracts*, vol. 27, February 1967, p. 2284A.

[21]Himmelweit, Oppenheim, and Vance. *Television and the Child.*

[22]Wilbur Schramm, Jack Lyle, and Edwin B. Parker. *Television in the Lives of Our Children.* Stanford, Calif.: Standford University Press, 1961, p. 16.

[23]John F. Savage. "Jack, Janet, or Simon Barsinister?" *Elementary English*, vol. 50, no. 1, January 1973, pp. 133–136.

[24]Rosemary Lee Potter. "Learning to Listen: TV Can Help," *Teacher*, vol. 95, no. 3, November 1977, p. 42.

[25]Clark M. Agnew and Neil O'Brien. *Television Advertising.* New York: McGraw-Hill, 1958, p. 22.

[26]Jimmie E. Cook. "A Study in Critical Listening Using Eight to Ten Year Olds in an Analysis of Commercial Propaganda Emanating from Television." Doctoral dissertation, West Virginia University, Morgantown, 1972.

[27]Thomas G. Devine. "The Development and Evaluation of a Series of Recordings for Teaching Certain Critical Listening Abilities." Doctoral dissertation, Boston University, 1961.

[28]Sara Lundsteen. "Teaching Abilities in Critical Listening in the Fifth and Sixth Grades." Doctoral dissertation, University of California, Berkeley, 1963.

[29]Alfred M. Lee and Elizabeth B. Lee, eds. *The Fine Arts of Propaganda.* New York: Harcourt, Brace, 1939, p. 105.

[30]Maurice Sendak. *Where the Wild Things Are.* New York: Harper & Row, 1963.

[31]Mel Evans. *The Tiniest Sound.* Garden City, N.Y.: Doubleday, 1969.

[32]Paul Showers. *The Listening Walk.* New York: Crowell, 1961.

CHAPTER EIGHT

Oral Discourse— Discussing and Presenting

PREVIEW QUESTIONS

1 How can a teacher improve the quality of oral communication?

2 What kinds of questions and what strategies of questioning produce responses from children?

3 What kinds of discussion groups are there, and for what purpose is each best?

4 How do you select materials and prepare for storytelling and choral reading?

5 How should teachers evaluate oral presentations?

Mr. Walker's sixth-graders had prepared for Richard Chase's visit to their school by reading some of his collection *The Jack Tales*,[1] listening to a record of him telling some tales, and listening to other storytellers as well. They themselves had asked their family at Thanksgiving about stories their parents, aunts and uncles, or grandparents had heard as children. They shared these in class—sometimes retelling the tale themselves and sometimes playing the tape recording they had made. A small group of students who weren't spending the holiday with relatives had gone to a retirement home nearby and "swapped" some songs for stories.

One student said his tale was hard to tell because it had too many characters, and so he got some friends to help do a dramatic reading of the story with different students taking different parts. Using different voices helped make it clear who was talking.

The day finally came when Mr. Chase arrived. He was everything they had expected. Looking like some ageless gnome, he told his stories and asked them to tell theirs. They talked together about what to say in games, and then exchanged irreverent school rhymes and chants and songs. He answered all their questions about collecting stories. The glow he sparked got them interested in finding out more about their stories and in finding more stories.

The librarian helped them search out some different versions of familiar tales, and they had great fun sharing and discussing these with each other. Mr. Walker had them do some detective work to explain differences in these versions and to infer why certain aspects of the stories that changed were appropriate for the country of origin. One group got out some of the Greek and Roman myths and compared these with each other and with Norse mythology.

Two of the girls who had gone to the retirement home found that one of the stories they heard there was much like a story told by another friend's grandmother who had grown up in eastern Canada. They decided to go back to their informant and find out some more about where he had heard the story and about his background.

These students were developing some important language skills—discussing, interviewing, analyzing, summarizing, storytelling, and dramatic oral reading—as well as learning a lot about a special genre of literature. They did more reading than anyone believed, reading stories and reading about the countries in which their tale originated to try to explain how the details of the story fit that nation. They delved into history and geography as they tried to explain why the versions differed in detail as they did. They developed some critical listening and reading skills in evaluating the stories they heard and read.

Such integrated learning with an emphasis on oral language development occurs also in primary classrooms. The topic may be different, but many aspects of learning are identical.

Ms. Clark's primary-graders took a walk around their school and looked for signs of various kinds. When they returned from their walk, Ms. Clark brought out some replicas of a few signs they had seen. After a brief discussion, the children decided to make copies of some other signs that the teacher had not constructed. When all the signs were completed, Ms. Clark brought out a pocket chart—a large poster-type sheet with narrow strips of paper stapled across it to make slots in which the sign replicas would fit. One row was for traffic signs, one was for advertisements, and the third was for information. The children selected a sign from the ones they had seen and went up to the chart to put it in the right place. The Burger King sign went into the "advertisements" pocket, the stop sign went into "traffic," the street sign went into "information," and then one of the children put *Buses Only* into "information." Some of the children protested that it should be in "traffic." A somewhat heated discussion followed. In the process of that discussion, they came to narrow their meanings of all three labels—advertisements, traffic, and information.

As a follow-up Ms. Clark had the group select one sign (*Railroad Crossing*) and write an experience story about the railroad crossing sign. They read and reread their story as they were in the process of composing it. When the story was just as they wanted it, she copied it on a large sheet of lined chart paper and they decorated it with cutouts done in poster paint of trains and tracks, of children and cars waiting at a crossing, and of the railroad crossing sign itself.

The next day one group used an assortment of small boxes, clay, toothpicks, colored paper, and paint to make a table display map of their walk. Three of the children who had wanted to do the experience story on the Burger King sign dictated their own story to a fifth-grader who comes to their room three days a week for thirty minutes. Two others decided that there should be a sign for children from their school telling them where to wait for the crossing guard at a busy street nearby. They talked to their teacher about their idea for a few minutes and then went off to get poster paper and paint to make a sign for this. The rest of the group wrote up their own advertisements for various products, getting help in spelling the words they needed from another fifth-grader.

What are the key characteristics of these two classroom situations that are important in language learning? First, *the students were actively involved in their learning*. The older children collected the stories from their families, told the stories they heard, and introduced and interviewed their speaker. The younger children found the signs they worked on during their walk, and built the map and made up new signs or advertisements.

Second, *the students went into this study in enough depth to develop real understanding*. The sixth-graders did not just read a few stories from one of Richard Chase's books before meeting him and then applaud and go on with their study of prepositions or Twain or whatever. His visit became a renewal of interest in a study of folklore that took them into several types of literature, into folklore research and literary analysis. The younger ones also went into their topic in some depth, categorizing signs according to their purposes and learning about some of the new international road signs, sign design, mapping, and advertising signs. It was much more than the conventional learning about *stop*, *go*, and *caution*.

Third, *the students had some choices within the learning situation*. Although both groups of students had some assignments in common, they both had some choices within the area of study. The sixth-graders split into groups, some studying Greek, Roman, and Norse mythology and others matching folktales with the country of origin. Some told stories, while others tape-recorded them. Some of the primary children wrote an additional experience story, while others made up their own sign or made up advertisements.

Finally, *the students worked primarily with concrete materials*. This was not a matter of "read these pages, answer the questions, and fill in the blanks"; instead, students at both grade levels worked from firsthand knowledge and collection. The middle school students interviewed informants themselves and became informants as they answered Mr. Chase. The younger children saw the signs in use, made a realistic model of their walk, and made their own signs. The level of learning was much deeper than it could have been if the children had just been told to "draw a line from each sign to the sentence that tells what it means." For these two groups of children, learning was vivid and complex.

THE ENVIRONMENT THAT PROMOTES ORAL LANGUAGE SKILLS

The best plans of the teacher and the most stimulating topics for oral language activities will be of little value if the classroom environment does not encourage students' free and active participation. What kind of environment is necessary?

A key component is the removal of criticism and pressure to conform to some predetermined standards. Although the teacher may want to remind students before the activity to talk loudly enough for others to hear or to keep to the topic, the main emphasis is on what the student says rather than how it is said. It is not the time to correct word usage, criticize students' ideas, or suggest that they did not prepare adequately. Although you may feel that you can listen to students and at the same time do some clerical task, don't. You would be communicating nonverbally that what is being said isn't important or worth hearing. Sometimes it is tempting to suppress a child who is dominating group talk. However, the verbal student may not be subdued for very long, and you may inhibit another student who is on the verge of adding something to the discussion. Too many standards and too much adherence to them can hinder discussion instead of improving it.

A second component of a classroom environment that encourages participation is the establishment of *talk* as a significant vehicle for learning. Often, owing to evaluative measures and grading policies, teachers tend to place a higher value on written work than on oral work. Because of this, both students and parents begin to think written work is the most important. By seeking new ways to apply information that is acquired orally, teachers can provide experiences that can be evaluated according to students' contributions in oral language situations.

Another reason that oral activities do not receive the same emphasis as written ones is because words, once spoken, are quickly gone. There does not seem to be time to reexamine them or evaluate them. It is possible, however, to tape-record or take notes during discussions. Summarizing orally as the discussion proceeds may help individual students realize that their ideas do make a difference, and that as a group they have accomplished something in the process of oral work. Finding a system such as a chart to record those who participate, distract, and so on, will also help in your evaluation.

The establishment of meaningful conversation as a general classroom pattern is another facet of an environment conducive to the development of oral skills. This does not mean that students should be allowed to detract from other learning activities. It does mean that students should be allowed to converse with those nearby as long as the conversation does not interrupt others who are working on something else. There are times when you will need to have all their attention focused on you. There are other times—while they are building a model, writing a composition, planning a puppet play, doing art work—when encouraging conversation is developmentally sound.

Students can learn from each other, and they can learn from working together. When you are evaluating your students, you need to know what they can do independently; however, a large portion of time, they can work together on assignments, projects, or papers.

The final component of a classroom rich in oral language activities and language expansion is the development of a real need for children to discuss, describe, compare, and categorize things orally. Discussions should be an integral part of the daily classroom routine because there is always a need for something to be shared, discussed, or decided. The teacher must be perceptive and recognize moments when talk needs to be encouraged. A teacher can structure the classroom, the presentation, or a situation so that it calls for some phase of oral discourse.

THE IMPORTANCE OF ORAL DISCOURSE

Schools tend to focus on written skills, perhaps because children come to school with considerable competence in oral communication skills. While we do need to recognize and incorporate these skills, we also need to develop the various kinds of speaking skills.

For children who are in the preoperational stage of development—approximately two to seven years old—oral discussion experiences are especially important. The egocentrism of children at this stage of development leads them to assume that others know and think the way they do. And when others show that they do not, young children are often exasperated by this lack of understanding. An important way for children to realize that words do not carry all the information they suppose is to allow them many chances to talk with others, to explain their ideas, and to describe their experiences.

At the next stage of development—the concrete-operational period from about seven to about eleven—egocentrism becomes much less apparent and the child develops a social awareness and the understanding of another's point of view. Discussion and conversation are still very important, because at this stage of development they serve to help children communicate their thoughts and refine their concepts. Students at this stage of development cannot work from abstract ideas; their thought processes are still grounded in concrete, firsthand experiences. Their thinking is facilitated by using real objects and events. Through communicating with others, their concepts and views are accommodated into the internalized organizational patterns.

What we are suggesting is not just that talk of various kinds is a nice thing to do in elementary and middle-grade classrooms; rather, talk is a critical part of the school experiences of children. Oral language activities cannot be dismissed as a nuisance or as unimportant. They need to be considered a major part of the school curriculum for every child—and they are especially important for children whose background of experience does not include conversations or discussions of various kinds with linguistically mature adults.

SHARING

This section is entitled *sharing* instead of *show-and-tell* for several reasons. First, show-and-tell is confined almost exclusively to the primary grades, and older children would feel that having show-and-tell was childish although they might like to share hobbies or collections if it seemed like a grown-up thing to do. Another reason for using the term *sharing* is that it is more descriptive of the activity at any age or grade level. Show-and-tell implies one person at a time showing something and telling about it without any interaction from those listening. And that is exactly what it usually turns out to be—except that those who are supposed to be listening usually are not. Young children are too egocentric to be totally interested in what others say and are really more interested in what they themselves have to say. Too often it is the same few children who get up to show-and-tell, and they may not be the ones who need the experience the most.

Sharing, on the other hand, is a very adultlike activity. Its name directly implies give-and-take, response from the listeners, a mutual participating in the topic. Sharing, however, cannot take place with an entire classroom very successfully. Twenty to thirty people of any age cannot participate in a discussion. When show-and-tell shifts from a speaker-audience situation to a sharing activity, it becomes an interactive situation where the listeners' responses, questions, and experiences are also of value. This means that the teacher needs to provide a small-group situation for sharing.

After reading a favorite book, these students created a mural to illustrate various episodes in the story. They are sharing their work with some classmates.

Teachers play an important role in sharing. It is their responsibility to encourage personal involvement in the sharing discussion. Through the questions they ask and the strategies of questioning they use, teachers can explore the topics dealt with in greater depth and can extend their students' contributions. The interaction between participants is also part of the teacher's role in sharing discussions.

Encouraging Personal Involvement

Getting students really involved in a discussion means selecting topics that interest them and grouping children together who have some common experiences. In the early primary grades many teachers have found that sharing is better placed at the end of the school day than at the beginning. During the day either children do things such as paint, write stories, and so on, that they would like to share with others, or they are reminded of ideas or experiences they wish to tell about. One successful teacher uses a "sharing basket" to encourage discussion. Children may put a note in the basket during the day about what they would like to share. This has a dual purpose: it reminds them of their ideas, and it points out a purpose for writing. Older students may enjoy and profit from sharing a book they have read or a movie or television program they have seen. Teachers have used this kind of sharing as a substitute for the formal oral or written book report with great success. For this, you could group children according to those who have read books by the same author, books dealing with the same time period, or perhaps books dealing with the same theme.

Using Effective Questions and Questioning Strategies

One very important factor in developing sharing discussions is the use of appropriate questions and questioning strategies. Research suggests that the level of teachers' questions determines the level of children's thinking. Cunningham[2] has developed a model of questioning, shown in Figure 8-1 that seems helpful in considering the various kinds that may be asked.

Narrow questions are divided into two subcategories, cognitive-memory questions and convergent questions. Cognitive-memory questions are those which require the person responding to recall or recognize information which has previously been made available. This kind of question involves only remembering the answer. On a topic such as punctuation, the following are examples of cognitive-memory questions.

Recall: What punctuation marks are used at the end of a question?
Identify-observe: How many periods are there in this paragraph?
Yes-no: Is this mark a colon?
Defining: What do you mean by a quotation?
Naming: What is this punctuation mark called?
Designating: Which of these marks is used before a list of things?

Convergent questions are the other type of narrow questions. These questions may involve more than simply remembering, but they lead to one specific

The teacher's role in questioning, then, is to ask questions that are penetrating and provocative. These are the questions that make one think at a more complex level and that elicit several answers or reasons. Of course you cannot predict ahead of time which way a discussion may lead, but as a teacher you should prepare ahead of time a *few* key questions to ask. During the discussion itself, you can supplement the key questions you planned with others that seem necessary because of the direction the discussion takes.

In addition to the particular questions that are used during a discussion, there are four strategies that are used to improve discussion.

Ask fewer questions and balance the ones you do ask between broad and narrow questions. Use narrow questions to establish a common area of information; ask broad questions to extend the thinking of your group.

Balance participation in the discussion by calling on students who do not volunteer as well as those who do. Do not let a few students who always raise their hands to answer close out others who could also contribute to the discussion. Many students who are less able because of problems with reading and writing are perfectly capable of responding orally within the discussion. They may be rather shy about answering a question, but they will gladly do it if called upon. You can even refocus a child who is not really involved in the discussion by saying his or her name and then asking a question. However, do not do this to trap someone. Ask a question you think the child can answer.

Use questions that not only allow but encourage several children to answer. Students are the world's greatest experts at determining what teachers actually want. If you can convince them that there is not a preset, predetermined answer for every question and that it is their job to find out what that answer is, your students will reward you with some highly original ideas or solutions.

Improve students' responses to questions by giving them time to think, and ask additional questions to make them correct, clarify, or extend their first answers. Silence is an uncomfortable element in a discussion. Too often the teacher who feels responsible for the discussion will give an answer or just go on to another question. If, however, the teacher will make an effort to be quiet, one of the children will break the silence. They often need some time to think, to figure things out, to make connections between the question and their experiences. Give them time. There will be moments when a teacher may want to extend an answer. A puzzled look and perhaps saying *Ohhh?* or *Explain a little more* will elicit additional information.

Questioning plays a very large part in teacher-led discussions. The questions themselves and the strategies of questioning that the teacher uses are significant. Through the questions posed, teachers raise the level of students' thinking and further their language development.

Promoting Child-to-Child Interactions

The questioning strategies above will help develop a pattern of discussion in which the students do more talking than the teacher. Asking questions that do not focus on a single short answer will also promote child talk. After all, the teacher does not really need the experience of explaining, describing, categorizing, and speculating; the necessity to use language in a variety of ways is a part of language development and therefore what children need. Teachers can deliberately promote interaction among class members by asking them to verify or add to what someone has said without implying that the first response is incorrect. Another way of facilitating interaction in the classroom is to make students responsible and comfortable in asking questions as well as in giving answers. With young children you can prompt their questions by suggesting what they might ask: *Who would like to ask George what other ways people use to display their collection?* With students of any age, teachers can praise the questions that students ask. If you can make your class feel that asking questions as well as answering them is important to you, they will try to do it.

A critical feature of good discussion as well as good conversation is a small group in which each participant feels comfortable. With the large group—and perhaps with a small group in the primary grades—children may need to raise their hands and be called on in order to limit constant interruptions. As children have more experience, this should gradually become unnecessary.

Some teachers have found other ways to control interruptions. A "speaker selector" is highly effective if not used excessively. This is an object, something intrinsically interesting such as a marble egg, feather, or large button that is passed around the group. Only the person having the speaker selector should be speaking. As the object passes around the circle or group, the person having it may talk and then hand it on when finished. If the person who has it does not want to contribute an idea or comment, it is simply passed on. This eliminates all the raising of hands and being called on, and it also guarantees that each person will have a turn. Even with young children it is workable idea—perhaps because of its visibility and its guarantee of a turn. It is difficult to get young children to take their turn and not interrupt because of their strong egocentric drive and because of the amount of competition for attention present in the classroom which is not present at home.

Because sharing is an important part of the emotional development of children and offers such potential for developing thinking skills and language skills, it should be more than the conventional show-and-tell. Try to make the sharing time a vital part of the curriculum by arranging it in a way that affective, cognitive, and linguistic skills are developed.

DISCUSSING

In addition to conversation and sharing, there are two other kinds of classroom discussion: planning discussions and presentational discussions. These should be used in your classroom when there is a real need to plan or to present something meaningful to the students.

Planning Discussions

Two kinds of discussions are appropriate for planning or generating ideas. These are brainstorming groups and buzz groups. *Brainstorming* has been successfully used by adults as well as by children and is effective in generating ideas, especially innovative or creative approaches to a problem. In brainstorming there is no need to come to a decision or agreement. Every idea is accepted as stated, although others may combine ideas or add to an idea which has been suggested. It is a freewheeling approach which may include a wide range of suggestions from the very practical to the improbable. Most teachers will use it with caution, clearly stating ahead of time that the object is to get a lot of ideas without coming to a decision. *Buzz groups* are also used to get ideas or to plan. In contrast to brainstorming, buzz groups focus on a particular conclusion or decision. A small group or several small groups of students are given a specific problem and a certain amount of time to reach their objective. The discussion may require them to consider a number of pros and cons, but the group eventually reaches closure on an idea or suggestion.

Planning discussions can be used for a wide range of topics in the classroom. Their content may be related specifically to the language arts as children plan, for example, the cover for an invitation to their parents to visit their room. These discussions may also be related to another content area, such as how to care for and record their observations of the gerbils as a part of a science experiment or how to set up a softball tournament between the sixth and seventh grades.

If you allow students to participate in planning activities, you should be willing to agree to any reasonable plan which they decide upon. If you feel there are constraints on what they might decide, then note these ahead of time. You may wish to say what theme should be followed in the invitation, what supplies are available, what the cost or time limits are, and so on. If you have already made some planning decisions, then announce them or state the alternatives from which the group may choose.

Presentational Discussions

These discussions are intended as a way for individuals or a group to present to others something they have learned or information they have gathered. The two main kinds of presentational discussions are round-table discussions and panel discussions. The more informal and less audience-oriented of the two is the round-table discussion. *Round-table discussions* involve a small group of students and a moderator. They are relatively informal, with the group members sharing ideas or findings with each other or an audience. The moderator's main responsibility is to keep the group moving along and on the topic. You may want to have the moderator summarize the discussion in some way, but keep in mind that summarizing an oral discussion is a rather high-level thinking skill and is fairly difficult even for adults. *Panel discussions* are clearly intended for presenting ideas to an audience. Each member of the panel takes responsibility for some aspect of the topic. The members tend to take turns in presenting their part, although panel members may add to one another's information as the presentation continues. After the panel has made its presentation, members of the audience may ask questions of the panel as a whole or of one individual panel member. The panel discussion, in contrast to the round-table discussion, is more formalized and requires more preplanning.

The topics for presentational discussions tend to be primarily in content areas such as science or social studies, although some topics in literature are appropriate. One classroom had been doing a combination study of the stars and constellations: astronomy, astrology, and mythology. Each of the subgroups presented their information in panel discussions. This was the fact-finding part of their work reported orally; later, they extended the activity in many directions. Some went into writing fictitious horoscopes and various kinds of poetry. One group improvised a play about the Pleiades (according to Greek mythology the seven daughters of Atlas who were transformed into a cluster of stars). Another group improvised brief scenes in the lives of famous astronomers as they made their discoveries. One trio actually built a telescope and recorded changes in the positions of the stars. In spite of all the different activities that followed, all the children gained a basic knowledge of astronomy, astrology, and mythology from the original panel discussions.

Discussion Procedures

The purpose for the discussion, whatever kind it is, should be clear to you and to your students. If students have not had much experience with discussion groups, you should move them into these oral discussions slowly and with a considerable amount of structure. Give clear directions, have some sort of signal to use to stop the discussion if it becomes necessary, and put someone in charge of each group. If the students have to get up and move around to get materials, perhaps at first you will want to assign one person from each group to be the messenger. Keep the early experiences with discussion rather simple with a clear-cut purpose and some guidelines which are discussed ahead of time. As children become more used to working in groups, less structuring is necessary and they can work on more complex or involved projects. Age is not as important a factor as being familiar with working in groups this way.

You may want to start with only one small group working on something jointly while the other students are involved in independent projects. This will leave you free to work with the discussion group and get things started. Then you can add a second group, and finally a third, fourth, or fifth—whatever seems appropriate for their interests and needs. It is important, though, that students' early experiences with discussion work well and that they feel good about the group work.

Students may want to set up their own evaluation of their group work, or you may want to set guidelines ahead of time and then comment on those that were followed and those that they need to work on more the next time. These might include such things as keeping on the topic, listening to others, giving everyone a chance to talk, and doing one's share to reach the group's goal. You might also decide not to evaluate a particular discussion session with your students. Usually, though, it is a good idea for the teacher to keep some record of the discussion session and how children participated in it. This might be done on a checklist basis with each child's name and labeled columns for their performance, as in Figure 8-2. As you move about the room working with the discussion groups, you can make mental notes of individual contributions or responses. These can then be recorded on the checklist. You will not get a chance to check on each student each time, but over a period of time you can record several sessions for everyone.

REPORTING

Two typical forms of oral reporting are discussed here: informational reports and book reports. These very words seem to summon visions of children coming, one at a time, to the front of the room and reading a written report (some

Evaluation: Participation in oral discussion

Children's names	Actively participates	Adheres to topic	Gives others a chance	Other comments

+ = Positive evidence observed (does this)
− = Negative evidence (does the opposite)

Figure 8-2   Evaluation of discussion.

of which is probably copied directly from another source). Surely, there must be a better way! The description itself suggests three things to be avoided: standing up in front of the room, reading a written report, and putting down on paper another writer's words. Avoiding the possibility that children will present reports orally in this way can make the reporting situation more appropriate and pleasant for children in elementary and middle school.

Informational Reports

Reporting may be done through a group presentation if students have worked on related informational reports. A panel discussion is less formidable to children than individual reports. If the report topics are not closely related and a group presentation seems unsuitable, there are other ways of helping them present interesting oral reports without reading a prewritten text.

One way to improve oral reporting is to show students how to take notes from the encyclopedia or from other reference materials using their own words. This is not a skill that develops independently without instruction. Note-taking skills can be taught by showing children short paragraphs of material on chart paper or an opaque projector. After they have had a chance to read the paragraph, remove it from their view and have them tell or write down one or two important ideas from the paragraph in their own words. These can be telegraphic in nature rather than written in full sentence form. Your students will need quite a few experiences like this with note taking before they are ready to work with their own research materials. When they make that step, they will still need some help and supervision before they can work completely on their own. Students need to develop confidence in their own ability to take notes in their own words instead of relying on copying sentences or even whole paragraphs from other sources.

By changing the format of oral reports, the teacher can do a lot to improve the reporting situation. One effective way is *not* to have the focus of attention entirely on the student giving the oral report. One possibility is to have students prepare chart paper strips, with each idea they are going to talk about on a single strip. These can then be pinned up one at a time as they give the report. This same idea can be accomplished by writing the main ideas on a transparency and using an overhead projector. It is reassuring for many children to think the audience is looking at the main ideas instead of at them. The information for the report can also be given in an interview-show technique. You can have your own class version of *The Today Show*. To do this, children who are reporting will prepare three to six questions about the topic for someone else to ask them. They can rehearse their answers with the master of ceremonies who will interview the guests for the day's show. The element of role playing involved in this makes most children more comfortable. A third possibility for some topics is to have the students prepare slides, gather printed pictures to use with an opaque projector or make their own illustrations to accompany their report. Students can talk about the pictures as they present information about their topic. Thus, the attention of the class is focused on the pictures—particularly when a projector is being used—instead of on the person giving the report. These are a few of the ways you can make children more at ease with oral reporting.

In evaluating students' oral reports, it is extremely important that the emphasis be on *what* the person says, not on *how* it is said. The whole purpose of oral reporting is the giving or sharing of information; it is not oral language usage, projection of voice, and so on. Many teachers like to list (on the board or on a chart) reporting guidelines for children to consider while preparing their reports. If you choose to do this, keep the guidelines very simple and few in number. Too long a list will make anyone feel that there is no way to live up to such expectations. After the report you will no doubt want to make some evaluative comments. Keep in mind that everyone needs to feel successful and good about the experience, and that your comments may serve as instruction for others. You can comment on one or two things that the student did well, and save any further suggestions for an individual conference. Think of evaluation as searching for value in what students do; after all, the word *value* is an inherent part of the word *evaluation*.

Discussing Literature

Teachers of all grade levels discuss stories and books with children. Often, as in the teachers' manuals, most of the questions asked are memory-level questions: *What was the little girl's name? What did her stepmother tell her to do? What did she have to do for her two stepsisters? What was her fairy godmother's warning? What did she use for a coach? What were the horses made from? Where did the coachman come from?* And on, and on, and on. When this happens, it is unfortunate because it offsets the impact of the book or story and suggests that literature is "only the facts." It denies affective response and does not increase children's understanding of the literary elements employed. It reduces literature to the narrative line.

An interesting study done with tenth-graders by Lucking[4] suggests that asking questions in hierarchical order increases students' responses. Experimental group teachers were trained to discuss literature starting with simple recall questions and then progressing to evaluative questions. Whether it was the sequence of questions or simply that the teachers got beyond the memory level and asked a significant number of analytical, interpretive, and evaluative questions is not completely clear from this study. However, it does seem to indicate that significant numbers of higher-level questions are important.

Teachers who want to elicit affective response for discussion may find some of the following questions helpful:[5]

What could you guess about the characters that is not told about them?
What did any character in the book do that you would or would not like to do?
Do you know any people who are like those in the book? Can you describe them?
What things happened in the book that you would like to happen to you?
How would you change the story if you could?
What parts of the book are about things which you know are important?

If you want to develop students' understanding about various literary elements in the text, the following questions may be useful:

Plot structure: Can you describe the parts of the book—the beginning, middle, and end?
Plot structure: What is the event that the main part of the book builds up to?
Characterization: How did you learn what each of the main characters was like? (Through what the author said? Through what they said or did? Through what others said or how they responded?)
Characterization: Do any of the characters change during the book, and if so, what causes the change?
Setting: Would this story be better or different if it had happened somewhere else?
Theme: What was the author trying to say in the book? Do you think he or she was right?
Theme: If this book had a moral, what would it be?
Mood: How did the author make you feel the way you did in this book?
Summary: What would you tell a friend this story was about?
Summary: How well does the title fit the story? What title do you think would be a better one?
Critical summary: What would you say to people who asked you if they would like this book?

These questions and those in the preceding group may help you ask questions about literature that ask students to go beyond the "what happened?" stage. Do not use them all in discussing an individual story or book. Select the ones that will highlight the literary aspects that are most significant. If you want to make sure that the children have understood the story, ask them to retell it. It is much better to ask: *What happened at the beginning of Cinderella? At the middle? At the end?* than to let loose a barrage of questions like those at the beginning of this section.

Sharing Books

This section is intentionally entitled "Sharing Books" instead of "Book Reports." Why? Because the term *book report* usually carries negative connotations. Did you ever have to write and turn in weekly book reports? And what was the purpose of all those book reports? to check to see if you had really read the book? Our intention here is to present ways that students can share their experiences with books and, at the same time, be motivated to continue their reading. Not every book the child reads has to be shared in some way. Just as adults sometimes read a book they don't find particularly meaningful or a book that is too close to them to want to share, so children should be able to choose what books they want to share.

There are a number of alternatives to formal oral book reports. Books may be shared orally in interesting ways, they may be dramatized, or they may be shared through art. Books may also be shared through enjoyable writing experiences. Consider the following suggestions as examples of alternatives that you might use.

Sharing through talking

1. Students who have read the same book or who have read books by the same author might discuss the books with each other and with you. This encourages both description and comparing or contrasting, which are important cognitive skills.
2. Once in a while students might enjoy giving sales talks for their books. A sales talk should be finalized with some kind of decision which can be a simple vote, or it can be done by listing others in the class who want to read the book after the sales talk.
3. Students might like to tell the story or a part of it to some musical accompaniment of their choosing. This can involve using cutout illustrations, drawings, or a flannelboard.
4. A student can read orally a short scene from his or her book. The reader should practice this first so that the oral reading is prepared and smooth.
5. Older students might like to hold an interview with one of the characters in the book. The reader prepares the questions for someone else to ask and then impersonates the character in the book, answering the questions as the character would.
6. Students might enjoy preparing a talking bulletin board that will motivate others to read their book. Suppose four children have read *Harriet the Spy* and enjoyed it. They might work together in making a display to show the main characters, a favorite scene or episode from the book, and so on. A brief dramatization following the content of the bulletin board would then be recorded on cassette tape.

Sharing through drama
Dramatic activities based on a book are an interesting and enjoyable way for children to share a book they have liked with others. Some possibilities for dramatizing are:

1. Make stick puppets to dramatize one scene from a favorite book. Students who have read the same book may share this, or one person can ask a friend to help with the presentation.
2. Students may pantomime characters from familiar stories they have read. This might include some simple costumes.
3. They might enjoy doing a television commercial for their book. This sug-

gests that less content of the book will be shared, but also that greater selection of ideas is required.

4. If the class has been reading books that are suitable for improvisation, a group who has read the same book might like to do some improvised scenes from the story. They would not memorize any lines, but use their own words in the dramatization.

5. Students who have read two different books can work in pairs and do puppet dramas showing the two main characters meeting and talking. This is particularly effective if the two characters have something in common, that is, having lived in the same area at different times, having been president, or having fought in different wars.

Sharing through art Art, as a creative medium, is appropriate for sharing responses to another creative medium. In working with art and literature, try to vary the media used. Crayons and manila paper get pretty tiring after a while and limit potential creativity. Think of painting, crayon engraving, color washes over crayon, chalk, modeling in clay and paper-mâché, collages, sculpture in soap or paraffin, dioramas, and printing using vegetables or corrugated cardboard. Some art work done on 9- by 12-inch paper is fine, but other times children need to work with very large sheets of paper. Let the students choose the materials they would like to use, or work with them to suggest various possibilities.

1. Students could make original illustrations for their story. This might be one illustration or a series of them.
2. They might make an original book jacket for their book.
3. They can create a cartoon strip of one special incident in their story.
4. Making a map or time line of events in historical fiction or biography can be an appropriate activity.
5. Students can make models or sculptures of characters or objects in the book. This idea can also be extended and children can create mobiles.

Sharing through writing There are many possibilities of writing something that relates to the book read, without doing the standard book report.

1. Write diary or journal entries for one of the characters in the book.
2. Write an outline for a sequel to this story.
3. Write a description of a person or place in the story. This may be done as a simple description or as specifications for sets for a film or play version of the book.
4. Write a letter to the author or to one of the characters.
5. Write end flaps for a new book jacket for the book.

Whatever means you select to have children share their reading, keep in mind two important suggestions: the focus of the reporting activity should be on sharing and stimulating reading, and children should have a choice of how they want to share their book.

STORYTELLING

There is a very special quality in storytelling that is not present in other kinds of oral experiences. Reading aloud to students is important in aiding language development and increasing their interest in literature and ways of using language in writing. Storytelling provides these same possibilities for development and offers a personal contact not present in reading aloud. The teacher as storyteller can focus attention on those listening and immediately respond to their reactions. When reading a story, the teacher is giving attention at least partially to the printed page. Storytelling is highly personal and intimate.

A teacher who has a number of stories tucked away and ready to tell is prepared for the kind of situations that seem to come up all too frequently. These are the times when a scheduled speaker is late or calls to cancel out at the last minute, when the bus is twenty minutes late picking your group up from a field trip, or when you have two classes settled in your room to watch a special film and the projector breaks. Teachers who have several stories ready to tell do not need a book or any other equipment. They can entertain, instruct, and enchant a group of children on the spot.

Selecting material for storytelling depends mainly on two factors: first, a story should have a relatively simple plot and sequence of events and clear characterization; second, the overall style or effect of the story should suit the personality of the teller. Because of the need for exciting but simple plot development and characterization, folktales are particularly suited for storytelling. Folktales were originally part of the oral tradition and served a number of functions, some of which are still appropriate. Some of the functions met by various kinds of folklore are those of education, social protest, escape from reality, and converting work into play. American folklore—as well as the folklore of other lands—offers a tremendous variety of materials to the teacher. There are myths, legends, fairy tales or *Märchen*, and tall tales. A teacher with a soft voice and a quiet way of moving about might be more comfortable with one of the fairy tales or wonder tales rather than the swaggering tall tales. What you choose to tell should seem comfortable for you.

Because folklore was originally part of the oral tradition and was passed from storyteller to storyteller, there are numerous versions of many folktales. How a particular tale with the same basic features can occur in places apparently removed from each other is one of the unsolved mysteries of folklorists. For example, versions of "Puss in Boots" can be found in Sweden, Spain, Poland, the Dominican Republic, Greece, Turkey, India, the West Indies, Africa, and Indonesia. While the basic features of a folktale are similar, the details will vary quite widely. In an Italian version of 1502,[6] the "Puss in Boots" tale begins with the death of a very poor lady named Soriana who leaves her three sons only a kneading-trough, a rolling-board, and a cat. In a Greek version[7] it is a king who dies after losing all his wealth. He offers his three sons a choice of a golden strap and his curse or the cat and his blessing. The two elder sons, of course, take the strap and the curse, but the youngest son takes the cat and the blessing. In the French version,[8] which is more familiar to most Americans, it is a miller who dies and leaves only the mill, his ass, and his cat. The eldest takes the mill, the second chooses the ass, and the youngest son is left with the cat. Although your introduction to the folktale may be in written form, you should feel perfectly comfortable changing any of the details of the tale to something more meaningful to the group you are telling the story to. You do not have to memorize the story, only the basic events and their order. Occasionally a story has a particular phrase that is "just right" for it that you will want to memorize. This is the case for most of us with, "Mirror, mirror on the wall, who's the fairest one of all?" from *Snow White and the Seven Dwarfs*.

Some advice from an expert storyteller is to strip away any pretenses of being good or exciting, and simply be yourself. If you try to recall the experience or story you are going to tell and get a vivid impression of it, you will find it much easier to tell. You don't have to tell every detail, but select one or two and let the audience fill in the rest.

Students in the upper grades may also enjoy telling a favorite story. They may want to use a flannelboard or shadow figures arranged and moved on an overhead projector to supplement their telling of the story. You can encourage them and help them be successful, but insisting on their doing it is probably counterproductive.

Some of the values in storytelling are so important that teachers should make the effort to become able to tell stories as well as to read them aloud. Perhaps the main value in storytelling is in developing students' desire to learn to read for themselves, because through storytelling the teacher introduces them to many kinds of literature. Storytelling is one of the few kinds of talk done by the teacher that offers experiences with rich, complex, vivid language. This is especially important in developing complexity of language and acquiring a wide vocabulary. For students who speak a lower-prestige dialect than the teacher, storytelling is an opportunity to expose these children to another more socially accepted dialect without interfering with communication between the teacher and the students and without suggesting that their own dialect (and that of their home environment) is unacceptable in any way. Storytelling is also a way of exposing students to stories that are still too difficult for them to read on their own. This is particularly true in the upper grades when the distance between what interests many students and their ability to read independently is very wide. Storytelling occupies a very special place in the realm of oral discourse and should be important in the classroom.

SUPPLEMENTAL ORAL LANGUAGE SKILLS

There are a number of other oral language activities that should be included in any elementary language arts program at some time, but which are not as basic as sharing, discussing, reporting, or storytelling. They include a wide range of proficiencies, such as oral directions, messages, interviews, and choral reading or speaking. Some may be such an integral part of other activities or of classroom management that they are not obvious to the teacher. This is perfectly all right, even desirable, as long as the children are given adequate help in developing the oral skills.

Making Announcements and Introductions and Giving Messages

Students of all ages can participate in making announcements orally. In the early primary grades or with children who have had little experience, the announcements should be very brief. With more age and experience, teachers can expect competence with more complex and lengthy announcements. These can be worked into other content areas or into the regular classroom procedures. Children might report on the temperature or weather or something special about the day or week in the morning "opening exercises." Teachers who use a calendar might incorporate these facts with the month, date, and day of the week. This could be a rotating duty all during the year. Other teachers ask someone at each table or group to announce how many are buying lunch, how many are bringing lunch or ordering milk, and who is absent from their group. In an informal classroom where students help plan some of the activities, individual children might announce special activities that they are planning and that others could share in. Teachers often make many announcements during the day that students in their classes could make, and students need the experience of making them.

Introductions are also part of classroom procedures. Appointing one child per week or per month to welcome visitors to the classroom and to introduce them to others is excellent practice. It also makes visitors feel welcome. Often children do not get any training at home about how to make an introduction, and so you will need to teach or at least remind them how to do this graciously. Instead of instructing the whole class at once in an artificial situation, why not take the three or four students who are the first to be hosts and hostesses and work with them? Role playing is especially effective here. Perhaps you will want to provide signs on strings. In that way, the person who is playing the role of a parent can quickly slip on a sign saying *parent* and enter the room to be introduced to others. Other signs for principal, room mother, guest speaker, university observer, intern or student teacher, and so on can be used. Role-playing a situation before it actually happens makes it much easier for students; and using those who will actually need to do the introductions establishes a meaningful learning setting. Sometime during the year every student should have an opportunity to assume introduction responsibilities.

Giving accurate messages orally is an extremely important skill for everyone. It requires careful listening and remembering, as well as the skill of relaying information accurately. Pick up on any opportunities that occur to have students practice this skill. As with announcements, the first experiences with this should be simple informational messages. If the information to be relayed is critical, you may want to send a written message along with a child who has had little practice. Every child needs the experience at some time; be careful, therefore, not to limit the privilege to only the more mature children in the group.

Giving Directions or Explanations

Anyone who has asked for directions at a service station or from someone walking by has at sometime thought the informant was deliberately making things difficult or even giving directions to another place. Giving directions is a highly skilled task which requires that persons giving the directions or explanations put themselves in the place of the person asking for help. This makes the task difficult for young children in the preoperational stage of development, since their egocentric view of the world makes taking another point of view virtually impossible. They naturally assume that everyone understands by a word or statement just what they do. *Go this way until you get to Julia's house, and then turn.* Experiences with young children at this stage of development should involve having them explain things by giving concrete demonstrations as they talk. Older children who are in the concrete-operational stage of development have less difficulty taking another's point of view, but they still need practice in using a step-by-step explanation.

Some teachers have found it very helpful, when involving the whole class in a project that requires following directions carefully, to work with five or six children first so that they can execute the steps correctly. Then these children can assist others in their group or at their table by supplementing the teacher's directions or explanations. It certainly precludes the teacher's being called on for help from every direction at once. Students should also be encouraged to take a leadership role in explaining things to other children. Older children may also work with directions when developing map-reading skills. This kind of map work often starts with mapping some familiar area. The students might then do some role playing in giving directions from one place to another on their map.

Using the Telephone

The telephone is such a vital part of our communications that even very young children should be taught to use it to obtain emergency assistance; and older children should be able to answer courteously, get the person asked for, take a message, or handle a wrong number. Many telephone companies provide a kit with working telephones that may be used in the classroom. If this is not available in your area, you can probably borrow a toy telephone from a student or a friend who has young children. Telephone courtesy can be handled in a learning center with a set of situation cards for older students or a tape-recorded problem for younger ones. Every child of school age should know how to call the fire and police departments and be able to give whatever information is necessary (name, address, telephone number, and the problem). If they cannot memorize the police number, they should know how to dial for the operator and explain what they want. In metropolitan areas, this means being able to ask for the correct city department that handles their area. Children need to learn not to tell strangers information about where their parents are or that they are alone in the house. Courtesy is certainly desirable, but safety is an absolute necessity. Using the telephone is not necessarily something that needs a full instructional unit each year, but teachers should verify that the students in their class can use the telephone for emergencies.

Choral Reading and Choral Speaking

Choral reading and speaking are very special oral language activities which are enjoyed by many students. Early experiences should involve very brief passages of material. If possible, the children involved should participate in choosing the selection they are to read or learn. You can easily identify a well-liked poem because the children will start to repeat part of it with you as you read or say it, and it will be the one they ask for over and over again. These early experiences should probably be done in unison to develop the idea of speaking in perfect time and rhythm. The important thing here is that children have some opportunity to respond to the poem and suggest ways of interpreting it. One poem that allows for a lot of unison work and illustrates the concept of choral reading or speaking is the nursery rhyme "One, Two." Have half of the children say the first line of each verse or couplet, and the other half say the second line. Even nonreaders in kindergarten or first grade can say the first of the pair of lines.

NUMERICAL NURSERY RHYME[9]

One, two,
Buckle my shoe;

Three, four,
Shut the door;

Five, six,
Pick up sticks;

Seven, eight,
Lay them straight;

Nine, ten,
A good fat hen;

Eleven, twelve,
Let us delve;

Thirteen, fourteen,
Maids a-courting;

Fifteen, sixteen,
Maids in the kitchen;

Seventeen, eighteen,
Maids a-waiting;

Nineteen, twenty,
My stomach's empty.

Please, Mother,
Give me something to eat.

Another poem that is suitable for reading and that does not involve a lot of difficult words is "There Was an Old Woman."[10]

THERE WAS AN OLD WOMAN

There was an old woman who swallowed a fly;
I wonder why
She swallowed a fly.
Poor old woman, she's sure to die.

There was an old woman who swallowed a spider;
That wriggled and jiggled and wriggled inside her;
She swallowed the spider to catch the fly,
I wonder why
She swallowed a fly.
Poor old woman, she's sure to die.

There was an old woman who swallowed a bird;
How absurd
To swallow a bird.
She swallowed the bird to catch the spider,
That wriggled and jiggled and wriggled inside her.
She swallowed the spider to catch the fly,
I wonder why
She swallowed a fly.
Poor old woman, she's sure to die.

There was an old woman who swallowed a cat;
Fancy that!
She swallowed a cat;
She swallowed the cat to catch the bird,
She swallowed the bird to catch the spider,
That wriggled and jiggled and wriggled inside her.
She swallowed the spider to catch the fly,
I wonder why
She swallowed a fly.
Poor old woman, she's sure to die.

There was an old woman who swallowed a dog;
She went the whole hog
And swallowed a dog;
She swallowed the dog to catch the cat,
She swallowed the cat to catch the bird,
She swallowed the bird to catch the spider,
That wriggled and jiggled and wriggled inside her.
She swallowed the spider to catch the fly,
I wonder why
She swallowed a fly.
Poor old woman, she's sure to die.

There was an old woman who swallowed a cow;
I wonder how
She swallowed a cow;
She swallowed the cow to catch the dog,
She swallowed the dog to catch the cat,
She swallowed the cat to catch the bird,
She swallowed the bird to catch the spider,
That wriggled and jiggled and wriggled inside her.
She swallowed the spider to catch the fly,
I wonder why

ORAL DISCOURSE—DISCUSSING AND PRESENTING

She swallowed a fly.
Poor old woman, she's sure to die.

Ther was an old woman who swallowed a horse;
She died, of course!

Traditional American and English

One poem that works well with a chorus and a single voice for inexperienced students is "The Witch's Song" by Lilian Moore.

THE WITCH'S SONG

Hey! Cackle! Hey!
Let's have fun today.
    All shoelaces will have knots.
    No knots will untie.
    Every glass of milk will spill.
    Nothing wet will dry.
    Every pencil point will break.
    And everywhere in town
    Peanut-buttered bread will drop
    Upside down!
Hey! Hey! Hey!
Have a pleasant day!

Lilian Moore[11]

John Ciardi has written a poem that simply cries out for some large-group participation. It is a perfect example of a poem that can be used for choral reading in front of an audience of other children. It allows the audience to participate in the reading by filling in the missing words.

SUMMER SONG

By the sand between my toes,
By the waves behind my ears,
By the sunburn on my nose,
By the little salty tears
That make rainbows in the sun
When I squeeze my eyes and run,
By the way the seagulls screech,
Guess where I am? At the. . . .!
By the way the children shout
Guess what happened? School is. . . .!
By the way I sing this song
Guess if summer lasts too long:
You must answer Right or. . . .!

John Ciardi[12]

Sound effects, such as a group saying *"Shhhh"* or whispering *Whisper, whisper, whisper,* can be used effectively with choral speaking as a kind of counterpoint to the words. "Whispers" works well with this interpretation.

WHISPERS

Whispers
    tickle through your ear
    telling things you like to hear.
Whispers
    are as soft as skin
    letting little words curl in.
Whispers
    come so they can blow
    secrets others never know.

Myra Cohn Livingston[13]

With older children, the poetry you read to them and the poetry they select to read chorally may be considerably more complex. You might use one of the following poems as an introduction and then let them choose and arrange the readings themselves. The process of doing choral reading or speaking is important; the end result is really not important as long as it pleases the children. The last two lines of each stanza of "This Old Hammer" make it especially appealing for choral reading.

THIS OLD HAMMER

This old hammer
Shine like silver,
Shine like gold, boys,
Shine like gold.

Well don't you hear that
Hammer ringing?
Drivin' in steel, boys,
Drivin' in steel.

Can't find a hammer
On this old mountain.
Rings like mine, boys,
Rings like mine.

I've been working
On this old mountain
Seven long years, boys,
Seven long years.

I'm going back to
Swannanoa Town-o,

That's my home, boys,
That's my home.

Take this hammer,
Give it to the captain,
Tell him I'm gone, boys,
Tell him I'm gone.

Traditional American[14]

Another poem with sound appeal is "The Ballad of Red Fox."

THE BALLAD OF RED FOX

Yellow sun yellow
Sun yellow sun,
When, oh, when
Will red fox run?

When the hollow horn shall sound,
When the hunter lifts his gun
And liberates the wicked hound,
Then, oh, then shall red fox run.

Yellow sun yellow
Sun yellow sun,
Where, oh, where
Will red fox run?

Through meadows hot as sulphur,
Through forests cool as clay,
Through hedges crisp as morning
And grasses limp as day.

Yellow sky yellow
Sky yellow sky,
How, oh, how
Will red fox die?

With a bullet in his belly,
A dagger in his eye,
And blood upon his red red brush
Shall red fox die.

Melvin Walker La Follette[15]

Choral reading or speaking is one way of enhancing students' responses to poetry, and this should be the prime concern of the teacher. A rich exposure to poetry of all kinds serves as a basis for enjoyment. However, today's children seem particularly fond of some of the newer poetry that uses modern language and content. The real learning and enjoyment in choral activities depend upon the children being involved in interpreting the poem through using low and high voices, soft and loud passages, and unison speaking contrasted with solo voices. The whole effect may not be as polished as one arranged by the teacher, but the learning involved will be considerably greater.

Other Oral Language Skills

Some of the other oral skills that may become part of the classroom activities are particularly appropriate for older students. These skills include conducting meetings or group discussions, using simple parliamentary procedures, making oral reviews of movies or television programs, and interviewing others. Many of them can be easily integrated with other content areas, but sometime during the middle grades the children should have experiences with each.

SUMMARY

Numerous oral skills need to be developed during students' years in elementary and middle grades. Many of these are used in various content areas as children discuss conflicting views on social problems, present information from their experiments in earth sciences, or simply discuss a new television program. We all spend so much of our time listening and talking, that students need to become proficient in using oral language effectively.

PRELIMINARY LEARNING ACTIVITIES

1. Suggest three questions for each of the following situations that you believe would generate responses from children in a sharing discussion.
   (a) Lee has brought several coins from her collection of early American money.
   (b) Tommy has brought his collection of ten arrowheads to share.
   (c) Kim has a new ship model of the *Mayflower*.
   (Some possible questions that might be asked are included at the end of this section. Check your questions to see what the answer might be. If they can be answered in a few words, try again.)
2. Select a book or short story appropriate for the grade you expect to teach and write down three or four questions that you would use to extend students' responses to it.
3. Read three to five children's trade books and suggest a different way to share each through writing, talking, drama, or art. (You may refer to the section "Sharing Books.")
4. Find a group of people and try doing some choral reading yourself. Use one of the poems from this text that has suggestions for ways to read it, and then select another of your own choosing.
5. Collect ten to fifteen poems that would be suitable for choral reading for the grade and age level with which you want to work. Print or type these on cards.

PARTICIPATION ACTIVITIES

1. Record several students participating in a discussion, using Figure 8-2 on page 161.
2. Prepare and tell a story to a small group of children. You might select a folktale or another story you particularly like.
3. Conduct a discussion with a group of students on some experience they have had. Get someone else to record or check off your use of strategies to encourage interaction and participation. If you prefer, you could tape-record the discussion and do your own analysis later. Look at the questions you ask, the time intervals left before going on to something new, and so on.

Answers to Preliminary Learning Experience, Activity 1

(a) *Lee's coin collection:*
    What things make particular coins especially valuable?
    What makes coins fun to collect?
    Which three coins are the most interesting and why?
(b) *Tommy's arrowhead collection:*
    How can you tell a real arrowhead from a piece of rock that is accidentally shaped with sharp edges?
    Where are the best places for finding arrowheads?
    If prehistoric hunters had lived in an area where there were no rocks, what might they have used for spear or arrow tips?
(c) *Kim's model of the Mayflower:*
    How would the *Mayflower* compare with ocean ships today?
    How do you go about putting a model ship like this together?
    What things would you change if you were designing models?

REFERENCE NOTES

[1]Richard Chase. *The Jack Tales* (Berkeley Williams, Jr., illustr.) Boston: Houghton Mifflin, 1943, 1971.

[2]Roger Cunningham. "Developing Question-Asking," in *Developing Teacher Competencies* (James Weigand, ed.). Englewood Cliffs, N.J.: Prentice-Hall, 1971.

[3]Lee Banton. "The Question: How to Produce Mentally Dull Students and Look Good Doing It," *Virginia Journal of Education*, October 1977, pp. 13–15.

[4]Robert A. Lucking. "A Study of the Effects of a Hierarchically-Ordered Questioning Technique on Adolescents' Responses to Short Stories," *Research in Teaching of English*, vol. 10, no. 3, Winter 1976, pp. 269–276.

[5]William Anderson and Patrick Groff. *A New Look at Children's Literature.* Belmont, Calif.: Wadsworth, 1972, pp. 229–230.

[6]Thomas F. Crane. *Italian Popular Tales.* Boston: Houghton Mifflin, 1885, p. 348.

[7]Laurits Bodker, Christina Hale, and G. D'Aronco, eds. *European Folk Tales.* Hatboro, Pa.: Folklore Associates, 1963, p. 197.

[8]Jacques Barchilon and Henry Pettit. *The Authentic Mother Goose Fairy Tales and Nursery Rhymes.* Denver: Alan Swallow, 1960, p. 59.

[9]Josephine Bouton, comp. "One, Two," *Poems for the Children's Hour.* Garden City, N.Y.: Garden City, 1927, p. 3.

[10]Traditional American. "There Was an Old Woman," in *Junior Voices, The First Book* (Geoffrey Summerfield, ed.). London: Penguin, 1970, p. 24.

[11]Lilian Moore. "The Witch's Ride," in *See My Lovely Poison Ivy*. New York: Atheneum, 1975.

[12]John Ciardi. "Summer Song," *The Man Who Sang the Sillies*. Philadelphia: Lippincott, 1961.

[13]Myra Cohn Livingston. "Whispers," in *Whispers and Other Poems*. New York: Harcourt, Brace, and World, 1958.

[14]Traditional. "This Old Hammer," in *Junior Voices, The First Book*. (Geoffrey Summerfield, ed.). London: Penguin, 1970, p. 42.

[15]Melvin Walker La Follette. "The Ballad of Red Fox," in *Junior Voices, The Second Book* (Geoffrey Summerfield, ed.). London: Penguin, 1970, p. 55.

CHAPTER NINE

Dramatic Expression

PREVIEW QUESTIONS

1 Why is dramatic expression preferable to doing a play?
2 How can a teacher get students involved in dramatic activities?
3 How do you select or plan motivational activities as well as major dramatic activities to extend students' understanding of concepts or of literary works?
4 In what ways can dramatic expression be evaluated?

A group of seventh-graders, investigating early coastal Indian life, have begun their study by dramatizing some scenes from Joyce Rockwood's *To Spoil the Sun*.[1] Today different students are exploring how it would be to meet men with light skins who wear peculiar clothing of bright colors and come in "floating townhouses" with great cloths hanging above them. Two warriors go out to greet the "immortals" and get into dugouts to go on to the "townhouse." After they return safely, almost all the warriors go out to visit. But the huge cloths are raised, and only the warriors' empty dugouts are left, floating free upon the water. What has happened? Who were the strange men who came? Will the warriors ever return? This class is using drama to explore possibilities and to recreate and make more vivid one aspect of history.

In the elementary school down the street, a group of third-graders have heard their teacher read *Caleb and Kate* by William Steig.[2] They decide to dramatize the story in pairs, improvising the lines as they go along. In the scene, presented by the first pair of children, Caleb and Kate have an argument.

Caleb: What do you mean I never help you?
Kate: You don't! You're always out hunting and stuff. That's not work. I have to cook and clean and wash all the dishes.
Caleb: You're crazy! I'm the one who does all the work while you just fool around in the house.
Kate: Then go out to the woods! See if I care. I'd be happy without you around.
Caleb: Not as happy as I'd be out of here. (He runs off.)

A second pair of children dramatize the same scene, but their argument is completely different: Kate complains about Caleb's not helping with the dishes. A third pair of children do the scene, arguing about the sale of their old horse.

The lines in these improvised scenes are not memorized or rehearsed. There are no costumes or props except for two yardsticks the seventh-graders used for canoe paddles and an old hat that Caleb throws on as he stalks out the door. There is no audience either, except for some of the other students in the room, who are taking these parts in another scene or in recreating the same scene. The students never perform the "play" for others; they simply enjoy doing their own dramatized version of the story.

The authors of the stories that the children choose to dramatize might well flinch at what has happened to their carefully chosen words, but they could not help reacting favorably to the children's enthusiastic responses to their books. This form of dramatic expression permits students to respond to a book that they love in a most meaningful way. In the enactment of the story, they are developing language skills—listening and speaking—as well as cognitive, affective, and psychomotor skills.

This is dramatic expression, not theater. Drama in the classroom is a way of exploring the world and oneself. It may be based on a story or simply on a situation. Each "performer" will do the same part differently—as he or she sees it, as experience suggests. The *doing* of the play or the scene is the important part. It does not need an audience; in fact, an audience usually inhibits children. It does not require practicing to "get it right," because there is no right way. Sometimes a suggestion of a costume or a prop will help children feel the character, but an old terrycloth towel will do for the wolf's furry back, a paper crown will do for Max as he sails to "where the wild things are," or a yardstick will do for the fishing pole Tom Sawyer uses while rafting downriver. The learning and fun come from participating and not from the applause of an audience. "Theater concerns performances before an audience, whose point of view is included and for whose benefit effects are calculated. Theater is a secondary effect of drama, an outgrowth appropriate only much later, after elementary school."[3]

FORCES ENCOURAGING DRAMATIC EXPRESSION

It is difficult to single out one factor that has changed the educational scene. Although an individual or a group may initiate a new program or a new emphasis, the "climate" must be ready to receive it. The climate was receptive in 1966 (after a period of emphasis on the scientific and the technological) for a more individualistic and humanistic influence. That was the year of the Anglo-American Conference on English Teaching at Dartmouth College, New Hampshire. The British participants had already become deeply involved with drama in the classroom in the process of academic desegregation. This same emphasis on drama existed at international conferences at York, England, in 1971, and in Sydney, Australia, in 1980, where participants from Great Britain, Canada, the United States, and Australia and New Zealand met to continue the dialog on English teaching. Reports from these conferences suggest a number of bases for renewed interest in dramatic expression.

Emphasis on Creativity

As we begin to accept diversity in life-style and values, it becomes more important for students to explore a variety of responses to their environment. In society today there is a wide range of attitudes, opinions, and values; some of these contradict one another. Children must learn to cope with these contradictions and even recognize and communicate their own diversity. They must find what is uniquely personal, what their potential is, and where they stand. Language arts teachers are becoming more interested in imaginative writing—in all areas of written composition—where there is an opportunity for original thought and expression. Dramatic activities in the classroom offer a comparable avenue for original and individual oral expression. Dramatizing offers the possibility of trying out attitudes, roles, and emotions and creating new possibilities for ourselves without real risk.

Emphasis on Oral Modes

School used to be a place for developing reading and writing skills (along with arithmetic) rather than oral skills. Information from the cognitive psychologists clearly suggests that students need to be active in the learning process, that children of elementary school age who are in the preoperational or concrete-operational stages do not learn by merely reading about things, but from doing them and from talking about them. Recent research also indicates such experiences are important for older students in the formal-operational stage. We also know from the language learning process that students need to use language in a variety of ways. Research on the amount of time most adults are involved in oral speaking and listening suggests that writing is not the prime communication channel in terms of functional use. Dramatics offers meaningful practice in both listening and speaking. One must listen to what the other person says in order to respond appropriately. What one says must be clear and meaningful so that someone else can reply. In addition, dramatic expression offers the "intellectual challenge of finding language true to one's subjective experience."[4] The need for developing students' ability to use language orally in an effective way leads directly to increased use of dramatic activities in the classroom.

Interdependence of Language-Based Arts

Language, and especially oral language, is an inseparable part of the entire language arts program. It is the basis for literature, for writing, and for vocabulary and thought development. Literature provides a special way of helping students interact with their surroundings and with others. Through literature they can discover that books offer special satisfaction.

> Part of the satisfaction comes from the knowledge, the information, available through literature. This knowledge is not the same as that on the reference shelf; literature is not factual as an encyclopedia article is factual. . . . Literature is concerned with why things happen, on the motivations of man.[5]

One of the ways of helping students respond more deeply to a piece of literature is through dramatizing it. In that process, the individual child moves one step closer to experiencing life in another time, another place, another situation. In the active oral response to the book, students come closer to its view of reality. They are in on the "doing" and are no longer passive receivers. They use the language of the book and make it their own.

Dramatizing stories or situations is an important factor in developing skill in using written language. Dixon asserts that "the neglect of talk and drama has had disastrous effects on writing."[6] Children write best from their own experience just as adults do. Their direct firsthand experience is limited, and they need additional input. Experiences with drama which place them in new situations are a rich source of material for writing. When they write stories of their own, characterization is richer for having experienced other people's ideas and personalities; setting or environment is more vivid from insight into other situations; plot is better developed from observing the patterns of events.

Language and thought are advanced through dramatizing. Moffett notes that "dramatic interaction [is] . . . the primary vehicle for developing thought and language."[7] Complex cognitive skills are involved in the process of selecting, interpreting, and arranging the material from which the dramatization evolves. Whether the students are working from a piece of literature or from a particular situation, they must choose the relevant and meaningful parts and arrange them so that they are significant. They must select words that carry this significance—words from the book or those directly related to the situation. The more familiar one is with a word and the more importance it assumes, the deeper and richer is its meaning.

These three forces—emphasis on creativity, emphasis on oral modes, and interdependence of the language-based arts—point to the necessity for developing dramatic interaction and expression in elementary classrooms. As we come to know more about how learning occurs, we find more need for active involvement and experience. Participating in dramatizing events, problems, situations, and stories is a uniquely appropriate way of providing this active involvement and experience.

LEVELS OF DRAMATIC EXPRESSION

There are two major levels of drama, the exploratory level and the performance level. In the exploratory level students can examine a variety of roles and possible situations. They can put on high heels or a racing helmet, jump into their car or plane, and zoom off alone or with some friends. At a later stage they can test their courage as they face a hostile band of Martians or join in the gold rush in California as they pan for gold at Sutter's Creek. At this level there is constant interplay between investigating and representing, finding out and trying on. It doesn't matter if someone else is there; there is no real attempt to communicate to anyone outside those participating. There is no sense of audience, no need to communicate with the audience. Exploring ideas and feelings and situations is all-important.

At the performance level in drama the players have gone through the exploring and are now trying to communicate with and to others their sense of the experience. Exact words become more important as they must express ideas and findings; certainly other information must be communicated to the audience so they can know what is happening. The "play" is formalized and structured—rehearsed for effects. The values in it shift from the players to the audience. Only the skilled performers participate. It becomes theater. The discovery and the exploration are over as the play is set. It is no longer a learning process, but has become a demonstration of specific sophisticated communicative skills.

FORMS OF DRAMATIC ACTIVITIES

Although there is no set sequence of dramatic activities that must be followed, there is usually a general progression from simultaneous participation by the whole group, to participation by parts of the group while others wait for their turn and are an "audience," to performance of scenes for the class or some other small audience. Dramatic expression may take one or more of several forms: dramatic play, movement, pantomime, improvisation, readers' theater, and puppetry.

Dramatic Play

Dramatic play is most often seen in the early childhood years either at home or in the nursery school or kindergarten. Opportunities for this kind of experience should be offered to children in the primary grades—particularly in areas where children have had little opportunity for this kind of play. Dramatic play involves playing out situations and taking roles. Children may play doctor, house, grocery store, and so on. It is highly informal and not directed by the teacher, although a teacher may intervene briefly to reinvolve a child or to suggest a possibility that may continue the play. All that is needed is some space in the corner of the room and a few simple props or materials for costumes.

Sometimes dramatic play may originate after the children have heard a story or when the teacher adds some new element to suggest an idea to the children. A few red firefighters' hats may stimulate a whole series of rescue scenes. An old jacket with some braid may get children involved in ships and sailing. Some empty boxes or cans (opened from the bottom) may initiate a series of grocery store scenes. A telephone, a small toy cash register, and an old typewriter are good props to have available. Hats and scarves, an apron or two, a crown, and some old jewelry help children become someone else. Through experiences with dramatic play, children learn to work with others to make the play more fun. They also have an opportunity to explore what roles various adults take and, in a very special sense, how it feels to be that adult.

Movement

This involves developing body-awareness as well as exploring differing ways of moving and expressing ideas through movement. It might be considered the forerunner of pantomime, although it is not as stylized. Children work on rhythm and moving to rhythms. They also learn about moving in various ways such as jumping, rolling, twirling, or gliding. An interesting book that may involve children in movement activities is Wildsmith's *Python's Party*.[8] In this, the python invites all the other animals to his party and suggests a competition to see who can do the cleverest trick. He slithers down a tree, the hyena wobbles along on two round melons, and the elephant comes along to rescue them with his heavy tread.

Poetry, as well as prose, is a good source for experiences with movement. The spaghetti in "A Round" almost demands action as it "wriggles."

A ROUND

Spaghetti,
spaghetti,
heaped in a mound;

spaghetti,
spaghetti,
winds and winds around;

spaghetti,
spaghetti,
twists and turns and bends;

spaghetti,
spaghetti,
hasn't any ends;

spaghetti,
spaghetti,
slips and dips and trips;

spaghetti,
spaghetti,
sloops and droops;

spaghetti,
spaghetti,
comes in groups;

spaghetti,
spaghetti,
no exit can be found. . . .

Eve Merriam[9]

Children can also develop skill in kinesics as they show through body actions and facial expressions various activities or feelings.

Pantomime

Pantomime is an outgrowth of movement, although it is somewhat more formal. It involves postures and facial expression as well as body movement to communicate an idea without using words. Very young children have a great deal of difficulty refraining from using language as well as mime to express themselves, but older children often enjoy the challenge—especially if it can be done in a game situation at first. The class might be divided into small groups, with each group selecting an action (riding a bike, climbing a ladder, and so on) and a way of doing something (quickly, cautiously, intensely, and so on) to pass on to another group. The object of the game is to recognize the action and guess the *-ly* word they are demonstrating.

Books too lend themselves to pantomime. *No Bath Tonight*[10] by Jane Yolen would be perfect for younger children to pantomime. It is an account of Jeremy's week and all his reasons for not taking a bath each night. On Monday he built a fortress in the sand and hurt his foot; on Tuesday while picking berries he sat down in a pricker bush; on Wednesday he fell over home plate and hurt his nose. Each day, he does some new activity and finds a new reason for no bath that night. Children could start with Jeremy's activities of the week and even go on to invent their own reasons for not having a bath.

Improvisation

Improvisation is probably the central activity in dramatic expression for elementary school children. It involves acting out events or situations without using a script and without rehearsing. It is an on-the-spot impromptu version of the events or the situation. Improvisations may be based on a familiar story or simply on a particular situation. Body actions and language are both used to carry meaning.

There may be some planning or discussion before a dramatization, but dramatizations are not planned to the point of becoming set situations. Students are free to use their own language and present their own arguments or reasons. The scenes are not show pieces; they still retain the flexibility and fluidity characteristic of improvisation.

One group of fifth-graders who had been studying ecology did a dramatization of a concept. Their teacher set up the problem: a large manufacturing company has purchased several hundred acres of land in their area and wants to build a factory. Company representatives will meet with interested citizens to discuss the matter. Some children are school board members, some are real estate developers, some represent homeowners' groups, and so on. After choosing roles, the children spent a few days doing some research on the problem; then the town meeting was held. This dramatized scene involved the children in taking a wide variety of community roles as they created the various characters they portrayed. The preparation for the drama involved the children in meaningful research activities. The dramatization itself served as a good evaluation for the teacher in examining the students' knowledge about ecology as it was presented in their arguments for or against building the factory.

Some second-graders dramatized scenes from Sendak's *Where the Wild Things Are*,[11] exploring the reasons for Max's being sent to bed without his supper. The children worked for a few minutes in pairs to figure out what they thought Max might have done to deserve that. One pair had him refuse to take out the garbage, one pair had him break something he wasn't supposed to touch, and another pair had him talk back to his parents.

Eighth-graders studying a unit of Greek mythology dramatized some of the myths they had been working on for their classmates. One group of four improvised Hephaestus, son of Zeus and Hera, who was thrown out of Olympus by Zeus when he interfered with his parents' quarrel. Another group chose Hermes and the time he traded his lyre for Apollo's herd of cattle and magic wand as well. Each group chose a different god or goddess to bring to life.

Readers' Theater

This form of dramatization is most appropriate for older students. In it a piece of writing—a story, poem, or section of a book— is brought to life by the readers. These readers typically use little costuming, scenery, or action as they try to recreate the piece of literature. Preparation for such a dramatization includes extensive discussion and analysis of the literature so that students can interpret the characters and project them to the audience. Coger[12] suggests that what occurs in readers' theater is that the readers share their insights into literature with others.

In a readers' theater presentation, a narrator usually fills in necessary information for those listening. The original piece of literature is turned into a script and carefully rehearsed so that the individuals playing the different characters are comfortable and secure in their interpretation. The audience will probably be the other members of the class, and so the presentation is still rather informal. As in the other types of dramatic activities, the learning occurs during the preparation and practice as students work on how a particular character would have said a special line, why some character behaves the way he or she does, and how to highlight a special part of the script.

Puppets and Masks

Puppets and masks of various kinds are fun for children of all school ages. In the earlier grades, because of their egocentricity, the children working the puppets will sometimes speak as well as the puppets, but this in no way diminishes the fun or the learning for them. In the upper grades the shyer, more self-conscious children may find working with masks or puppets more comfortable. The teacher may want to provide some basic puppets which can be transformed into the characters needed, or the children can actually make the puppets they need. Facial masks can also be used. Another possibility is the "body mask" made from a large sheet of posterboard or a carton with cutouts for the face and arms—like the old-fashioned scenery boards for funny photographs at the beach. In any case, the puppets and masks do not have to be beautiful. A simple cutout figure mounted on a stick or a stuffed paper bag will do as well as a complex papier-mâché creation. A large refrigerator box with a cutout area will do perfectly well as a stage. The students should be involved in the planning and making. This involvement stimulates the learning that comes from puppetry and is more important than having a professional-looking stage or fancy puppets.

INITIATING DRAMATIC EXPRESSION

There are no hard and fast rules to follow that will guarantee success as you begin working with drama, but there are some general guidelines that should help you work effectively. The activities at the end of this chapter also provide specific examples of how to plan classroom drama.

First of all, select stimuli for dramatizing—whether stories or situations—that have appeal for both you and your children. You should be genuinely enthusiastic, for your enthusiasm will be conveyed to your students. Heathcote, who has done extensive work in improvisational drama, speaks of the need to arrest students' attention.[13] She insists that drama should not be watered down; it should not be fairies and flowers prancing around in leotards, but real situations and real problems to solve.

A second guideline is to start small. Begin with something simple, not an improvisation of an epic by the whole class. In the primary grades, this might be some movement to music or very brief improvisations of scenes from a favorite book you have read to your class, or perhaps pantomimes similar to charades of events in the unit of stories they have just finished. In later grades, you might start with improvisations of one or two favorite scenes from a book, or pantomimed actions and feelings described earlier in the section on pantomime, or stick-puppet scenes of the most exciting part of the library book the students have read (instead of a book report). Be sensitive to what the students are comfortable doing, and try to make these early experiences a successful, satisfying contact with drama.

A third guideline is that you should do extensive planning of the dramatization even though what the students do will be spontaneous. Unless you have a great deal of experience with the theater and with dramatization, you need to do some careful planning to make the experience work for your students. You need to consider what arrangement of furniture in the room will be best, what warm-up or motivational activities might prepare them and make them more comfortable, what extra materials you may need such as music, fabric pieces for costumes, paper, sticks and paint for puppets. If you plan to have your students dramatize a story, you should analyze the story carefully for possible scenes, characters, movement patterns, and appropriate motivational techniques. If you are working with the whole class in the story dramatization, consider how you can give each one an opportunity to have a part and participate in the dramatization. Selecting a story with a large cast, adding characters or scenes to stories with small casts, or repeating a scene two or three times with a new cast of characters each time would solve this problem. Although you would not take students through all of this process, you need to do it yourself. Even though they may take a somewhat different direction from what you expected, your plans can be adjusted and modified as you go along. The thinking-through that you experienced while planning will help you adapt to their ideas; when they need direction, you can be confident that you will be able to provide it.

Role Playing

Role-playing familiar experiences is an ideal starting point for young children. It is one way that they have of verbalizing what has happened to them and finding out that some children have shared similar events while others have had different experiences. To the very young, family customs appear to be universal experiences, and at first it will be hard for them to believe that others do

Any dramatization requires careful planning. With the help of their teacher, these students are practicing role playing based on particular situations.

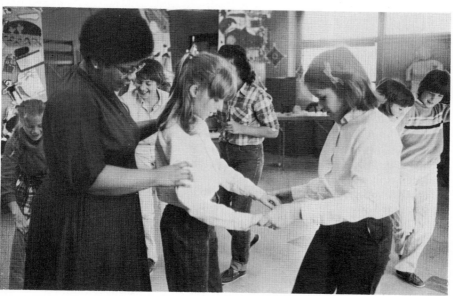

DRAMATIC EXPRESSION

things differently. The role playing may begin with something that just happens in the classroom, or it may evolve from a discussion of a story or a picture.

Some situations which lend themselves to this kind of role playing with young children are celebrating a birthday, going shopping, going out to a restaurant to eat, getting ready for Thanksgiving or Christmas, buying a new pair of shoes, having a new babysitter, meeting someone new who's moved into the neighborhood, and planting a garden. The children should have experienced the situation themselves, and the role playing should result from their familiarity with it. The role playing will probably need to be done in small groups since young children all want to participate at once in the dramatizing. The teacher may guide them by asking questions or proposing variations or complications to extend the dramatization.

With older children the situation for role playing should be somewhat familiar, but it need not evolve from firsthand experience. Some situations that might be appropriate for role playing in these grades could develop from unfinished problem stories or from situations that they might face some time. The role playing could be such things as returning merchandise to a store, working in an office, selling products door to door, taking a job as a babysitter, taking a driver's license examination, or flying in a plane during an emergency. The role playing will need some discussion of the possible situation first, and again the teacher may intervene to guide the experience or extend it. There should be some problem involved in the role playing that needs resolution and that might be resolved in several ways. For example, if the group were doing something about a babysitting job, perhaps one of the children gets very ill or there are warnings of a tornado on the television or some friends drop in for a visit and break something. This is no time for preaching morals; it is a time for students to discover what alternatives there are in a situation and what the consequences of taking a particular alternative are. It is a way of exploring danger and reality in a safe situation.

Dramatizing Literature

Dramatizing stories is an exciting way to develop children's skill in exploring new ideas and at the same time reinforce and enhance the impact of a particular book or story. The first dramatizations you do may just be of one scene in the story that particularly interests your class, or some movement or pantomime related to something in the book. Think back through the general guidelines given at the beginning of this section on initiating dramatic expression and select something that appeals to both you and your class, start with something small, and do some extensive planning before you start to work with the children.

When you do get ready to dramatize the whole story, you still will need to do some motivational or warm-up experiences before the children are involved enough to lose themselves in the dramatization. These warm-up activities may involve heightening the children's awareness of the sensory environment through discussion: *Close your eyes. You are sitting on the bridge the three billy goats will cross. Reach down and feel the bridge. What is it like?* (wood, concrete, cool in the shade, warm in the sun). *What things can you hear?* (water running over the stones, boughs of trees scraping the bridge railings, a bullfrog down below). *What things can you smell?* (sweet grasses in the field nearby, apple blossoms, clover). It might involve pantomiming actions that will come in the dramatization or ones related to those in the story: *Without saying anything, see if you can be the smallest goat. How would you walk? How would you run? Now be the biggest billy goat! You are big and heavy. Your feet really clomp down.* The warm-up activities might include some dialog—or perhaps monolog. *Be the troll. Say what you would to the littlest billy goat.* Then move into pairs and one partner take the troll's part and one take the smallest billy goat gruff. *Now switch parts. The one who was the billy goat is now the troll, and the troll is now the biggest billy goat. Say what you think they should say.* These warm-up activities might involve moving to music or to a particular rhythm, developing the sensory environment, pantomime, monolog, or working on dialog with a partner. The extensiveness of the warm-up depends on the particular group of students and how easily they become involved in the dramatization. The warm-up activities need to be carefully thought out by you, the teacher, so that they build the children's self-confidence and prepare them for participation in the story dramatization itself.

Dramatizing Concepts

Rather than building a dramatization on a familiar story, you may choose to dramatize an idea within a situational context. One illustration of this was mentioned earlier in the chapter in which a class dramatized a problem in ecology. This kind of dramatization correlates very well with social studies.

A series of these dramatizations involving the whole class or a group within the class may explore universal themes. "Daring to Face the Unknown" might involve a dramatization of a Roman centurian off to face the fierce Pictish tribes in Great Britain or Columbus on his first voyage to America or a pioneer family crossing the United States to California in a covered wagon. "Decisions" might range from a contemporary of Louis XIV not wanting to participate in revolutionary activities, to Robert E. Lee resigning his commission in the U.S. Army to fight with the Virginia Militia, to someone in the late 1960s deciding not to accept his draft notice during the Vietnamese fighting.

The dramatization of the concept should present some sort of conflict that must be resolved. Although the children may need to search out some information on the topic, their speeches or lines are not planned. And if the dramatization is repeated with another group of children, a different argument may be presented. A minor character one time may become a major character another time. The drama may or may not be repeated depending upon the children's interest and enthusiasm.

As an early experience with drama, this kind of dramatization may be a bit overwhelming for both students and teachers. For most teachers it is more successful after the children have had some other experiences with dramatic expression of various kinds and subsequently feel more comfortable with the less structured situation.

CRITERIA FOR DRAMATIC EXPRESSION

There are three major criteria for dramatic expression that the teacher can use as a general guideline in working with students: *concentration, interchange,* and *involvement.* These are key elements in the success of a dramatic experience.

Concentration

Students must be able to stay within the confines of the drama and not break out of the situation. They should feel as though the situation is real and they are the actual characters being portrayed. They need to persist in continuing the dramatic experience. Concentration implies an intensification of feeling and a focus on the task at hand. The following questions may help you evaluate their concentration:

Are the students reacting to the drama as if it were real?
Can they continue the dramatization and extend it beyond a superficial level?
Are they beyond the point where minor distractions will interfere with the
    drama?

You will never be successful with drama if you permit someone to interfere with another student's interpretation of a role or situation. Laughing at someone will not only affect that person but also make the others reluctant to participate if they know they may be ridiculed. When this first happens, the teacher must firmly, but not punitively, stop the laughter.

Interchange

Drama cannot be a solitary experience. Dramatic expression in the classroom involves many students—whether a whole class or just a group of children. The participants in the drama must respond to each other in a meaningful way. This means that cooperation is one of the key concerns of the teacher. As the students interact with each other, they participate mutually in the experience. In the interchange process, they come to explore how they react in certain situations and how they respond to others. The verbalizing that goes on in the drama absolutely requires good listening and speaking skills. Since there is no script, there is nothing to fall back on. One must express ideas clearly and listen to what others say. It is at this point that listening and speaking skills develop. To evaluate interchange, these questions may assist you:

Are students working together in the dramatization, or is it one idea versus
    another?
Do the students listen to others and respond to what they have said?
Does one student pick up on what another has said and repeat or extend the
    idea?

The teacher may choose to intervene in a dramatization to clue students into an effective idea. This may be done by taking a role within the dramatization for a moment, or simply by making a quick suggestion. It is also possible to wait until the scene is finished, and then discuss a variety of ideas. After this, the students may even decide to exchange parts and replay the scene.

Involvement

This is probably the keystone of all experiences with dramatic expression. If students are not really involved and committed to what they are doing, the whole experience becomes unreal. Dramatizing should provide a real learning experience for students. Dramatizing should not be just playing at being someone; it should be actually becoming that person. Of course it should be a pleasurable experience, but it should be more than just fun. Professional actors cannot really become this involved in a performance, because they must be concerned about conveying feelings to the audience. Participants in classroom dramatizations do not have to worry about conveying feelings to an audience. The drama is done for their sake, not for someone else's sake. These questions should help you evaluate children's involvement:

Do you see changes which fit the character each student is playing, or do the students retain their own personality and way of doing things?
Is there the quality of intensity, of becoming someone else, present during the dramatization?

If you continually find the quality of involvement lacking in the students' dramatic expression, it may be that the situation they're dramatizing does not seem right for them. Perhaps you are choosing stories or situations that are too superficial. It may also be that a particular group needs more motivational or warm-up activities before getting into the drama. Go back to basics and start doing some shorter, simpler dramatizations. Perhaps adding some costuming or props will help children become more involved. Try a different time of day or try working in smaller groups. Like so many other worthwhile educational experiences, dramatic expression is not easy and there is no simple formula for success.

SKILLS DEVELOPED IN DRAMATICS

Although dramatizing stories or concepts is usually an enjoyable activity for children, this is not the primary reason for including dramatics in the language arts program in elementary schools. Drama has a potential for developing language ability that is not paralleled by any other single language arts activity. It offers possibilities for developing more general skills in the cognitive, affective, and psychomotor domains that few other activities possess. It is also an especially fine way to integrate the language arts with each other and with content areas.

Language Skills

One of the two main implications for teaching coming from the psycholinguistic theory of how children develop language is that they need to use language in a variety of ways. Dramatizing stories or situations calls for just this kind of language use. The participants must find language that is true to the character and to the situation they are playing. Through playing a variety of roles, students should experience the language that a variety of people would use. Their language in the dramatization becomes a creative oral composition. Even when the situation being dramatized comes from a story or book that they have heard or read, the language that they use in the dramatization is not taken verbatim from the original; they take the idea of what happened and create the language to fit it. Few stories actually require memorization of particular lines; and these lines should be chosen by the students rather than by the teacher. One student teacher whose group was dramatizing the "Three Billy Goats Gruff" tried and tried to get the child playing the troll to say, "I'm going to gobble you up!" He finally was able to repeat the line and the dramatization started. When the moment actually came, he shouted out in a frightening voice, "Hey, man, I'm gonna eat you up!" It was so right for him and for the rest of the children, and they were so involved in the dramatization that the student teacher just smiled to herself. When a situation arises that children think requires the exact language of the original story, they either will have it down pat or will ask for it. One specific case where this happens is in dramatizing the "Three Little Pigs." The children want to say, "I'll huff and I'll puff and I'll blow your house down!"

Vocabulary development is another area of language that is increased through drama. In story dramatization there is a double occasion for this: the vocabulary presented through the story or book itself and the vocabulary used in the dramatization. Students in drama feel the need to express just the right shade of meaning in the words they use. Thus, new words may be presented in the story in a meaningful context, and these words or others may be used in the later dramatization. Meeting words in a meaningful context and then having an opportunity to use them immediately is an extremely effective way of building vocabulary.

The nonverbal elements of communication are also developed in drama as we use body movement, gestures, and space to develop the characters. *How can you show that Caleb and Kate are really angry with each other? How close would they stand when arguing? How could Caleb show that he was turned into a dog—without barking? When Caleb comes back home (as a dog), how does he try to let Kate know? How close would he stand to her then? How would the robbers move about their house at night?*

All these elements of language are developed through dramatization. They are the expressive part of oral language. The corresponding receptive part—listening—is also well developed through dramatization. Students need to listen to each other in the dramatization in order to respond meaningfully to each other. They need to extend the ideas or refute the arguments presented by others. In story dramatization, they also need to listen carefully to the story to be able to work with it later. Thus, the whole range of oral language skills is represented in dramatic experiences.

Other Skills

Knowledge or cognition can also be developed through dramatizations as students demonstrate their knowledge at various levels of complexity. Abstract ideas can be shown in a specific context, and students can pull together ideas to form a unique communication. Drama is also a vehicle for exploring affective components. Drama may influence students in their interests, attitudes, and values as well as develop appreciations. Within the framework of a dramatization, students can explore how they feel about various ideas and personalities and how others feel. By playing a scene several different ways, they can explore alternative emotional responses. They can see the consequences of certain behaviors as they take on various roles. Psychomotor skills are also developed through dramatization as children respond to music or rhythm and other sensory stimulation and relate their actions to the sensory stimuli in performing the physical movements.

Creative activities such as role playing and dramatic play are very important in preparing children for the academic work of school. Beaven says,

> Apparently, talk alone is not enough to help children organize their concepts and develop their language. They need a structuring activity such as building, creative art and movement, or dramatic play into which they can cast their impressions of the world. A wide variety of studies indicates that one-to-one adult-child play interactions, story-telling, and sociodramatic play using the manipulation of objects, are all good ways to foster growth of language and thought in children.[14]

SUMMARY

An understanding of the skills—language skills of oral speaking and composing, vocabulary development, language structure development, and listening as well as other cognitive, affective, and psychomotor skills—that are developed through early and continuing experiences with dramatic expression seems to show clearly that dramatizing is more than just fun. It offers opportunities for developing children's abilities in a multitude of ways. Every teacher at every level of elementary and middle school should consider dramatic expression a key area of the language arts. It is a connecting point between language and literature and also serves as a basis for composition.

PRELIMINARY LEARNING ACTIVITIES

I. There are four main kinds of motivational or warm-up exercises which often help children get into the mood of the situation or story that they are going to improvise. You will probably not want to use all four kinds each time you do some improvisation, but might use each of the four kinds at some time or other. These four kinds of motivational exercises are sensory exploration, movement to music, pantomime, and imaginary situations.

Below are examples of each kind of warm-up or motivational exercise related to a particular topic. Look at these carefully and then try to think of examples of your own on a second topic.

Downtown in the City

The following warm-ups are related to a topic of being in the center of a large city. They might be done before improvising a story that takes place in the city or before improvising a problem dealing with living in a city.

1. *Sensory* Sensory exercises try to help children get a sense of the physical environment the drama will explore through discussing the various senses.

   Sight   What buildings do you see?
                  What other things? (buses, taxis, crowds of people) Any more?
                  (a park, pigeons)

Smell	Close your eyes and tell me what you can smell in the city. (fumes from cars, smog) What good smells? (someone selling candied apples)
Taste	What can you taste? (bubble gum from a machine, hot dogs)
Touch	Sit down on that low wall near the building. What does it feel like? Hot or cold? Rough or smooth? Rub your foot on the ground below. What's there?
Hearing	What can you hear in the city? (horns, people's feet, pigeons cooing, sirens, the whistle of a police officer)

2. *Movement to music* This kind of warm-up works on two things at the same time: setting the mood of the story or situation and working on rhythmic movement.
   (a) You walk across the street—wait at the corner for the light to change—now quickly cross the other way. Walk along with the crowd; stop to look in a store window.
   (b) Now you are an old man with a cane walking up to the corner.
   (c) This time you are a college student on the way to meet your date.
   (d) Finally you are a mother with a young child who has been downtown shopping for three hours—Wow! Do your feet hurt!

3. *Pantomime* Pantomime may be done simultaneously so that all the children are pantomiming the same thing at the same time. In doing this the children may show their different reactions to the situation without the pressure of an audience watching. This motivational exercise—like any of the others—may be used alone as a dramatic activity or as a warm-up for something else. Pantomimes may also be done with small groups and, therefore, with some audience as the children appear to be comfortable with it.
   (a) Simultaneous: a police officer directing traffic on a busy corner where there is no traffic light; someone walking a dog on a leash through the crowded streets
   (b) Small groups: trying to get a taxi to stop for you; trying to get bus fare out of your pocket while your arms are loaded with sacks; a child in the back of an elevator trying to see what floor it is over the heads of the people in front

4. *Imaginary situations* These are very similar to pantomime except that they may involve monologs or dialog. When members of the group are working on simultaneous situations, each member develops a monolog. In small-group situations the dialog is loosely planned and the children would respond to each other.
   (a) Simultaneous: asking directions of people who do not know or will not answer
   (b) Small groups: a shoeshine boy or girl trying to get some customers; riding your bike on a busy city street; having a flat tire on your car while you are in the center lane of traffic.

Now that you have read some examples of things which might be done for each of the four kinds of motivational or warm-up exercises, try to suggest various kinds of warm-ups for an improvised story or scene involving an amusement park.

At an Amusement Park
1. *Sensory*
   sight
   smell
   taste
   touch
   hearing
2. *Movement to music*
   (a) Whole group
   (b) Small groups
3. *Pantomime*
   (a) Simultaneous
   (b) Small groups
4. *Imaginary situations*
   (a) Simultaneous
   (b) Small groups

II. Whatever warm-up activity or main dramatic activity you choose to do, it should be related to the main topic or story you have chosen. It should highlight and enrich the children's experience with the book and their response to it. Supposing that you did not want to do an entire story dramatization of the following two books, what dramatic activities might you do with each that would be particularly appropriate for it? We give some possible activities as an example.
1. For younger children:

   Miss Nelson is Missing! by Harry Allard and James Marshall.[15] Boston: Houghton Mifflin, 1977.

   (a) *Description*   The children in Miss Nelson's room were the worst-behaved class in the whole school. She was *so* nice, but they whispered and giggled and refused to do their lessons. Miss Nelson decided something would have to be done, and the very next day a new teacher appeared wearing an ugly black dress. She put them to work immediately, and they could see she was a real witch. The children really missed Miss Nelson. When it seemed that they would never find her and they would be stuck with Miss Viola Swamp forever, they heard footsteps in the hall and someone said, "Hello, children," in a sweet voice. Miss Nelson noticed a lovely change in her class; and that night when she took off her coat at home and hung it up in the closet (right next to an ugly black dress), she sang a little song.
   (b) *Possible activities*   This story, with its school setting, is full of action. It moves quickly, and there are lots of characters. Two kinds of dramatic activities that would be appropriate are movement and pantomime.
   (1) *Movement.*
       Miss Nelson: Walking into class
                      Trying to get children to listen to story hour

| Miss Swamp: | Assigning homework |
| | Walking around the room |

Children:	When Miss Nelson is the teacher at the beginning
	With Miss Swamp as the teacher
	With Miss Nelson when she comes back

(2) *Pantomime.*

| Miss Swamp: | Coming home after school |
| | Getting up in the morning and getting ready for school |

Children:	At their desks at the beginning of the story
	The first day Miss Swamp appears
	Seeing Detective McSmogg
	Going home after school with Miss Nelson—before
	Going home from school when Miss Swamp was teacher
	Looking for Miss Nelson

2. For older children:

The Eyes of the Amaryllis by Natalie Babbitt.[16] New York: Farrar, Straus & Giroux, 1977

(a) *Description*   Jenny comes to stay with her grandmother Geneva (for whom she is named) while her Gran's broken ankle mends. Her grandfather was captain of a sailing brig, the *Amaryllis,* which carried a likeness of his wife holding an amaryllis as the figurehead. Thirty years before, as Geneva and her son watched, the ship and crew were flung against the rocks in a sudden storm just off the beach and all were lost. Ever since, Gran has searched the beach at high tide looking for a sign. Jenny joins in the search and learns about the mysterious Mr. Seward who also searches for things from the sea. They find their sign, part of the figurehead, and nearly lose it again in the terrible hurricane which almost claims Gran's life too.

(b) *Possible activities*   There is a quality of the supernatural in this, as well as a real sense of character change and development as Jenny grows up, Gran finds her "sign," and Jenny's father confronts the sea again. It seems appropriate to explore some of the changes through imaginary scenes (especially those not in the book) and through pantomime.

(1) *Pantomime.*

Jenny:	Going to the beach for the first time
	Dressing at midnight to go out to search
	Finding the figurehead
	Taking care of Gran during the storm

Gran:	Going out to the edge of the beach with a bad ankle
	Seeing the figurehead Jenny found
	Seeing Mr. Seward at the beach

(2) *Imaginary scenes.*

Mr. Seward and Gran's conversation when he tells her who and what he is

Jenny's mom and dad discussing whether or not to let her stay with
  Gran
Mr. Seward meeting Jenny on the beach the day after the storm

PARTICIPATION ACTIVITIES

1. Choose a book that would be suitable to read to students and plan one or
two dramatic activities as a follow-up. Try your lesson with a small group
of students.
2. Make a list of five to ten books with a summary of each and brief notations
of dramatic activities for each book that you could use with children of the
age you plan to teach.
3. Take one of the books you have chosen above and write out full plans for
dramatizing the entire story. Plan the warm-ups or motivational activities
and the main scenes and characters for each, including your plans for each
person to have a part in the dramatization.

REFERENCE NOTES

[1]Joyce Rockwood. *To Spoil the Sun*. New York: Holt, 1976.
[2]William Steig. *Caleb and Kate*. New York: Farrar, Straus & Giroux, 1977.
[3]James Moffett. "Acting Out." *A Child-Centered Language Arts Curriculum K-6: A Handbook for Teachers*. Boston: Houghton Mifflin, 1968, p. 35.
[4]Benjamin DeMott. *Drama in the English Classroom* (Douglas Barnes, ed.). Champaign, Ill.: National Council of Teachers of English, 1967.
[5]J. N. Hook, Paul H. Jacobs, and Raymond D. Crisp. *What Every English Teacher Should Know*. Champaign, Ill.: National Council of Teachers of English, 1970, pp. 39–40.
[6]John Dixon. *Growth through English*. Reading, England: National Association of Teachers of English, 1967.
[7]James Moffett. *Drama: What Is Happening*. Champaign, Ill.: National Council of Teachers of English, 1967.
[8]Brian Wildsmith. *Python's Party*. New York: Franklin Watts, 1975.
[9]Eve Merriam. "A Round," *Finding a Poem*. New York: Atheneum, 1970.
[10]Jane Yolen. *No Bath Tonight* (Nancy Winslow Parker, illustr.). New York: Thomas Y. Crowell, 1978.
[11]Maurice Sendak. *Where the Wild Things Are*. New York: Harper & Row, 1963.
[12]Leslie I. Coger. "Staging Literature with Minimal Props for Maximal Meaning," *Scholastic Teacher*, October 1971, pp. 24–25.
[13]Dorothy Heathcote. *Three Looms Waiting*. Time-Life Films.
[14]Mary Beaven. "Learning through Inquiry, Discovery, and Play," in *Discovering Language with Children* (Gay Su Pinnell, ed.). Urbana, Ill.: National Council of Teachers of English, 1980, pp. 15–16.
[15]Harry Allard and James Marshall. *Miss Nelson is Missing!* Boston: Houghton Mifflin, 1977.
[16]Natalie Babbitt. *The Eyes of the Amaryllis*. New York: Farrar, Straus & Giroux, 1977.

CHAPTER TEN

Written Discourse— Self-Expression and Communication

PREVIEW QUESTIONS

1 How do you determine whether a piece of writing is done primarily for self-expression or for communication, and does it matter what the purpose is?

2 What preparation for writing should the teacher make?

3 How can children's writing be shared with other children and with adults?

4 What components make up a sequential program of composition?

5 How should children's writing be evaluated so that it promotes further skill development?

Although we often think only of stories and poems when we think of imaginative writing, all written composition involves the imagination. In composing stories or poems writers try to express their ideas and experiences in a unique and highly personal way. A well-written report or letter, however, also requires some of the same elements of imagination and creativity. Evidence of this is shown in the following story, note, and poem, which were composed by elementary school children.

IF I WERE A STAR

If I were a star I would go to the moon or Venus or Mars and have a good time. But if I want to go to the sun, I would have to get a lot of sleep. But I do not want to — not me, not me. But I am not a star, so that's that!

February 20

Dear Mom and Dad,
    Thank you for the nice valentine card you gave me. I liked it. It's just like me, especially when it says giggly. I love you and thanks for being my valentine.
Love,

BIRDS

Birds fly while I try
To learn and read
Birds are show-offs!

PURPOSES OF WRITING

Many adults have unpleasant memories of their own writing experiences in elementary school. Maybe you can remember a few. On the first day of school, you could count on writing about "My Summer Vacation." You could also be sure the teacher would red-pencil any spelling or punctuation errors. You probably learned to dislike writing instead of finding it to be a way of communicating your ideas or expanding your imagination. Today's teachers need to avoid perpetuating unpleasant and unproductive writing experiences.

   The purpose of writing determines the ways that the teacher stimulates students to write and the kind of response that the student gets back. The authors of *They All Want to Write* suggest that writing serves at least two needs for the writer and the audience: first, that of artistic self-expression and, second, the communication of functional ideas.[1] The first function is personal, individual, imaginative, and highly perishable and is best kept alive by allowing complete freedom to experiment and complete acceptance of the piece regardless of its nature. The second function is utilitarian, realistic, or intellectual, and needs the discipline of correct mechanics to be socially acceptable. Although a writer should observe certain conventions of spelling and punctuation as a courtesy to the reader, the teacher must realize that much ego involvement exists in communicative writing; and that it, too, must be handled very sensitively. When a child decides to share some of his or her expressive writing with others, it may be revised to meet conventions of writing. This should be the writer's decision with the teacher helping as an editor in an individual conference.

INDIVIDUALIZING WRITING EXPERIENCES

Just as children vary in their ability to read, they also vary both in their ability to write and in the experiences they have had to write about. An individual child may write easily and fluently one day, but spend much time thinking and experimenting the next day before starting to write. This indicates that the teacher should provide a multitude of experiences and stimuli from which children may choose, as well as the opportunity to go off in some independent direction in writing. It also means there should be some flexibility in time for writing.

Teachers may want to provide some group or whole-class experiences to talk about or dramatize before writing, but they should also be ready to make suggestions and stimulate independent thinking in individual conferences with students. A writing center somewhere in a quiet corner of the room with plenty of paper and sharpened pencils, a good dictionary, a thesaurus, and some suggestions or questions to provoke thinking may aid in developing writing.

Writing should be directed primarily by the student rather than by the teacher. Topics that present a problem, challenge the imagination, and are particularly interesting lead a child to become a writer. Children need to learn how to express things in their own way, rather than in their teacher's way. They require reactions to their efforts, and these should come from other students as well as from the teacher. Too much composition work is done with the teacher as the only reader. In real life almost no one would take the time and effort that children expend to write something for only one other person to read. Children, as well as adults, must write for a real audience and get some kind of response from that audience.

Children do best when they experiment with their own ideas and are not confined by an assigned topic. One week they may want to write several things, and the next week they may not be in the mood to write much. Flexibility to pursue writing in these ways is basic to the writing program suggested in this chapter. Flexibility, however, should not be interpreted as the right to choose never to write.

Writing is such a complex task that composition must be taught just as its complementary mode, reading. Composing or writing involves getting thoughts on paper for the writer or someone else to read later. It is difficult to convey in writing exactly what you want to say without any of the verbal and gestural cues used in speech. Yet we probably give very little instruction to school children in how to express their ideas or how to communicate in writing with others. This chapter explores various activities to help children start writing and information on teaching strategies to improve children's writing.

SOME RESEARCH ON WRITING

Research studies in imaginative or creative story writing are somewhat limited in both number and scope. The following reported studies correspond with authoritative opinion and theoretical views on stimulating children's stories or compositions. General trends in research, theory, or opinion can indicate procedures that are helpful for the individual teacher to follow.

A major study in stimulating writing at the elementary school level was conducted by Carlson,[2] who sought to determine if special materials (as opposed to assigned topics) would provoke more original stories from fourth-, fifth-, and sixth-graders involved in the study. The children in the experimental group, who had the special stimulus materials, wrote longer and more original compositions and used a more versatile vocabulary than the children in the control group, who were writing on assigned topics. The research indicates that books, pictures, records, and toys appear to be better stimuli for writing than a single title.

The view expressed by Holbrook[3] is that actual objects, photographs, and news items are less likely to prompt "involved" creativity because they have too little unconscious content and symbolic quality. He contends that the examples that prompt creative work should be creatively symbolic in themselves—that is, pieces of music, poems, paintings, stories—rather than real objects or accounts of real events.

Research data on elementary school children which examine frequent practice in writing and composition quality are not available, but two experimental studies explored this relationship using junior high school and senior high school subjects. Both Burton and Arnold's study[4] and McColly and Remstad's study[5] found that more frequent experiences in themselves did not improve the children's writing, but that functional instruction improves composition. Although we cannot apply these findings directly to elementary school children, they suggest that writing and more writing without instruction and positive feedback in the way of suggestions is of doubtful value. What is needed is a carefully planned program of instruction.

THE WRITING PROGRAM: PHILOSOPHY AND PLANNING

Any plan should be based on a sound philosophy about composition. Therefore, in developing and organizing writing experiences for students, consider the following philosophical statements. They are based on theory, research, and the experiences of teachers. And they also reflect the thinking of those who have been involved in the Bay Area Writing Projects. These nationally recognized projects grew out of a "deep concern that inadequate attention had been focused on the need to teach young children to write."[6] (The Instructional Laboratory at the University of California, Berkeley, acting as a link between expertise of the university and the needs of public schools, has been the facilitating unit for the Bay Area Writing Projects.)

Surround the act of writing with talk.
The quality of the preparation for the act of writing is decisive in determining the quality of the result.
People write better by rewriting. The process of rewriting may involve several drafts of a composition.
Students should engage in postwriting activities. Besides rewriting, students should share, appreciate, and evaluate each other's work.

The teacher's response to a student's writing should be swift—immediate, if possible.

Student-teacher conferences that focus on meaning produce improved writing. Conferences should occur regularly.

The teacher's response should make sense to the student; comments such as *good organization* or *awkward* are of little value to students.

Different intensities of grading do not significantly affect the quality of students' writing.

Liberate writing from the confines of the "reading period" and the "language arts period"; let writing span the curriculum.

Reading and the study of written prose have a positive influence on the quality of student writing.

Sentence-combining exercises, as an approach to composition, can increase sentence maturity (refer to Chapter 6).

Allow the classroom to be a laboratory for experimentation with language. Try to design your classroom for interaction among students (refer to Chapter 1).

Ideas grow out of specifics. First teach students to write about specifics; then teach them to write about abstractions as their ability to abstract increases.

Mere writing does not teach writing; the act of writing alone and increasing the number of writing opportunities fail to bring significant improvement in writing skill. Less writing in conjunction with better teaching of writing will produce measurably superior results.

Teachers should, at least occasionally, write assignments along with students. Students should see their teachers' writing.[7]

MOTIVATING WRITING

Early Writing

Young children are normally self-motivated to experiment with print. They may scribble marks on a page or drawing and then attempt to tell their written message to a nearby adult. This behavior indicates that the child is aware that written signs are intended to communicate meaning. Marie Clay,[8] in her book *What Did I Write*, discusses young children's development and understanding of print. If teachers observe early writing closely, they will notice that during one stage of development children repeat patterns. These may be repeated marks, letters, or words. Clay, referring to this as the "recurring principle," suggests that "repeating a word produces a long statement of which one must be proud."[9] It shows a sense of accomplishment and learning. Figure 10-1 is an example.

"Children turn letters around, decorate them, and evolve new signs as they explore the limits within which a sign can vary."[10] Common examples of this may be seen as part of children's drawings. As young children progress in their knowledge and understanding of print, they begin to develop and use invented spellings, and many times they display these on their drawings. Clay says, "When children discover that words are built up out of signs they know, they can invent words from signs they know."[11]

Figure 10-1 Repetitions in early writing.

Teachers of young children should make a point of observing the writing that these young students initiate themselves. Much can be learned about a child's concept of print and writing development through such observations. And this knowledge may be used effectively to extend a child's learning and growth in writing.

Two major studies have begun to examine the writing processes in younger students. King and Rentel have a NIE (National Institute of Education) grant and are examining the very beginning stages of writing, particularly the link to oral language, the organizational patterns of story structure, the role of cohesion in generating texts, and the role of social-linguistic contexts.[12] The other study of children's early writing is being conducted by Graves.[13] His work and that of his colleagues have already indicated that young children can be successful writers in a workshop situation where they share their writing with each other and learn mechanics of writing as they find them necessary.

Dictated Writing

The very earliest experiences with composition should serve two purposes: communicating the idea and helping children realize that what they say may be written down for others to read. This means that the teacher, an adult, or an older child will print what children want to say—perhaps about a picture they have created or something they have made. It is important to transcribe exactly what a child says—the words and word order—using conventional spelling. From dictating titles or captions, the next step would be to dictate short stories. As the children begin to print, they may want to copy part of the message themselves. As the students become more capable of writing on their own, they may go on to writing stories by themselves or with a friend. When writing in pairs, the children may decide to do the writing completely by themselves, or they may decide together on their ideas and dictate the story to someone else.

Dictation, especially in the early stages of writing, is necessary because children just learning the mechanics of writing are not physically capable of getting down their myriad ideas. Dictation, however, should not be limited to the primary grades. There are many older children whose ideas run far ahead of their skill in putting them down on paper. They might choose to compose a group story and share the writing chore just as they have shared the composing. Here, too, is the possibility of using an adult to write for them or tape-recording the story for later transcription.

One primary teacher initiated dictated compositions by asking the students to tell about growing up. After the children had dictated their stories, they illustrated them. These stories were bound into a book so that all the class members could read them. Here are three of the dictated stories:

GROWING UP

When I grow up, I want to be a gymnast. I will work very hard when I grow up. I will teach other children to grow up to be just like me. I want to take training. I like the way they move and it is fun and I want to be a pro. The end.

Danielle Russell

GROWING UP

When I grow up, I want to be a ballerina and have a pretty dress. When I go to college I will be a ballerina, because they are pretty. I like it because it is nice. When I have a child, I will show her ballerina things that I do. The end.

Felecia Counkle

ELEPHANT

I would like to be an elephant. An elephant is big. I want to be big. I like peanuts to eat. My brother couldn't beat me up any more if I was an elephant.

Johnny Hall

Encouraging Children to Use Their Experiences

Although children become more capable of writing on their own, they still need ideas to stimulate them. Their writing may be based on a variety of experiences—personal experiences both outside and within school, literature that enriches writing, and other creative modes such as drama, music, and the visual arts.

Children bring a wealth of experiences with them, just as they bring a wealth of language. The one piece of advice given beginning authors is to write about what they know best. This applies to children as well. For primary school children, early experiences with writing should explore further the world they already know. Most young children have gone shopping, been to a party, ridden bicycles, or been to a park or playground—that is to say, what they know best is the world around them. And if you take advantage of this knowledge as one first-grade teacher[14] did, you will have children who want to write. Her students made booklets with titles such as "Me," "My Favorite Toys," "My Favorite Foods," "My Hobbies," and "What I Watch on TV." To make the booklets, the teacher stapled a considerable number of blank pages between covers of colored construction paper. The children were encouraged to make first drafts, revise, or even begin their story again by simply pulling out an unwanted page and writing on the next clean page. When they completed their story, perhaps after several rewritings, they usually illustrated it in some way. After the children had finished several booklets, they could decide which one they wanted "published." The term *published* meant in this instance that they could choose which story they would like to have placed in the classroom library area for other students to read.

Older children will have an even wider range of experiences on which to base their stories. Capitalize on these experiences and encourage children to write about what they know intimately.

Making observations—careful and continued exposure to something interesting—often prompts children's writing. Wright includes two samples of writing from the same child who had had the opportunity to make some careful, close observations of a pet iguana who lived in a cage on his table.[15] The children watched the iguana, photographed it, and then wrote about it. Jon's first writing was:

Creeping
Crawling
Walking down the sandy beach
the green scaly iguana
makes his way
toward the forest.

Several days later, after he thought of the word *stoutly* to describe the iguana's walk, he wrote:

As the iguana walks stoutly
small animals step
from his way.

The input of interesting things, such as animals and plants, and time to ponder ideas, leads to good writing.

Children need to become consciously aware of their senses, and they should be encouraged to observe closely and accurately. Children can become more alert to the subtle contributions made by one sense to another. On a rainy day we are often unaware of how much the sense of smell adds to that of sight; or when we are popping corn, we may be unaware of how our sense of hearing adds to the enjoyment of the smell. Developing more accurate and more sensitive powers of observation and perception contributes to the child's experiences and thus to the process of imaginative writing.

Providing New Experiences

There are also ways to add new experiences or new ways of viewing past events. There are the kinds of experiences that explore things outside the classroom. These may be actual field trips—to the water-treatment plant, to a nearby lake or river, or to a farm—or they may be informal explorations of nearby places such as a new department store, an area of the playground, the neighborhood, or the kitchen in the cafeteria. The new experiences may be objects brought into the classroom to see and touch, or a classroom activity such as making popcorn balls or nut bread, planting seeds, or making pinecone wreaths for candles.

Just having new experiences is not sufficient in itself, as Lane and Kemp[16] point out:

> The teacher will find it hard to provide stimuli for talking and writing . . . but she must seek regularly to do just this. She cannot continue to draw indefinitely on the

capital of the children's haphazard experience of living; she must always feed in new experience to the child, which should be so presented as to affect him deeply and touch him through the life of the senses, the emotions, and the imagination.

In working with sensory stimuli, a teacher is attempting to refine and extend children's awareness of their senses as well as to explore the various senses in imaginative ways. How about darkening the room and then using a floodlight and a revolving color disk shining on an aluminum foil sphere fastened to the ceiling as background and stimulation for writing about space voyages? Add some eerie music, and get out the pencils and paper. A sequence of sounds may also suggest a story. For example, the sounds used for the story below are a door opening, a ripping sound, a police siren, and a scream. Colin Miller used this sequence in the first draft of his story.

THE MURDERING MUMMY

As Joe Wilson returned home he felt that somebody or something was watching him. He opened the door to get another pair of shoes.

As he bent down reaching for his shoes, something knocked him back. He saw that it was a whitish figure. The figure pounced on Joe. There was a sound of a dagger ripping through a man's body.

The next day the police were trying to identify the killer. They only found a piece of white cloth. This kept on happening until one day the thing got shot with a gun.

A policeman heard a scream. It was from a house on the other side of the road. He ran as fast as he could go. The lady was dead. The whitish figure kept on running across the yard. The policeman yelled, "Stop or I'll shoot."

The whitish figure fell. He walked over to the whitish figure. "Omigod," the policeman yelled. "A Mummy!"

The teacher must be careful not to overdo the stimulus or to structure it too tightly. The stimulus should serve as a springboard and not as an enclosure that limits children's creativity. Just saying *Write a story* is not enough. Moffett suggests, "They need definite stimulants and frameworks that prompt the imagination. Their original stories are recombinings of familiar stories in more or less new ways."[17]

Structured comparisons are one way to break through clichés and stimulate the imagination. Two dissimilar things may be compared: *A fire is like a snowstorm because . . .* or, *A paper clip is like a sweet roll because. . . .* Another way of structuring comparisons is suggested in *Making It Strange.*[18] This set of materials is a four-book series of creative writing based on the conscious use of metaphor. One type of question posed is exemplified by the following: *Which weighs more — a cough or a sneeze? Which is louder — a smile or a frown? Which is thinner — day or night? Which is rougher — yellow or purple?*

Giving children an opportunity to be someone else can force them to look at the familiar with unfamiliar eyes. The teacher may start with objects in the room, classroom pets, or various animals. Each child can decide what he or she wants to be. Figure 10-2 shows stories composed by a second-grader (Betsy), a third-grader (Myra), and a fifth-grader (Denise).

I'M A LEAF

I'm a little leaf hanging on the tree all alone. I wish someone else would grow in spring. But everyone else is one the gound. I wish I'd fall, too! But I can't! Why, oh why can't I fall? I'm all different colors—red, yellow, and brown. It's atum now and I still haven't fell! All this time I still want to fall. Wish me luck!

Betsy's first draft

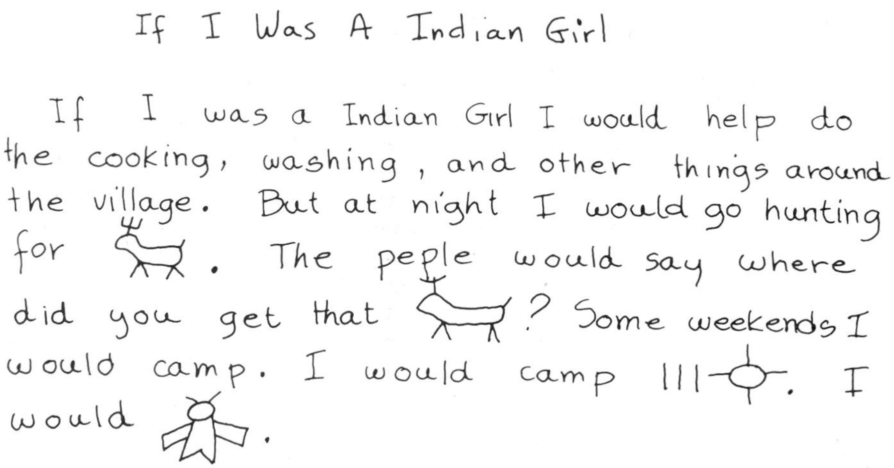

If I Was A Indian Girl

If I was a Indian Girl I would help do the cooking, washing, and other things around the village. But at night I would go hunting for [drawing]. The peple would say where did you get that [drawing]? Some weekends I would camp. I would camp III—[drawing]. I would [drawing].

Myra's first draft

I'M SANTA CLAUS

I'm Santa Claus and I've got a lot of letters this year and I'll have to make a lot of stops. Here's a letter from a boy in Africa who wants a stuffed tiger. But oh dear how will I get there when my deer are used to cold. I'll have to send some magic pills that will make zebras fly. I'll tell him to send eight zebras to pull my sled.

So now don't be suprized if santas makeing zebras pull his sled. You proble want to know what I do with the deer. I still use them only in places where it's cold.

Denise's first draft

Figure 10-2   Top: Betsy's first draft; middle: Myra's first draft; bottom: Denise's first draft.

All the stories in Figure 10-2 show the ability to imagine being someone or something else. The children have used interesting details to make their "Being Someone or Something Else" stories their own.

Using Literature as a Basis for Writing

Literature that has rich language and is sensitive to children's interests can serve as a springboard to imaginative writing. Books present another view of life and experience to compare with one's own sense of reality. Through literature one may also experience on a very personal level events, people, and times far removed in place or time from one's own life.

Inductively the child can adapt or assume the form, style, or scheme of a particular piece of literature. This does not happen from a story heard once a week; it does not come from reading unimaginative or simplified books. It does result from daily exposure to excellence. The need to hear good literature does not end when the child can do some independent reading. It is just as necessary in grades 4 through 8 as it is in kindergarten through grade 3.

Literature provides familiar stories to draw upon in imaginative writing, and can be important as a specific starting point for writing. Children may draw upon their familiarity with particular kinds of stories and write their own versions. Younger children may compose their own ABC or counting books after listening to some and looking at or "reading" several examples. An ABC book

These students created a television roller movie to accompany their original written story about a favorite book character.

composed by some first-graders and illustrated by them has "Crayons begin with C, dog begins with D, Easter egg begins with E, and fence begins with F." Another group of first-graders did their book using a wide variety of fabrics, paper, buttons, etc. They even had a nickel on the N page.

Not all ABC books are intended for young children. Some sixth-graders became intrigued with the words and pictures in *Hosie's Alphabet*.[19] The book inspired them to create their own ABC books illustrated with water color drawings. One student wrote in his book, "D is for devine devilment, L is for the loquacious locust, and Q is for quadrophonic quadruplets." Older students want to write accumulative stories patterned on *The House That Jack Built* or *The Judge*.[20] They can write their own versions of *Chicken Soup with Rice*,[21] using their favorite food and doing either months of the year or days of the week.

Older students also enjoy writing their own tall tales, parodies of fairy tales, newspaper columns, or Mother Goose rhymes, and explanatory tales. One fourth- and fifth-grade group wrote their own Paul Bunyan stories in small groups, with Paul solving the problem of a gigantic snowstorm. These are two of their solutions:

Paul told the mother snowstorm to tell the father snowstorm to tell the baby snowstorm on the ground to come home or he would spank him!

Paul ate up all of the pepper they had except for one plateful which he put under his nose. Then he sneezed and sneezed. He couldn't stop sneezing and he sneezed the snow away.

The *Whole Mirth Catalog*, suggested for older students, contains a variety of activities that may be extended through writing. Several sixth-graders added eight of their ideas to the list entitled "Ten Ways to Get Your Parents to Stop Smoking." After sharing *Robbers, Bones and Mean Dogs*,[22] a collection of students' essays about what scares them, a teacher discovered that her fifth-graders wanted to compile their own book on the subject.

Preceding any such writing there should be extensive reading of the story and considerable inductive discussion of its form, format, or characteristics. Books may also inspire writing about a new character, a new adventure, a new event, or an ending to a well-liked story or tale.

A second-grade teacher read *John Brown, Rose, and the Midnight Cat*[23] to her children. Since this sensitive story leaves the reading audience wondering about the fate of the household when the Midnight Cat is allowed inside, children can write their own endings. One young student, showing a knowledge of fairy tale endings, wrote the ending shown in Figure 10-3, on page 210.

Some sixth-graders created a new character—the seven dwarfs in "Snow White and the Seven Dwarfs" became eight as Wiggley joined the story. Children in another group were unhappy with the ending of *Dazzle*[24] because they thought the small birds were too nice to Dazzle who, in turn, had not been very nice to them. They wrote a different ending in which Dazzle served as the birds' cook for a while.

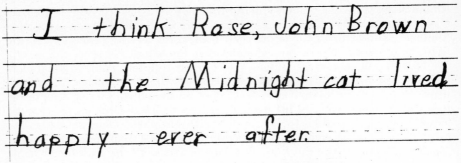

Figure 10-3 Student's ending for *Rose, John Brown, and the Midnight Cat.*

These are very direct uses of particular pieces of literature; however, literature also indirectly influences children's writing as they become more familiar with many well-written and enjoyable stories. For example, a group of first-graders were enchanted with the Winnie the Pooh stories and wrote many of their own based on different characters. Here are three that illustrate what an average group of first-graders can write when they have had many experiences constructing sentences and dictating stories.

RABBIT INVITES POOH OVER FOR A TEA PARTY

One day Pooh was going for a walk. He met Rabbit and Rabbit invited him over to his house. Rabbit had a tea party. Pooh went out the front door and he got stuck. Rabbit pushed and pulled but Pooh wouldn't move an inch. Pooh said, "Why don't you make your door a little wider?" Rabbit went to find the strongest animal he knew. Pooh was still stuck. Then Rabbit and everyone in the forest pushed and pulled and Pooh shot out like a rocket. And they didn't see Pooh for three years.

David

KANGA-ROO IS LOST!

Kanga was jumping with Roo in her pocket. Then she stopped. Kanga thought that Roo was lost but she was stuck in the pocket. Then Kanga went to Pooh and said, "Pooh would you look in my pocket?" "What for?" said Pooh. "For Roo!" So he did and he found him. He took Roo out. Then they lived happily ever after.

Sissy

EEYORE LOSES HIS TAIL

One day Eeyore was walking along the grass. He heard something fall. He didn't know what it was. He didn't know it was his tail. Eeyore went home and took a nap. When he woke up, he figured out that his tail was missing. He went to Pooh and told him what was wrong. Pooh went to owl. Then Pooh went for a walk. Pooh saw Eeyore's tail lying on the grass. He took the tail to Eeyore. Eeyore said thank you. Pooh put Eeyore's tail back on.

Rob

LANGUAGE SKILLS: SUBSTANCE AND STRATEGIES

Other Creative Media

Another way of developing both the senses and the emotions is through opportunities to share new experiences, ideas, or feelings with others. We all view what we see and do through our own personal background of experiences, and sharing reactions with someone else gives us the ability to place a novel experience in perspective and to view other aspects of the experience.

Dramatic activities are also a way of dealing with new ideas. In talking about improvisation as a part of drama, Summerfield suggests:

> It is a means of sharing one's own sense of the world, one's own sense of reality, with others and comparing with other's sense of reality. The imagining, the fantasy is made public, and once it's seen and shared by other pupils, the authenticity, the reality, the truth, the convincingness of an individual realization is something that can be assessed and discussed when the appropriate moment comes. . . . They can be observed and they can be extended and they can be refined and they can be rendered increasingly subtle, increasingly adequate, increasingly full.[25]

Drama then becomes another way of talking about one's experiences, another way of sharing new ideas and new observations. Dramatizing an experience or extending that experience into the unknown but imagined in an unstructured drama may suggest a variety of ideas or avenues of approach to write about. One possibility is to use props, such as different kinds of hats, gloves, and perhaps shoes. The students can choose a hat, for instance, and pantomime certain characteristics that might be associated with the personality that would wear the hat—a hard hat and a construction worker, a felt hat and an elderly woman, a baseball cap and a baseball player, a Stetson and a Texan. Then the students can write about their character, describing both physical and personality traits in their creative compositions. As a postwriting activity, hats and accompanying compositions might be displayed on a bulletin board.

Just as drama is one way of sharing new experiences and making them personal, there are other ways of sharing. Music, painting, sculpture, and other creative media become both a way of viewing new insights and new experiences and a fresh foundation for creativity in composition. The creative arts can serve jointly with imaginative writing to express one's senses, emotions, or imagination, or they can serve as a stimulus for writing.

Many teachers have had success using music to motivate writing. Simply playing a record and asking children to write about what comes to their mind is usually not sufficient structure. March music might suggest a parade or a football game, and a few questions before the writing may provoke additional ideas.

Zavatsky and Padgett say to avoid rock and roll and jazz or you will have the students bopping around in their seats, and no writing will get done. Instead, they suggest that "most children do not have the habit of listening to symphonic music, so almost any orchestral piece with variations of tempo works well."[26] Igor Stravinsky's *Firebird Suite* and *Le Sacre du Printemps (The Rite of Spring)* are possible choices. Piano pieces by Liszt, Debussy (the *Etudes*), and Chopin should be considered; and the symphonies of the American composer Charles Ives are inspirational and well worth a try.

The visual arts may be used as a stimulus for writing, and most children enjoy writing a story to go with a picture or poster. Pictures that present an element of strangeness or an apparent contradiction work well. Children do need to be able to select the picture they want to write about. They may also use their own pictures, prints, or crayon etchings as the basis for a story. One group of second- and third-graders painted large poster-type pictures of what they would like to be someday. Then they wrote about their paintings. Here are two of their stories:

I'd like to be a policeman because I'd patrol the area in search of crime. I'd tell the patrol what to do.

I'd like to be a preacher because I could tell the services and hypnotize babies.

One upper primary teacher had a large aquarium in her classroom. All the children were fascinated watching the fish and snails move about. One boy drew a picture of his favorite fish in the tank and then wrote this story:

I am a fish and my name is Twish gurgle-gurgle. I like swimming through the weads because it tickles. I am a gold fish. It fils funny wene bubles hit me. The water is blue. people try to catch me but I am to fast for them. THE END

This unrevised first draft shows how familiar he was with fish, and at the same time exemplifies many elements of good writing and creativity. He has given the fish a perfect name, has used details about the weeds and bubbles to add a sensory impact, and has included a clever ending.

Vaneta drew the picture shown in Figure 10-4 and then wrote a story (also shown) about dressing up—a familiar experience for many children.

Figure 10-4   Vaneta's picture and story. The story has been edited for spelling and punctuation.

THE BIG HAT

Hello, my name is Cindy. See my hat. Well, it's not mine; it's my mother's. I'm just playing house and dress-up in one. I'm the mother. The hat swallows me whole. It's so big Mother has to tie it. I found it in our cedar chest. I think I'll find another hat to play with that doesn't stink like cedar. Bye now!

Pictures that are used as a basis for writing should be somewhat unusual; they should pose a problem for the writer to solve. This kind of picture often can be found in advertising which uses the unusual to attract attention. For example, advertisements that have been successful are an elephant carrying a typewriter, a dining room table set with china and crystal in the center of a busy street, a sweet grandmotherly woman sitting on a sofa holding a rifle, and some Madison Avenue types in business suits flying kites in Manhattan.

An unfinished line drawing may also stimulate children to write. They can finish the drawing and make anything of it they want and then write about it.

Many middle- and upper-grade children love comic books, and these may be used by a teacher to facilitate story writing. They are particularly good for developing plot structure and the conversation or dialog in children's stories. You can begin with simple figures with a number of empty balloons for the children to complete. Also, newspaper comics work very well with the words eliminated from the balloons. It is much easier to make the transition from the balloon wording into quotations and from descriptive captions into descriptive paragraphs once the ideas have been clearly established through the cartoon.

DEVELOPMENTAL TRENDS IN WRITING

This section will examine some of the developmental trends that one finds in children's writing. Before we look at some of these trends, it should be made clear that there are no "stages at certain ages" associated with imaginative writing. The trends in the use of language when writing and the development of conventional story technique do not follow a pattern of particular items at particular grade levels. They indicate, rather, the progression that most children follow in development, and children at any one grade level will vary greatly.

Language in Writing

The two most general trends in written language are from the simple to the more complex and from the more general to the more specific. These trends are manifested by increasing sentence length, changes in structure from simple sentences to more coordination to more subordination and embedding, increasing use of a variety of pronouns and synonyms, increasing precision of words used, and greater fluency and overall length.

Development of Conventional Techniques

Analysis of children's imaginative writing reflects the same two general trends of increasing complexity and specificity: a change from basic description to the development of events, movement from the view of self to the view of others, development from single to multiple events, increasing use of dialog, increasing use of details, and the addition of minor events and explanations.

Sample stories   Perhaps it would clarify the trends suggested above to examine some samples of children's stories written about the same picture.

A FIRST-GRADER'S STORY

I have a Siamese cat. I like my Siamese cat. I like butterflies. They are pretty. Leaves are pretty too. I like them. Sometimes they are brown. I like them. I love animals. I have blue eyes. I have red hair. I like looking at butterflies. I like to catch them. My cat likes to eat them. My cat likes to catch them. Sometimes I catch them. I put them in cages sometimes.

A SECOND-GRADER'S STORY

It has big green leaves, and the girl is looking at the big butterfly, and the cat's looking at it, and the girl has red hair, and the cat's brown, and it has big blue eyes. It looks like the cat is trying to get a butterfly.

A THIRD-GRADER'S STORY

Once there was a girl with long red hair and big blue eyes. She was walking through the forest with her Siamese cat. When she saw a big red and black butterfly, she stood there looking at him. She was thinking it was pretty. Her cat was thinking, "Boy would I like to catch him!" All of a sudden he ran after the butterfly. The girl decided to walk back out of the forest because the butterfly was gone.

A FOURTH-GRADER'S STORY

I have red hair and blue eyes and a pet cat, and I like to go in the woods and look at butterflies and try to find out what kind they are, and try to find out what kind the leaves are and collect the leaves and look at other animals. One day when I went along with my cat, I saw a butterfly with orange and brown spots; but it flew away, and I never saw anymore like it. One day I saw one almost like it, but it had red spots. But it flew away too. One day I got a butterfly that had all different colors in it, and I kept it for a pet. One day it flew away, but I knew it was happier there with other butterflies so I wasn't too sad.

A FIFTH-GRADER'S STORY

There was once a girl who was lost in the woods and couldn't find her way out. She had a pet cat who followed her in the jungle, and the butterfly showed her the way home. After that she made a little place in the woods where the butterfly showed her the way home. When she got older, she lived in this place where the butterfly lived. When winter came, the butterfly had to fly down to Florida; and the girl was sad because he had to fly down south, and she didn't think it would fly back. After winter was gone the butterfly flew back. Then they decided to move to Florida so the butterfly wouldn't have to fly away, and that's where they lived from then on.

Analysis   *A change from basic description to the development of events*   Both the first- and second-grade stories are entirely descriptive. In the third-grade story, the cat chases the butterfly and the girl leaves. The fourth-grade story is similar in that the butterfly leaves, but its author adds other butterflies to the story. In the fifth-grade story we see the development of a crisis when the butterfly goes to Florida for the winter and the girl fears that she won't see it again. Happily, the butterfly does return and they move south so that they can be together.

Movement from view of self to the view of others The first-grader uses the first person, but—more important—many personal notes are added as "I" becomes the central character. "I love animals," "I like them (leaves)," or "I put them in cages sometimes" all appear to be the author speaking. The second-, third-, and even fourth-grade stories may use first or third person, but seem to involve the author as a participant in the stories. The fifth-grader's story is told more from the viewpoint of a disinterested person; certainly there is less involvement of self.

Development from single to multiple events In the first two stories, the events are not developed. The third-grade and fourth-grade stories suggest a single and similar event—the butterfly goes away. In the fifth-grade story, the butterfly leaves, but when it returns, they all go south to be together.

Increasing use of dialog Unfortunately for illustrative purposes, only one of the stories uses dialog—the third-grader's story. In order to use some dialog, the story must be viewed as separate from the storyteller, and this is not typical of the early primary grades. It could well have been added to the fourth- or fifth-graders' stories, but was not. This may be an individual developmental item, or the result of infrequent opportunities to tell or write stories.

Increasing use of details In the first-grader's story, the descriptive details included the word "pretty" and the naming of colors. In the second-grader's story, additional details are given—"big, green leaves" and "the cat's brown, and it has big blue eyes." The third-grader's use of details is more frequent and more extensive, with "long red hair and big blue eyes" and "A big red and black butterfly." Both the fourth- and fifth-graders do use descriptive adjectives, but they more frequently supply details in other ways. The fourth-grader adds, "I like . . . to find out what kind they are," "I never saw anymore like it," and "I knew it was happier there . . . so I wasn't too sad." The fifth-grader adds similar details such as "a girl who was lost in the woods and couldn't find her way home," and "made a little place in the woods where the butterfly (had) showed her (the) way home."

The addition of minor events and explanations This is closely related to the use of details discussed above. We see in the third-grade story an example of the addition of explanations as we find out what the girl and the cat were thinking. In the fourth-grader's piece, there is the idea of the girl as a scientist looking at butterflies and other animals or leaves to identify them. There is also the addition of other butterflies previously seen, "a butterfly with orange and brown spots" that flew away and "one almost like it, but it had red spots" and it flew away too, and finally a butterfly with "all different colors on it, and I kept it for a pet." The fifth-grader adds a series of events as the butterfly shows her the way home; she builds a place in the woods; when she is older, she lives in that place; winter comes and the butterfly goes to Florida; after winter, it flies back; and finally they move to Florida so that it won't have to fly away in the winter.

The trends toward more maturity in the development of story technique and in the language used in writing really need to be examined in multiple samples of children's writing. They indicate the pattern of development, and maturity will be most evident in the older or more mature children's writing, and with those who have had a fine composition program.

IMAGINATIVE WRITING: CHILDREN'S STORIES

Evaluation of Story Writing: General Considerations

In evaluating student's writing of any kind, and particularly story writing, the thrust of the evaluation should be to look for value. The emphasis in evaluation should be on the positive, on what was beautifully conceived or expressed. Measurement in the sense of making comparisons with others or with some set standard is completely inappropriate. Evertts[27] states that stories are "not exercises to be corrected, scored, rewritten or graded. (*Never* graded! Who can grade imagination, especially that of a young child with a lifetime of growing to do?)"

The legitimate purpose of evaluation is twofold: to express to the child what you value in the composition, and to seek what is valuable to use as a basis for future growth. Because imaginative writing is so intimately tied to one's own personal experiences and views of reality, it is very painful to be criticized by someone else. Future improvement and growth come from the basis of what is done well or expressed well. The teacher's evaluation should be confined to two purposes: communicating to the child what is good about the writing and using observations of the child's work to plan helpful writing experiences.

Evaluation, then, involves looking for what is valuable in children's work and communicating this to them to foster future writing development. The teacher must be very specific in communicating what is successful to the author. Was it the idea itself or an interesting event or explanation? Was there an interesting beginning or a particularly effective ending? Did the child use details well to build an effect, was there some unique touch that made it personal, or was there some humorous aspect that gave it life? Was there some interesting dialog, or were some especially effective words used? One of the best methods of communicating with a student about a piece of writing is through an individual conference. Questions such as these may be posed and discussed between teacher and author. The results of each conference may vary. For example, the student may rewrite the composition, implementing the suggestions that were made during the conference, or specific goals may be established for improving the quality of future pieces of writing. Teacher-student conferences, held on a regular basis, can help students become better writers.

Good record keeping is an essential part of any writing program. Dated notes and comments following each writing conference should be placed in a folder with the student's name on it. Sometime during each month, the teacher also might file a sample piece of writing in each of the folders, thus establishing an ongoing, sequential record of each student's writing progress. Compositions written at different times throughout the school year may be compared to determine a student's growth in writing ability. Each folder becomes essentially a permanent record of students' writing achievement and can be made available during teacher-student conferences as well as teacher-parent conferences.

Evaluating children's writing on the basis of what was well done does not mean that the teacher should ignore conventions of written language, such as spelling, punctuation, capitalization, and so on. Problems with supportive writing skills should be noted for future instruction. Some writing will be corrected completely in conference with the teacher, and other pieces will remain as uncorrected first drafts. This whole area of conventions of writing and revision is discussed later in the chapter.

Two methods of evaluating the writing performance of a group of children may be of interest to teachers and administrators. These are holistic assessment—an evaluation process used by the Educational Testing Service and the National Assessment of Educational Progress[28]—and the use of rating scales in which various aspects of writing are evaluated, typically on a 1 to 5 basis, and a total score is derived. Neither procedure is intended for children's use, but both procedures can be used by teachers or school systems to chart progress in writing over a period of time.

In holistic assessment, several teachers or evaluators read a set of compositions, giving each a single score—usually from 1 (the lowest) to 4 (the highest). The raters practice this scoring on sample papers to make sure they agree on what is expected. When all the compositions have been scored by two readers, the widely divergent scores should be reconciled, usually by a third rater. Such ratings may be of help to the teacher in several ways. Horner suggests:

> Scores show how an individual student's writing compares to the group's, and they reveal how well the group writes as a whole. Scores converted to simple percentages tell what proportion of a group falls into each of the four classifications: poor, below average, above average, and excellent. This information can effectively be used for program evaluation when systematically planned into pre- and post-testing.[29]

Although there are many scales to evaluate writing, a commonly used one was developed by Paul B. Diederich, Director of Research in English, Educational Testing Service.[30] This scale has three main sections: content and organization, which count 50 percent; aspects of style, which are 30 percent; and mechanics, which are 20 percent. Each subcategory is rated on a scale of 1 to 5, from poor to excellent. While this scale was developed for older students, it may also be useful for evaluating groups of younger students. Although it is a 100-point scale, teachers should be cautious about considering scores as percentages. Such an evaluation is helpful at the beginning of the year to indicate areas to be developed during the year, and a pretest and posttest use of the scale can assess the semester's or year's progress.

Evaluating Elements of Creativity in Story Writing

Creativity in writing is more difficult to evaluate than the mechanics of writing. Whereas it is relatively easy to judge the correctness of punctuation, capitalization, and spelling, it is much harder to assess structural elements such as sequence of ideas, an interesting beginning or ending, the use of descriptive details, and the use of dialog. However, some specific qualities that a teacher might look for in imaginative story writing are suggested by various originality scales developed for rating compositions.

Yamamoto[31] developed such a rating scale with six major parts: organization, sensitivity, originality, imagination, psychological insight, and richness.

Sample subdivisions listed for imagination are richness of imagination, fantasy, abstraction, identification, and reasoning. This scale was supplemented by Torrance[32] in a two-section rating for evaluating originality and interest. The originality section includes picturesqueness, vividness, flavor, personal element, original solution or ending, original setting or plot, humor, invented words or names, and an unusual twist in style or content. The section on interest includes naturalness, variety of kinds of sentences, personal touches, questions and answers, conversational tone, use of quotations, and humor.

Another scale for evaluating originality in children's writing was developed by Carlson.[33] This scale has five main divisions: story structure, novelty, emotion, individuality, and style of stories. Then each of these is subdivided into numerous items. Story structure, for example, has five subsections: unusual title, unusual beginning, unusual dialog, unusual ending, and unusual plot. The section on novelty has sixteen divisions, some of which are novelty of names, new words, new objects created, picturesque speech, unusual related thinking, and quantitative thinking. The Carlson Analytical Originality Scale was developed after extensive sampling of children's stories and has a six-point rating scale for each subitem. Four of the six points for each are illustrated with samples from children's writing. The main sections and subsections are listed as an appendix to this chapter.

Kantor[34] suggests that we may find some realistic guidelines for criteria to use in evaluating creative writing in the psychological literature on creativity. The first concept of creativity, divergent thinking, was suggested by J. P. Guilford. A second concept, which comes from Freudian theory, is playfulness and fantasy. The third quality that may be found is risk taking and skepticism about convention. The fourth category, openness to experience, is described by various theorists such as Carl Rogers and E. G. Schachtel. It involves the inclusion of original concrete details, perhaps in unusual combinations with each other. The fifth quality suggested comes from Jerome Bruner—effective surprise, a shock of recognition caused by connections between previously unrelated realms of experience. The last quality is symbolic expression, which involves using the metaphor to suggest deeper relationships. Kantor adds a final caution that seems particularly appropriate here:

> In adopting these concepts of creativity as guidelines for evaluation, we run the risk of bringing about a regime as rigid and dictatorial as the old one. In short, if students begin to write more imaginatively solely to satisfy the teacher's expectations and not because they find it personally worthwhile, then we haven't come very far.[35]

It seems clear that we must help our students find more pleasure in their own writing and provide them with opportunities for a real audience as an alternative to the teacher as the sole audience for writing. The scales and concepts of creativity should indicate to the teacher some of the aspects of creativity that may be found in children's writing that need encouragement. They may serve to help the teacher specify precisely what a child did well in a piece of writing so that the child can apply the learning in additional stories.

Improving Mechanics in Story Writing

The first thing the teacher needs to do is to become convinced that the purpose for the writing determines what should be done about editing or correcting any mechanical aspects of writing. A general rule of thumb would be that if the child or the teacher is going to share the story by reading it, there is no need for correcting mechanical errors. If others are going to read it and would have difficulty, it should be corrected as necessary. Editing or correcting for no real purpose does not teach correct mechanics, nor does it advance imaginative writing.

The second thing that the teacher should do is to help the child avoid making as many mechanical or spelling errors as possible. Then correction becomes less necessary and less frequent. A good program of instruction, as outlined in Chapter 11, should gradually reduce difficulty with conventions in writing. In the meantime, there are two main ways of making corrections less necessary and less frequent: dictating imaginative writing and helping the children while they are writing. Burrows[36] reports that research plainly indicates that young children should be given plenty of opportunities to dictate stories, reports, verse, titles, questions, plans, and other forms of composition. She adds that research also indicates that "it's more desirable to cherish fluency and uniqueness of expression than complete correctness."

As children begin to become independent writers, they still need someone to transcribe part of their story before they make additions to it or finish it. Students in the upper grades also need opportunities to dictate stories from time to time. Various people may take the dictation—parents, aides, and older children as well as the teacher—or the dictation may be tape-recorded for later transcription.

Spelling errors are frequent problems in children's writing, but there are a number of ways they can be avoided. Children should be encouraged to keep a separate sheet of paper nearby when they are writing to note any words they need to know how to spell. Then they leave blank spaces in their writing for those words to be added later. If you circulate around the room while the children are writing, you can supply the spelling for these words. The children should also have a personal word dictionary with one or two pages for each letter. Then as they obtain the spellings for the unknown words, they can write them in their personal dictionary for later use. It's amazing how children learn to spell the words they look up frequently. If children are writing about a similar experience, the teacher may put some of the words they think they may want to use on the board. A caution here is that this kind of group listing may limit the ideas which the children use in their writing if they feel confined in any way to the words on the board. There is also the possibility that children may ask someone else near them how to spell a word or that they can simply go ahead and write the word the way they think it is spelled. If the piece of writing is going to be shared orally, there may not be a need for correct spelling. Burrows[37] suggests that this kind of writing needs to fulfill only the child's desires, except upon those extremely rare occasions when correct form is necessary out of consideration for others or when the product is to be permanently preserved.

When it is necessary to put imaginative writing in correct form, the teacher should edit the writing with the child in a person-to-person conference. At this time, the teacher can supply the corrections while explaining what the revision is or by asking how the child wants to solve a particular problem.

The most important way for a teacher to help improve children's imaginative writing is by truly appreciating and cherishing what children write. If the teacher delights in children's ideas and is not dismayed by their form, the children will freely use their imaginative and creative powers and write. Moffett[38] suggests that "children should begin their careers thinking of the class as more the audience than the teacher, who should avoid making himself (or herself) the source of evaluation."

One teacher shared some imaginative writing about Thanksgiving with the parents of the children in her room without any editing changes. Along with the publications of their writing was the following note:

> I would like to take this opportunity to pass on to you a sampling of our creative writing. The results this week have once again shown me that there is always thanks in the hearts of children.
>
> Let me tell you about creative writing. It is not natural or spontaneous for some children. The mood must be set and the child must be led carefully and skillfully to express himself. All children have deep thoughts and feelings, but the difficulty lies in getting these thoughts and feelings from the minds and hearts to the paper. If a child knows that every incorrect word is going to be circled in red—he will not write! I did not change these stories because to tamper with the form is to destroy the spirit and charm which the author intended.
>
> Read the following with humor and taste and the knowledge that you have had a rare opportunity to look (for a few seconds) into the minds and hearts of these beautiful children.[39]

How could anyone fail to enjoy these children's writing? They were second-graders, and much of their spelling reflected good second-grade-style guessing; but the warm reception of their teacher was reflected in the enthusiasm with which they wrote.

To emphasize once again, if the teacher is to become a source of improvement for students, there must be accurate diagnostic records of each child's writing. The teacher must look at the growth of both individual children and the entire class. One way of keeping records is through anecdotal notes. As the teacher circulates around the room when children are writing or when they share their stories, he or she may note particular strengths or particular problems that the children are having.

Another way of keeping track is for teachers to develop a checklist. Then they can keep one for each child—recording and diagnosing each story written—or they may use such a checklist for the class on particular pieces of writing in order to select children for small-group instruction. In the vertical columns teachers would list the particular aspects of structure and originality they are looking for. These might be such things as development of an idea, effective beginning or ending, use of vocabulary, use of dialog, novelty or ingenuity of ideas, variety of sentences, and humorous incidents or touches. In mechanics one might examine spelling, punctuation, usage, capitalization, and sentence form. Then in that column opposite the name of a particular piece or an individual child, one would indicate the diagnosis by a comment or by a symbol. A sample checklist is shown in Figure 10-5.

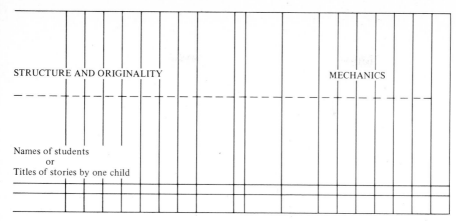

STRUCTURE AND ORIGINALITY   MECHANICS

Names of students
or
Titles of stories by one child

Figure 10-5   Sample checklist.

Once the teacher has had an opportunity to examine several pieces of imaginative writing from the students in the class, a brief look at the checklist will show if there are several children with a similar problem. These students may be grouped for instructional purposes to work on this specific area.

The key point in any discussion of mechanics or spelling in story writing is that the teacher should look for and respond to improvement in the imaginative quality of the writing and not emphasize the correctness of the form in which it is written. Form may be dealt with separately. Imaginative writing is not reserved for just a few students in the class. Moffett points out that creative writing is a staple of learning for all children, not just Friday afternoon fun for advantaged children who are mastering the basics on schedule. "The testimony is ample from many hard-working teachers in urban ghettos that deprived children can learn 'basics' only *after* they have become persuaded that the world of letters has something in it for them."[40] Imaginative writing is a vehicle for students to use in dealing with their ideas and their fears—their own personal reactions to their world.

WRITING POETRY

Poetry is another kind of imaginative writing that should be an important part of every student's school experience. It should be an alternative way for children to express their personal reactions, feelings, and observations. Interest in poetry and interest in writing poetry need to be developed and expanded during these early years.

Developing Children's Interest in Poetry

Two main factors are involved in developing children's interest in poetry: increasing familiarity with various kinds of poetry and extending responses to poetry. An important part of stimulating children to write poetry is to increase their familiarity with all kinds of poetic expression by reading a wide range of poems to them and by understanding what is shown about their interest in poetry.

Increasing familiarity with poetry   Anthologies will certainly provide some material, but these often contain older, traditional poems and only rhymed, metered poetry. Because of copyright laws, the anthologist is somewhat limited in the selection of poems which are available and financially feasible to include. The major source for modern poems is the individual collection written by a particular poet. Any number of these collections are available—beautifully illustrated and comprising the best of the poet's art.

Children need to have a variety of books of poetry available to read and examine. Special favorites may be displayed in a book bound by the class or on a special bulletin board. Teachers should make a point of reading poetry to children frequently. If teachers keep and organize copies of poems they may want to read to their class, they can easily find the one about dandelions on the very same day these bloom outside. A "sharing time" report of fixing breakfast could trigger the teacher's reading "Mummy Slept Late and Daddy Fixed Breakfast."[41] Poetry should never be just "the words we copy from the board for handwriting practice." Poetry should become an integral part of talk and response in the classroom. Children need to know that poetry is a way of reacting to something very real in their lives, and that it is a meaningful response.

Extending the response to poetry   Children's response to poetry may be enlarged by various activities that encourage the children to become more involved with a particular poem. Some of these activities are making media presentations of poems, doing choral reading of poetry, and setting poems to music.

Media presentations of poems are a way of visualizing the poem in one of the graphic arts. Children may select a poem they particularly like and illustrate it in some way. Chalk, finger paints, crayon and crayon engravings, mobiles, clay sculpture or soap or paraffin carvings, dioramas, models, murals, collages and mosaics, torn-paper illustrations, or homemade slides—all these media presentations help make the poem more meaningful to the child who creates them. Directions for making your own slides are as follows:

1. Place transparent contact paper over a 2- by 2-inch color (clay base) picture from a magazine.
2. Rub contact paper with spoon until picture is clear.
3. Cut out.
4. Put in warm soapy water and peel off paper that originally had picture on it.
5. Place between slide frames.
6. Iron or glue frame closed.

If children are allowed to select a poem to read chorally and plan how the lines will be read, there is a great deal of learning and involvement in the activity. Groups of three to five children can work together in planning the readings, which may be tape-recorded or given orally. In the process of planning the reading, deciding which lines should be emphasized and how gives children a lot of insight into the poem.

Setting poems to music is an additional way of extending the mood or feeling of the poem. Children may make up their own musical accompaniment and play it while the poem is being read, or they may choose some professionally recorded music as a background for their reading. Rhythmical instruments rather than a full musical background may be more appropriate for some poems.

Research on children's interests in poetry Children's interests in poetry—the kinds of poems or qualities in poetry that they prefer—have remained surprisingly stable over the years. A study by Terry examined children's interests and preferences in listening to poetry.[42] She analyzed fourth-, fifth-, and sixth-graders' responses to over one hundred selected poems and found the following characteristics in the poems liked and disliked by the children in this national survey.

Characteristics Liked	Characteristics Disliked
Humorous poems	Sentimental or serious poems
Rhythm, rhyme, sound	Imagery and figurative language
Enjoyable familiar experiences and animals	Unenjoyable familiar experiences
Contemporary poems	Traditional poems
Familiar poems	Free verse
Narrative poetry	Haiku
Limericks	

There appear to be several important implications from Terry's study that relate to children's writing poetry. One of the things that children liked to hear was familiar poetry. Unfortunately, this same study revealed that three-fourths of the teachers read poetry to their classes only "occasionally" or "once a month." Writing poetry was not a common practice in these classrooms, as over 90 percent of the teachers in the study had their children write poetry only "occasionally" or "very seldom."

In replicating Terry's study at the primary level, Fisher and Natarella[43] obtained similar results. Information from the participating teachers indicated that young children had very little exposure to reading and writing poetry. This study revealed that children of primary school age are very similar to older students with regard to their preferences in poetry. There are only two exceptions: young children tend to prefer traditional poetry and enjoy poems about strange and fantastic events.

Two other studies just over forty years apart relate to children's interests in poetry and to what teachers read to children. Coast[44] in 1928 examined the poems that a group of teachers most enjoyed teaching and the poems that children in these classrooms preferred. She concluded that the poems which teachers prefer are the ones most frequently chosen by children. Tom[45] conducted a survey in 1969 to determine what poems were read to children in the fourth through sixth grades. Almost six hundred questionnaires from five states showed that the majority of the forty-one most popular poems were in narrative form, and that all but four of them were written before 1928. The poems most often read by teachers were "Paul Revere's Ride," "Stopping by Woods on a

Snowy Evening," "A Visit from St. Nicholas," "Casey at the Bat," "Little Orphan Annie," "Fog," "The Village Blacksmith," "My Shadow," and "Hiawatha." Unfortunately, many of the poems represent the traditional poetry that Terry found children dislike and frequently do not understand.

Children's overall interest in poetry decreases throughout the elementary grades, perhaps because we are not capitalizing on their preferences for poems. It is also difficult to determine if their preference for rhymed metered poetry is a reflection of what they think poetry should be because of the poems they have been exposed to or a preference which is independent of previous experience with poetry. We also need to distinguish between what students enjoy listening to and what they enjoy and are capable of writing.

Poetic Forms

Children need many experiences as a base for writing poetry. They need to play with words and with sounds and images. Typical of this is the seven- or eight-year-old who leaned out over the swimming pool watching a bug on the water and made up a wordplay poem which he repeated over and over.

Bug off, bug
Go away
Who needs you
On a sunny, summer day?

Another example of this fun with wordplay and with sounds of words that younger children enjoy so much occurred while children were working on a task of combining two simple sentences into a single sentence. The children, a second-grade group, were shown these two sentences: *My hat is blue. My hat has flowers on it.* One child, after hearing the sentences read, responded immediately, "My hat is blue, my hat just flew, up in the sky so high."

The starting point of poetry is developing experiences—direct experiences that create an impression on children and also a need to say something about the experience. Another part of stimulating children to write poetry is providing them with a rich and varied background of knowledge about poetry by reading a wide range of poems to them. The third part of getting children started in writing poetry is to have reasonable expectations of their abilities and introduce poetic forms that enable them to be successful. There should, of course, be a feeling of willingness to try new or different things because the teacher has set up a warm and responsive climate in the classroom in which children can experiment and take risks.

Children's first attempts at writing poetry are far from being really fine poetry. Before they reach this point, they need frequent opportunities to express themselves poetically. The following suggestions for writing free verse, concrete poetry, invented unrhymed forms, and simple rhymed forms are beginning points in writing. The final objective is the ability to use poetry—rhymed or not—as an alternative to writing prose for those ideas that are especially suited to poetic expression.

Parallel poems and lists   The editors of *The Whole Word Catalogue*[46] suggest parallel poems and lists as good ways to begin writing poetry. This kind of initial poetry is based on repetitions; the poems have consecutive or parallel lines that begin or end with the same words. This is a form that many poets have made use of because of its rhythmic, chantlike effect. The structure is there as something to be relied on, and yet its open-endedness invites writers to explore their imaginations. "The beauty of these parallel poem ideas is that they allow students to plug into them at their own level of skill and sophistication."[47]

I Wish

Write a poem in which every line begins with *I wish. . . .*

Colors

Write a poem with a color in every line.

Lies

Write a poem with a lie in every line.
Write a poem with a whopping lie in every line.

I Remember

Write a poem in which every line begins with *I remember. . . .*

Dreams of the Future

Write a poem in which every line begins with *I am going to. . . .*

Comparison Poems

_____ *is like* _____. For example: *Thunder is like bowling. Clouds are like a feather.*

Metaphor Poems

Same as comparison poems, except without the word *like.*

Equivalent Poems

In the past they _____, *but now we* _____.

I Used to Be

Has the form *I used to be (a)* _____, *but now I'm (a)* _____. For example, a first-grader wrote: "I used to be a cookie, but now I am a crumb."

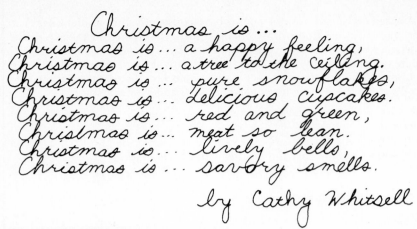

Christmas is . . .
Christmas is . . . a happy feeling,
Christmas is . . . a tree to the ceiling.
Christmas is . . . pure snowflakes,
Christmas is . . . delicious cupcakes.
Christmas is . . . red and green,
Christmas is . . . meat so lean.
Christmas is . . . lively bells,
Christmas is . . . savory smells.
by Cathy Whitsell

Figure 10-6 Definition poem by a fourth-grader.

Definition Poems

Spring is. . . .
Love is. . . .
Fear is. . . .
Magic is. . . .
Misery is. . . .
Beauty is. . . .
Gold is. . . .
Loneliness is. . . .
Alone is. . . .
Thanksgiving is. . . .

Using *Christmas is . . .*, a fourth-grader wrote the poem shown in Figure 10-6.

Some group compositions by students use the list form and create free verse.

HAPPINESS IS:

two kinds of ice cream
learning to whistle
knowing a secret
having a sister
climbing a tree
singing together
learning to tell time
finding your skate key
playing the drum
walking hand in hand
  Anyone and anything at all
  That's loved by you.

WHAT IS EXCITING?

> *Christmas*
> *parties*
> *making all A's*
> *polka dots*
> *birthdays*
> *getting an allowance*
> *knowing a movie star*
> *long fingernails*
> *new records*

Exciting is different things to different people.

Free verse   The first writing by children should be very free—something we might call *word pictures*. An example from a first-grader is a poem about time.

THE CLOCK

The clock tells time
  Bedtime
    Suppertime
      Playtime
The best time of all.

Barry

Inspired after the teacher had read and talked about free verse, an older student composed the following poem. Notice that he was also interested in experimenting with form—something that may happen when a student has been exposed to reading and writing a variety of poems.

The earth is a large round ball
  Circling the sun, never to be
                      stopped
By the Human Race . . .

Jeff

This kind of writing, as it develops, becomes the kind of free verse written by a seventh-grader.

The sky never ends　　　　　　*The morning comes thin*
up and up forever high　　　　　*and pinkish paint soaks the sky*
reaching for the top　　　　　　*The sun wakes us up*

Darkness spreads like ink
Till the stars shyly peep through
And extend their light　　　　　Christine

```
B
I
R
D
S
```
Birds fly high, birds fly low

Birds fly slow, birds fly fast
```
B        F
I        L
R        Y
D
S        F
         R
         E
         E
```

Figure 10-7   Concrete poem by Mark Davis.

Figure 10-8   Concrete poem by a third-grader.

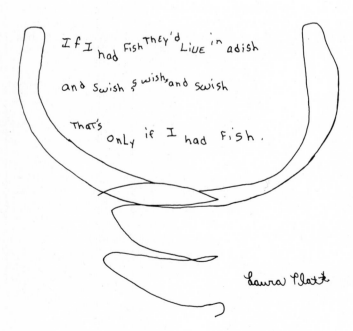

LANGUAGE SKILLS: SUBSTANCE AND STRATEGIES

Concrete poetry A kind of poetry that may appeal to children throughout the elementary grades is a special kind of picture writing. In concrete poetry the words either outline a visual picture of the topic or form a more solid picture of the idea of the poem. Mark Davis's poem about birds, shown in Figure 10-7, is a fine example of concrete poetry. Laura, a fifth-grader, contributed the concrete poem shown in Figure 10-8, about fish.

Concrete poetry can be one of the easiest kinds of poetry for young people to write because there is so much appeal inherent in the visual picture and because there is so little structure that is predetermined. Since the poet sets the pattern of the concrete poem, it may also have a very complex form and be a most demanding kind of poetry to write.

Invented unrhymed poetry Several of the invented forms of poetry that do not depend upon rhyme give children some structure for composing without being too difficult to use. After seeing several examples of a particular kind of poem, students can compose their own poems without knowing the technical names of the parts of speech. An easy form of poetry is the *cinquain*. This is a five-line poem: line 1 is the name of something or someone; line 2, two words that describe; line 3, three *-ing* words that show an action like *running* or *shaking*; line 4, a four-word comment or feeling; and line 5, one word which is either a repeat of line 1 or a synonym for that line. Betsy's cinquain is about a candle.

Candle
Bright, light
Glowing, shining, sparkling
Such a pretty sight
Fire

A group of first-graders dictated the following poem about a cat.

Cat
Furry, cuddly,
Walking, meowing, scratching
Likes people petting him
Kitten

A group of older students became interested and involved in writing their own forms of cinquain poetry. Here are three of their poems.

Stamps
Small objects
Colorful bits of paper
A hobby full of geography
Money

Kathy

Lady
Small, red
Crawl, slow, tired
Cute, darling, and nice
Polkadotted

Robin

Sun
Red, hot
Bursting with flames
It makes me hot
Burning

David

Another group of children decided to make an even smaller cinquain and came up with the following poems about some fish in their room.

Fish	*Fish*
Big, little	*Big, small*
Swimming, eating, hiding	*Swimming, floating, eating*
In water	*Sliyme-things*
Blurp!	*YUK!*

The rather unconventional spelling of *slimy* doesn't really detract from the poem; in fact, it makes it seem even slimier.

Another invented form which is a bit more difficult is the *diamante*, so called because of its diamond shape. The first three lines follow the cinquain pattern. Line 4 has four nouns which start to form opposites between the second and third. Then line 5 is like line 3, line 6 is like line 2, and the seventh line is a noun which is the opposite of line 1. Carolyn, a sixth-grader, wrote the following diamante:

Enemy
Strange, untried
Challenging, teasing, ignoring
Opponent, competitor—teammate, pal
Playing, sharing, giving
Nice, new
Friend

Shay has taken a few liberties with the fourth line, but his poem certainly makes his own comment:

Flag
Stars, stripes
Waving, flapping, symbolizing
Expressing leadership—battle torn
Declining, splitting, weakening
Fight, die
War

Children may also enjoy making up their own invented forms of poems. They can vary the number of words in various lines, and can use certain kinds of words like color words, action words, -ly words that describe like *slowly* or *cautiously*, and so on. They might enjoy working on these poems with a partner at first. One group of fourth- and fifth-graders who were studying about their state wrote the following poem in their own invented form:

Georgia
Pines
green and brown
waving, rustling, murmuring
Earth
orange and red
warming, feeding, encouraging
Growth

Rhymed forms   When you begin to introduce writing rhymed poetry, you should begin with very simple forms. One that has had special appeal and considerable success is *terse verse*. These poems consist simply of two rhymed words with a rather long explanatory title. Start with the pair of rhymed words and then add the title to it. Children throughout elementary and middle school or junior high school have had fun and success with terse verse. Lee Nichols wrote:

WHAT THE GIRL SAID TO HER MOTHER IN THE SPRINGTIME—

Green
Scene.

At Christmas time Angela Kentonicks wrote:

WHAT SANTA SAID TO THE ELVES—

Toys
Boys

and Darren Gates wrote:

WHAT THE REINDEER SAID TO SANTA CLAUS—

Weird
Beard!

Another form of rhymed poetry which children have enjoyed is the *clerihew*. Clerihews are four-line poems; line 1 is (or ends with) a name and rhymes with line 2, and then lines 3 and 4 rhyme. These poems are considerably more difficult than terse verse, however; and when they are introduced to children who have had little experience with poetry, the result is often loss of meaning or convoluted word order. In the attempt to meet the rhyme scheme, the children alter their normal language patterns or come up with nonsense verse. This is one important reason for introducing unrhymed poetry to children. You will also want to caution students about substituting rhyme for meaning in their poems. The following examples are two clerihews written by children who have had some experience with poetry and who were not restricted by the rhyme scheme.

Casey Jones　　　　　　　*Santa Claus*
Broke all of his bones　　　*Had to pause*
He did it fast　　　　　　　*Bringing toys*
Before he crashed.　　　　*To girls and boys.*

Tammie　　　　　　　　William

Another rhymed form of poetry is the *triplet,* or three-line rhymed poem. Again, this form is a bit more difficult because of the need to come up with three rhyming words that make sense together at the end of the lines. Here are two written by a group of ten- and eleven-year-olds who succeeded quite well:

As I sat under a tree
Along came a bee
And said, "Hi" to me.

There was a bear
Who had a lot of hair
But he did not care.

There are, of course, additional forms of rhymed poetry with various patterns of rhyming lines. As children become more at ease with poetry, and as they develop a larger and larger vocabulary, they are more able to write rhymed poetry.

Found poetry　"Found poetry" may be a kind of poetry that children will enjoy discovering. Found poetry comes from prose—a segment of prose that can be rearranged into poetry. You can find poetry in any number of types of prose—advertising, descriptive writing, stories, and so on. The piece of prose, when rearranged in some format, may take on a shape much in the same way concrete poetry does, or it may be set out like free verse.

Here is an example from an article by William F. Herrnkind, "Strange March of the Spiny Lobster," in the June 1975 *National Geographic.*

> A prickly forest of legs and feelers seethes under a rock ledge 25 feet down in the warm Gulf Stream washing the Great Bahama Bank. Spiny lobsters—hundreds of them—cram a single den no bigger than a pool table. Slowly, several leaders emerge, drawing others into bustling podlike clusters. Gradually the pods string out into lengthening files. . . .
>
> Then it begins: a relentless head-to-tail march, a mysterious impulse that drives these crustaceans day and night for miles along the sandy, unprotected shallows.

This might be arranged into a free verse poem by selecting certain phrases and rearranging them into a poetic form, as shown on the opposite page.

A prickly forest
of legs and feelers
    h
 ee e
s   s
   t
under a rock ledge.
Spiny lobsters
cram
a single den.
S l o w l y
several leaders emerge.
Then it begins
a relentless
head-
to-
tail
march.

With a shorter passage, the entire passage might be used as a found poem.

Working with found poetry is good experience for many children. It may make them more aware of writing styles and phrasing, and also be a good introduction to poetry that says something that is not about trees and flowers and fairies. For children who are unsure of their ability to write poetry, found poetry may be an intermediate step to original writing.

A note on haiku and tanka We have not included the oriental forms of haiku and tanka in this section, although they are often recommended as forms of poetry for children. Both haiku and tanka, which are syllabic arrangements, make a comment on life in such a way that the whole poem is really a metaphor. Since we have considerable evidence that children have a great deal of difficulty understanding metaphorical language and since writing haiku and tanka calls for making a seventeen- or thirty-one-syllable metaphorical comment on life, we feel that both of these forms are too abstract and may be far too difficult for many elementary school children. Also, accepting any seventeen syllables arranged in five-seven-five syllable lines without the additional characteristics of the haiku seems to be cheating children by letting them think they have written a haiku when they really have not.

Initiating Poetry Writing

Motivating poetry writing through books of verse and poetry There are a number of books that may be shared with students to motivate writing. *A Twister of Twists, A Tangler of Tongues*[48] might inspire the use of alliteration and the writing of tongue twisters. *The Queen of Eene*[49] contains humorous poems about characters such as "Pumberly Pott's Unpredictable Niece," "Aunt Samantha," and "Curious Clyde." Students can develop their own comical character

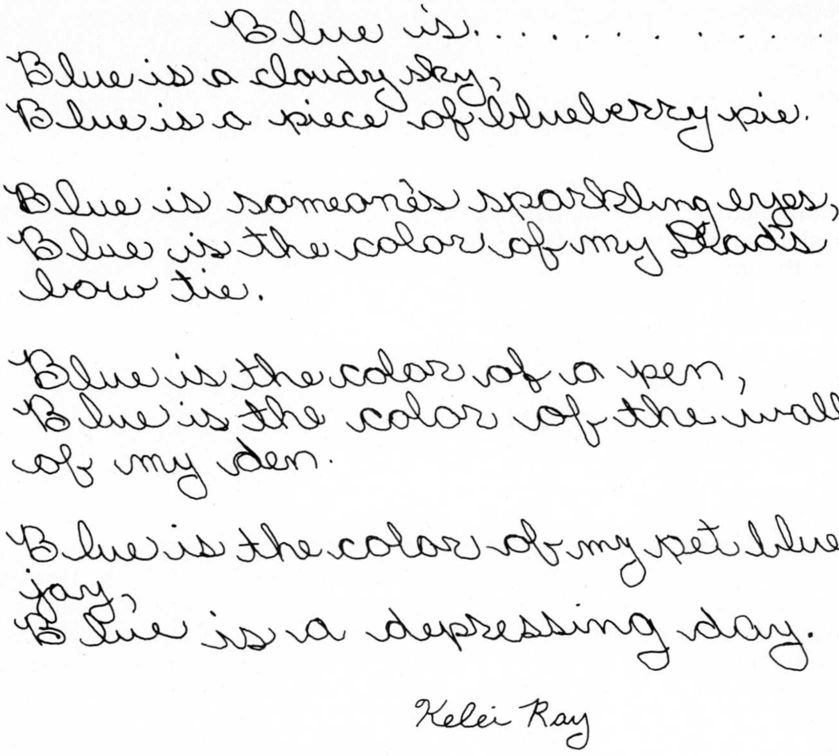

Blue is..........
Blue is a cloudy sky,
Blue is a piece of blueberry pie.

Blue is someone's sparkling eyes,
Blue is the color of my Dad's
bow tie.

Blue is the color of a pen,
Blue is the color of the wall
of my den.

Blue is the color of my pet blue
jay,
Blue is a depressing day.

Kelei Ray

Figure 10-9   Poetic writing by a fourth-grader.

and write a poem in the style of those found in this delightful book of poems by
Jack Prelutsky. Mary O'Neil's *Hailstones and Halibut Bones*[50] offers another
opportunity for writing poems. Using colors, O'Neil writes in picturesque language: "What Is Red," "What Is Yellow," "What Is Blue," and so on. The example by a fourth-grader shown in Figure 10-9 illustrates the kind of poetic writing
that might occur after sharing this book of colorful poems.

Group poems   In the primary grades children have many more wonderful
ideas than they are capable of writing down. This is a good time for group compositions where all the children can add ideas and feel they have shared in the
writing of the poem. One child's contribution often will stimulate another child
to add a really special touch. In addition, it gives the children the knowledge
that poetry is not something lofty and untouchable, but rather that it is one way
to share ideas and experiences with others.

Group writing is also a good way to introduce children to poetic form. After
seeing and discussing many examples of the form, the group can write several
poems together. Group writing may also mean pairs or trios of children writing
together without the teacher's direct supervision or help. Some children really
enjoy this kind of experience and feel less self-conscious about their own con-

tributions. In the process of writing together, the discussion of what words to use, which order of ideas is best, or which form fits the idea leads to new knowledge and increased interest in writing.

One of the most important things for the teacher to recognize is that no one can simply turn on creativity. Creative writing of stories or poems cannot be done in thirty minutes neatly scheduled for Friday afternoon. Giving children longer periods of work time with a variety of activities to choose from is much more productive. There will be some children who will nearly always choose to write alone, and others who will prefer some kind of group writing. That's just part of the individuality of children. Sometimes children will get very excited about writing and produce a great deal; at other times, they may write very little or nothing. That, too, is a part of individuality.

Poetry writing and the composing process Before children actually begin writing poetry, a teacher can do a number of things to facilitate matters. Children need to have a wide background of experience from which to write. A teacher can make various experiences in school and out of school more meaningful by asking questions that challenge children's thinking and that help children relate new experiences to familiar ones.

Children also need to have another kind of experience—real familiarity with poetry of all kinds. They need to hear poetry of all kinds: poetry that is metered and rhythmical; poetry that is free and unstructured; poetry written by professional poets and poetry written by other children or by their teacher; poetry that touches children's everyday experiences and poetry that stimulates their dreams; poetry that tells a story and poetry that describes a mood, a feeling, or a place.

Because poetry is so highly condensed, every word is very important. Teachers can help children write by helping them enlarge their own vocabularies and by aiding them in seeing various shades of meaning. Discussing an experience the children have had and asking children to make close observations help with this process. If there is an aquarium in the room, what words could describe how the various fish move? The small ones *dart* or *dash* or *spurt about*. The larger ones may *float* or *glide* or *slip from weed to weed*. The catfish on the bottom may *laze along* or *drift* or *hover about*. They don't just *swim!* Having the range of words to express just the right feeling or picture helps children with writing poetry, in fact, with any writing.

Selecting the right kinds of form to introduce to children, while still allowing them to use whatever form they like or whatever seems right for their ideas, is an important part of the teacher's job. A certain amount of form or structure may help children write, but too much demand for meter and rhyme is frustrating and may destroy children's enthusiasm for writing poetry. Sometimes children may be anxious to share their writing—at other times they may appear uninterested. This should be their decision. There should be opportunities for sharing with the teacher or another adult and opportunities for sharing with other children. Some poems may be copied in edited form in individual or classroom books, bound, and kept to share with others. You want children to develop an interest in reading and writing their own poetry. The long-range goal is for students to express their thoughts and feelings freely through poetry without the help of motivational devices.

Evaluating Children's Poetry

Evaluation of poetry is a particularly difficult task for anyone, and it is especially important for the teacher not to impose adult standards on children's writing. One practice that might help in guiding and evaluating children's progress in writing poetry is for the teacher to write. Also, as in story writing, emphasis on valuing (instead of on grading) is a way to heighten interest and ability. The following guidelines may help in indicating the kinds of things teachers may look for and appreciate in children's poetry.

An awareness of an experience: There is a sense that the child has written about an event that meant something.
Sincerity of feeling: There is an impression of honesty and genuine expression.
Appropriate and natural language: The words are the child's own and fit the topic; there is no obvious straining of sentence structure to make a rhyme; the words are precise without seeming unnatural.
Creation of a response in the reader to the poem: The reader of the poem is somehow touched, amused, or made conscious of something new.

Responding to children's poems by telling them what you particularly liked in the poem and having other children hear and read their poems and tell what they liked stimulates interest in writing poetry and growth in writing. Encouragement does far more good than any grading or evaluation system.

INFORMATIONAL WRITING: RECORDING AND REPORTING

One of the most difficult tasks for children in elementary school is writing an informational report. Part of their problem is that reporting calls for a more formal style of language than they are accustomed to using, and another part of the problem is that they are told to write a report without being given enough help in how to do this. What too often happens is that they look up information in an encyclopedia or other reference books and then copy whole paragraphs or sections for their report. We would like to suggest that an earlier kind of informational writing should precede report writing—recording. In written recording children begin to develop skills necessary for more formal reporting.

Recording

Defining recording   Written recording involves some kind of data gathering on a firsthand basis and then converting the information in these data into written sentence or paragraph form. As a beginning step in informational writing, the information that the children use is something they themselves have observed and recorded or something they have found out personally by surveying, measuring, and so on. Since we know that children of elementary school age do not learn from abstract sources, it is particularly important to involve them in collecting the information they will be writing about.

The observations or survey results should be categorized by the children on some type of chart or graph. This grouping or categorizing helps to consolidate the information they have gathered into a manageable form. Then they are ready to write sentences or paragraphs about their observations.

Learning to record is an important process for children. They learn how to use information and how to organize and write their observations on paper. Not until they have had a lot of opportunities to use the recording process are they ready for written reports which involve library materials and other secondhand sources for their information.

Written recording is an appropriate activity for children in all grades, but is especially valuable for older children who have not had previous experiences with recording. It should be a regular part of the writing program for younger children, who need many experiences with written recording before moving into report writing.

Classroom recording experiences The kinds of recording experiences that children have should be related to the other activities they are doing; they should not simply be unconnected exercises intended for practice. Recording relates very well to science and social studies where children are observing, comparing, and surveying anyway.

Comparisons Young children are very perceptually oriented, and the teacher can capitalize on this by challenging them to compare two items. These might be two shells, two rocks of different types, or two plant cuttings. More mature children can compare three or four samples, looking for similarities and differences. An occasional question or suggestion from the teacher may help them make finer distinctions among the items they are comparing.

In comparing plant cuttings, the children will quickly notice the colors of the leaves, their general shape, and perhaps whether they are fuzzy, smooth, or waxy. They may not notice if the leaves grow opposite one another or if they alternate, whether the stem is round or square, and whether the plants have a distinctive odor or not. These are the kinds of cues the teacher may suggest when the children appear to have finished their comparison.

Observations Children make many, many observations that can be used for experiences with recording. These may involve observations of the living things in their classroom or on the playground. They may involve observations about the experiments they are conducting in science. As children observe, they should keep some type of log, journal, or chart. If they are recording an event over a period of time, the observations need to be made at regular intervals.

One group of second-graders made observations about changes that took place during the fall season. They each took a particular tree on the playground area and went out every two weeks to see what changes were taking place. Some others kept track of the average daily temperatures and amounts of rain during those same two-week periods. By mid-November they were ready to put together their observations and write about the changes that take place in the fall.

A group from a fourth-grade class made daily observations of the baby gerbils born in their classroom: growth of fur, when the eyes opened, when they began to eat independently, how much they weighed, how well they walked, etc. After five weeks the gerbils were grown, and the children wrote their description of the growth of the baby gerbils based on their recording.

Surveys   Occasionally a disagreement over something or the mention of a favorite program or pet may lead children to take a survey of some kind. Any number of things may be surveyed—favorite sports, foods, colors, television shows, birthday months, transportation used in getting to school, or state capitols visited. The results of the survey can be easily graphed and written about.

Taking a survey is the beginning of interviewing and is an important way of gathering information for reporting. At first the children can make the survey within their own room; later, they may survey children in other rooms, the teachers or other school personnel, or people within the community.

Measuring   Still another kind of recording experience involves taking measurements of various kinds and recording the results. Children may compare standard measures (foot, cup, inch) against nonstandard measures (span of a hand, a glass, a piece of yarn). They may work with various standard measures—cup, pint, quart, gallon—to find out for themselves how many cups are in each of the others, or how many pints in the quart, gallon, or half-gallon. Their measuring could involve comparisons between measures in use now in the United States and metric measurements.

Recording experiences: A final word   Any number of regular activities that children do can be used as a basis for recording. Children need many experiences with recording as a basis for the more formal written reporting that they will be called on to do later. If they can learn to depend on their own observations and ideas in the early stages of reporting, they will not be as prone to copy pages and pages from encyclopedias. Also, some children are much more oriented toward the realistic than toward the imaginative. They need opportunities to write stories and poems. The kinds of close observation used in recording form a solid basis for descriptive writing.

Reporting

Moving into reporting   There are several ways of easing the transition from informal recording activities into more formal reporting. The first written reports might involve topics closely related to the students' interests which could be easily illustrated. The main part of the information could be conveyed with a series of illustrations or a display of some kind. The children could set up a model or diorama or collection on a table display or a series of illustrations on a bulletin board. The labels or explanations along with the illustrations would constitute their report.

The first uses of reference materials might involve informational books which could be shared. Too often we think only of encyclopedias or similar reference books for reports when there is a wide variety of well-written illustrated informational books with a range of reading levels. The first reports that children write might be a review or summary of one of these informational books.

Developing reporting skills   Three major skills are involved in writing reports: taking notes, organizing ideas for writing, and using reference materials. These skills need to be taught. You cannot just send children to the library with a topic for a report and a set time period and expect them to be able to write a good report. Each skill needs to be taught before the children are required to use it.

Taking notes Much of the problem with copying portions of encyclopedias and giving them as reports starts with children's inability to take notes in their own words. Although selecting the main idea from a paragraph or even a larger portion of material is a reading skill that is tested throughout the school years, much of the time the main ideas are chosen from a predetermined set of choices. In order to prepare children for stating the main idea from a range of materials in their own words, a great deal of preliminary work needs to be done.

One workable way to do this is to write out on chart paper or on a transparency a paragraph of material from a source similar to the ones the children will be using. Have the children read through the paragraph carefully; then remove it from their sight and ask them to write down one or two of the main ideas that were in the paragraph. The instruction may be more effective if done in small groups. When they have finished writing (or nearly finished), ask them to take another look to fill in any details or ideas they missed. Discussion is very helpful. You will want to talk about the main ideas and details that are important to include.

When they have become proficient at selecting the main ideas from materials that you control, they are ready to work with duplicated materials on their own. This is a critical time to make sure that they are not reverting to copying whole sentences from printed sources, but rather formulating the ideas in their own words. After they have mastered the skill, they are then ready to take notes independently from library sources.

Organizing ideas There are a number of ways to organize the material collected for writing—many of them highly individualistic. We will suggest one way of pulling ideas together so that they form a kind of rough outline. Mature writers may not need to go through this kind of process as they are more able to handle abstractions and organize mentally without resorting to paper and pencil.

This process of organizing material before writing has four main steps: listing ideas, grouping ideas, ordering the ideas within groups, and then ordering the groups of ideas. At first the child lists all the ideas to be included in the report (each one in a word or short phrase). Then the child groups together the ideas that somehow go together. After this, the ideas within each group are put in sequence for writing. The final step in organizing is to decide which group of ideas will be dealt with first, second, third, etc. When that is finished, the child has a rough outline of the report. At any time in the process, a particular idea may be discarded or changed to another group.

Teachers may want to go through this process several times before expecting children to be able to do it independently. The first two steps are really categorizing, and are most appropriate activities for younger children to do simply as a way of organizing information.

To illustrate this in a more concrete manner, consider what a group of fourth-graders did to organize material based on their favorite foods. In groups of four, they listed their favorite foods on 3- by 5-inch cards. Items such as the following appeared on the individual cards: steak, hamburgers, baked potato, fried chicken, pecan pie, chocolate ice cream, fried shrimp, pizza, broccoli, nachos, cherry cheesecake, peanuts, and broiled lobster. They then categorized the items according to appropriate labels—entrees, vegetables, desserts, and snacks. Afterward, they decided to write descriptive words on the back of each card—for example, for *pizza* they wrote "cheesy, spicy, thick, and chewy." Finally, adding necessary information along with selected descriptive words, they wrote four paragraphs to correspond to the four categories. The first paragraph is shown here.

When thinking about dinner, who can pass up spicy pizza, crispy fried chicken, tasty fried shrimp, or juicy, buttery broiled lobster. And what about a tender steak or an old fashioned hamburger with lettuce, pickles, and tomatoes? Those have to be favorites!

Using reference materials   Before starting to use reference materials independently in the library, children need some help in knowing what kind of information is in what kind of book and how to find out whether a particular book covers the topic of interest. If you can obtain a small collection of reference materials in the classroom, you can help your students learn to use an index and table of contents. Skimming is an important skill in working with reference materials, especially skimming through a segment and reading only the titles and subtitles of the various sections.

Informational books may provide pertinent material about a subject and at the same time present a format that can be modeled for writing reports. Also, informational books should be available in the classroom as reference sources when students are studying specific topics. Since a wide variety of informational books exists today and their presence offers attractive, readable material for different age levels, teachers should consider them as significant reference materials for students' research and reports. Too often, unfortunately, the encyclopedia becomes the single source for information gathering on a research topic.

Evaluating Informational Writing

Report writing and recording are primarily information and not particularly personal or emotional in nature, so that the teacher is somewhat more free to suggest revisions and help with editing. The general purpose of the report or recording is to communicate information to others rather than to express individual ideas. Because of this, it should be easily read by others. Conventional spelling, punctuation, and mechanics aid the reader and should be correct as a courtesy to the reader.

Marking the report with *Sp* (for spelling errors) or *P* (for punctuation errors) is not a very helpful way to go about making the child's report better mechanically. Corrections should be made in individual conferences with students. One idea that may help your students accept the idea of correcting their reports is to always refer to their first writings as the "first draft." If one knows from the beginning that there will be revisions and corrections—that one is writing a first draft instead of the final copy—it is much easier to revise and rewrite.

Keeping some kind of record of the kinds of problems particular children are having will help you group for instruction. You may want to keep their first drafts in a folder for future reference. However, attaching a note of items for instruction may save time in the long run. A column or chart similar to the one suggested earlier for recording children's work may be even more helpful. As with any kind of writing, pointing out what the children did well does help improve the quality of recording or reporting. It also may serve as valuable information for others in the class.

PERSONAL WRITING

Personal writing includes all the kinds of writing that might be called *social correspondence* in etiquette books as well as the writing one does for oneself—reminders, journals, or diaries, and messages—and personal notes. Because most personal writing is very private, it presents special problems for the teacher. What writing of this kind should be checked and what should be private? How do you encourage children to freely express themselves in writing, much as they would in an intimate conversation, without being an intruder? How important *is* form? Perhaps two samples of letters written to an author will clarify the issue.

January 15, 1982
Dear Mr. Burch,
  Our teacher read Queenie
Peavie *to us. It was a nice
book. Thank you for writing it.
We liked it.*
              Sincerely,
              Julianne

Dear Mr. Burch,
*Our teacher read us the story
you wrot about that girl who
was so mean and I wanted to
tell you that lots of girls are
that way cause the boys are so
mean to them that they half to
be that way. You just made it
seam so real that I could believe it.*
            Your friend,
            Julianne

If you were Mr. Burch, which letter would you prefer to get? The first letter is in perfect form, and probably that student could name the parts of the letter: the heading, greeting, body, and closing. The second letter has a few spelling errors, no date, and some other mechanical errors, but it certainly lets one know that the child has been touched emotionally by the story, that she really did like it.

    Certainly proper form does need to be learned, but not at the expense of individuality and ideas. Acquiring form may be a slow process that takes place over a number of years. Provide children with a sample of the form, and let them emphasize individual ideas. The form becomes an instrument like the sample letters in manuscript or cursive writing over the chalkboard, something to refer to when needed. It should not be the whole focus of the experience.

Providing Experiences for Personal Writing

The most important thing that children have to learn about letter writing, personal notes, invitations, announcements, or messages—all the kinds of personal writing that will be sent to someone else—is that one can communicate ideas through writing. Writing can get something done, can get an idea across. This means that writing these kinds of things for practice—just for practice— is self-defeating. Writing needs to be real.

Letter writing   Both personal letters and what might ordinarily be termed *business letters* may be somewhat informal during the elementary school years. If children are writing for information of some kind or wish to order something, you will need to remind them to put their addresses and their full names in the letter, suggesting the proper placement. You may offer to check over the letter if they would like you to, and to help them with spelling as they are composing it. However, probably the most important thing that you can do is to use meaningful situations that call for writing a letter.

You may be able to establish pen pal relationships with a class in another city or a different part of the country. When one of the children or a group has enjoyed a particular story or book, suggest a letter to the author. If you need some free or inexpensive teaching materials, recruit some of the children to order them for you. Keep the addresses of children who move away during the year so that their friends can correspond with them. Adopt some patients in a nearby veteran's hospital or nursing home. You can encourage the children to write to the subject or author of articles (in the children's magazines they subscribe to, in *TV Guide,* or in your local newspaper) in which they seem particularly interested.

After studying problems concerning mass transit, these two students volunteered to write letters to several city officials. They are editing the first drafts before writing the final letters.

Personal notes   Instead of being upset when children write notes to each other, capitalize on their interest and channel it into good practice in writing. Set up mailboxes for each child somewhere in the room, where they may put notes for one another and where you may also put notices, reminders, or notes for them. A special note from the teacher once in a while may be cherished, and writing only two or three a day does not take much time. It's a nice way to compliment someone who does not often get compliments.

Invitations   Children of all ages can help write invitations to others asking them to visit the classroom for something special. If they are too young to write the invitation in letter form, compose some that they can complete: *Please come to* _____, *Where* _____, *Time* _____, *etc.* Even beginning first-graders can copy in the necessary information and make the decorations for the covers. When the children are older, they can write out the full invitation. You will need to remind them of what information is needed, but they can do the actual wording themselves. Perhaps there should be a writer or secretary on the "helpers" chart each week to take care of invitations and thank-you notes. Be sure to give the secretary something to write during the week, even if it is a thank-you note to the cooks for an especially good lunch.

Announcements and messages   Children need to be able to make announcements and take down messages in written form. The key is providing opportunities for them to have real practice in doing this. However, be sure to have alternative plans for those really crucial pieces of information until your children have had enough practice to be completely reliable.

Keeping a diary or journal   Keeping a diary or a journal which is completely private or one that may be shared is a valuable experience for elementary or middle-grade students. In this book they can keep notes for themselves on something interesting they have observed, a new word or phrase they like, an idea for a story or poem, something they have wondered about and would like to check later, or just how they felt about the day or what they did.

The journal may be completely private; if so, perhaps you can provide a file drawer or other locked closet or drawer where they may be stored. If they are not so private, the students may wish to keep the journal at their desk or storage spot. Sometimes a diary with space for every day for a whole year is rather intimidating. Instead, they could make their own bound book and fill in the days or dates as they have something to write. They might like to try out the idea first just for one month, and bind a booklet with the days and dates for that month.

At the end of a week or a month, you might like to take some time with them to talk over the good times and the bad times you have had as a class. Their journals can serve as a reminder and also as a chart of their growth. They will need time, though, to write in their journals. Some teachers who have blocks of time for a variety of activities find that the children can take care of this writing during that time. Others with a more structured schedule like to take a quiet time at the end of the day for the students to make their journal entries, get homework assignments, and generally catch up on the day before the bus leaves or the bell rings.

Evaluating and Improving Personal Writing

The main key to improving personal writing is giving children ample opportunities to use this kind of written communication. A secondary factor is your availability to help when help is needed. This help may be in the form of individual consultation, sample formats, or suggestions about content. A quick *Be sure to tell Tim about the softball game* or *I think Sally would be interested in what we learned about quilting from Mrs. Sommers* really helps children with ideas to use in their letters. If you do not know the people your students are writing to, you may suggest some more general ideas about things you have done as a class and then ask the children for further ideas. Encourage them to write their letters and their journals as though they are telling someone about their experiences. This kind of writing is the closest to "talk written down" that exists.

As far as evaluating personal writing is concerned, the evaluation must really be done by the writer and not by the teacher. Asking students to write one thing they have done well and one that they need to work on may help them examine their own strengths and weaknesses.

SUMMARY

Composition should not be a hit-or-miss portion of the elementary school experience. Just as reading skills are carefully developed throughout the different grades, so composition skills should be developed. We have suggested in this chapter some writing experiences of each type that are appropriate for all the various age groupings of children.

One of the two main things to consider in planning a writing program is to provide a balance of writing experiences. Students need many opportunities to write stories and poems, record or report, and undertake a variety of kinds of personal writing. There should be some kind of sequence that will ensure variety in the writing program. Just as they should not hear the same book read to them each year, no matter how much their teachers may enjoy reading it, they should not write just cinquains or terse verse year after year. Teachers also need to provide for individual children's abilities and growth. Some children are ready to move into more formal aspects of writing earlier than others; options and choices need to be provided along with guidance from the teacher.

We have not set up a sequence of writing activities on a grade-by-grade basis because there is so much variation from one classroom to another and from one child to another within an individual class. Students do not have to write one story every week and one poem and one report and one letter. They do, however, need meaningful opportunities to write each of these kinds of compositions sometime during a larger block of time.

The second factor to consider in developing the writing program is that much of students' writing can and should be integrated with other aspects of the language arts program and with other content areas. The children's individual interests and preferences come into consideration here. If the teacher is alert to the possibilities for writing inherent in other content areas or those associated with the units of stories in the basic reading program or the books children are working with in an individualized reading program, it is easy to structure a variety of writing experiences that may be integrated with other work and with students' interests.

Our obligation to the children we teach is to make them not only competent writers, but also adults who find pleasure in writing and who can easily communicate in writing.

PRELIMINARY LEARNING ACTIVITIES

1. In each of the dictated compositions below, suggest two specific things the child did well.

WHAT I WOULD DO IF I WENT TO THE MOON

If I went to the moon, I'd take a friend and we'd jump over the craters and we'd eat cheese and crackers and drink cokes. We'd visit the stars and jump over their points. We'd sleep in a rocket and go back to earth.

THE ROAD TO GRANDMA'S HOUSE

One morning we were on the way to Grandma's house and we always liked to sing songs on the way. And sometimes when we come to a big bump, we take off our seatbelts and go flying in the air. And you can look up in the sky and look how blue it is. And there's a bunch of green trees along the way.

We go riding on a horse at Grandma's house and in the night-time Grandma tells us stories about people who lived in the house before they did. And how they killed wolves who got in the back door. And once my brother had to go to the outside bathroom and when he came out, he got chased by a lion. And Mom didn't believe it!

2. What elements of originality do you see in the following unedited stories? List the original elements and write out a brief note to the child who wrote each piece.

SAVED

One day I was camping out in back of my yard. Suddenly it turn night. I was afraid of the dark and so I went to sleep. I heard creeping noises and the wind blowing. Then I heard footsteps. And suddenly I saw something on the ground. It was a dead body. Then I turnn into a detective. I heard the footsteps again. I saw green man from Mars, but he didn't see me and I shot him with my 22, 38, 49, 50, 58 shotgun. And thats how I solve my mystery.

JUNIOR

Junior is a bug with eight legs. He's a very nice bug and likes to climb trees. and he bites them to. But one day there was a man standing very still. Junior thought he was a tree and bit hem. It hurt so bad, the man jumped, and through Junior off! That taught Junior a leson. Allways check good before you bite.

3. Give examples from the stories at five grade levels of the developmental trends in children's writing that pertain to language development.
4. Draw up a chart similar to the one suggested in the section on evaluating children's story writing and check off or record what you think should be recorded for the story below.

LISANINEING SECRETLY

Once a pome a time a hippo was liveing in a zoo. He was tired of hearing the same old thing (Hot Dogs) (Hurry folks step right up.) It was makeing him sick. So he decied to run away from the zoo. that night he herd strange noisees! He said, (Who goses there.) So the next day was almoset here! he had to hurry if he was going to run away. the next day, the zoo keeper was going to hippo's cage. Hippo wasen't there! He left a note the note read,
> *Dear Zoo,*
> *I was tired of hearing the same old thing. So I ran away.*
> > *Hippo*
He found lots of new things to hear a policeman's wishle, Beeps of cars, oh just lots of things! But he missed all the people watching him, splashing all day. And even the loud noeises! So he said, the zoo is my home, I miss it there. So he went to the zoo. All the people was glad to see him! But he relised that after you are use to someing you will miss it if you leve it! the end

5. Suggest a children's book for K–second, one for third–fourth, one for fifth–sixth, and one for seventh–eighth grades that you might use directly in an imaginative writing experience. Indicate also how you would use each of the four books and what discussion or dramatization might precede the writing.
6. Try writing some poetry using three or four of the different forms. Indicate what kinds of problems they might present to children trying to use them.
7. Conduct a recording experience by making some comparisons or observations, taking a survey, or doing some measuring. Put your results into some kind of chart or graph and write the results in a paragraph or two.
8. Keep a journal that you might share with your class when you start teaching.

PARTICIPATION ACTIVITIES

1. Have some children dictate or write some stories using a variety of stimuli, and evaluate them to see which stimulus prompts the most creativity and involvement on the part of the children.
2. Try teaching (inductively) one of the poetic forms that is appropriate for the children with whom you are working. Do some group compositions, and encourage children who would like to try writing some on their own.
3. Set up some comparisons or experiments related to what the class is studying in science and have the children record them. After the children have set up their chart of observations or similarities and differences, have each small group write what they discovered in paragraph form.
4. Have the children do some kinds of personal writing—diaries, journals, etc.—whatever is appropriate considering other classroom activities.

APPENDIX TO CHAPTER 10:

CARLSON ANALYTICAL ORIGINALITY SCALE

I. Story Structure
   1. Unusual title
   2. Unusual beginning
   3. Unusual dialog
   4. Unusual ending
   5. Unusual plot

II. Novelty
   1. Novelty of names
   2. Novelty of locale
   3. Unique punctuation and expressional devices
   4. New words
   5. Novelty of ideas
   6. Novel devices
   7. Novel theme
   8. Quantitative thinking
   9. New objects created
   10. Ingenuity in solving situations
   11. Recombinations of ideas in unusual relationships
   12. Picturesque speech
   13. Humor
   14. Novelty of form
   15. Inclusion of readers
   16. Unusual related thinking

III. Emotional Aspects
   1. Unusual ability to express emotional depth
   2. Unusual sincerity in expressing personal problems
   3. Unusual ability to identify self with problems or feelings of others
   4. Unusual horror theme

IV. Individuality
   1. Unusual perceptive sensitivity
   2. Unique philosophical thinking
   3. Facility in beautiful writing
   4. Unusual personal experience

V. Style of Stories
   1. Exaggerated tall tale
   2. Fairy tale
   3. Fantasy turnabout of characters
   4. Highly fantastic central idea or theme
   5. Fantastic creatures, objects or persons
   6. Personal experience
   7. Individual story style

REFERENCE NOTES

[1]Alvina Treut Burrows, June D. Ferebee, Doris C. Jackson, and Dorothy O. Saunders. *They All Want to Write.* New York: Prentice-Hall, 1952.

[2]Ruth Kearney Carlson. "Recent Research in Originality," *Elementary English,* vol. 40, October 1963, pp. 583–589.

[3]David Holbrook. "Creativity in the English Programme," In *Creativity in English* (Geoffrey Summerfield, ed.). Champaign, Ill.: National Council of Teachers of English, 1968.

[4]Burton and Arnold. *U.S. Office of Education, Cooperative Research Project No. 1523.* Florida State University, 1963.

[5]McColly and Remstad. *U.S. Office of Education, Cooperative Research Project No. 1528.* University of Wisconsin, 1963.

[6]Jack Hailey. *Teaching Writing K–8.* Berkeley, Calif.: Instructional Laboratory, University of California, 1978, p. vii.

[7]Ibid., pp. 57–60.

[8]Marie M. Clay. *What Did I Write.* London: Heinemann Educational Books, 1975.

[9]Ibid., p. 22.

[10]Ibid., p. 26.

[11]Ibid., p. 28.

[12]Martha L. King and Victor Rentel. "Toward a Theory of Early Writing Development," *Research in Teaching of English,* vol. 13, no. 3, October 1979, pp. 243–253.

[13]Lucy McCormick Calkins. "Children Learn the Writer's Craft," in Donald H. Graves, "Research Update." *Language Arts,* February 1980, pp. 207–213.

[14]Mary Ellen Giacobbe, Team Leader. New Hampshire Writing Project.

[15]Evelyn Wright. "Wishes, Lies and Dreams: Pedagogical Prescriptions," *Elementary English,* vol. 51, April 1974, p. 553.

[16]S. M. Lane and M. Kemp. *An Approach to Creative Writing in the Primary School.* London: Blackie, 1967, Preface.

[17]James Moffett. *A Student-Centered Language Arts Curriculum, Grades K–13: A Handbook for Teachers.* Boston: Houghton Mifflin, 1968, p. 118.

[18]Teacher's Manual, *Making It Strange.* New York: Harper & Row, 1968, pp. 33–34.

[19]Hosea Baskin, Tobias Baskin, and Lisa Baskin. *Hosie's Alphabet* (Leonard Baskin, illustr.). New York: Viking, 1972.

[20]Antonio Frasconi. *The House That Jack Built.* New York: Harcourt, Brace, 1958; Harve Zemach. *The Judge.* New York: Farrar, Straus, 1969.

[21]Maurice Sendak. *Chicken Soup with Rice.* New York: Harper & Row, 1962.

[22]Barry Berkey and Velma Berkey, comps. *Robbers, Bones and Mean Dogs,* (Marilyn Hafner, illustr.). Reading, Mass.: Addison-Wesley, 1978.

[23]Jenny Wagner. *John Brown, Rose and the Midnight Cat.* (Ron Brooks, illustr.). Scarsdale, N.Y.: Bradbury, 1978.

[24]Diane Redfield Massie. *Dazzle.* New York: Parents' Magazine Press, 1969.

[25]Geoffrey Summerfield. "About Drama in England," *Elementary English,* vol. 47, no. 1, January 1971, pp. 20–21.

[26]Bill Zavatsky and Ron Padgett, eds. "Writing to Music," *The Whole Word Catalogue 2.* Published in association with Teachers & Writers Collaborative, McGraw-Hill Paperbacks, New York, 1977, p. 210.

[27]Eldonna L. Evertts, ed. *Explorations in Children's Writing.* Champaign, Ill.: National Council of Teachers of English, 1970, pp. 86–87.

[28]The address of ETS is Educational Testing Service, Princeton, New Jersey 08540. The address of National Assessment is 1860 Lincoln Street, Denver, Colorado 80203.

[29]Judith Horner. "How Do We Know How Well Kids Write?" *English Journal,* vol. 67, no. 7, October 1978, pp. 60–61.

[30]Paul Diederich, John French, and Sydell Carlton. "E.T.S. Composition Evaluation Scales," in *Measures for Research and Evaluation in the English Language Arts* (William T. Fagan, Charles R. Cooper, and Julie Jensen, eds.). Urbana, Ill.: National Council of Teachers of English, 1975, p. 190.

[31]K. Yamamoto. *Scoring Manual for Evaluating Imaginative Stories.* Minneapolis: Bureau of Educational Research, University of Minnesota, January 1961.

[32]E. Paul Torrance. "Supplementary Scoring Guide for the Evaluation of Originality and Interest," *Scoring Manual for Evaluating Imaginative Stories.* Minneapolis: Bureau of Educational Research, University of Minnesota, January 1961.

[33]Ruth K. Carlson. "An Originality Story Scale," *The Elementary School Journal,* April 1965, pp. 366–374.

[34]Ken Kantor. "Evaluating Creative Writing: A Different Ball Game," *English Journal*, April 1975, pp. 72–74.

[35]Ibid., p. 73.

[36]Alvina T. Burrows, "Teaching Composition," *What Research Says to the Teacher* (Sidney Borrow, ed.), no. 18. Washington D.C.: National Education Association, 1959, p. 11.

[37]Burrows, Ferebee, Jackson, and Saunders. *They All Want to Write.*

[38]Moffett. *A Student-Centered Curriculum*, p. 126.

[39]Mrs. Blazer. *Madison Local School District.* Columbus, Ohio.

[40]Moffett. *A Student-Centered Curriculum*, p. 242.

[41]John Ciardi. "Mummy Slept Late and Daddy Fixed Breakfast," *You Read to Me and I'll Read to You.* Philadelphia: Thomas Y. Crowell, 1962.

[42]Ann Terry. *Children's Poetry Preferences: A National Survey of Upper Elementary Grades.* Urbana, Ill.: National Council of Teachers of English, 1974.

[43]Carol J. Fisher and Margaret A. Natarella. "Of Cabbage and Kings: Or What Kinds of Poetry Young Children Like," *Language Arts,* vol. 56, no. 4, April 1979, pp. 380–385.

[44]Alice B. Coast. "Children's Choices in Poetry as Affected by Teacher's Choices," *Elementary English Review*, vol. v, May 1928, p. 145.

[45]Chow Loy Tom. "What Teachers Read to Pupils in the Middle Grades" (unpublished Ph.D. dissertation). Ohio State University, Columbus, 1969, p. 194.

[46]Rosellen Brown et al., eds. *The Whole Word Catalogue.* New York: Virgil Books, 1972, pp. 49–50.

[47]Ibid.

[48]Alvin Schwartz, comp. *A Twister of Twists, A Tangler of Tongues* (Glen Rounds, illustr.). Philadelphia: Lippincott, 1972.

[49]Jack Prelutsky. *The Queen of Eene* (Victoria Chess, illustr.). New York: Greenwillow, 1978.

[50]Mary O'Neill. *Hailstones and Halibut Bones* (Leonard Weisgard, illustr.). Garden City, N.Y.: Doubleday, 1961.

CHAPTER ELEVEN

Supportive Writing Skills

PREVIEW QUESTIONS

1 When should students' writing be corrected or revised?

2 How can the mechanics of writing, spelling, and handwriting be taught within a meaningful context?

3 In what ways can spelling instruction be individualized and made meaningful?

4 How can handwriting instruction—both initial instruction and skill development—be improved?

SKILL DEVELOPMENT IN CONTEXT

Understanding the Importance
of Writing Skills

When we talk about supportive writing skills, we are referring to capitalization, punctuation, spelling, and handwriting. Our effective use of these skills enables others to read easily and understand our written language.

It is sometimes quite difficult to read the writings of young children who have developed their own ways of writing ideas down, because they do not use conventional spellings or perhaps letter forms. Figure 11-1 shows a letter from Cortney.

Although it is a natural step in the development of writing and reading skills to devise a personal system for writing, it is important later to learn conventional letter forms, spelling, and punctuation. Using standard punctuation and spelling and legible handwriting is a courtesy to the reader.

We need to help students understand how the acquisition of writing skills is essential to their written communication. Too frequently students are asked

Figure 11-1 Letter from Cortney.

to memorize isolated rules that they do not see a need for in their own writing. Rules learned out of context with little explanation are rarely remembered. Students are more apt to develop and use good writing skills when they need them and when they have a part in figuring out how the various writing skills are actually applied.

To help students understand the relationship between effective written communication and the use of correct writing skills, it is essential for students to read their own writing aloud and to have others read it. When students try to read an unedited first draft, they will very quickly see the need for more conventional mechanics of writing, for accurate spelling, and for more legible handwriting.

Using a Functional Approach to Teaching Writing Skills

If we view writing skills as tools that we use to make our written language more readable for others, then we must use a functional approach to teaching these skills. Skills taught in isolation from content or the composition process are meaningless. First, we must have the thoughts or ideas that we wish to express. These are the basis for our composition. We already know that young children have difficulty keeping more than one thought in mind. To ask them to express on paper ideas and thoughts while at the same time remembering commas, question marks, periods, and so on is asking too much. Older students may experience the same difficulty, or they may have decided from what their teachers emphasize that spelling, handwriting, punctuation, and capitalization are more important than the ideas in the composition. Therefore, the handwriting may be neat and legible, every word may be spelled correctly, periods may be in their right places, and question marks may appear at the end of questions, but the composition itself has suffered.

A functional approach allows both younger and older students to express themselves freely while attending to correct spelling, legible handwriting, proper punctuation, and capitalization. Neither the quality of the composition nor appropriate skills are slighted when the writing experience is done in several steps. Students are encouraged first to put down their thoughts and ideas on paper. The emphasis is upon the quality of content in the first draft, not correct writing mechanics. After they are satisfied with the content and there is a need to edit, emphasis is then given to correct spelling and proper placement of punctuation or capitalization items in the composition. After the necessary corrections have been made, the final draft of the composition is prepared. This final writing is done in the student's most legible handwriting and is then shared with others.

Chris's poem, shown in Figure 11-2 and 11-3, illustrates this process. The student first wrote his thoughts and feelings, giving little attention to writing mechanics, poetry form, or spelling (Figure 11-2). Afterward, he rewrote the poem to make it readable for others (Figure 11-3). The poem became part of a growing collection of students poems that have been placed in the classroom library area.

A ~~young~~ animal ~~standing~~ eating
grass in the meadow
Looking ~~straight~~ down at the
fresh green grass.
His feet so steady with fresh
brown fur
He is listing for any movement
in case of danger,
A little crackle of a twig
breaking.
A split second it was off in
a ~~core~~. flash
A hunter was coming out to a
bush. ~~He fired.~~
~~It fell to the ground~~
~~It was a perfect eight point~~
~~buck.~~ He got away in a flash

by Chris Gowan

Figure 11-2 Above: Original version of Chris's poem.

Figure 11-3 Below: Revised version of Chris's poem.

An animal eating grass in a
meadow,
Looking down at the fresh
green grass,
His feet so steady with fresh
brown fur.
He is listening for any movement
in case of danger,
A little crackle of a twig
breaking,
A split second later he was
off in a flash.
A hunter was coming out to
a bush.
He fired —
But he got away in a flash.

(deer)

by Chris Gowan

Whenever students recopy their writing, the recopying should be done with a purpose in mind. If we stress the importance of making a paper "letter perfect" for others, then we need to provide a means for sharing the piece of writing.

Here are a few ideas that may be used in a classroom situation.

1. Have mailboxes in the classroom where students can actually receive mail from one another. Names can be placed on the boxes, and students can deliver their own letters or notes. To make sure that all students write and receive mail, they may each have a pen pal within the classroom.

2. Students can write and illustrate their own stories. A film from Weston Woods, *The Lively Art of the Picture Book,* may be shown to students to demonstrate how an author or illustrator first makes a dummy before producing a book in its final form.

3. Students who are interested in reading and writing poetry can be responsible for a poetry bulletin board. They can share their poetry by attractively displaying it, and some poems may be recorded on cassette tape to accompany the bulletin board. Information regarding poetry content, children's poets, or ideas about writing poetry can also be posted on the bulletin board.

4. Older students can be encouraged to have a pen pal in another part of the country. Or you may be able to arrange pen pal assignments with another class.

5. Stories written by individual students may be collected and kept in a special book. This compilation of their stories may be placed in the classroom library area for others to read. If some students wish, they can keep their own book of stories to share with their parents and friends. (See directions in Chapter 13 for making a book.)

MECHANICS OF WRITING: PUNCTUATION AND CAPITALIZATION

Learning to Punctuate Written Material

To illustrate how punctuation assists us in writing, a teacher may tape-record materials for students to punctuate. The recorded material may be typed on a ditto sheet without punctuation marks and then distributed to the students. As they listen to the tape they can hear a pause, the stress at the close of a question, and an exclamatory remark calling for an exclamation point. If you wish, a key may be provided for children to check what they have done at the end of the recording. Small-group instruction may also take place using this method of punctuating material. For example, if a few children are having difficulty in remembering to place commas in a list, specific material may be recorded that contains a series of listed items. The teacher discusses the pause that occurs between each item and how a comma is used to indicate the pause. It is a way of separating one item from another.

Besides punctuating tape-recorded material, students may be taught to read their writing aloud to determine if punctuation is needed. When we read material orally, we frequently pause where it seems most natural. If a question mark is missing at the end of a question, reading the material aloud may call the error to our attention. Students can learn to listen for this when they are reading their own material.

In considering the punctuation items, or "rules" as they are frequently called, we certainly do not expect the child to learn and apply all of them during the first years in school. We need to teach those items that the children actually need to use, remembering that not all children need the same things. Perhaps we should look at the kinds of writing that children do at different levels to determine what punctuation items they need to know.

In the early stages of writing, the preoperational child primarily uses uncomplicated sentences. These children begin writing their names, the date, the name of their school, etc. They may also compose or copy notes and invitations to take home to their parents. They are probably dictating and writing experience stories that require only periods, question marks, and commas. We should consider teaching only what they need to use. Asking children to do more than this may be expecting too much at their developmental level.

From seven to eleven in the concrete-operational stage, children are writing more and more. The sentence structure becomes more complex as the child gets older, requiring more sophisticated mechanics of writing. According to research, dialog appears in children's compositions at about the age of nine. Older children are attending to more detail, and their ability to use a variety of punctuation marks has increased. As they begin to use more complex structures and their writing becomes more detailed, children need instruction on the aspects of punctuation they are actually using and need for their writing.

In the formal-operations stage from about eleven to fifteen years, students are writing more formal kinds of papers to increasingly distant audiences. They are beginning to develop elements of an individual style in their writing, and consequently have need for a greater variety of punctuation marks. They begin to get into specialized punctuation for specialized purposes.

Following are three lists of items of conventional punctuation that children in elementary school and middle school may need to use in their writing.

Simple Punctuation

Period at the end of a sentence that states something
Period after abbreviations or initials
Question mark at the end of a sentence that asks something
Comma between day and year in writing a date
Comma between city and state
Comma after salutation and closing in a note or personal letter
Comma to separate three or more items in a list
Apostrophe in common contractions like *isn't* or *don't*

More Complex Punctuation

Period after number when listing items. For example:
    1. A box
    2. A couch
Period after numerals or letters in an outline
Comma with a conjunction such as *and* or *but* in a compound sentence

Comma to set off an appositive or noun of direct address
Comma after an introductory phrase or dependent clause
Comma before a quotation within a sentence
Apostrophe to show possession
Apostrophe in less common contractions like *she'll, he's* and *weren't*
Exclamation mark at the end of a sentence requiring it
Quotation marks before and after a direct quotation
Quotation marks around titles of poems and stories or chapters within a book
Underlining book titles
Colon in writing time (1:25 P.M.) or after salutation in a business letter
Colon to set off a list that follows
Hyphen when dividing a word at the end of a line
Semicolon between compound sentence clauses when there is no conjunction
Parentheses to set off supplementary matter

Advanced Punctuation

Question mark to indicate uncertainty or lack of information, as in Brutus, Marcus Junius, 85?–42 B.C.
Comma to set off transitional words or expressions, like *on the contrary* and *moreover*
Comma to set off brief and closely related clauses instead of a semicolon
Comma to indicate the place of an omitted word or word group, such as *The 2500 model is used for racing; the 1200, for city use*
Comma to set off inverted names on a list, like *Johnson, Sally*
Comma to prevent misreading, such as *Inside, the cottage was cozy*
Semicolon to separate items in a series that have commas within the items
Colon to introduce a quotation, especially when quotation marks are not used
Colon to separate numbers in ratios (12:6) and in bibliographic references of volume and page or chapter and verse
Dash between quotation and author's name and also to indicate omission
Suspension points (three periods or asterisks) to indicate long pauses or an unfinished sentence.

Why are these particular items frequently not applied in children's writing? There may be a number of reasons: the method of instruction, the amount of practice or experience a student has in using these items, and when and how the item is introduced.

What can a teacher do to help children learn and use punctuation skills? We have already mentioned a few significant ideas, but the following list presents a range of possibilities.

1. Tape-record material for children to punctuate.
2. Have children read their writing aloud in order to hear intonations and pauses that indicate a need for punctuation.
3. Conduct instruction in small groups for children having similar difficulties in using particular punctuation items.
4. Teach punctuation inductively and let children see how it works and state their own rules.

5. Prepare written materials for children to punctuate or in which to find punctuation errors only after the rule is discovered inductively.

6. Use devices that will illustrate certain punctuation items:

(a) Show children that a series such as *the wet, cold, icy winter* is the same as saying *the wet and cold and icy winter*.

(b) When an appositive is taken out of a sentence, the sentence remains complete and meaningful: *Mary Smith, the girl next door, is waiting for you (Mary Smith is waiting for you); He sat in the chair, the one with the broken arm (He sat in the chair)*.

7. Prepare transparency materials to use on an overhead projector for children. These may be writing samples that require punctuation, or they may contain errors that can be identified and discussed.

Learning to Capitalize Written Material

The need to learn specific capitalization skills also parallels children's writing needs. The young child will be concerned only with the most frequently used skills such as capitalizing the first word of sentences. Older students, whose writing needs are more varied, will require a wider knowledge about capitalization.

The following suggests simple, more complex, and advanced items your students may need.

Simple Capitalization

The first word of a sentence
The child's first and last names
The word *I*
The teacher's name
The month and day of the week
Other people's names
The name of the school
The name of the city and state

More Complex Capitalization

Proper names such as streets, cities, states, countries, oceans, common holidays, and trade names
The first word of the salutation and closing in notes or personal letters
Mother and *Father* when used in place of their name
Names or abbreviations of titles, such as *Mr., Reverend, Ms.,* and *Dr.*
Names of organizations to which the children may belong, such as *Girl Scouts* and *Little League*
First and important words in titles of books, stories, poems, compositions
First word in a line of verse in poetry
Names of the deity; the Bible and other sacred writings
The first word of a sentence being quoted
Capitalization as used in outlines

Advanced Capitalization

Derivatives of proper nouns, like *Americanism* or *Bostonian*

Names of peoples, races, tribes, and languages, like *He studied mathematics, Latin, chemistry,* and *English*

Names of planets, constellations, stars, and asteroids except sun, earth, and moon unless they are listed with other such names

Letters indicating academic degrees: *A.B.* or *Ph.D.*

To help students learn capitalization skills, there are a variety of ways teachers can introduce this instruction.

1. Before children are writing independently, teachers should point out capital letters as they write on language-experience charts or on labels, or when taking individual dictation.
2. Have students help each other edit compositions that will be recopied for a final draft.
3. Teach capitalization inductively, letting students discover what the rule is and state it in their own words.
4. Work with small groups of students who have difficulty with a specific capitalization item.
5. Provide writing tasks that will cause students to need to use particular capitalization skills.

Rule Books

Students can keep their own punctuation and capitalization rule books, either as a section at the front of their personal spelling books or as a separate book. As rules are being used and introduced, the students would write particular items of capitalization or punctuation down in their books. Illustrations of the rule being used should be included, and it would be helpful to have the punctuation categorized by type of punctuation mark. This should make the rules accessible for reference. When the student feels he or she is consistently applying the rule, it can be checked off. Figure 11-4 might be a page from Jeff's book.

Figure 11-4 Jeff's rule book.

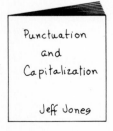

SPELLING INSTRUCTION

The ability to spell correctly is necessary if we are to communicate effectively with others in writing. There is steadily growing concern that too many students are graduating from high school and college who are poor spellers. An instructional program in spelling that is based on research evidence available today along with tried and proven teaching methods can be provided to help all students become better spellers.

First, we must recognize that spelling is a writing skill. No one spells out loud, except perhaps teachers, who *should* not. This means that spelling practice should be written practice, and that any games or activities intended to teach spelling should involve writing the words or seeing them in written form. As adults we actually use different strategies for spelling words than we teach to children. When students ask how to spell a word, the most frequent answer is "sound it out." Yet when we aren't sure of how to spell a word, we don't sound it out; we write it down to "see if it looks right." That's just what students should do. They should write the word down—using what they know about sound-letter relationships—and look at it to see if it looks right.

When we examine what good spellers do, we find that they are not just smarter. They are persistent and care about spelling correctly. And their characteristic strategy is to write down the word, sometimes three or more ways, and then to look at it to see which is right. When you ask them how they know which one is the correct spelling, they say that they read a lot. They just know the right way when they see it.

That is exactly what most adults who are good spellers do. Unfortunately, the children who use this approach must figure it out on their own. Few are taught to use this method of spelling. Mostly spelling is memorizing a list of words from the spelling book presented on Monday and taking a test on Friday, and then quickly forgetting the words.

Early Experiences with Spelling

Some new research and reports of classroom activities that involve beginning students in spelling must be considered. In an article entitled "Write Now, Read Later" Chomsky suggests that children ought to learn how to read by creating their own spelling of familiar words using sets of plastic letters or alphabet blocks. Instead of words resembling a secret code that only others can break, writing words becomes a way of expressing something that the child knows. She points out,

> If we concede that word recognition, or even just the sounding out of words, appears so much more difficult for children than composing words, why do our reading programs as a matter of course expect children to deal with it first? The natural order is writing first, then reading what you have written. To expect the child to read, as a first step, what someone else has written is backwards, an artificial imposition that denies the child an active role in the whole process.[1]

In the beginning stages, when children are trying to represent words with letters their spelling is not conventional. Instead, it reflects their knowledge of the sounds the letters stand for and the ways that they pronounce words.

Many children start with their own names and change initial sounds. Mike put some plastic letters together to spell his name, saying, "That's me, I'm Mike." When asked how he could change it to *like*, he quickly put an *l* at the beginning to replace the *m*. Another Michael, age 5, wrote I NO MI ABC WOT U PLY WF ME—his version of *I know my ABC, won't you play with me*.[2]

Montessori also used this method with children in Rome. She worked in a very directive manner, but the process was essentially the same. The children were given a box with all the consonants and vowels they knew; and while the directress pronounced a word, the child selected the letters to compose it. Montessori comments,

> But the reading of the word which he has composed is not so easy. Indeed, he generally succeeds in reading it only after a certain effort . . . But once he has understood the mechanism of the game, the child goes forward by himself, and becomes intensely interested.[3]

One concern might be that such prolonged exposure to highly individualistic spelling patterns might make children poorer spellers in the long run. Chomsky points out that standard spelling finds its way gradually into the children's writing from reading, use of the dictionary, and direct instruction.[4] Look again at Cortney's note, shown in Figure 11-1 (page 251). Cortney is using many invented spellings: *mie* (my); *sore* (sorry), *longr* (longer), and *der* (dear). But she is also using some standard spellings for words that she sees frequently in books and that she uses frequently in her writing. We find this in *no, love,* and *I'm*.

Using invented spellings in early writing experiences does not appear to be harmful. A study in which the spelling subtest of the California Achievement Test was given to a group of children who had spelled inventively all through first grade showed grade-level scores in second grade and above-grade-level scores in third grade in spelling.[5]

In many ways, encouraging children to start writing using their own ways to represent words makes spelling more parallel to the acquisition of language. It also fits with Piaget's view that children understand best what they have figured out for themselves. Once children have invented a system of spelling, the principle of how such a system works is theirs, and converting to standard spelling is quite easy. What characteristics do learning to spell this way and learning a language have in common? First, approximations are rewarded. When children are first learning to talk, we do not expect or demand adult form. We hear, *Me going dere?* and we answer as if it were a perfect sentence. When we can understand what writing means, why not take the same approach? We need to respond more to children's meaning, and less to the form it takes—especially in the beginning stages. A second parallel is that practice should mean engaging in the activity in a real way. Students should practice spelling in the way that a doctor practices medicine or a lawyer practices law—not pretending, but using the skill in meaningful ways. Finally, just as children are active in processing the language from their surroundings and figuring out how it works, they should be active in examining how words are spelled and how sounds are represented in writing, and in figuring out the letter-sound system too. We have considerable evidence that figuring out the rules helps one remember them better; that is inductive teaching.

Regularity in Phoneme-Grapheme Relationships

While many delight in pointing out the irregularities in our language, actually it is quite systematic. One or two letters will account for a very large percentage of nearly all sounds. Further, the fact that our sound-letter relationships are not in perfect correspondence allows for divergent dialect pronunciations. If people wrote words just as they pronounce them, we would have real trouble reading what someone speaking a different dialect had written. Here are some groupings of the consonant sounds and short and long vowel sounds with corresponding spellings; you may find them useful. The information comes from Hanna, Hanna, Hodges and Rudorf's study[6] of 17, 310 commonly used words in English.

Consonants are the most regularly spelled. Tables 11-1, 11-2, and 11-3 show three groups of consonant sounds with the percentage of time each is spelled as indicated.

Vowels are not spelled as regularly as consonants, but there is enough regularity with both long and short vowel sounds that students can use such information to help them become better spellers. Of these two, short vowel sounds (Table 11-4) are more regularly spelled than long vowel sounds (Table 11-5).

Table 11-1. Consonant sounds spelled primarily with one letter/letter combination

Sound	As in	Letter(s)	Percentage
/h/	*hit*	*h*	98
/hw/	*when*	*wh*	100
/kw/	*quick*	*qu*	97
/əl/	*riddle*	*le*	95
/v/	*very*	*v*	99
/w/	*wet*	*w*	92
/th/*	*then* or *think*	*th*	100

*Voiced or unvoiced.

Table 11-2. Consonant sounds spelled with matching single or double letter

Sound	As in	Letters Used	Percentage
/b/	*bat* or *rubber*	*b* or *bb*	99
/d/	*dog* or *fiddle*	*d* or *dd*	99
/f/	*fin* or *puff*	*f* or *ff*	87
/g/	*go* or *giggle*	*g* or *gg*	93
/l/	*like* or *fill*	*l* or *ll*	99
/m/	*my* or *hummed*	*m* or *mm*	98
/n/	*no* or *runner*	*n* or *nn*	99
/p/	*pet* or *clipped*	*p* or *pp*	100
/r/	*red* or *purr*	*r* or *rr*	99
/t/	*to* or *putt*	*t* or *tt*	99

Table 11-3. Consonant sounds spelled with different letter combinations

Sound	As in	Primary Letters	Percentage		Secondary Letters	Percentage
/ch/	check	ch	55	and	tch	31
/j/	gym	g	66	and	j	22
/k/	cat	c	73	and	k	13
/ks/	fix	x	90	and	cs	9
/ng/	ring	ng	59	and	n	40
/s/	so	s	72	and	c	17
/sh/	ration	ti	53	and	sh	26
/y/	yes	i	55	and	y	44
/z/	was	s	64	and	z	23
/zh/	fusion	si	49	and	s	33

Table 11-4. Short vowel sounds spelled with matching alphabetic letter

Sound	As in	Letter	Percentage
/a/	pat	a	96
/e/	pet	e	90
/i/	pit	i	68
		or y	23
/o/	pot	o	93
/u/	putt	u	86

Table 11-5. Long vowel sounds spelled with matching alphabetic letter or matching alphabetic letter and diacritic e

Sound	As in	Letters Used	Combined Percentage
/a/	acorn or cake	a or a-e	79
/e/	media or scene	e or e-e	72
/i/	idea or hide	i or i-e	74
/o/	roll or pose	o or o-e	86
/u/	unit or tune	u or u-e	89

How could teachers use such information in teaching students to spell? Good spellers know how a word could be spelled as well as what it should look like. This is the approach we recommend for all children. Learn how the word might be spelled, that is, what letters might be expected to spell the sounds; and then write the word down one or more ways to see which looks right. Let's take the color of the paper this book is printed on. It should be *whit* or *white*. Do either of those look right? Yes, the second one: *white*. Even if it's not that easy, the process is effective.

Suppose a word includes a vowel sound that is not represented by the most frequent spelling. While a long *a* sound is spelled with *a* or *a-e* 79 percent of the time, it can also be spelled numerous other ways. Students will need to learn some of these as they go along; *ai, ay, ai-e, eigh, e, ea, ei,* and *ey* are spellings that are found in ten or more words with this sound. Now, let's take the word that means "to hurt," "to ache," "to be very sore." First, we try *pan* and *pane.* Those aren't right; *pan* has the short *a* sound, and *pane* is a piece of glass, a homophone. Well, what next? *Pain, payn, paine?* The only one that looks right is *pain.* An added benefit of this procedure is that students become increasingly able to look up spellings in a word book or dictionary because if the word isn't spelled as they think at first, they now have an alternative letter combination or two to check. The basic strategy, then, is:

1. *How could it be spelled?*
2. *Which looks right?* (If you're not sure, check.)

Sources of Words for Study

Several sources for spelling study need to be considered. Each contributes to the spelling program in different ways at different grades. Selection of words from different sources helps to build a complete program.

Spelling texts   Spelling texts present words in some sort of sequence and may be used to provide continuity from grade to grade. Although commercial textbooks differ, the organization of the basic instructional program usually follows a similar pattern. The test-study plan is basic to these spellers and can be a very effective method of learning words—providing that students correct their own tests. The main shortcoming is that such texts encourage all students to study the same words and to do so in the same way—in spite of the fact that students differ considerably in the words they can or cannot spell. In addition, texts do not usually provide ways to relate the study of their word lists to students' writing needs in other areas.

Students' writing   Since the purpose of learning to spell words correctly is to communicate with others effectively in writing, the students' own writing is a logical source for spelling words. In fact, a writing component is essential to an effective spelling program. By selecting and writing words, students develop the ability to spell the words they need to use. As needs arise, new words are written, learned, and added to their growing spelling vocabularies.

Younger children may enjoy the way of keeping records suggested by Dunkeld and Hatch.[7] The teacher prepares three envelopes for each child, with the child's name in red on one, in yellow on the second, and in green on the third. As the teacher discovers words that are consistently misspelled in children's writing, he or she writes these words on strips of paper and places them in the red envelope. When the student is in the process of studying the word, it is placed in the yellow envelope; and when it is completely mastered, it is placed in the green envelope. This method gives the teacher a chance to select words for study on the basis of students' actual errors; frequently misspelled words receive special attention; and students can evaluate their progress by seeing how many problem words have been put in the green envelope.

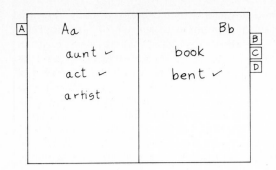

Figure 11-5
Individualized spelling dictionary.

Older students should be encouraged to keep individual spelling dictionaries of their own words. A notebook is alphabetically tabbed for each student, and then when students ask for spellings, when they look words up, or when they make mistakes in their writing, the words are placed on the appropriate page. Periodically students should select words from this book for study, checking off the ones mastered, as in Figure 11-5. Teachers often use these books, too, as they circulate around the room during writing or editing time to write down the correct spellings of words their students need help with (instead of trying to spell aloud).

Word lists Frequency of use of words is another criterion for choosing words to learn to spell. Researchers have found that about 3,000 words make up 95 percent of all words most commonly used by individuals in their writing. Ten words account for 25 percent of all the running words in the writing of adults— *I, the, and, to, a, you, of, in, we,* and *for,* and one hundred words represent approximately 60 percent of all the words used in an average person's writing.[8] Unfortunately, frequently used words are sometimes difficult to learn because they have so little appeal and because few of them represent concrete objects.

In Cunningham's "Scratch, Scribble, and Scribe"[9] such frequently used words are written on individual large strips and put up around the room—a few at a time—in alphabetical order. Each day the teacher tells the students to take out a sheet of "scratch" paper, and then dictates a test of five words. These may be some of the new words for the day or week or words from earlier sessions. Of course, if students need to look at the word cards, they can; but soon the words are learned and there is no need. This technique or something similar is particularly effective in helping students with those frequently used but uninteresting (and often irregular) words.

Rinsland conducted a study to determine what words children use most commonly in their writing.[10] The list of words that he found most frequently used by children should prove helpful to the teacher of spelling.

Rinsland's List of First Words of Highest-Frequency Use

a	again	also	an	any	as
about	all	always	and	are	asked
after	along	am	another	around	at

away	do	help	more	room	today
baby	dog	her	morning	run	told
back	doll	here	most	said	too
ball	don't	him	mother	Santa Claus	took
be	door	his	much	saw	town
because	down	home	must	say	tree
bed	each	hope	my	school	two
been	eat	house	name	see	until
before	every	how	never	she	up
best	father	I	new	should	us
better	few	if	next	sister	very
big	find	I'm	nice	snow	want
black	first	in	night	so	wanted
book	five	into	no	some	was
boy	for	is	not	something	water
boys	found	it	now	soon	way
bring	four	its	of	started	we
brother	friend	just	off	summer	week
but	from	know	old	sure	well
by	fun	large	on	take	went
called	gave	last	once	teacher	were
came	get	let	one	tell	what
can	getting	letter	only	than	when
car	girl	like	or	that	where
cat	girls	little	other	the	which
children	give	live	our	their	while
Christmas	glad	long	out	them	white
close	go	look	over	then	who
cold	going	looked	people	there	why
come	good	lot	place	these	will
coming	got	lots	play	they	wish
could	grade	love	played	thing	with
country	great	made	please	things	work
daddy	had	make	pretty	think	would
day	happy	man	put	thought	write
days	has	many	ran	three	year
dear	have	me	read	through	years
did	he	men	red	time	you
didn't	heard	milk	right	to	your

Spelling words taken from content areas Content areas, such as social studies and science, can be sources for spelling words. However, a word of caution is needed here. Words selected for study should be useful to students long after a given topic is completed in a subject area. Too frequently time is spent learning to spell words that will not be needed again for writing. If a child wants to learn some of the more unusual words, this is fine. But a required list of such words to commit to memory is unnecessary. They can simply be listed on chart paper for everyone's use during that unit of study.

SUPPORTIVE WRITING SKILLS

Word families There are groups of words that can be most profitably studied together. These "families" are of two types: phonic groupings in which a sound is spelled with the same letter combination or semantic groupings in which the words are related by both meaning and spelling. The phonic groupings are commonly used and help students focus on a particular phoneme-grapheme correspondence such as *hey* and *they* or *few, grew, new, pew,* and *stew.* When using such groupings, it is generally counterproductive to use different spellings of the same sound in one lesson.

Semantic families help children focus on words that come from the same base, carrying similar spellings even when pronunciation changes. The first vowel sound in *courtesy* is difficult, but not when you know that the word comes from *court* and the manners that were appropriate there. Thus, *court, courtesy,* and *courteous* are learned at one time. How is the second vowel in confidence spelled? To many, it sounds as if it would be an *a* or an *e.* If you associate it with *confide,* however, you know right away that you should use an *i.* Thus *confide* becomes the key to *confidante, confidence, confident,* and *confidential*—all of which carry the *i* in the second syllable.

Both types of groupings can provide children with information to use in selecting the correct spelling. And having several different strategies to use helps students make the correct, conventional choice.

Methods of Studying Words

One of the priorities in developing good spellers is to help students see the need for correct spelling themselves. Consequently, it is important to set spelling study within a framework of writing and sharing one's writing with many other people—other students, the teacher, parents, visitors, or students in other classes. No amount of lecturing by the teacher is as effective as seeing someone else unable to read your story because of misspellings.

The steps that a child may take in studying a word are listed below.

1. Observe the word and pronounce it.
2. Close your eyes and mentally picture how the word looks. Write it.
3. Look at the word again and check the spelling with yours.
4. Write the word thinking about how it looks.
5. Check your written spelling of the word.
6. Try writing the word correctly one more time.

Notice that these study rules involve looking at the word, visualizing it, and checking it in written form. It is not necessary to write the word many times; three times in one study period is about maximum. Concentrated study while writing the word fewer times really works.

For many years we have attempted to teach spelling rules or generalizations to help children learn to spell. Phonic generalizations are not really helpful, except perhaps to check a word after it is written. For example, one rule that is quite regular is that words having double *e* usually have the long *e* sound. For the speller, the problem is not what sound *ee* makes, but what letters to use in writing down the long *e* sound; and a study by Hanna et al.[11] indicates that *ee* is used for that sound only 9.8 percent of the time. Because spelling and reading are opposite processes, generalizations that may be helpful in reading are usually not helpful in spelling. Furthermore, many of the generalizations taught do not work well enough to justify teaching them at all. In a study of the applicability of spelling generalizations to words in six major spelling programs, Davis[12] considered the commonly taught rule "When there are two vowels side by side, the long sound of the first one is heard and the second is usually silent." She found this to be applicable only 32 percent of the time: in 1,893 words with two vowels side by side, 612 conformed to the rule and there were 1,281 exceptions. Applying this rule, then, you would be wrong more than two times out of three. But even if the rule worked most of the time, how would it tell you to put two vowels together—let alone which two vowels?

The "rules" that do seem to work are those that can be induced from the charts of sound-letter correspondences given earlier in the chapter.

1. Short vowel sounds are most often spelled with the matching alphabetic letter.
2. Long vowel sounds are most often represented by the matching alphabetic letter or by the matching letter and a diacritic *e*.
3. Consonant sounds are most often represented by the matching alphabetic letter.
4. Consonants are often doubled at the end of words and sometimes in the middle of words.
5. Some consonants double by changing letters: *k* becomes *ck*, *ch* becomes *tch*, and *j* becomes *dge*.

The practices which help students learn to spell involve using a test-study-test program so that students can identify which words they need to study. Research clearly shows that students learn best to spell if they correct their own papers, thus focusing attention on the mistakes they have made as soon as possible. Frequent practice which involves writing the word about three times at a session is more effective than one session in which words are written ten or fifteen times. All practice should involve writing the word, not spelling it out loud. Games may be used for additional practice and for motivation.

Spelling Games and Activities

Occasionally a spelling game or special activity will add motivation and interest to learning to spell. All games should meet two criteria: the spelling should be done in written form and *all* children should participate throughout the activity. This eliminates the spelling bee, at least in its traditional format. An acceptable spelling bee would allow teams to consult on the spelling of a word and the word would be written on the board instead of being spelled orally.

Some children enjoy word puzzles of various kinds, and for them crossword puzzles may prove enjoyable. These must be very simple at first as most children do not understand how they work. Early puzzles might have only two or three words but illustrate different spellings of the same sound, as in Figure 11-6.

Another old-fashioned game that still has a great deal of appeal for students is hangman. In playing this game the players try to find out what word the teacher or another student has selected by guessing what letters might be in it before they are "hung." Figure 11-7 shows what would be drawn for a five-letter word before the game begins. Each wrong guess allows another part of the person to be added to the noose. The students must guess the word before the figure is completely drawn. The teacher may vary the number of guesses allowed by

How can you spell the sound /f/ ?

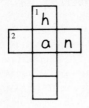
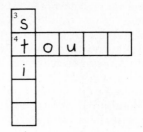

Down:
1. A part of a whole is a _____.
3. Synonym for rigid.

Across:
2. Something used to circulate air.
4. Synonym for difficult (slang).

Answers:

half
fan
stiff
tough

Figure 11-6 Spelling puzzles.

Figure 11-7 "Hangman."

1   2   3   4   5   6   7
n   o   d   d   i   m   e

Clue	Answer: Position	Word
a. ten cents	4	*dime*
b. strange or peculiar	2	*odd*
c. word that means you	6	*me*
d. opposite of bright	4	*dim*
e. shake your head	1	*nod*

Figure 11-8 Classroom version of a television game.

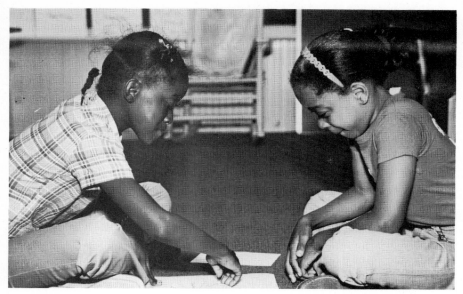

Games for spelling practice are excellent for developing a student's interest in spelling.

varying the number of parts to the person being hung. That is, only the head, torso, arms, and legs may be used, giving six incorrect guesses; or hands, feet, and so on may be added to the list.

Classroom versions of television game shows can be worked out to provide interesting spelling games. One such game calls for the contestant to locate words in a line of continuous letters. This is good practice in developing a visual set toward spelling. You can use one line of letters or several rows depending on the students' age and ability. After you give the clue, the students must identify the word by giving its position and saying or writing it. An example of this is shown in Figure 11-8.

Another version of a television game requires a spinner on a wheel with varying numbers of points marked off around the circle. A preselected title, person's name, or object is shown with a dash for each letter. The players from each team alternate, trying to guess which consonants might be in the mystery word. They may use some of the points they have accumulated to "buy" a vowel (they guess which one), or they may guess the word. If they make an incorrect guess, the next player takes over. The object is to get as many points as possible. If there are two or more repeated consonants in the word, they get the number of points spun multiplied by the number of times that consonant appears.

Team competitions may also be set up by asking students to alternate in listing words that have a particular prefix, suffix, or compound part. This could also include writing synonyms or antonyms. For example, use the prefix -*un*:

Team A: **1.** *unfriendly*   **3.** *unhappy*   **5.** *unclean*

Team B: **2.** *unable*   **4.** *unnecessary*   **6.** ?

Team A wins the first round and team B starts the second round. This game is good not only for practice in spelling, but also for vocabulary development.

The commercial game of Scrabble can also be an enjoyable spelling activity. To score points, players are required to think of a variety of word choices that contain letters or a specified number of letters. Students also use a dictionary to check word spellings as well as the existence of words.

Games for spelling practice are intended to develop interest in spelling and make spelling study more enjoyable. They are an excellent alternative to looking up the meaning of each word in the dictionary or to writing each word in a sentence week after week, two common practices that have little relation to spelling.

Testing in the Individualized Spelling Program

If the spelling words that children are learning are from completely individualized lists, then the testing must also be individualized. If you have an aide or teaching assistant, he or she may give the tests; otherwise the children may test one another. Some teachers prefer to individualize spelling study by using reading groups and alternating which group has individual lists. If this is the case, the teacher may dictate the spelling tests for the various groups on the weeks when they are working on the same words. The test words and sample sentences may also be put on tape by the teacher or by each individual child, and the cassette tape can then be used to test whenever the child is ready. If it is possible to have a cassette for each student, there are many possibilities for reviewing words.

Perhaps this is an appropriate time to point out that it is not necessary to work with a new group of words each week; there is nothing sacred about Friday spelling tests. Some children may use a four-day study period; others a seven- or nine-day period. Having some variation in when children start a new list to study and when they are tested on the words may help you individualize their learning.

Analyzing Spelling Problems

An individualized spelling program depends upon the teacher's ability to determine what kinds of problems students are having in spelling. Typically, students use particular spelling strategies that cause them to make the same kinds of errors repeatedly. When you can find a pattern in their errors, you can often help your students spell a great many words more quickly.

Some errors indicate less trouble with spelling than others. For example, although *afrade* is not the conventional spelling of *afraid*, we can still recognize the word. Recognizing *thaitch* as *though* is almost impossible and indicates a more serious problem. The types of errors that children make can be classified into seven categories.

1. *Not using the English phoneme-grapheme system:* Children who spell *though* as *thaitch* or who spell *favorite* as *falort* aren't using letters that could represent the sounds in the word.
2. *Spelling the homophone:* Many words that are pronounced the same have dif-

ferent spellings. These are pairs like *blew* and *blue, threw* and *through,* or *see* and *sea.* There are also pairs of words that within some dialects become homonyms: like *on* and *own, pin* and *pen,* or *ant* and *aunt.* When children pronounce two words in the same way—whether or not this pronunciation is correct—they are apt to misspell them: like *witch* and *which, then* and *than,* or *ask* and *ax.*

3. *Making the wrong choice among options: Cream* could be spelled several different ways: *creme, creem, kreme, criem, creame,* etc. When students choose one of the alternative ways, they are using the English phoneme-grapheme system; they just didn't make the right choice. While this means that the word is not spelled correctly, it is usually still readable and shows that the student knows something about spelling.

4. *Reversing letters in a word:* Often reversing letters occurs when one hurries and the mind is going faster than the pen or pencil. A common reversal is spelling *girl* as *gril* or *also* as *aslo.* This frequently happens when words are studied aloud; children know what letters belong, but have not developed a sense of their order or appearance.

5. *Adding or deleting letters when combining words or affixes:* Children often make errors in spelling when they combine two words—*drivway* instead of *driveway*—or when they add an affix to a word and fail to double or drop a letter when they should, or do so when they should not. Thus we get *slideing* instead of *sliding, sliping* instead of *slipping,* or *realy* instead of *really.*

6. *Making mispronunciations that lead to errors when children depend on the sounds in the word:* If you pronounce the word *library* as *lieberry,* you are apt to spell it *libary. February* is also often mispronounced and therefore spelled *Febuary.* Some dialect pronunciations can also lead children into misspellings: *idear* for *idea* in the Northeast or *den* for *then* among speakers of black dialect.

7. *Other errors:* There are other errors that do not readily fit into one of the preceding categories. Some seem to occur when children first learn about a diacritic (silent) *e.* They add *e*'s to everything, and so we find *am* spelled *ame* or *stop* spelled *stope.* Then there is *unclet* for *uncle;* perhaps the *t* from *aunt* got transferred here, or perhaps this is creativity appearing. Such unexplainable errors seem to need an "other" category.

Teachers should keep a record of students' errors—or have the students do so—by listing the misspellings along with the correct spelling. Then you can see what patterns emerge in the kinds of errors that individual students are making. Those who are making errors in category 1 need to learn sound-letter representations and proofread their work to see if they can read it back. Mnemonic devices and special lessons or games may help children who use the wrong homophone, category 2. Working on developing a visual sense of the word and regular proofreading will help children in choosing the right option, category 3. Reversing letters, category 4, and other errors, category 7, may both be helped by careful proofreading and studying words in writing. Category 5, adding or deleting letters when adding affixes or combining words, should be helped by practice with groups of words that drop or add letters. Different groups of these should be separated in time, so that each is learned thoroughly before encountering another group. Individualized study and concentrating on written forms should help children with errors in category 6, which relate to word pronunciation.

Some words seem to be particularly difficult for students, even those in the middle grades. Unfortunately, many of these difficult words are among the more frequently used words. Many have little intrinsic interest or content; many do not use the most common letters to represent their sounds. Here is a list[13] of the one hundred words most commonly misspelled by elementary school children. Those checked are also on Rinsland's list of words most frequently used in students' writing.

One Hundred Words Most Frequently Misspelled

their ✓	February	something ✓	running	its ✓
too ✓	once ✓	named	believe	started ✓
there ✓	like ✓	came ✓	little ✓	that's
they ✓	they're	name ✓	thing ✓	would ✓
then ✓	cousin	tried	him ✓	again ✓
until ✓	mother ✓	here ✓	all right	heard ✓
our ✓	another ✓	many ✓	happened	received
asked ✓	threw	knew	didn't	coming ✓
off ✓	some ✓	with ✓	always ✓	to ✓
through ✓	bought	together	surprise	said ✓
wanted ✓	getting ✓	you're	before ✓	swimming
hear	going ✓	clothes	caught	first ✓
from ✓	course	looked ✓	every ✓	were ✓
frightened	woman	people ✓	different	than ✓
for ✓	animals	pretty ✓	interesting	two ✓
know ✓	because ✓	went ✓	sometimes	jumped
decided	thought ✓	where ✓	friends	around ✓
friend ✓	and ✓	stopped	children ✓	dropped
when ✓	beautiful	very ✓	an ✓	babies
let's	it's	morning ✓	school ✓	money

A Final Word About Spelling

The discussion in this section has centered on a variety of methods and approaches that may be used to facilitate spelling instruction. We need to recognize that an effective spelling program does not adhere to a single approach. A method that helps one child spell better may not help another. And when all is said and done, it is not the method per se that makes good spellers; it is how well the method is implemented and children learn.

HANDWRITING INSTRUCTION

The manuscript style of writing often called printing first appeared in this country in the early 1920s. After its debut in suburban and private schools, the teaching of manuscript writing spread throughout the public schools. By 1950, this style of writing had become widely accepted in the primary grades, replacing the cursive style of writing which had been learned by young children for years and years.[14]

Teachers, who were concerned with teaching children to read, were delighted to see manuscript writing come into vogue. There was no longer a problem of dealing with two styles of writing—cursive for the purpose of writing and manuscript for the purpose of reading. Now children could focus on one style of writing—print—when first learning to read and write.

Beginning Handwriting Instruction

It is widely accepted that young children should begin to write in manuscript or print. The rationale for initial instruction in manuscript is aptly stated by Herrick.[15] If we consider young children's eye-hand coordination and motor development, the straight lines and circles which are used to make manuscript letters are best. The first-grade child is learning to read, and manuscript symbols correspond to the print children are asked to read. Finally, children's writing is more legible when they use manuscript.

Prewriting experiences Before formal instruction in manuscript writing, young children can benefit from prewriting experiences. The kindergarten child has not yet fully developed coordination of the smaller muscles in the hands and fingers. Experiences which consider children's physical development and help them prepare for writing can be an integral part of the learning environment.

The following activities illustrate the kind of prewriting experiences that might be provided for young children.

Painting: Children need frequent opportunities to paint, either at an easel or on the floor. Children consistently use strokes similar to those needed for manuscript writing when they paint their own pictures. You will readily find simple straight lines and circles, basic strokes in manuscript writing, in their paintings.

Making designs: Children can design their own book jackets, borders for bulletin boards or pictures, fabric for beanbags, and so on. Ideas for using designs that incorporate basic writing strokes are many.

Sand or salt trays: Sand or salt trays are easy to make and loads of fun for children. Using their fingers for drawing, children can make pictures and designs one after the other.

Finger painting: Finger painting offers children the opportunity to explore in a tactile manner lines, curves, ovals, squiggles, and so on.

Children's designs, paintings, or finger paintings can be used in a variety of ways. Those on heavy paper like Figure 11-9 may become book covers or placemats for lunch, snacks or a party. Designs done on long strips like those in Figure 11-10 may form a border for a bulletin board or decorate a learning center. Basic writing strokes like those in Figure 11-11 may frame a story, a poem, or a picture. Designs on cloth as in Figure 11-12 may be sewn into a cushion, a beanbag, or even a pocket on a cover-up shirt. Experiences making these should continue throughout kindergarten, and, for some children, during the first grade in

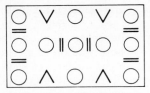

Figure 11-9   Overall design.

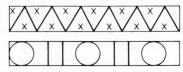

Figure 11-10   Border designs.

Figure 11-11   Design as a frame.

Figure 11-12   Fabric design.

school. Because young children develop physically at different rates, some students will not be ready for formal writing instruction when they enter first grade. They will need many more experiences that will get them ready to write.

Assessing writing readiness   The teacher who is concerned with initial writing instruction needs to determine which children are ready to learn manuscript. Berry [16] has developed a list that can be helpful in assessing writing readiness. She says that children may be taught to write when they show some interest in writing their own names; when they have developed facility in the use of scissors, crayons, the paintbrush, and the pencil in a variety of informal activities; when they can copy simple geometric or letterlike characters with proper orientation; when they have established a dominant hand; and when they sense a personal need to write.

Close observation of each child's physical or motor development is needed in order to make an accurate evaluation of his or her abilities. It is important for a teacher to understand that certain children, because of their stage of development, cannot be expected to write as well as those children who are already well coordinated.

Appropriate Materials for the Beginning Writer

Paper   Beginning writers will perform best if they are given large sheets of unlined paper. Newsprint or butcher paper works very well because young children need the freedom to use their large muscles for writing. Small sheets of paper require children to use small hand muscles, and may lead to fatigue and frustration. Because children's eye-hand coordination is still developing, unlined paper is recommended for use throughout grade one. Also, writing without lines helps beginners focus attention on letter formation.

Easels and chalkboards Children can write on paper that is attached to an easel or practice manuscript strokes or letters on the chalkboard. Both provide the area that young children need when beginning to write.

Writing instruments Large crayons or primary pencils are frequently recommended as writing instruments for young children. The primary pencil or readiness crayons are approximately twice the thickness of a conventional no. 2 pencil and are intended to be easier for beginning writers to hold. However, research studies indicate that most young children do very well with a standard-size writing instrument, and many children are already familiar with these because they have used them at home.

A manuscript alphabet Sample alphabet cards are familiar in the elementary school classroom. You will frequently find them placed above the chalkboard in the front of the room. To make the manuscript alphabet easier for children to see and use, try taping a sheet containing the alphabet to the top of each student's desk or table. Looking up to the front of the room and back to one's paper is difficult. The alphabet sheets may be laminated or covered with clear contact paper for protection from wear and tear, and this way children can see the letters as often as they wish.

Teaching Handwriting within a Meaningful Context

Instruction in handwriting should occur within a meaningful context. Practicing and mastering isolated strokes and letters before writing words belongs to the past. Young children can first learn to write their names, addresses, telephone numbers, the name of the school, and their teacher's name. They can keep their very own book or diary for recording each day's date along with something special to remember for the day. Meaningful writing experiences may also include writing notes to parents, labeling objects, recording observations of the classroom hamster or fish, writing messages to a pen pal within the class, or attaching captions to their drawings and paintings. Children may copy dictated experience stories or begin writing their own stories using their own spelling system.

Styles of Writing

There are many different styles of writing, and teachers should learn to form their letters—both manuscript and cursive—according to the writing system adopted in their school system. There is a surprising amount of difference in the letter shapes. Herrick compared nineteen commercial writing systems in 1960[17] and found agreement only on i and o in lowercase manuscript; only on P in uppercase manuscript; and only on a, i, e, m, n, s, and t in lowercase cursive. There was no agreement on any uppercase cursive letter. In manuscript, there were five forms of the lowercase letters y, p, and g; q had 7 forms. In lowercase cursive writing, the greatest variations were with *c* and *r*, which had six forms, and *g* and *y*, which had five forms; uppercase letters were even more varied.

Two styles of writing commonly used today are reproduced as an appendix to this chapter for your reference. One is the more traditional "ball-and-stick" style of print from Zaner-Bloser; the other is an "italic" style from Scott Foresman.

Manuscript Writing

Letter groupings of manuscript It is critical to start children off well so that they will develop correct writing habits. For children to begin writing properly, the teacher needs to show them individually how to form the letters, where to start each letter, and what makes one letter different from another similar one.

Often in handwriting, "similar" and "different" take on somewhat new meanings. In geometry, a triangle is a three-sided shape, and no matter how you turn it, it is still a triangle. But now children are confronted with the following:

The same: a a A a a

Different: d b p g g

What differences do make a difference? To help them learn what we know about this, it is important to teach letters in groupings that will contrast what is similar yet different. The emphasis in beginning writing must be on the order and direction of formation of the letters, not on similarities of appearance in the finished letter.

Manuscript lowercase letters There are five basic groups of letters in lowercase manuscript, according to direction and order of formation.

Group 1. o a d g q   Around to the left. Down.

Group 2. c e s • f   Around to the left, but not complete.

Group 3. l t i j • k u   Straight down. Another stroke.

Group 4. n m r h b p   Straight down. Push up and around to the right.

Group 5. v w x y • z   Down at an angle.

Teaching letters in these groupings will help children avoid confusion and prevent many reversals. *b* and *d* are widely separated, and the emphasis on *d* being like *a* (except with a longer line) and *b* being more like *h* (except completely closed) helps to separate that troublesome pair. S is often reversed as ᴢ; associating it with c and therefore making the first curve in the same direction as c should help prevent reversed s's. Sometimes children are unsure about the second line of y, making it ⋎. Again, association with a v-w-x whose first stroke is the same should help.

Manuscript capital letters   Most capital letters will be taught after the lowercase letters, although children may know a few—the ones in their name, the name of their school, etc. We recommend three groups of letters based on similarity to a corresponding lowercase letter, with subgroupings by direction of formation.

Group 1. Similar to lowercase.

COS · TKPU · VX · Z

Group 2. Partly similar to lowercase

FJ · MNW

Group 3. Different from lowercase

AHILE · DBR GQ · Y

Beginning instruction in manuscript   The beginning instruction in forming manuscript letters should be done carefully, with the teacher checking each child individually to make sure each letter is being formed correctly—that is, in the proper direction and order. You cannot look at OO and tell which was formed clockwise starting at the bottom and which counterclockwise from the top. You need to be walking around while children are practicing—checking their letters, the way the pencil is held, and the way the paper is placed. No more copying from the board while the teacher takes lunch count or works with reading groups!

After children have gone through the initial stages of learning to form the letters in manuscript, the teacher needs to individualize handwriting instruction. Some children may be reversing letters, others may need help with spacing, and a few may simply be unable to write certain letters. Children who have similar writing problems can be grouped together for instruction. Using the overhead projector, chalkboard, or prepared worksheets, the teacher can easily give these children special help.

Starting the left-handed writer   Because most children in elementary school classrooms are right-handed, those who are left-handed frequently get slighted. Without special guidance, the left-handed writer will naturally follow the instructions for right-handed writers. Too often, left-handed children develop the habit of hooking their wrist when they write because they have learned to slant their paper in the same direction as right-handed children.

It is the primary teacher who gives children their start in both manuscript

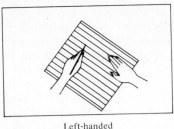

Left-handed   Right-handed

Figure 11-13   Positions for writing paper.

and cursive writing. What must this teacher be concerned about when teaching the left-handed writer? According to Enstrom, the left-handed student should be taught the following:

1. The paper for the left-handed writer should slant about 30 degrees to the right for both manuscript and cursive styles of writing, or slightly more slanted than for a right-handed person and in the opposite direction. Getting the child to position the paper in the proper direction is the first step toward making a successful writer. See Figure 11-13.
2. The left-handed child should hold the pencil farther back from the point than the right-handed child.
3. The child's elbows should be kept rather close to the body.
4. The blunt end of the pencil or pen should be directed back over the shoulder.
5. The desk should be high enough for the child to see the pencil or pen as it touches the paper.[18]

Working with children with special needs   Children with learning disabilities of various kinds may need special help with writing. If there is a specialist who works with such children, he or she may be able to suggest specific approaches to be used. If not, try using multisensory practice and reduce as many distractions as possible.

While most children do not need tactile or kinesthetic practice—making letters in sand or salt, tracing around sandpaper letters, or making large letters in the air with the whole arm—such practice may be helpful to children with learning disabilities. Lined paper is distracting, especially the kinds recommended for young children by companies producing handwriting materials that are filled with rows of straight lines in two colors with dotted lines interspersed. Such paper is disastrous for learning-disabled children. To reduce distractions, use unlined paper or paper with single lines. Children who are color-blind will also have trouble with lined paper using two colors; give them unlined paper or paper with only single-color lines, or mark the line they should write on until they can distinguish the special shade of gray that denotes the line.

While most manuscript systems have letters that are made with separate strokes, it may be helpful for some children to do more retracing or to use an italic system that is more similar to cursive letters. See Figure 11-14. A special focus on legibility rather than perfect letter form seems appropriate here.

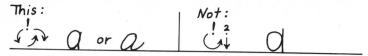

Figure 11-14 Modified letter forms for special children.

Cursive Writing

Although nearly all schools convert children from manuscript to cursive writing, there are several arguments for some children, if not all, to continue writing in manuscript style. Using research and theoretical evidence, those who favor continuing manuscript[19] point out:

There is no difference in speed between manuscript and cursive writing when children have had comparable practice in both.
Under pressure to write quickly, manuscript writing remains more legible.
A signature does not have to be done in cursive writing to be legal.
Children who develop slowly could benefit from continuing manuscript writing throughout elementary school.
Time spent in instruction in cursive writing could be better spent in creating, composing, and expressing ideas in the writing style that children have already mastered.
The primary concern of secondary schools is legibility, and manuscript writing is more legible than cursive. Note the frequency of "PLEASE PRINT" on forms.

In spite of numerous logical reasons for continuing manuscript writing, it is difficult to break with tradition. Many parents want their children to learn cursive style; and many children look forward to the time when they will learn to write in "real writing." Certainly all students should be taught to read cursive writing and many would choose to learn to write it if they could. Since it is somewhat unrealistic to consider eliminating cursive writing from the elementary school curriculum, we are including suggestions for teaching it.

Suggestions for teaching the reading of cursive handwriting Reading cursive should begin before formal instruction in this style of writing. The second-or third-grader will initially find cursive writing difficult to read and will need some special help. Several weeks before instruction in cursive, do the following:

Write the day's date on the chalkboard each morning in cursive:

Monday, April 1

If you are writing brief instructions on the chalkboard for children to read, write them in both manuscript and cursive, as in Figure 11-15.
Prepare ditto sheets that have sentences written in both manuscript and cursive writing styles. As a whole-class activity, read and discuss the sentences. A comparison may be made between the formation of corresponding manuscript and cursive letters.
As the children become more adept at reading cursive writing, start writing more of your instructions or announcements entirely in this writing style.

SUPPORTIVE WRITING SKILLS

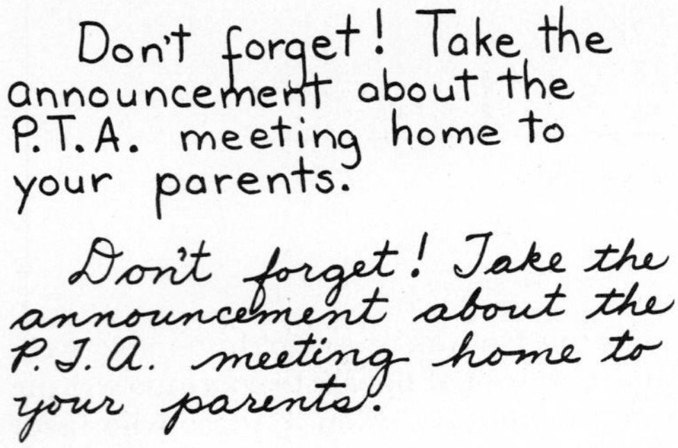

Don't forget! Take the
announcement about the
P.T.A. meeting home to
your parents.

Don't forget! Take the
announcement about the
P.T.A. meeting home to
your parents.

Figure 11-15 Instructions written in
(top) manuscript and (bottom) cursive.

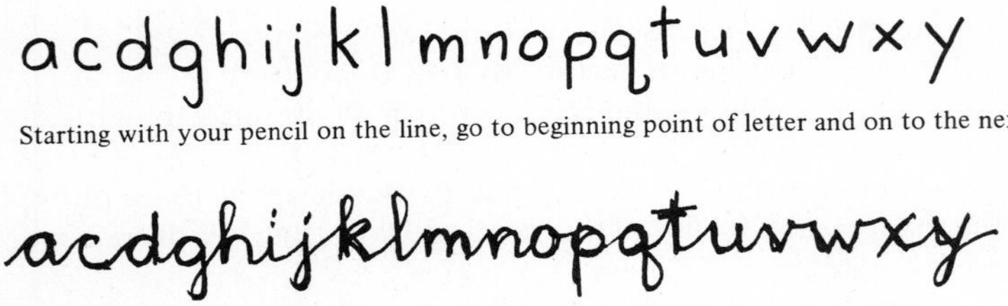

a c d g h i j k l m n o p q t u v w x y

Starting with your pencil on the line, go to beginning point of letter and on to the next.

acdghijklmnopqtuvwxy

Figure 11-16 Connecting manuscript letters to form cursive letters.

Teaching children to write in cursive style   Most of the letters in cursive writing are very similar to their corresponding manuscript form except for the connecting strokes or loops which help join the letters within a word.

Letter groupings of cursive writing   *Cursive lowercase letter groups*   All but six
lowercase letters can simply be connected and we have instantaneous cursive
writing. Look at Figure 11-16.
  Show the children this. Let them try it a few times. Then take these twenty
letters in groups of four or five and practice. Now make words and write them.
Try *all, at, that, chain, cat, dog, chicken, pig, cow, goat, toad, big, two, dot, can,
no, not, milk, jump, cold, cool,* and *yowl.* Have your students go on a word hunt
for words without *s, r, f, e, z,* and *b.* Practice writing all the words that they find,
gradually slanting a bit and working without the print first.
  Then go on to teach the six letters that look different in cursive writing or
are made in a different order-direction. Take time with each letter and practice
using them in words as you go along.

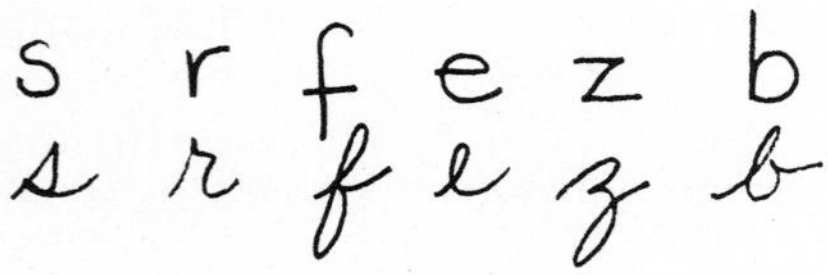

s   r   f   e   z   b
s   r   f   e   z   b

Group 1: Similar to lowercase letters

a c e o · m n v u y z w · p

Group 2: Partly similar to lowercase letters

K X

Group 3: Different from lowercase letters

B R · F T · G S · I J · L · E · H · 2 · O

Figure 11-17   Groups of cursive capital letters.

Cursive capital letter groups   For a while the students can use their manu-script capitals as they develop skill in the cursive lowercase letters. When you are ready to teach the capital letters, consider the groups and subgroups shown in Figure 11-17.

Midpoint connectors   One other group of letters in cursive writing may need special attention. These are the midpoint connectors:

b   o   v   w

All the other letters start and end at the baseline; these four end at midpoint and cause students great difficulty when they are followed by *s*, *e*, and *r* in particular, but sometimes also *k*, *l*, and *i*. When the upstroke from the line is not present, the letter changes appearance. These combinations need special practice.

Bring, bite, tubs, bean, black   *br*

Ostrich, toe, ore, coke, old, coin   *os*

Very, vivid, village   *ve*

Flows, west, wring, winter, wise   *wr*

Some children have trouble with *m* and *n*; this can be somewhat alleviated by starting all letters at the baseline and emphasizing that *m* has three down strokes and *n* has two down strokes — true even after a midpoint connector.

m   n   am   an   omit   on

Students need to observe how letters are formed. A teacher may use both an overhead projector and the chalkboard to demonstrate such things as letter for-mation, uniformity of size, slant, and how particular letters are connected.

Some thoughts on practice   Practicing handwriting is not a very exciting task, and anything the teacher can do to make it more interesting seems worthwhile.

Children may use the chalkboard or an overhead projector to work on particular groups of letters. They also enjoy using colored felt-tip pens and brightly colored paper. Even while they are learning to write in cursive style, they need opportunities to keep up some facility with manuscript writing. Making signs, labels for displays, or titles for bulletin boards helps keep them in practice.

Assessing Legibility in Writing

Early evaluators of handwriting emphasized its esthetic qualities, and instruction emphasized "beautiful" writing. Current methods emphasize teaching for legibility, since the entire purpose of writing is its readability. What factors influence legibility? Four factors are the most important in determining legibility: letter formation, spacing, size or proportion, and slant. Two other factors may affect legibility: alignment and line quality. The letters formed should be the correct shape, well rounded, and properly connected. Spacing should be even and appropriate between letters, words, and lines of writing. The size of the letters should be even, not too large or too small, with enough contrast between tall letters and middle-size ones. The slant should be regular, not too far forward or backward. (Some backward slant may be appropriate for left-handed writers.) Alignment means that the letters are on the line, not above or below it. The line quality of the writing should be even and not too light or too dark.

To complete the evaluation of students' writing, the teacher should check the position of each student's body and paper as well as how the writing instrument is held. This should be done often in the early grades and less frequently in later grades. When you are teaching an upper grade and have students holding a pencil incorrectly or left-handed students writing with their wrist hooked, it may be difficult to get them to change. This is why it is so critical to get students started correctly in the lower grades.

Improving Handwriting

One of the main ways to improve handwriting is to improve the quality of instruction in the initial stages of writing. Developing legibility and speed is then an individual problem. Conferences with the teacher are helpful in getting children to see what particular problems they have and how they can make their handwriting more legible. Before such a conference, the teacher should actually observe the child writing. This helps in assessing handwriting speed and facility as well as helping to determine if that child is forming letters correctly. After such teacher-student conferences to determine what particular skills the children should work on, there is direction and purpose to their practice.

Just copying something from the board will not improve students' writing. They must focus their practice on the one major problem they are having. If they need to work on the c-e-s-f group in manuscript, they need words with lots of those letters. If they need to work on midpoint connectors in cursive followed by an e or an r, they need words with b-o-w-v plus e or r. Don't have them copy poetry; it makes for poor handwriting practice and turns them away from poems.

Students should be involved in evaluating their own writing. A quick way is to have a set of samples ranging from excellent to poor. These may be prepared by you or may be available from publishers of handwriting materials such as Zaner-Bloser.[20] To use such a scale, students simply compare a sample of their writing with the writing specimens given on the scale. When they find a specimen that closely resembles theirs, they read the corresponding rating score and evaluative comments. Students can help determine what factors, such as letter size and slant, can be improved in order to increase the quality or speed of their writing.

Students should also keep samples of their writing to be used for evaluative purposes. It is best to begin a handwriting folder for each person at the first of the school year. From time to time, new handwriting samples are added to the folder. By dating each sample, students can compare papers written in September with those placed in the folder in October, November, December, and so on. The growing collection of handwriting samples can be used by students to assess their own handwriting progress. When later samples are compared with earlier written samples, students can determine if the quality of their handwriting is steadily improving. They also can diagnose problem areas that need further improvement. Individualization, allowing students to work on their own handwriting problems, is essential to an effective handwriting program.

SUMMARY

Children learn the more mechanical aspects of writing—punctuation and capitalization, handwriting, and spelling—when they see the need for such things in their own writing. Whenever you can provide instruction within such a framework, it is certainly desirable to do so. Using conventional spelling and standard punctuation and capitalization and writing legibly are a courtesy to your reader. Although we may pull out some part of these skills for practice, the initial impetus for study should evolve from students' needs. Furthermore, the supportive writing skills should never divert the focus from the presentation of ideas.

PRELIMINARY LEARNING ACTIVITIES

1. Look at the excerpt from a child's story in Figure 11-18 (page 284), in her own writing. List the words spelled correctly; then categorize the mispelled words according to the probable cause of the error.
    (a) Not using the phoneme-grapheme system
    (b) Spelling the homophone
    (c) Using the system, but choosing the wrong option
    (d) Reversing letters
    (e) Adding or deleting letters when combining words or affixes
    (f) Mispronouncing words, causing misspelling
    (g) Other, not clearly explainable
    These should be applied in order, categorizing the misspelling by the first one that applies.

Im a quartersiting in a coke
mashih. And thin a bent up
dime dropse on my back and
scrachis it. Thin it kep on
happaning and boy did I look
uglee. And in a week on every sentam
eeter of my body I had a
scrach.

Figure 11-18 Sample for spelling analysis.

2. Now look at each of the lists of errors below and try to determine the major kind(s) of errors each student is making.

Kim

really/realy
writing/writting
particular/particuler
cried/cryed
trouble/truble
babysitter/babysiter

Lee

field/fild
ankle/anckool
straining/stranning
yelling/yealling
crawl/croll
helpless/helpliss
while/will

Marty

Christmas/Chrismas
would/whould
different/differnt
similar/simular
said/siad
life/live
could have/could of

3. Handwriting analysis involves the six factors discussed earlier in the chapter. Examine the handwriting samples—both print and cursive—in Figure 11-19 (pages 286–287) and analyze them using the factors that apply.

Letter Formation

Not correct shape
Not rounded
Not connected

Slant

Not regular
Too forward or backward

Spacing

Between letters
Between words
Between lines

Alignment

Not even
Not on line

Size and Proportion

Not even
Too big
Too little
Not enough contrast

Line Quality

Uneven
Too light
Too dark

4. Prepare a cassette tape of a series of short pieces of material involving punctuation skills appropriate for the age level you would use them with. The students who listen to the tape should be able to use your voice and timing as a guide. They could have a copy of the same material (without punctuation present) and add the appropriate marks or write the material down as dictation, both words and punctuation. (Start with one simple skill and gradually increase complexity and length.)

PARTICIPATION ACTIVITIES

1. Select one of the spelling games or activities and try it out with a group of children. If you wish, you can devise a game or crossword puzzle of your own. (Be sure it involves writing the words or seeing them in print and that all children can continue to participate and learn.)
2. Teach inductively some element of punctuation or capitalization that a group of children need to learn so that they discover the "rule" from the examples that you give.
3. Take some children who are having difficulty with handwriting and analyze their legibility problems. Keep a sample from before you start and then take another sample after working with them several times. See what progress they have made.

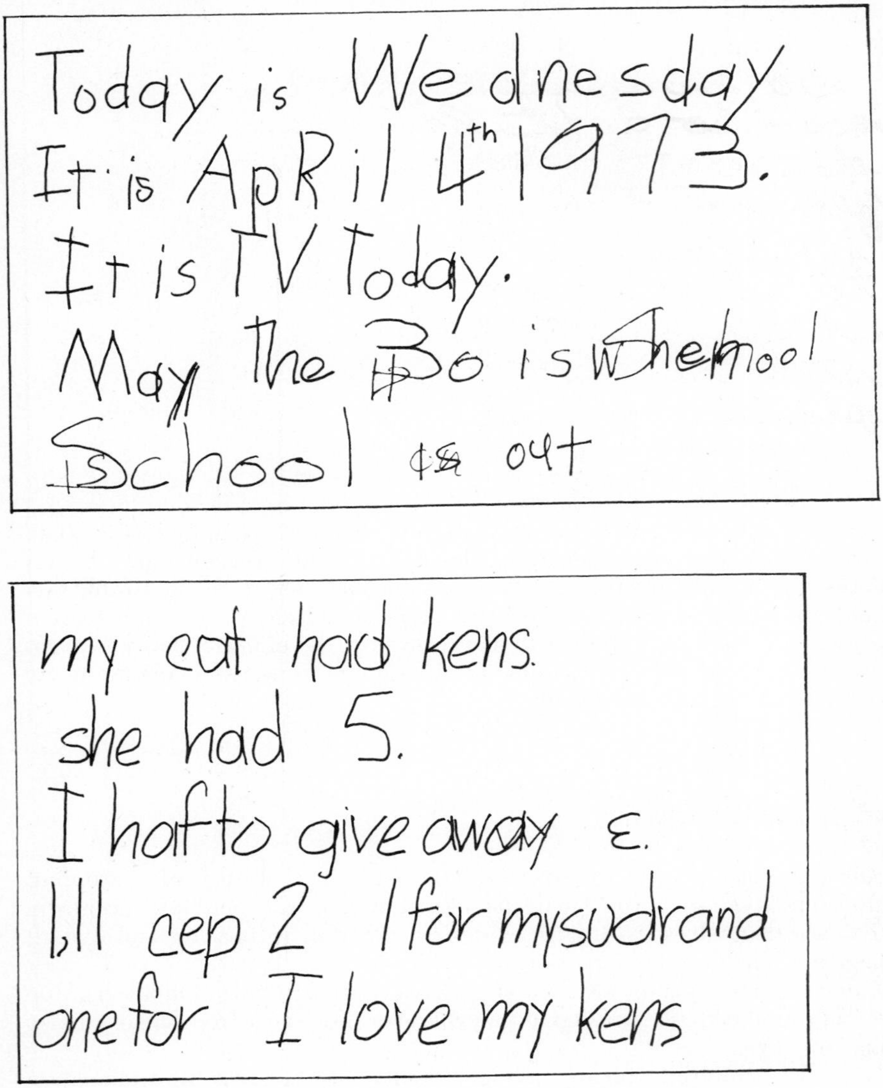

Today is Wednesday
It is ApRil 4th 1973.
It is TV Today.
May the Bo is Whehool
School is out

my cat had kens.
she had 5.
I hofto give away 3.
I,ll cep 2 I for mysudrand
one for I love my kens

Figure 11-19 Samples for handwriting analysis.

So now those zebras
now so don't be surprised
if santas makeing
zebras pull his sled.
You proble want
to know what I do
with the deer. But I
still use them only in
places where its cold.

The End

The zooger is very mean,
He will get you,
He sees something,
He said I'm going to kill it.
He runs after it,
The thing said help!
He kills it with the nife,

Figure 11-19. Samples for handwriting analysis (*continued*).

APPENDIX TO CHAPTER 11: HANDWRITING MODELS

From Parker Zaner Bloser[21]

From D'Nealian[22]

D'Nealian™ Manuscript Alphabet

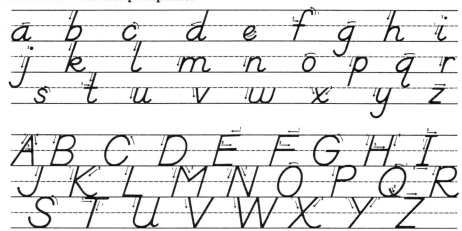

D'Nealian™ Cursive Alphabet

D'Nealian™ Numbers

REFERENCE NOTES

[1]Carol Chomsky. "Write Now, Read Later," in *Language in Early Childhood Education* (Courtney B. Cazden, ed.). Washington, D.C.: National Association for the Education of Young Children, 1972, p. 120.

[2]Carol Chomsky. "Invented Spelling in First Grade," unpublished paper, Harvard Graduate School of Education, May 1974, pp. 1–2.

[3]Maria Montessori. *The Montessori Method.* Cambridge, Mass.: Robert Bently, 1967, p. 283.

[4]Chomsky. "Invented Spelling," pp. 11–12.

[5]Ibid.

[6]Paul R. Hanna, Jean S. Hanna, Richard E. Hodges, and Edwin H. Rudorf. *Phoneme-Grapheme Correspondences as Cues to Spelling Improvement.* U.S. Dept. of Health, Education and Welfare, 1966.

[7]Colin Dunkeld and Lynda Hatch. "Building Spelling Confidence," *Elementary English*, vol. 52, no. 2, February 1975, p. 227.

[8]Ernest A. Horn. "A Basic Writing Vocabulary—10,000 Words Most Commonly Used in Writing," *University of Iowa Monographs in Education*, First Series, no. 4. Iowa City: University of Iowa, 1926.

[9]Pat Cunningham. "Scratch, Scribble, and Scribe: Can't-Fail Writing Recipes" (mimeographed). Alamence County Schools.

[10]Henry D. Rinsland. *A Basic Vocabulary of Elementary School Children.* New York: Macmillan, 1945.

[11]Hanna, Hanna, Hodges, and Rudorf. *Phoneme-Grapheme Correspondences as Cues to Spelling Improvement.*

[12]Lillie Smith Davis. "The Applicability of Phonic Generalizations to Selected Spelling Programs," *Elementary English*, vol. 49, no. 5, May 1972, pp. 706–713.

[13]Leslie W. Johnson. "One Hundred Words Most Often Misspelled by Children in the Elementary Grades," *Journal of Educational Research*, vol. 44, October 1950, pp. 154–155.

[14]Gertrude Hildreth. "Manuscript Writing after Sixty Years," *Elementary English*, vol. 37, no. 1, January 1960, pp. 3–13.

[15]Virgil E. Herrick. "Children's Experiences in Writing," in *Children and the Language Arts* (Virgil E. Herrick and Leland B. Jacobs, eds.). Englewood Cliffs, N.J.: Prentice-Hall, 1955, pp. 271–272.

[16]Althea Beery. "Readiness for Handwriting," *Readiness for Reading and Related Language Arts.* Champaign, Ill.: National Council of Teachers of English, 1950.

[17]Virgil E. Herrick. "Manuscript and Cursive Writing," *Childhood Education*, vol. 37, February 1961, pp. 264–267.

[18]Eric A. Enstrom. "The Extent of the Use of Left Hand in Handwriting and Determination of the Relative Efficiency of the Various Hand-Wrist-Wrist-Arm-Paper Adjustments," *Dissertation Abstracts*, vol. 27, no. 5, 1957.

[19]Modified list taken from Hildreth. "Manuscript Writing after Sixty Years," pp. 3–13.

[20]*Guiding Growth in Handwriting Scale.* Columbus, Ohio: Zaner-Bloser Company.

[21]Reproduced with permission of Zaner-Bloser, Inc., from the series *Creative Growth with Handwriting,* © 1975, 1979.

[22]From *D'Nealian*™. *Handwriting* by Donald N. Thurber, copyright © 1978, Scott, Foresman and Company; reprinted by permission.

PART THREE

Components: A Comprehensive Language Arts Program

In a comprehensive language arts program, children's literature and reading are fundamental components. However, because both are usually dealt with in separate and complete courses at the college level, the discussions presented in this text are primarily devoted to the relationship of language, literature, and reading.

There are strong indications that children who are surrounded with books and encouraged to read widely will develop broader vocabularies, will become more fluent speakers, and will be more proficient readers. If books can offer these advantages, then literature programs should be commonplace in elementary school classrooms. As is suggested in Chapter 12, such programs would include reading books aloud, sharing poetry, listening to recorded stories and poems, participating in small-group discussions of books, and sharing favorite stories through various creative projects.

Reading instruction is often separated from the natural development of language skills. In Chapter 13, the use of children's language is emphasized as a basis for reading instruction, and a description of the reading process according to psycholinguistic theory is presented. The discussion describes the teaching of reading using the language-experience approach. It outlines specific ways of helping children learn word-attack skills, since all too often teachers spend time eliciting stories from children for experience charts but devote very little time to using them in the instruction of basic reading skills.

Chapter 14, the final chapter, summarizes the linguistic and cognitive bases for the language arts program presented in the text. Guides which emphasize the interrelatedness of all the language arts are included in Chapter 14 to help with the planning of a balanced and integrated program. Suggestions for involving parents and teachers' aides are also an integral part of both this chapter and the individualized instructional program developed within the text.

CHAPTER TWELVE

Literature in the Language Arts

PREVIEW QUESTIONS

1 In what ways does literature—both prose and poetry—relate to language development?
2 What special opportunities does poetry offer for speaking and writing creatively, as well as for personal enjoyment?
3 In what ways can poetry be shared with children?
4 What are some books that will contribute to growth in language?
5 How is a literature program developed and implemented?

Children enjoy hearing stories read aloud. "Read me a story. Read it again!" And after three times, "Just one more time, just one!" Their attention is just as rapt the fourth time as the first—and they may correct you on a misread word or a section accidentally omitted.

Children's interest in stories is good for them. Parents who respond to children's requests to read aloud are helping their young children become verbally proficient. There is a strong chance that learning to read will be easier, vocabularies will be larger, and greater fluency in language usage will occur.

LANGUAGE DEVELOPMENT THROUGH LITERATURE

How can something as simple as reading aloud be so helpful to children? How can the language of books influence a child's development to that extent? Looking closely at literature, we see that the language may be as emotional as:

> "Go out and hold that mongrel if you don't want him shot." He held the door ajar the width of the boy's body and thrust him out. The boy fell on the back of the dog, whose snarling jaws had pushed into the light between the boy's legs. A heavy boot half pushed, half kicked the entangled feet of the sprawled boy and the nose of the dog and slammed the door. "Get that dog out of my way and hold him if you don't want him dead."[1]

The language may be as rhythmical as:

THE MODERN HIAWATHA

He killed the noble Mudjokovis,
With the skin he made him mittens,
Made them with the fur side inside,
Made them with the skin side outside,
He, to get the warm side inside,
Put the inside skin side outside:
He, to get the cold side outside,
Put the warm side fur side inside:
That's why he put the fur side inside,
Why he put the skin side outside,
Why he turned them inside outside.

George A. Strong[2]

The language may be as descriptive as:

> In the city everything is squeezed together. The buildings are so close they have to stretch up into the sky to find enough room .... A city sky is caught between tall buildings, with only a little bit showing.[3]

From literature, children learn the complexities of language, the diversity in its usage, the emotions of its tones, the softness of its beauty.

Related Research

Several research studies support the use of books to stimulate children's language and vocabulary development. Courtney Cazden[4] conducted an experimental study to determine if the finding of certain grammatical constructions in young children's oral language was related to parents' frequent expansion of the children's telegraphic speech. In reviewing her findings, she reported that children whose statements were extended by adult responses gained more than two other groups on six measures of language development. The significance of this finding, as it relates to literature, is that stories were read aloud to this group to stimulate conversation and discussion. The investigator, in citing implications of the research, suggests that children be given extensive opportunities to discuss ideas out loud and that books are excellent for creating talk about the pictures or story content.

A related study was conducted at New York University. Over 500 black children, kindergarten through grade 3, were involved in the year-long research effort. Approximately half the children (ten classrooms) assigned to the experimental group "participated in a literature-based oral language program intended to expand experience, conceptual ability, control over the structure of language and the range of language used."[5] Selected books were read aloud each day, followed by activities emphasizing the use of children's oral language. The control group, comprising the remaining half of the participating children, enjoyed a literature program, but the enrichment activities were intentionally not based on oral language. The results of the research indicated that literature expanded language skills for both groups of children. The greatest gains, however, were evidenced by students in the experimental group, with the most significant increase in kindergarten. In view of these findings, director of the study, Bernice Cullinan, makes the recommendation that a literature-based oral language program begin early. She further states that emphasis on oral language enhances children's mastery of standard dialect while maintaining facility in their own dialect.

From these two studies, we can conclude that reading books aloud—and then allowing time for plenty of conversation and discussion—stimulates children's oral language development. It would appear that students also are given a greater opportunity to become proficient in a more socially acceptable dialect when participating in this kind of language environment. The earlier a literature-based oral language program is provided, the better.

As a second part of a linguistic study, Chomsky directed an investigation that involved children from five to ten. Extensive information was gathered about each child's exposure to reading. Specifically, data were compiled regarding the amount a child read and was read to, and the complexity of the reading material itself. Further information was obtained using Huck's *Taking Inventory of Children's Literary Background,*[6] a measure indicating a child's knowledge of the content of sixty well-known books for children. The primary purpose of the study was to determine the relationship between reading exposure and a child's rate of linguistic development. The investigator considered written language to be potentially of a more complex nature than oral speech. Therefore, the assumption was made that children who read and hear a variety of rich and complex materials receive greater linguistic benefits than children who are non-literary. The study's findings on all reading measures were highly significant, resulting in the conclusion that reading exposure and linguistic stages of development are definitely related. Huck's inventory proved an excellent measure, consistently showing a positive relationship between scores and linguistic stages. Chomsky's summary of the results and implications of research speaks profoundly to the classroom teacher:

> Our reading results indicate that exposure to the more complex language available from reading does seem to go hand in hand with increased knowledge of the language. This would imply that perhaps wider reading should find a place in the curriculum. The child could be read to, stimulated to read on his own, not restricted to material deemed "at his level" but permitted access to books well "above his level" to get out of them whatever he may. Perhaps he should be encouraged to skim when he reads, to skip uninteresting portions and get to the "good parts" instead of concentrating at length on controlled texts. In general it may be that the effort should be towards providing more and richer language exposure, rather than limiting the child with restrictive and carefully programmed materials.[7]

The last piece of research to be discussed in this section is related to literature and reading with a special emphasis on vocabulary development. Conducting an extensive study to determine the influence of literature on vocabulary and reading achievement, Cohen identified second-grade classrooms containing children who were slow to learn to read. Each of the experimental classes received fifty books to be read aloud during the year, with some selections being read more than once. The books chosen for the study dealt with universal experiences, allowed for emotional identification with characters, and contained language that flowed smoothly and best conveyed the idea or image to the child. No limitation was placed on vocabulary when selecting the books. Throughout the academic year teachers read stories aloud, followed by a variety of activities, while the control group received no special attention. The results of the study showed that the experimental group increased significantly over the control group in word knowledge, quality of vocabulary, and reading comprehension.[8]

Implications

The following implications for teaching in the elementary school classroom can be drawn from these four research studies.

1. A literature-based language arts program should begin in kindergarten and continue throughout the elementary grades.
2. A variety of rich and complex reading materials should be provided for children.
3. It is important that teachers consistently read books aloud to their children. Oral language activities—such as discussions of the story, role playing, or puppetry—should frequently be used as follow-ups to reading aloud.
4. Children should be encouraged and motivated to increase their independent reading.

SELECTING BOOKS FOR
A LANGUAGE-BASED LANGUAGE ARTS PROGRAM

When you recognize the significance of books and their language, selection becomes increasingly important. Approximately 2,000 books for children are published each year, and certainly not all are books of high quality containing language of high quality. The teacher must be able to distinguish between those books that are deserving of children's attention and those that are not. If a primary purpose is to select books for their language value, then it is incumbent upon teachers to become discriminating and knowledgeable about the language offered in books for children.

Metaphorical Language in Books

Metaphorical language is found frequently throughout books for children. Authors creatively turn the familiar into the unusual by comparing unlike objects or personifying the inanimate. The Caldecott Award Winner *White Snow, Bright Snow* is an excellent example of such creativity with language. In describing the effects of a heavy snowfall, Alvin Tresselt writes in metaphorical language:

> *In the morning a clear blue sky was overhead*
> *and blue shadows hid in all the corners.*
> *Automobiles looked like big fat raisins*
> *buried in snowdrifts.*
> *Houses crouched together, their windows*
> *peeking out from under great white*
> *eyebrows.*
> *Even the church steeple wore a pointed*
> *cap on its top.*[9]

Hearing and discussing language that is used in an interesting manner contributes to a child's own use of language. Merely exposing children to creative language by reading various books may not be enough. If children are to become aware of how an author has used language, a certain amount of discussion needs to take place. The imagery Tresselt creates may not be overtly noticed or appreciated unless attention is somehow drawn to it. Rewriting the passage in a reporting style and then comparing it with the original is one method of helping children understand the importance of using language creatively. However, paraphrasing a creative effort such as this should be done only to emphasize the effectiveness of such language. It should not be a technique that becomes a part of the daily classroom routine. The rewritten passage might be:

The morning sky was clear and blue with some shadows.
Automobiles were buried in snowdrifts.
Houses were covered in snow and their windows could hardly be seen.
Even the church steeple was snow-covered.

Older students may be asked to rewrite the passage and then make the comparison by responding to certain questions. An effective method for doing this is to pair students, have them read their piece of writing and then the original from the book. To bring these differences out in the discussion, the following questions might be asked: *How would you describe the language that the author, Alvin Tresselt, chose to use? How does this compare with the way you used language in your writing? If you want to visualize the scene in your mind, which piece of writing helps you the most? What is it about metaphorical writing that creates images?* As a follow-up to this discussion, students may wish to try changing the language of a recently written piece of their own writing. Or using the reporting of some event in a news article, they may want to try their hand at writing it more creatively.

A considerable number of books for children are available that offer the kind of creative language that we have been talking about here. The following is a beginning list to help you become acquainted with a few of them. As you review and read other books that belong with these, extend the list. More important, however, read them to your students, encourage your students to read them, and intervene at appropriate times to call attention to the interesting ways language is used.

Bourne, Miriam. *Emilio's Summer Day*. New York: Harper and Row, 1966.
Goble, Paul. *The Girl Who Loved Wild Horses*. Scarsdale, N.Y.: Bradbury, 1978.
McCloskey, Robert. *Time of Wonder*. New York: Viking, 1957.
Tresselt, Alvin. *A Thousand Lights and Fireflies*. New York: Parents' Magazine Press, 1968.

Repetition in Books

Young children enjoy repetition. They enjoy the rhythm of language when words are creatively strung together and repeated. They like saying and hearing rhythmical patterns of words over and over again, much as they enjoy repeating nursery rhymes. Actually, the activity of repeating refrains or rhythms can be described as language play. Children like the way particular words sound when they are put together. For example, "I'm in the milk and the milk's in me. God bless the milk and God bless me,"[10] from Maurice Sendak's book *In the Night Kitchen*, is learned and said repeatedly by children because they enjoy the sound of the language. The refrain is adopted by the child and hence becomes very personal. It is taken out of its original context and added to a storehouse of rhymes, jingles, and enjoyable word patterns to be conjured up during an evening meal, at bedtime, or on the school playground.

Books are excellent sources for providing the repetition children find so enjoyable. *Millions of Cats*, by Wanda Gag, is a favorite among young children. Its repeated refrain is especially treasured:

Cats here, cats there,
Cats and kittens everywhere,
Hundreds of cats,
Thousands of cats,
Millions and billions and trillions of cats.[11]

Numerous books for children contain repetitions and refrains. Become acquainted with some of the more outstanding ones, and be prepared to read them more than once to young children. When you come to the refrain in a book, encourage children's participation. Let them say the refrain along with you. Let them enjoy the sounds of language. You may want to start with the following list:

Banchek, Linda. *Snake In, Snake Out*. New York: Thomas Y. Crowell, 1978.
Brown, Margaret Wise. *Goodnight Moon*. New York: Harper & Row, 1947.
Gag, Wanda. *Millions of Cats*. New York: Coward-McCann, 1928.
Lindgren, Astrid. *The Tomten*. New York: Coward-McCann, 1961.
Piper, Watty. *The Little Engine That Could*. New York: Platt, 1954.
Preston, Margaret Mitchell. *Monkey in the Jungle*. New York: Viking, 1968.
Sendak, Maurice. *The Nutshell Library*. New York: Harper & Row, 1962.
Slobodkina, Esphr. *Caps for Sale*. New York: Scott, 1947.
Smith, Mary, and R. A. Smith. *Long Ago Elf*. New York: Follett, 1968.
Westcott, Nadine Bernard. *I Know an Old Lady Who Swallowed a Fly*. Boston: Little, Brown, 1980.

The Language of the Accumulative Tale

The language of the accumulative tale is closely related to the kind of language found in books containing repetitions and refrains. Children enjoy the built-in rhythm created by the plot structure of such a tale. Specifically, a pattern is established and repeated each time an event or character is added to the developing story. This continues until the climax or end of the tale. In *The Great Big Enormous Turnip*, by Alex Tolstoy, the old man finds that the turnip he planted has grown so big and strong that he cannot pull it out of the ground by himself. He first asks the old woman to help him.

> The old woman pulled the old man.
> The old man pulled the turnip.
> And they pulled and pulled again,
> but they could not pull it up.

Next, the granddaughter is called to help the old man and woman.

> The granddaughter pulled the old woman,
> The old woman pulled the old man,
> The old man pulled the turnip.
> And they pulled and pulled again,
> but they could not pull it up.[12]

When the three are not successful in pulling it up, others, one by one, lend a hand until the turnip comes up at last.

Accumulative tales are excellent for getting children involved in the language. Students can repeat the refrain together, "And they pulled and pulled again, but they could not pull it up." Accumulative stories may also be role-played by children or retold using felt characters and a flannelboard.

To become more familiar with the language and enjoyment of the accumulative tale, the following books should be helpful:

Bowden, Joan Chase. *The Bean Boy*. New York: Macmillan, 1979.
Duff, Maggie. *Rum Pum Pum*. New York: Macmillan, 1978.
Emberly, Barbara. *Drummer Hoff*. Englewood Cliffs, N.J.: Prentice-Hall, 1967.
Frasconi, Antonio. *The House That Jack Built*. New York: Harcourt, Brace, 1958.
Hogrogian, Nonny. *One Fine Day*. New York: Macmillan, 1971.
Zemach, Harve. *The Judge*. New York: Farrar, Straus, 1969.

Books That Lend Themselves to Conversation and Discussion

We have already talked to some extent about the value of discussion. Verbal interaction among children or between children and their teacher fosters the development of language, concepts, and ideas. Certain books for children invite conversation and discussion. In fact, an experience with books of this nature is incomplete if, after they are read, no conversation about them takes place. Books demanding discussion can be categorized in the following three ways: books requiring close observation and attention to detail; books having surprise endings; and books having several layers of meaning.

Books requiring close observation and attention to detail   An amusing book by Ellen Raskin, *Nothing Ever Happens on My Block*, [13] is an outstanding example of a book in this category. Chester Filbert claims that he lives in an unexciting place and yet, while he sits and ponders this, innumerable events are occurring all around him: a house catches fire, is rebuilt, and then struck by lightning; a thief is caught in the neighborhood; and a parachutist falls to the ground, landing almost directly on top of Chester. Happening after happening takes place, each completely unnoticed by Chester Filbert. The illustrations are a myriad of discoveries and demand more than one glance through the book. Asking the question, *What do you notice on this page that Chester doesn't?* can stimulate closer observation and enjoyable conversation that develops and extends children's language and thinking.

Books requiring close observation demand a keen eye and are few in number when we consider the quantity of books available for children. Therefore, you may want to become acquainted with the following:

Brown, Marcia. *Once a Mouse*. New York: Scribner, 1961.
Burton, Virginia Lee. *The Little House*. Boston: Houghton-Mifflin, 1942.
Hoban, Tana. *Is It Red? Is It Yellow? Is It Blue?* New York: Greenwillow, 1978.
———. *Look Again*. New York: Macmillan, 1971.
Kraus, Robert. *Owliver*. New York: Dutton, 1974.
Mitsumasa, Anno. *Anno's Counting Book*. New York: Thomas Y. Crowell, 1975.
———. *Anno's Journey*. New York: Collins, 1978.
Raskin, Ellen. *Spectacles*. New York: Atheneum, 1968.
Scheer, Julian. *Rain Makes Applesauce*. New York: Holiday, 1964.
Wildsmith, Brian. *Puzzles*. New York: Franklin Watts, 1971.

Books containing surprise endings   Have you read a book and been completely surprised by its ending? Or can you remember a movie with an unexpected ending and your total surprise at the finish? How do you feel when this happens? If you are like most of us, you immediately want to share the experience with another person. The same thought occurs to young children when they hear stories having surprise endings. Conversation about what has happened is spontaneous and natural. For example, reading aloud the book *One Monday Morning*,[14] children are surprised and delighted when they discover a boy's daydream about a royal family coming to visit him was all started while playing with a deck of cards. The chatter that begins at the end of reading such a book can be guided and extended by asking questions. Other books with surprise endings:

Balian, Lorna. *The Aminal*. Nashville, Tenn.: Abingdon Press, 1972.
————. *I Love You, Mary Jane*. Nashville, Tenn.: Abingdon Press, 1967.
DePaola, Tomie. *The Clown of God*. New York: Harcourt, 1978.
Holl, Adelaide. *The Runaway Giant*. New York: Lothrop, 1967.
Mahy, Margaret. *The Boy Who Was Followed Home*. New York: Franklin Watts, 1975.
————. *The Dragon of the Ordinary Family*. New York: Franklin Watts, 1969.
McPhail, David. *The Magical Drawings of Moony B. Finch*. Garden City, N.Y.: Doubleday, 1978.
Smith, James. *The Frog Band and Durrington Dormouse*. Boston: Little, Brown, 1977.
Spier, Peter. *Oh Were They Ever Happy*. Garden City, N.Y.: Doubleday, 1978.

Books having several layers of meaning   Some books for children have several layers of meaning and consequently different levels of interpretation. *The Velveteen Rabbit*, a long-standing favorite, is enjoyed by all age groups. Young adults recently adopted the book and have made it a popular gift item for close friends. The theme of the story has far-reaching implications, making it possible for varying age groups to enjoy and discuss the book. The following excerpt illustrates this point. The sawdust-stuffed Rabbit asks the Skin Horse:

> "What is REAL?" asked the Rabbit one day. . . . "Does it mean having things that buzz inside you and a stick-out handle?"
> "Real isn't how you are made," said the Skin Horse. "It's a thing that happens to you. When a child loves you for a long, long time, not just to play with, but REALLY loves you, then you become Real."
> "Does it hurt?" asked the Rabbit.
> "Sometimes," said the Skin Horse, for he was always truthful. "When you are Real you don't mind being hurt."
> "Does it happen all at once, like being wound up," he asked, "or bit by bit?"
> "It doesn't happen all at once," said the Skin Horse. "You become. It takes a long time. That's why it doesn't often happen to people who break easily, or have sharp edges, or who have to be carefully kept."[15]

Another book having several layers of meaning is *Crow Boy*,[16] a story frequently recommended for second-grade children that appeared in a basal reading series at the fourth-grade level. It is that kind of story—enjoyable and appropriate for more than one age group. Chibi, a small frightened Japanese boy, is not accepted by other children in his class. He gradually withdraws into his own world, and it is not until sixth grade and Mr. Isobe that Chibi is viewed by others as someone worthwhile with something to contribute in life. The book ends with Chibi being called Crow Boy, the change in name depicting the change and growth in Chibi. He is no longer the scared, withdrawn little boy who hid under the school. Huck[17] says that this is one of the few picture books for children that show character development.

Books such as *The Velveteen Rabbit* and *Crow Boy* stimulate provocative, sensitive discussions. They allow the reader or listener to confront the content of the story at a personal level and talk about it. The sensitive message and theme conveyed in each book makes it beg to be discussed. These books and others like them can make a significant contribution to the rich language environment of your classroom. If you are not yet acquainted with *Frederick*[18] and *Swimmy*,[19] or *John Brown, Rose and the Midnight Cat*,[20] you may want to get to know them, too.

ESTABLISHING A LITERATURE PROGRAM IN THE ELEMENTARY SCHOOL

The daily curriculum already seems to bulge at the seams with content and skill requirements. Teachers frequently complain about the amount of material that has to be covered and the short amount of time for doing it. Somehow, when the priorities get weighed, reading books aloud or independently falls at the bottom of the day's list.

How can a teacher be certain that time is provided to make books and language an integral part of the daily learning environment? The best insurance is to plan a literature program at the very beginning of the academic year. In broad terms, such a program means surrounding children with books and providing a wide variety of activities that make reading an enjoyable experience. In more specific terms, however, the following plan might be used as a guideline and source for establishing a successful literature program in the classroom.

Components of a Literature Program

Establish a relaxed and comfortable atmosphere for reading An attractive library center in the classroom can create an environment conducive to reading books for enjoyment. A rug, soft pillows, or maybe a comfortable chair or rocker, will turn the traditional reading area into a warm, cozy place for pleasurable reading. Think about the kind of comfort you want when you decide to spend an evening reading the most recent best seller. You certainly do not select a straight-back chair behind a desk. Many children have been discouraged because they have never found reading an enjoyable experience. Establishing a relaxed atmosphere that invites children to read just for the sheer fun of it is one step toward making readers out of them.

Make books freely and constantly accessible to children Within such a library center a wide variety of books should be available to children. The size of the collection will vary. However, a minimum of three or four books per child seems essential if children are to have a reasonable choice. New books should be talked about and continually added to the existing collection. Research shows

Paperback collections provide students with many book choices within the classroom setting.

that if a teacher introduces a book to children, interest in reading it is stimulated. If certain books, time and time again, appear uninteresting to youngsters, remove them from the shelves and replace them with books you feel will be more appealing. The most important thing to remember is to have books that children want to read. To do this and keep children's interest high, you will more than likely need to change the entire collection several times during the year. If there is not a library within the school, public libraries are usually willing to lend a number of books to teachers for their classrooms.

Provide time for children to read books As an elementary student, did you ever have a book taken away from you because you were reading it during a lesson in mathematics, social studies, science, and so on? If it did not happen to you, do you remember it happening to another student? Were you ever given time to simply sit and read that book you were so engrossed in? Frequently, the only reading children are allowed to do in school is related to content subjects and the basal reader. Children rarely discover that reading can be enjoyable, and many teachers seldom discover that their best readers are those who constantly enjoy reading. It may well be worth considering that children learn to read by reading, and children learn to enjoy reading by reading. This being the case, time allotted to reading books for pleasure is never wasted.

One method that offers possibilities for providing time in the classroom for reading is an "uninterrupted sustained silent reading program." What is it? It means that you set aside a certain thirty- or forty-minute time period each day for pleasurable reading. Children and teachers alike read books of their own choosing—or magazines, comic books, and newspapers can be brought in to give a choice of reading material. The point is that everyone reads! What about reluctant readers—children who refuse to read during this time? Give them a variety of books you think they can read easily and will enjoy. Some children may refuse for a while, but if everyone else is reading, they will join in before long. These children may first begin by browsing but will eventually be captured by material that they have found interesting.

Read books aloud to children   Children throughout the elementary grades benefit from hearing books read aloud. We know children's language is developing at least through age ten. Consistently hearing complex language of high quality contributes to this development. Reading stories aloud not only enhances language facility but also stimulates children's interest in reading books independently. Many will want to reread a book that has been read aloud to the class or may be inspired to read another book written by the same author.

A read-aloud program can be planned at the beginning of the year. First, a time needs to be set aside each day for reading aloud. Many teachers seem to read to children after the lunch or recess break before other work or activities are started. Second, books for reading aloud must be carefully chosen. Certain books for children simply lend themselves to being read aloud while others do not. Considerations about the appropriate age level, interest, and appeal of the book enter into the selection process. The size and quality of illustrations would be relevant considerations for picture books. The following questions may be useful when you are choosing books to read aloud: Will the story interest your children, both boys and girls? Is the sequence of the story easy to follow? Is the language enjoyable? Does it flow smoothly for reading aloud? Does the book avoid stereotyping? If it is a picture book, can the illustrations be readily seen by and shared with children as you read the story? Do the illustrations enhance the enjoyment of the book? Before reading a book aloud to children, it is crucial that a teacher read the book first and decide if it is suitable for the class. Familiarity with a book promotes a smooth, enjoyable reading and prevents stumbling over words or phrases. An excellent book can be ruined when it is read aloud poorly.

Conduct small-group discussions about books   Children who are not egocentric can readily become involved in small-group discussions of books. Paperback books are numerous and inexpensive. Several copies of the same book may be purchased for the classroom and read by interested students. A discussion of a book that has been enjoyed by four or five children can often be provocative and stimulating. For such a discussion to be productive, however, it is necessary that the teacher or students prepare questions about the plot, characters, specific incidents, or even the ending of the book. For example, an excellent book for small group discussion is Armstrong Sperry's *Call It Courage*,[21] a Newbery Award winner. The main character of the story, Mafatu, leaves his native island to prove his courage to his father and to himself. The author develops the character in many different ways by the end of the first chapter. The reader gets to know and understand Mafatu by hearing his friends talk about him and through comments made by his father, and certain thoughts and perceptions are revealed by Mafatu himself. Children, when asked, *How did you get to know Mafatu?* can identify an author's technique in developing a central character. Questions directed toward interesting discoveries in books can enhance the enjoyment and quality of a discussion; however, questions that consistently probe for recall answers about a story may create a test situation and destroy both the discussion and the book for children.

Make books memorable for children Enjoyable activities following the reading of a book can be effective in making books memorable to children. Formal written book reports are passé and it's to be hoped that they have seen their last days in the classroom. Required book reports probably have done more to turn children away from reading than any other single source. Art activities such as the creation of a wall hanging, mobile, box movie, diorama (three-dimensional scene), or series of puppets relating to the story or characters heighten children's enjoyment of the book. Much constructive, enjoyable learning takes place while doing such activities. Children must plan and develop a creative work—decisions have to be made about materials that will be used, how things will be put together or displayed—and throughout it all, language is a vital, living part of the process. Enacting a story is still another way of sharing and making a book memorable. Tape-recording book reviews or retelling the story from one character's point of view may be interesting activities. (A more extensive discussion of ways to share and interpret books can be found in Chapter 8.)

Make records, cassette tapes, and filmstrips available when possible Many schools provide listening centers for teachers to use in their classrooms. If not, a tape recorder placed in a corner of the room will suffice. Having such a center means that several children can hear a particular recording at the same time. You can make a recording of a story for children to listen to while looking at the book. More and more literature for children is being offered commercially on record or cassette tape—some with accompanying filmstrips. School libraries frequently order and store such materials for teachers' use. However, if you are interested in obtaining brochures or catalogs or purchasing literature-based materials for yourself, following are some companies which produce them:

Random House School Division
Department 0177E
400 Hahn Road
Westminster, Maryland 21157

Scholastic Book Services
50 West 44th Street
New York, New York 10036

The Viking Press, Inc.
625 Madison Avenue
New York, New York 10022

Weston Woods Studios
Weston Woods, Connecticut 06880

Planning and Using a Literature Web

Books are sources for numerous activities and experiences. For instance, one book may stimulate a discussion, a piece of writing, an art project, or a comparison with a similar story. The more planning that occurs to discover the possibilities of a book, the more able a teacher is to find and use appropriate activities that suit students' interests. A helpful way of planning the various activities that might surround one book can be shown in a diagram called a *web*. A teacher will not want to use all the ideas that are displayed in a web for fear of ruining a book; instead, a teacher will select from the various choices some activities that are appropriate for individual, small-group, and whole-group experiences.

The two webs shown in Figures 12-1 and 12-2 display possibilities for the picture book *Amos and Boris* (Figure 12-1, pages 308–309) and the Newbery Award–winning book *Bridge to Terabithia* (Figure 12-2, pages 310–311). The web for *Amos and Boris* was developed by Sibley Veal; the one for *Bridge to Terabithia* was presented in the periodical *The Web*.[22] As you can see, the webs differ in that the activities are categorized according to different headings. The teacher has the freedom to develop and organize a web in a manner that seems most appropriate for the book and its purpose. A web simply may be viewed as a visual mapping of the potential of a book, and particular activities are then selected from it by using one's knowledge of students' interests, developmental levels, and past experiences.

Poetry in a Rich Language Environment

Poetry, perhaps better than any other type of literature, presents the very essence of creative language. According to Huck, "Poetry is language in its most connotative and concentrated form. Each word must be chosen with care, both for its sound and meaning."[23] It is a poet's thoughtful and imaginative use of words that creates a poem.

Reading poetry aloud and sharing poetry offer students an opportunity to hear creative language at its very finest.

Selecting poems If we want children to enjoy poetry and the language of poetry, then we must first select poems that will interest them. In the past, required memorization has dulled children's enthusiasm for poetry. However, an inappropriate or poor selection of poems can be just as deadly. Reading condescending or sentimental poems to students may cause them to reject poetry. Choosing only the older, more traditional poems to share with students may also hinder a developing interest in poetry.

If teachers begin poetry at the level of the children's interest, they have a better opportunity of sustaining children's enthusiasm for poetry. The first task is to have students wanting to read, write, and hear poetry. After this accomplishment, a teacher can gradually introduce poems that raise the quality of children's tastes and appreciation. But first it's necessary to get them to like poetry.

Sharing poetry in the elementary school classroom Poetry may be shared in a variety of ways in the elementary classroom. Children can listen to poems on record or cassette tape, certain poems may be compared and discussed, or some children may wish to put poems to music. A teacher has the opportunity to be creative in how poetry is presented and enjoyed in the classroom. A few suggestions follow to illustrate the kind of diversity that is possible when sharing poetry.

Reading poetry aloud Poetry is meant to be read aloud, and poems containing the qualities of rhythm and sound are particularly enjoyable. The appeal of such poetic characteristics is well illustrated in David McCord's "Song of the Train."

SONG OF THE TRAIN

Clickety-clack,
Wheels on the track,
This is the way
They begin the attack:
Click-ety-clack,
Click-ety-clack,
Click-ety, clack-ety
Click-ety
Clack.

Clickety-clack,
Over the crack,
Faster and faster
The song of the track:
Clickety-clack,
Clickety-clack,
Clickety, clackety,
Clackety
Clack.

Riding in front,
Riding in back,
Everyone hears
The song of the track:
Clickety-clack,
Clickety-clack,
Clickety, clickety,
Clackety
Clack.

David McCord[24]

ORAL ACTIVITIES

Interview the elephants about their heroic rescue.

Discuss other ways Amos might have rescued Boris.

Share a time when you helped someone and it made you feel good.

Compare the shape of the boat and the shape of Boris. Stress similarities.

Arrange a choral reading of the attached list of poems.

Read some of the related stories, and compare and contrast.

Show paintings and sketches about whaling from *The Story of Yankee Whaling*.

Glue beans and peas on boards in whale shapes.

Make papier-maché whales.

Carve soap in the shapes of elephants, mice, or whales.

Make a ship model.

RELATED BOOKS TO READ

The Fables of Aesop: 143 Moral Tales
Andy and the Lion
The Lion and the Rat
"Stand back" Said the Elephant; "I'm Going to Sneeze"
My Friend John

ADDITIONAL ACTIVITIES

List unfamiliar words in vocabulary notebooks.

Using the *Third Junior Book of Authors*, find out what William Steig has done besides children's books.

Show filmstrip "Creating a Fable" from *English Composition for Children* (Pied Piper Productions, 1975). Create an original fable.

GEOGRAPHY

Locate the Ivory Coast of Africa on a map or globe.

Pinpoint the Seven Seas on a map or globe.

Show the typical migration routes of sperm whales on a map or globe.

Figure 12-1 Literature web (developed by Sibley Veal) for *Amos and Boris*. Books mentioned are listed as an appendix to this chapter.

WRITING

Write a list of items *you* would take on a long trip.

Write a paragraph about a good friend and what you like about him or her.

Write a journal that Amos might have kept.

Write another title for the story.

AMOS AND BORIS
by William Steig

SCIENCE AND MATHEMATICS

Make a chart on the characteristics of mammals and discuss why all the characters in the story belong to this group.

Make a transparency showing a size comparison between an average sperm whale and familiar items such as cars, school buses, desks, and classrooms.

Find out why whales must sound and live in water.

Find out how the sperm whale population has fluctuated over the years.

LISTENING ACTIVITIES

Listen to the tape of William Steig reading his own story (*Famous Author/ Illustrator Filmstrip Library*, Miller-Brody Productions. 1975)

Listen to a tape of the voices of hump-back whales.

Listen to a recording of *La Mer* by Claude Debussy.

DRAMATIZATION

Make the four characters into sock or stick puppets and act out the story.

Act out three scenes:
(1) The first time Boris sounds
(2) Amos finding Boris on the beach
(3) Amos and Boris saying good-bye

Pantomime the whole story.

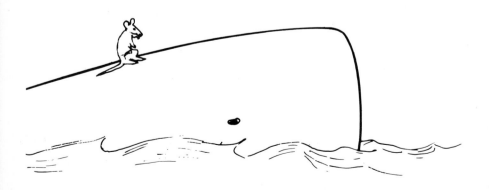

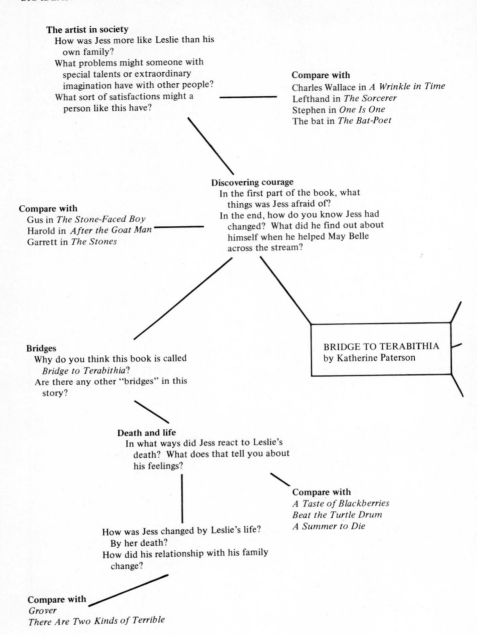

The artist in society
How was Jess more like Leslie than his
own family?
What problems might someone with
special talents or extraordinary
imagination have with other people?
What sort of satisfactions might a
person like this have?

Compare with
Charles Wallace in *A Wrinkle in Time*
Lefthand in *The Sorcerer*
Stephen in *One Is One*
The bat in *The Bat-Poet*

Discovering courage
In the first part of the book, what
things was Jess afraid of?
In the end, how do you know Jess had
changed? What did he find out about
himself when he helped May Belle
across the stream?

Compare with
Gus in *The Stone-Faced Boy*
Harold in *After the Goat Man*
Garrett in *The Stones*

BRIDGE TO TERABITHIA
by Katherine Paterson

Bridges
Why do you think this book is called
Bridge to Terabithia?
Are there any other "bridges" in this
story?

Death and life
In what ways did Jess react to Leslie's
death? What does that tell you about
his feelings?

Compare with
A Taste of Blackberries
Beat the Turtle Drum
A Summer to Die

How was Jess changed by Leslie's life?
By her death?
How did his relationship with his family
change?

Compare with
Grover
There Are Two Kinds of Terrible

**Figure 12-2 Web for *Bridge to Terabithia* (presented by Huck and Hickman). Books mentioned
are listed as an appendix to this chapter.**

COMPONENTS: A COMPREHENSIVE LANGUAGE ARTS PROGRAM

A BOOK LOOK

What does the seal on the cover tell
  you about this book?
What sense do you make of the dedica-
  tion at the front of the book?
What clues to the story are given in
  the chapter titles ("The Giant
  Killers," "NO!")?
Which illustrations do you really like?
  How does the illustration on page 92
  make you feel?

Create a coat of arms.
  What do your symbols and colors
    mean?
Map the terrain.

Chapter 5 and Chapter 12 have no
illustrations. Choose a scene in one of
these chapters and make an illustration
for it.

IMAGINARY KINGDOMS

Where is Terabithia? What does it look like?
  What are the "rules of the land"? What
  ceremonies and rituals are there?
Why do you think Jess and Leslie like
  to go to Terabithia?
What is imagination good for?

Create your own imaginary kingdom.
  What name would it have?
  Where could it be?
  What could you do there?

Other imaginary kingdoms
Narnia—*The Lion, the Witch, and the
  Wardrobe*
Oz—*The Wizard of Oz*
Prydain—*The Black Cauldron*
Earthsea—*The Wizard of Earthsea*

WORDS

Why does the author say things like "mad
  as flies in a fruit jar" instead of "very
  angry"? Can you find other examples?
Do Jess's parents use the same kind of
  language as Leslie's parents? What
  differences do you see?
What can you tell about the characters
  from the way they talk? What can
  you *not* tell?

Make up your own list of similes to
  describe how you feel, how something
  looks, etc.
Compare with the similes in *Jack and
  the Wonder Beans*

Write your own ceremonial pronounce-
  ment or prayer to the spirits of the
  grove.

Discuss other books that use
  language in a special way. E.g.:
  Enchantress from the Stars
  Carrousel
  Abel's Island

Humorous poems are fun, and children like them. Reading poems that bring laughter into the classroom not only enhances the enjoyment of poetry but also promotes a wholesome atmosphere. School should be a pleasant place where learning is an enjoyable rather than painful experience for children. Poems such as John Ciardi's "Mummy Slept Late and Daddy Fixed Breakfast" and the limerick "There Was an Old Man of Blackheath" will certainly contribute to this kind of learning environment.

MUMMY SLEPT LATE AND DADDY FIXED BREAKFAST

Daddy fixed breakfast.
He made us each a waffle.
It looked like gravel pudding.
It tasted something awful.

"Ha, ha," he said, "I'll try again.
This time I'll get it right."
But what I got was in between
Bituminous and anthracite.

"A little too well done? Oh well,
I'll have to start all over."
That time what landed on my plate
Looked like a manhole cover.

I tried to cut it with a fork:
The fork gave off a spark.
I tried a knife and twisted it
Into a question mark.

I tried it with a hack-saw.
I tried it with a torch.
It didn't even make a dent.
It didn't even scorch.

The next time Dad gets breakfast
When Mummy's sleeping late,
I think I'll skip the waffles.
I'd sooner eat the plate!

John Ciardi[25]

THERE WAS AN OLD MAN OF BLACKHEATH

There was an old man of Blackheath,
Who sat on his set of false teeth.
Said he, with a start,
"Oh, Lord, bless my heart!
I've bitten myself underneath!"

Unknown[26]

Listening to poetry on cassette tapes or records As mentioned earlier, a variety of commercial recordings of literature for children are now available; poetry seems to have received greater emphasis in the last few years. Therefore, not only is there choice, but the quality of such presentations is usually excellent. For example, a recording of "Over in the Meadow" may be obtained from Scholastic Book Services with an accompanying paperback book illustrated by Ezra Jack Keats. The poem is set to music; and by the third stanza, everyone who is listening is nodding to the beat. Here are the first few stanzas:

OVER IN THE MEADOW

Over in the meadow, in the sand, in the sun,
Lived an old mother turtle and her little turtle one.

"Dig!" said the mother.
"I dig," said the one.
So he dug all day,
In the sand, in the sun.

Over in the meadow, where the stream runs blue,
Lived an old mother fish and her little fishes two.

"Swim!" said the mother.
"We swim," said the two.
So they swam and they leaped,
Where the stream runs blue.

Over in the meadow, in a hole in a tree,
Lived a mother bluebird and her little birdies three.

"Sing!" said the mother.
"We sing," said the three.
So they sang and were glad,
In the hole in the tree.

Ezra Jack Keats[27]

Not all recordings of poetry for your classroom have to be commercially produced. You can record poems on cassette tapes for children to hear in a listening center, and children can record favorite poems for others to hear. Poetry can also be read and recorded with a musical background that contributes to the tone, mood, or rhythm of a poem.

Interpreting poetry through art Poetry is personal. What one person mentally pictures when reading the poem may not be exactly what another pictures. Therefore, interpretation of a poem through art is individualistic. Children may illustrate particular poems using a variety of media. When art materials are limited, creative work is limited. Supply children with a choice of materials: tempera and an assortment of brushes, water colors, materials for collage, pastels, and oil-based crayons, to name a few. Poems containing imagery or picturesque descriptions lend themselves to interpretation through art. For example, how might *you* illustrate the following poem? What media would best picture what you see in this poem?

FAR AND NEAR

Farther away than a house is a lawn
   A field and a fence and a rocky hill
   With a tree on top, and farther still
   The sky with a cloud in it gold at dawn.

Closer than dawn in the sky is a tree
   On a hill, and a fence and a field and a green
   Lawn and a house and window screen
   With a nose pressed against it—and then me.

Harry Behn[28]

Encouraging interest in poetry through popular music lyrics   Many older children, for one reason or another, have become disenchanted with poetry. Haviland and Smith comment, "How natural and harmonious it all is at the beginning; and yet what happens along the way later to make poetry to many children the dullest and least enjoyable of literary expressions? It is usually about fifth grade in our schools that children decide poetry is not for them."[29]

Because popular music lyrics appeal to children of this age, they may be used to stimulate or renew an interest in poetry. Lyrics from folksongs or popular rock music may be selected and typed copies given to students. Playing a recording while seeing the lyrics to a particular piece of music is helpful in making the experience more enjoyable. Students can be led to see how lyricists in actuality are poets. Content of some of our more contemporary poems for children often parallels that of contemporary songs. Both poets and songwriters frequently address the problems of society through their creative endeavors. By gaining an interest in poetry through musical lyrics, students may be encouraged to write their own poetry and set it to music.

Many other ways of bringing poetry into the classroom exist. The discussions of poetry in Chapters 8 and 10 on choral reading and writing poetry should add to your growing collection of ideas. And as a creative, imaginative teacher, you will think of many more on your own.

SUMMARY

A literature-based language arts program should begin in kindergarten and continue throughout the primary and middle grades. Reading books followed by meaningful discussions and activities promotes (1) a love for reading, (2) development of oral language and vocabulary, and (3) reading comprehension. Since over 2,000 children's books are published each year, the books should be selected carefully for the program. The teacher should plan the program to include a wide variety of literature experiences and activities that will stimulate students' learning and enjoyment of books.

APPENDIX TO CHAPTER 12:
BOOKS IN THE SAMPLE LITERATURE WEBS

Books Mentioned in the *Amos and Boris* Web (Figure 12-1)

Daugherty, James. *Andy and the Lion.* New York: Viking, 1938.

de Montreville, Doris, and Donna Hill. *Third Junior Book of Authors.* New York: H. W. Wilson, 1972.

LaFontaine, Jean de. *The Lion and the Rat* (Brian Wildsmith, illustr.). New York: Franklin Watts, 1966.

Shapiro, Irwin. *The Story of Yankee Whaling.* New York: American Heritage, 1959.

Spriggs, Ruth, ed. *The Fables of Aesop: 143 Moral Tales* (Frank Baber, illustr.). Chicago: Rand McNally, 1976.

Steig, William. *Amos and Boris.* New York: Farrar, 1971.

Thomas, Patricia. *"Stand Back," Said the Elephant, "I'm Going to Sneeze."* New York: Lothrop, 1971.

Zolotow, Charlotte. *My Friend John* (Ben Shecter, illustr.). New York: Harper, 1968.

Books Mentioned in the *Bridge to Terabithia* Web (Figure 12-2)

Alexander, Lloyd. *The Black Cauldron.* New York: Holt, 1965.

Baum, L. Frank. *The Wizard of Oz.* New York: World, 1972 (1900).

Byars, Betsy. *After the Goat Man* (Ronald Himler, illustr.). New York: Viking, 1974.

Cleaver, Vera, and Bill Cleaver. *Grover* (Frederic Marvin, illustr.). Philadelphia: Lippincott, 1970.

Compton, Ann Eliot. *The Sorcerer* (Leslie Morrill, illustr.). Boston: Little, Brown, 1971.

Engdahl, Sylvia Louise. *Enchantress from the Stars.* New York: Atheneum, 1970.

Fox, Paula. *The Stone-Faced Boy* (Donald A. Mackay, illustr.). Scarsdale, N.Y.: Bradbury, 1968.

Greene, Constance C. *Beat the Turtle Drum* (Donna Diamond, illustr.). New York: Viking, 1976.

Hickman, Janet. *The Stones* (Richard Cuffari, illustr.). New York: Macmillan, 1976.

Jarrell, Randall. *The Bat-Poet* (Maurice Sendak, illustr.). New York: Macmillan, 1964.

Kroeber, Theodora. *Carrousel* (Douglas Tait, illustr.). New York: Atheneum, 1977.

LeGuin, Ursula. *Wizard of Earthsea.* Emeryville, Calif.: Parnassus, 1968.

L'Engle, Madeleine. *A Wrinkle in Time.* New York: Farrar, Straus, 1962.

Lewis, C. S. *The Lion, the Witch and the Wardrobe.* New York: Macmillan, 1961.

Lowry, Lois. *A Summer to Die* (Jenni Oliver, illustr.). Boston: Houghton, Mifflin, 1977.

Mann, Peggy. *There Are Two Kinds of Terrible.* Garden City, N.Y.: Doubleday, 1977.

Paterson, Katherine. *Bridge to Terabithia* (Donna Diamond, illustr.). New York: Crowell, 1977.

Picard, Barbara Leonie. *One is One.* New York: Holt, 1966.

Smith, Doris Buchanan. *A Taste of Blackberries* (Charles Robinson, illustr.). New York: Crowell, 1973.

Steig, William. *Abel's Island.* New York: Farrar, 1976.

Still, James. *Jack and the Wonder Beans* (Margot Tomes, illustr.). New York: Putnam, 1977.

REFERENCE NOTES

[1]William H. Armstrong. *Sounder.* New York: Harper & Row, 1969.

[2]George A. Strong. "The Modern Hiawatha," in *Favorite Poems Old and New* (Helen Ferris, comp.). Garden City, N.Y.: Doubleday, 1957, p. 337.

[3]Alvin Tresselt. *A Thousand Lights and Fireflies.* New York: Parents' Magazine Press, 1965.

[4]Courtney B. Cazden. *Child Language and Education.* New York: Holt, 1972, pp. 121–125.

[5]B. E. Cullinan, A. Jagger, and D. Strickland. "Language Expansion for Black Children in the Primary Grades: A Research Report." *Young Children,* vol. 29, January 1974, pp. 98–112.

[6]Charlotte S. Huck. *Talking Inventory of Children's Literary Background.* Glenview, Ill.: Scott, Foresman, 1966.

[7]Carol Chomsky. "Stages in Language Development and Reading Exposure." *Harvard Educational Review,* vol. 42, February 1972.

[8]Dorothy H. Cohen. "The Effect of Literature on Vocabulary and Reading Achievement." *Elementary English,* vol. 45, February 1968, pp. 209–213, 217.

[9]Alvin Tresselt. *White Snow, Bright Snow.* New York: Lothrop, 1947.

[10]Maurice Sendak. *In the Night Kitchen.* New York: Harper & Row, 1972.

[11]Wanda Gag. *Millions of Cats.* New York: Coward, McCann & Geoghegan, 1928, 1956.

[12]Alex Tolstoy. *The Great Big Enormous Turnip.* New York: Franklin Watts, 1968.

[13]Ellen Raskin. *Nothing Ever Happens on My Block.* New York: Atheneum, 1968.

[14]Uri Shulevitz. *One Monday Morning.* New York: Harper & Row, 1967.

[15]Margery Williams. *The Velveteen Rabbit.* New York: Doubleday, 1926.

[16]Taro Yashima. *Crow Boy.* New York: Viking, 1955.

[17]Charlotte S. Huck. *Children's Literature in the Elementary School,* 3d ed., updated. New York: Holt, 1979.

[18]Leo Lionni. *Frederick.* New York: Pantheon, 1967.

[19]————. *Swimmy.* New York: Pantheon, 1963.

[20]Jenny Wagner. *John Brown, Rose and the Midnight Cat* (Ron Brooks, illustr.). Scarsdale, N.Y.: Bradbury, 1978.

[21]Armstrong Sperry. *Call It Courage.* New York: Macmillan, 1941.

[22]Charlotte S. Huck and Janet Hickman, eds. *The Web,* vol. II, no. 3, Spring 1978, pp. 28–30.

[23]Huck. *Children's Literature,* p. 386.

[24]David McCord. "Song of the Train," *Far and Few.* Boston: Little, Brown, 1952, p. 87.

[25]John Ciardi. "Mummy Slept Late and Daddy Fixed Breakfast." *You Read to Me and I'll Read to You.* Philadelphia: Lippincott, 1962.

[26]Unknown. "There Was an Old Man of Blackheath," in *Laughable Limericks* (Sara Brewton and John E. Brewton, comps.). New York: Thomas Y. Crowell, 1965.

27Ezra Jack Keats. *Over in the Meadow*. New York: Four Winds, 1971.

28Harry Behn. "Far and Near," *The Wizard in the Well*. New York: Harcourt, Brace, 1956.

29Virginia Haviland and William Jay Smith. *Children and Poetry*. Washington, D.C.: Library of Congress, 1969, p. v.

CHAPTER THIRTEEN

Language-Based Development in Reading

PREVIEW QUESTIONS

1 How does a child's own language fit into reading instruction?

2 In what ways does reading relate to the other language arts?

3 How is instruction in word-attack skills and comprehension handled within a language-experience approach?

4 How can some language experience be included with a basal reading program?

The content of this chapter, as in others, is based on developmental theory. Written from a psycholinguistic point of view, the text of the chapter focuses on the relationship among language, thought, and learning to read. Because the discussion in Chapter 13 is limited to the topic indicated by the title—"Language-Based Development in Reading"—only one method of teaching reading is addressed: the language-experience approach.

The following tenets are basic to this approach.

Reading is language: Goodman states that reading is language, in fact, that it is one of the four language processes: reading, writing, speaking and listening.[1] How we use oral and written language may vary, but the purpose is the same—communication. While speaking and writing are productive processes, listening and reading are receptive language processes. And in reading, as in listening, the primary aim is the comprehension of meaning.

Readers are competent language users: The beginning reader comes to school an able language user. The child is already an effective listener and speaker, demonstrating real skill in language. When confronted with learning to read, this same child brings to the task an ability to use and understand language. Goodman explains that children:

> . . . can process an aural language sequence, get to its underlying structures, and construct meaning. They are limited in doing so successfully only to the extent that cognitive development and relative lack of experience limit them. They have mastered the system of language, its symbols, rules and patterns. If they lack vocabulary, it is more a result of limited experience and cognitive development than a cause of lack of comprehension.[2]

The child's language strength cannot be ignored in the teaching of reading; rather, language competence, if understood and encouraged by teachers, becomes a primary means of helping children become proficient readers of their language.

Language communicates meaning: The purpose of both oral and written language is to communicate meaning. If children are to make effective use of their own linguistic ability when learning to read, their reading material must contain relevant and meaningful language. "Any attempt to reduce the complexity of language in reading by sorting out letters or word parts increases the complexity of the learning since it substitutes abstract language elements for meaningful language."[3] Any sorting out or categorizing must be done by children as they work out a systematic approach to the problems they encounter.

THE PSYCHOLINGUISTIC VIEWPOINT AND THE TEACHING OF READING

If we adhere to the basic psycholinguistic principles regarding the relationship among language, thought, and the teaching of reading, the reading programs in our elementary schools may need some alterations. In evaluating a reading program, we need to ask several questions.

Does the program respect and make use of children's language competence? Does the reading material contain natural sentence patterns that you would expect a child to use? Young children use sentence patterns that show a knowledge of language. Their use of syntax is not as complex as that of an older child or an adult, but they do not speak or write entirely in simple sentences. For example, a group of kindergarten children were involved in sand play. As you examine a transcription of their conversations, you can identify a variety of complex sentence patterns—sentences that are structurally similar to mature adult speech.

I've got two sets of people and they all live in one house.
Yeah, if we get more water in it, it will be soaked.
If I had a bucket, I could make a sand castle.
Dale and me and my friend in Richmond has the toad and it belongs to us.
I know how he feels because my sister and I had a toad before.

Young children's written compositions also illustrate knowledge and control of their language. A first-grade class enjoyed writing *I wish* poems that were later compiled in a book and placed in the classroom library area. Kim's poem, taken from this source, reveals not only her ability to use language but also some of her private and inner feelings.

I wish I had a guitar to play—
I love the way it sounds.
I wish I could go to my Grandmother's house.
I wish, I wish I was 23 years old
Because I would be able to live my own life—go where I wanted to go.
I wish my older sister was here.
But now she can live her own life.

Children bring much more mature language to the reading process than what is sometimes presented in commercially produced reading programs. It is important that the reading material reflect children's natural language patterns.

Does the reading program consider children's background of experience? Children's past experiences and their understanding of concepts are significant considerations when we teach reading. To give a child who has never been to the ocean a story containing such words as *jellyfish, starfish, evening tide, sand crabs, pier,* and *sandbar* may create some unnecessary reading difficulties. Both children and adults apply knowledge of past experiences to the reading process. Engineers have no difficulty in reading material concerned with their profession; but the average layperson, who has had very little experience in the engineering field, will find the same reading material difficult to comprehend. Even *sand* and *tide*—two relatively simple regular words—are difficult if there is no match with conceptual development.

Does the reading program consider how children acquire and use language when teaching word-attack skills? Piaget's studies suggest that "the line of development of language is from the whole to the part."[4] And psycholinguistic theory says that the teaching of reading must deal with whole, natural, meaningful language. Goodman points out that "the actual importance of any letter, letter part, word or word part at any point in reading is totally dependent on all other elements and on the grammar and meaning of the language sequence."[5] Any reading program strictly adhering to a decoding approach that requires children to learn first sounds, then lists of words, and finally the reading of sentences violates everything we know about children's acquisition of and knowledge about language.

THE LANGUAGE-EXPERIENCE APPROACH TO READING

Of all the many approaches to teaching reading, language experience offers many advantages in capitalizing on children's oral language skills and in developing a well-integrated language arts–reading program. Language experience may be the basis for reading instruction or a supplement to the regular reading program. Why?

We consider four reasons especially important.

1. *The content is meaningful, and thus predictable:* Children dictate and write about experiences that are meaningful to them. Suppose a class is having a cooking experience—for instance, baking cookies for a classroom party. The recipe is first written on a chart for everyone to read. The children and teacher discuss the necessary steps in preparing the cookie dough. These are then written below the recipe for everyone to read. Finally, while the cookies are baking, the children dictate a group story about the experience. This is copied by each child and placed along with other experience stories in a special book. The stories may be read to the teacher or a reading partner or perhaps taken home and read to a parent. The content of experience stories is meaningful to children. This is very important to note since past experience is so much a part of the reading process. Children are writing and reading about things they know and understand; and because the concepts and vocabulary are familiar, they can easily comprehend their own written language. Also, a key to making reading easier for the beginning reader lies in finding materials for initial reading instruction that are not only easy and meaningful, but predictable. Kenneth Goodman suggests that among the most important characteristics of early reading material is its predictability. Therefore, when students read material that originates from their own experiences and matches their own personal language, they are better able to predict the words as they read them.

2. *Children read their own language:* Because the reading material is dictated or written by the children themselves, the written language is their own. A student dictates a story or experience to the teacher, and it is recorded exactly as it is said. If the student says, *He be going to the store,* the teacher writes *He be going to the store.* If a child says, however, *I'm goin' to the stowe in the mornin',* the teacher would write the dictated sentence using the correct spellings. Children need to see their words as they will actually appear in printed reading material. Children's linguistic ability is recognized and used in teaching them to read. Children experience success at the very beginning of reading instruction. Because they use their language and their experiences, children can immediately read what has been written. They realize that reading is not some esoteric process only adults know about; they can actually see how language and reading are related.

An experience story begins with an experience—here, a walk through a nearby wooded area.

The teacher answers questions and points out things to observe.

Eating outside is part of the experience.

After returning to the classroom, the teacher meets with small groups of children to discuss the walk.

The experience story is begun as the children dictate to their teacher what they want to say.

A Walk In The Woods
It was a shiny day.
And we went out into the woods. We had lots of fun.
We saw a river. We went across the river on a log.
It was easy.
We left some bread for the birds to eat. And we ate a snack.
The river had some teeny, teeny fishes. All the way back we had fun.

After the story is completed, the children take turns reading it. Then the story is hung on a special rack in the library area to be reread later.

3. *The language-experience approach involves all the language arts:* Hall states, "The language experience approach is based on the interrelatedness of language and reading. Pupils learn to read in a communication context where reading occurs in conjunction with talking, listening, and writing."[6] When using language experience in the classroom, a teacher naturally integrates all four language arts areas, and each contributes to the development of the other.

4. *Reading is an active process:* The language-experience approach makes reading an active process. Children become personally and actively involved in reading. The students participate in a wide variety of direct experiences, conversations and discussions as a part of this approach; and they have many opportunities to write about those things that interest them. They find in their own individual stories and in group compositions that meaning is the essential element of reading. They formulate their own rules, seek out their own patterns, develop their own ways to identify unfamiliar words.

Research on the Language-Experience Approach

As part of the National First Grade Studies, a number of investigators chose to compare the effectiveness of the language-experience and basal reading approaches. Findings reported by Stauffer and Hammond show language experience to be an effective reading approach in grade 1, and children taught with this method excel in written communication over those taught with a basal reader.[7] An extension of their study suggests that it is also an effective method in both second and third grades.[8] Studies conducted by Hahn[9] and Kendrick and Bennett[10] also favored the language-experience approach.

Language experience has its limitations, and a teacher must guard against some of the inherent pitfalls. There is no manual or teacher's guide to follow. A teacher must rely on a knowledge and understanding of the reading process. It is certainly not an easy way to teach reading. A teacher needs to provide for individualized instruction, grouping children for needed skills, personalized record keeping, and continual diagnosis and evaluation of each student's reading capabilities.

Another pitfall is that learning to read may become incidental. If a teacher has children read and reread the same experience charts or stories, expecting the sheer repetition of words to teach students to read, it will not work. There is more to the language-experience approach than the mere reading of experience stories.

Teaching Reading Using Language Experience

Basic to this approach is the writing of experience stories. At first, young children can dictate their stories to the teacher, a teacher's aide, or a parent who has volunteered to help in the classroom. An experience story may be dictated by a small group of children or by an individual child. As children mature, they can begin writing their own experience stories.

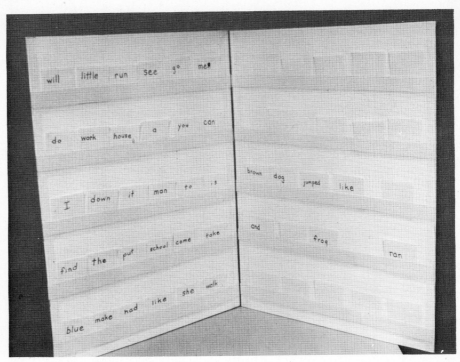

Word boards are easy and inexpensive to make. Children can use them to build and write sentences for their language-experience stories.

You can help children become independent writers if you provide special individual word boards and encourage their use each day. Printed on one side of the board is a list of basic sight words. Small cards containing the same words are slipped into a pocket below the printed words on the board. On the other side of the board, there are pockets and blank cards for children to write their own words. These are special words which they need in their individual writing. The small cards are taken from the board and strung together to construct sentences for the child's story. After a sentence is completed, the child writes it in a special storybook. The cards are then returned to the pockets as children prepare to build and write the next sentence for their story. As this process continues, children learn to use configuration clues, recognize that words and sentences are read from left to right, and find that language is related to reading.

Word boards are very similar to the word banks that are usually associated with the language-experience approach. Both help the beginning reader establish a sight vocabulary. Either method of collecting words, if consistently used, will contribute toward children's vocabulary development and ability to spell words correctly.

Basic sight words for children's word boards may be obtained from a variety of sources. You may want to choose words appearing frequently in children's group experience stories or words from their basal reader. The Dolch Basic Sight Word List[11] of 220 words has long been used and recommended by most reading authorities. It is still a useful list of words, but there are others that have been published more recently. The American Heritage List[12] is a highly recommended source, since the 500 words included in the list are those that appear most frequently in printed materials for children. Another good list, developed by Kucera and Francis,[13] contains 220 high-frequency words, 82 of which are not included in the Dolch Basic Sight Word List. It is shown here as one possible source that you may use in selecting words for individual children to learn.

220 Words of Greatest Frequency in Kucera and Francis's Study

the	here	since	home	war	before
of	between	against	small	until	must
and	both	go	found	always	through
to	life	came	Mrs.	away	back
a	at	right	thought	something	years
in	by	used	went	fact	where
that	I	take	say	though	much
is	this	three	part	water	your
was	had	her	once	less	way
he	not	all	general	public	well
for	are	she	high	put	down
it	but	there	upon	thing	should
with	from	would	so	almost	because
as	or	their	said	hand	took
his	have	we	what	enough	head
on	an	him	up	far	yet
be	they	been	its	two	government
each	which	has	about	may	system
just	one	when	into	then	better
those	you	who	than	do	set
people	were	will	them	first	told
Mr.	being	more	can	any	nothing
how	under	no	only	my	night
too	never	if	other	now	end
little	day	out	new	such	why
state	same	states	some	like	called
good	another	himself	could	our	didn't
very	know	few	time	over	eyes
make	while	house	these	man	find
world	last	use	school	me	going
still	might	during	every	even	look
own	us	without	don't	most	asked
see	great	again	got	made	later
men	old	place	united	after	knew
work	year	American	left	also	does
long	off	around	number	did	
get	come	however	course	many	

Children's experience stories can be written on large sheets of chart paper. They can then be taped to coat hangers and hung on a special rod in the classroom. Children can select their favorite stories, spread them out on the floor, and read them to partners or friends.

Students enjoy reading and collecting their own stories. Individual books can be made for each child's compilation of experience stories, or a teacher may choose to compile a book of classroom stories or poems. Each child submits a piece of writing to be placed in a large bound book. Books may be kept in the classroom library area for everyone in the class to read and enjoy.

Making Books

Books are easy to bind, and children feel that they are very special. They can also provide a purpose for children's writing. To make a book, fold the paper in half for the pages as in Figure 13-1 (A). Then sew along the fold with a needle and thread or with a sewing machine. If sewing the pages is not possible, they may be stapled together along the folded line. See Figure 13-1 (B). Next cut cloth or wallpaper one inch larger on all sides than the book pages. Lay the pages open and flat to measure as in (C). Heavy wrapping paper or contact paper may also be used for the cover. Then cut two pieces of cardboard about the weight of a shirt cardboard a little larger then the pages as in (D). Two pieces of dry mounting tissue are cut to fit and placed between the cardboard and the cloth cover material. If you prefer, glue works well also and may be spread evenly with a damp sponge. See (E). There should be some space between the two pieces of

Children can make and enjoy their own books.

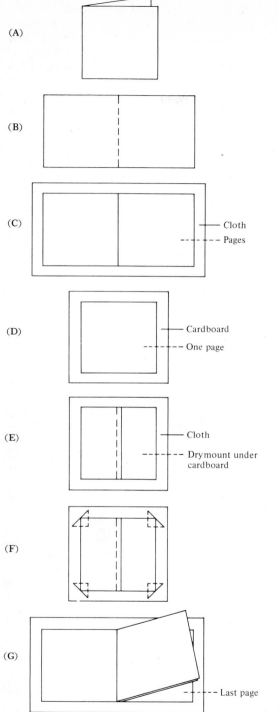

(A)

(B)

(C)
— Cloth
----- Pages

(D)
— Cardboard
----- One page

(E)
— Cloth
----- Drymount under cardboard

(F)

(G)
----- Last page

Figure 13-1 Binding a book.

cardboard to allow the book to open and close easily. If you are using dry mounting tissue, press with an iron in a few places to hold the cardboard in place. Then fold the corners of the outer covering in, fold the top down and in, fold the bottom up and the sides in, and iron or glue as in (F). The final step is to glue or use dry mounting tissue and iron the first and last pages to the cover, as shown in (G).

Using Wordless Books

Wordless books or books with very few words are excellent sources for stimulating children's oral and written language. These books were rare at one time, but today many are available, both in hardcover and in paperback. In her book *Literature and the Child,* Cullinan states that wordless books:

> . . . are used at many levels: very young children who do not yet read can tell the stories through the pictures, while beginning readers "read" them since they do not tax decoding skills, intermediate-grade students use them as models for story writing, and junior-high-school students use them to delineate the elements of fiction.[14]

As part of language experience, children may dictate or write their own text to accompany the pictures of a wordless book. As you read your students' story texts, you will notice variations. Children can look at the same book, and yet see and write about it in original ways. You may find that some students observe more closely and that their stories contain many details. Children's word choices will not always be the same, and certain portions of the story may even be interpreted differently by some pupils. You may also be aware of variations in sentence structure as well as differences in text originality.

Children's stories, such as those from wordless books, provide excellent opportunities for evaluation by the teacher. For example, considering the complexity of language, what can you say about a child's language development? Looking at various word choices, what do you know about a child's vocabulary development? Answers to these questions and others will enable you to plan additional needed experiences to improve the quality of a child's oral and written language. A checklist may prove useful as a more formal measure for evaluating and answering such questions. The appendix to this chapter presents and discusses a model checklist.

The following is a compilation of picture books that contain few or no words. Consider this merely as a representative list of books that you may use with students. A number of years ago wordless books for children were rare, but today, quantities are available in both hardcover and paperback editions.

Picture Books with Few or No Words

Aruego, Jose. *Look What I Can Do.* New York: Scribner, 1971.
Briggs, Raymond. *The Snowman.* New York: Random House, 1978.
Brinckloe, Julie. *Spider Web.* Garden City, N.Y.: Doubleday, 1974.

Burningham, John. *Come Away from the Water, Shirley*. New York: Thomas Y. Crowell, 1977.

———. *Time to Get Out of the Bath, Shirley*. New York: Crowell, 1978.

Carle, Eric. *Do You Want to Be My Friend?* New York: Crowell, 1971.

Carrick, Donald. *Drip Drop*. New York: Macmillan, 1973.

DeGroat, Diane. *Alligator's Toothache*. New York: Crown, 1977.

DePaola, Tomie. *Pancakes for Breakfast*. New York: Harcourt, Brace, 1978.

Goodall, John S. *Creepy Castle*. New York: Atheneum, 1975.

———. *The Midnight Adventures of Kelly, Dot, and Esmeralda*. New York: Atheneum, 1972.

———. *Naughty Nancy*. New York: Atheneum, 1975.

———. *Shrewbettina's Birthday*. New York: Harcourt, Brace, 1971.

———. *The Surprise Picnic*. New York: Atheneum, 1977.

———. *Paddy's Evening Out*. New York: Atheneum, 1973.

Hutchins, Pat. *Changes, Changes*. New York: Macmillan, 1971.

———. *Rosie's Walk*. New York: Macmillan, 1968.

Krahn, Fernando. *April Fools*. New York: Dutton, 1974.

———. *The Self-Made Snowman*. Philadelphia: Lippincott, 1974.

Mayer, Mercer. *A Boy, a Dog, and a Frog*. New York: Dial, 1967.

———. *Ah-Choo*. New York: Dial, 1976.

———. *Frog Goes to Dinner*. New York: Dial, 1974.

———. *Frog, Where Are You?* New York: Dial, 1969.

———. *Hiccup*. New York: Dial, 1976.

———. *One Frog Too Many*. New York: Dial, 1975.

Spier, Peter. *Noah's Ark*. Garden City, N.Y.: Doubleday, 1977.

Turkle, Brinton. *Deep in the Forest*. New York: Dutton, 1976.

Ward, Lynd. *The Silver Pony*. Boston: Houghton Mifflin, 1973.

Winter, Paula. *The Bear and the Fly*. New York: Crown, 1976.

Structured Language and Repetition

According to Emans,[15] "children may be able to learn to read naturally when enough repeated examples of written language are presented so children are able to extract necessary generalizations." Several research studies substantiate this statement. Carol Chomsky,[16] conducting a study in which children memorized stories by listening to them repeatedly on a tape recorder as they followed along in the written text, reports reading improvement. Also reporting positive results, Forester[17] suggests a similar process in which the teacher reads stories and nursery rhymes from wall charts. Finally, Hoskisson[18] reports significant results in using assisted reading for instructional purposes. He identifies three stages in assisted reading. The first stage consists of reading to the children and having them repeat the phrases or sentences after the person doing the reading. The second stage begins when the children begin to notice that some of the words occur repeatedly in the stories they are reading. In this stage the readers leave out some of the words they think children know. They have the children fill in the blanks left as they read. Stage 3 is entered when the children do the reading and the reader fills in the words the children may not know or may have trouble recognizing.

Memorization appears to play an important role in the process. "It may be," says Hoskisson, "that while children are memorizing the language, they are storing the meaning of the story. It is during this memorization phase that children must be working out what the words are."[19]

These conclusions suggest that an important part of an early reading program is reading and sharing stories. Applebee's[20] studies support and extend the evidence that stories can play an essential role in learning to read. His findings indicate that by the time children enter school, they have a firmly developed "sense of story" that influences their responses to new stories that they hear and read:

> Children's knowledge of the conventions of storytelling develops rapidly and finds expression at many different levels. These include syntax, word choice, and text structure, as well as such things as appropriate character types, settings, and events.[21]

Because young children have firmly established a set of expectations about what a story is, they possess a knowledge that can be applied in learning to read and comprehend stories. And this knowledge seems especially significant, since most formal reading programs are developed around stories.

Along with stories that are repeated over and over, rhymes, chants, jingles, and songs can provide additional sources of enjoyment. And because many children have already memorized their favorites, a teacher can begin writing them on wall charts, and individual booklets may be developed. They may be recorded on cassette tapes for a listening center or written on transparencies and shared on an overhead projector, or a favorite rhyme or jingle may be written on the chalkboard and read throughout the week.

COMPREHENSION:
READING AND RETELLING EXPERIENCES

Books are an inherent and basic component of any reading program. The teacher should read books to the entire class, to small groups, and to individual students. The classroom should contain a variety of good books and reading materials for students to read on their own. Given this environment, many stories will be read and reread by both the children and the teacher. Favorite stories that are enjoyed over and over again can provide the perfect motivation for storytelling.

Students can retell stories in small groups or record them on cassette tape for the classroom listening center. The stories may be retold as flannelboard stories, puppet plays, or brief dramatizations. Retelling experiences throughout the elementary grades enables students to sequence and organize reading content, demonstrate their knowledge and understanding of stories they have heard or read, refine oral language skills, and use new vocabulary in a meaningful context.

Teaching Recognition Skills

The beginning reader needs to develop a sight vocabulary. Repetition of basic sight words needs to be provided for the young reader. Word boards with experience stories read over and over again will help, but experience charts may be cut up and individual word cards created. Children can practice reading the words to partners, and finally, the words may be used to reconstruct the original story.

The beginning reader also needs to develop the concept that words are made up of letters and each letter has a name. What better way is there to learn this than by seeing your dictated words written letter by letter on paper? A teacher can easily discuss letters that spell various words in a child's experience story. Children's ABC books, such as *Helen Oxenbury's ABC of Things*,[22] *John Burningham's ABC*,[23] *Brian Wildsmith's ABC*,[24] and Robert Crowther's *The Most Amazing Hide-and-Seek Alphabet Book*,[25] also can be shared for learning and fun.

Phonics   Phonic instruction can coincide with the writing of experience stories. For example, children can look for words within a story which have the same beginning, middle, or ending sounds. If phonic generalizations are taught, only those which have high utility value should be considered (see research by Bailey,[26] Clymer,[27] and Emans[28]). A teacher should recognize that not all children will require the help of all phonic generalizations—the instruction should be personalized.

An inductive approach is best for teaching phonic generalizations. Have children look at a representative group of words that follow particular generalizations. After a discussion of the words, children can state their own generalizations.

For example, a teacher might say, *Look at the following words that begin with the letters kn. Let's read each of the words. What do you notice about the k in each of the words? What rule might we follow when reading these words that begin with the letters kn?*

knee	knife	known	knew	knack
know	knit	knock	knight	kneel

Context clues   Children need to be helped to recognize how context clues can be used to "unlock" strange or unfamiliar words. If a child does not recognize a word, the entire sentence should be read leaving out the unknown word. Using the context of the sentence, the student should be encouraged to *predict* the unknown word. The number of contextual clues appearing within a given sentence influences how accurate a child may be in making predictions. For example, consider the following sentences. The same word is missing in each. Why is it difficult to predict the missing word in the first two sentences? Why is it easy to predict the missing word in the third sentence?

I'm going to buy some _____ at the store.
She makes her own Christmas _____.
The _____ he drew were both aces.

Therefore, in the sentence below, for the child who is unfamiliar with the word *camel,* the context of the sentence tells the child that the word is a name of something that lives on a hot, dry desert.

The camel *lives on a hot, dry desert.*

The child should be encouraged to make predictions about the word. A teacher might say, *What animals live on a desert? What might this be living on a hot, dry desert?*

A form of the cloze procedure may help children understand the usefulness of context clues. Exercises, such as the following, may be given to children, or you may type their own experience stories leaving out key words for them to write in using the context of their own sentences. Students may be asked: *What words tell you the missing word? Why are these words helpful clues?*

Sue was _____ about going to Mary's birthday _____. She could hardly wait until Saturday. What should she _____ Mary for her birthday? Perhaps some_____ for her _____. Or maybe the _____ that she had been wanting to read.

A Model for Organizing and Teaching Skills

In order to organize the teaching of skills in a more systematic way, a teacher may find a model helpful. The one shown in Figure 13-2 provides a format for developing instructional or extension lessons to accompany a language-experi-

Figure 13-2
Model for instructional or extension lessons for a language-experience story.

Dictated group story

I like the circus because it is fun. My favorite part is the lion tamer and the lions. I like the leopards because I like cats. And I like the dancing bears and the horses, but I like the clowns best of all.

Word-analysis extensions

Context clues:

(1) Cover the word *dancing;* ask what other words might make sense in its place.

Phonics:

(1) Find the word *fun.* What other words in the story begin the same as *fun?*

(2) Find the word *bears.* Can you find other words in the story that begin the same as *bears?*

Comprehension extensions

(1) Reread the story. Ask each student to think of another title that would describe what the story is about.

Reading and language extensions

Oral language and vocabulary:

(1) The word *like* is used several times in the story. Let's read the story again and then decide what other word(s) might be used in its place but still have about the same meaning.

(2) Share the following wordless book: Brian Wildsmith. *The Circus.* London: Watts, 1969.

Have the students tell a sentence to describe the action in each picture.

Writing:

(1) Suppose we were to rewrite the first sentence. Can you think of another beginning sentence that would say about the same thing?

Other reading:

(1) Share the verse in the following book:

Jack Prelutsky. *Circus* (Arnold Lobel, illus.). New York: Macmillan, 1974.

ence story. Of course these lessons should be planned according to students' learning needs and abilities. To illustrate, one teacher used the model to create a lesson to reinforce and extend certain skills among a small group of students who had dictated a story entitled "What I Like about the Circus." You will notice that three major categories related to skills development appear on the sample model: (1) word-analysis extensions, (2) reading and language extensions, and (3) comprehension extensions. And subsumed under each labeled category are instructional or extension activities that pertain to the experience story. Using this model, a teacher may develop lessons for individual children, small groups, or the whole class.

COMBINING LANGUAGE EXPERIENCE WITH A BASAL READING PROGRAM

Reading in many schools today is taught using primarily a basal reading approach. If you are interested in language experience but expect to use a basal reader, there are effective ways of combining the two methods. Two are mentioned here—using the basal reader as a resource and using language experience as well as a basal reader—and you may explore other possibilities.

The Basal Reader as a Resource

It is possible to use basal readers as resource books along with the language-experience approach. For example, children can read a story from their basal reader and then retell it in their own words. This may be done by having students dictate the retelling or write it themselves. Children may enjoy writing new episodes or adventures for stories. The following are examples of individual children's telling of a new episode after reading a basal reader story. In this particular case, the teacher read the story aloud to a group of beginning readers. Then after discussing the story, they each dictated their very own. (If you are not working with beginning readers, you may want your students to read the story silently and then dictate or write their stories.)

GOING TO THE COUNTRY

In the morning Ting-a-ling and Soo Ling were going to see their cousins, but first they must get a good night's sleep.

Finally, it was morning and they were on the way. When they arrived at their cousins, it was time to go trick or treating. After that they spent the night with their cousins. The next day they all went to church.

While they were in church, Ting-a-ling ran away. Everyone chased around looking for Ting-a-ling. They found Ting-a-ling and chased her all the way home. They stayed for dinner. After dinner they talked. Ting-a-ling ran away again. The children cried and cried.

Teresa Fisher

LANGUAGE-BASED DEVELOPMENT IN READING

SOO LING GOES TO THE SEA

Today Grandfather and Soo Ling were going to the sea. They were so happy they decided to sing some songs on the way. Suddenly the car ran out of gas. It was a good thing they were on a hill. They went down the hill so fast that Grandfather lost all his hair.

Mike Kohlman

Each child's story was typed and placed in a special booklet. The teacher also included a few questions about each story on the second page of the booklets. The following day, the children were handed their booklets and encouraged to share their stories with one another. When the last reader had finished, the children asked if they could illustrate the front cover of their booklets. The reply was *yes*, and they went immediately to get a variety of art materials for their project. Later, as they cut, glued, and painted, the teacher moved from child to child discussing the questions on the second page of each booklet.

That evening the teacher read through the reading skills section of the basal reading manual and selected several exercises and activities that would be useful to these children. The next day the students found new pages in their booklets. One showed their original story with several missing words, as in the example below.

IN THE COUNTRY

Ting-a-ling was supposed to go to school tomorrow. He was not happy about going to _____. Ting-a-ling decided to_____ away. He thought the country would be a good place to hide.

It was 1:00 a.m. and Ting-a-ling _____ the house. He walked and walked. At last he saw the country. Ting-a-ling was very _____ and hungry. He didn't have any _____ and looked around. Ting-a-ling wished he was home. Just then he saw Soo Ling. He ran to her. Soo Ling smiled and took him_____.

The children read the stories silently filling in the missing words. They were instructed to read each sentence and then predict the missing word based on the context of the sentence.

Using Language Experience in Addition to a Basal Reader

A second way of combining the two approaches is to use a basal reading series supplemented with language experiences. For example, children can dictate or write experience stories about baking cookies, art projects, classroom visitors, handcraft demonstrations, model constructions, group dramatizations—the list is infinite. The stories may be read or shared, placed in special books for the library area, or written on large sheets of chart paper and displayed in the classroom. Students may also have their own writing books and word boards.

There are many ways to use components of the language-experience approach while teaching in a basal reading program. As you reread portions of this chapter and also learn more about language experience through additional readings, other ideas will come to you.

SUMMARY

In the psycholinguistic view of the reading process, some basic tenets are important for the teacher to understand: (1) reading is language, (2) beginning readers are competent language users, (3) beginning reading material should contain relevant and meaningful language, and (4) children's backgrounds of experience should be considered when planning a reading program. All four tenets are incorporated into the language-experience approach to teaching reading. A teacher may choose to use the language-experience approach for beginning reading instruction, as an integral part of the language arts program, or as a supplement to the basal reading series.

APPENDIX TO CHAPTER 13: USING A LANGUAGE-EXPERIENCE CHECKLIST

Figure 13-3 (on page 338) shows a language-experience checklist;[29] let's examine it in detail.

Consider the first category, *observable behaviors.* Here, five questions are explored: (1) Does the child observe the words as they are written? (Watching the words closely as they are written indicates a child's awareness of the relationship between oral and written language.) (2) Does the child pace the dictation to the writing speed of the scribe? (Such pacing indicates once again that the child recognizes the relationship between the spoken word and the written word.) (3) Does the child pause at the end of a phrase or sentence? (A positive demonstration of this behavior shows that the child recognizes the relationship between phrases and sentences in both oral and written language.) (4) Is the child able to give the story an appropriate title? (In giving a story a proper title, the child is demonstrating a knowledge of how stories are structured and also an understanding of the controlling idea of the story.) (5) Does the child attempt to read the story after the dictation is completed? (This last step allows you to identify children who have some reading skills or who are willing to try reading.)

The second category, *global language usage,* refers to verbal skills that are easily evaluated. This category and the next are based on the premise that the greater facility a child has with oral language, the greater ease the child will have in learning to read. Three considerations in language usage are evaluated in this portion of the checklist: (1) Does the child use complete sentences? (2) How many total words are used in the dictation? (3) How many different words are used in the story?

The third and final category, *refined language usage,* involves a more in-depth evaluation of the complexity of the child's language. There are four considerations: (1) How many adjectives are used? (2) How many adverbs are in the story? (3) How many prepositional phrases are included? (4) How many embed-

I. Observable behaviors:

  1. Watches when words are written down

(usually)	(sometimes)	(seldom)

  2. Paces dictation

(usually)	(sometimes)	(seldom)

  3. Pauses at end of phrase or sentence

(usually)	(sometimes)	(seldom)

  4. Appropriate title

(very)	(acceptable)	(poor)

  5. Attempt to read back

(most)	(some)	(none)

II. Global language usage:

  1. Complete sentences

(all)	(some)	(none)

  2. Total words

(31+)	(16–30)	(0–15)

  3. Total different words

(30+)	(15–29)	(0–14)

III. Refined language usage:

  1. Number of adjectives

(9+)	(4–8)	(0–3)

  2. Number of adverbs

(3+)	(1–2)	(0)

  3. Number of prepositional phrases

(4+)	(1–3)	(0)

  4. Number of embedded sentences

(2+)	(1)	(0)

        Total   ___ ×3   ___ ×2   ___ ×1

        Total points

        Grand total _____

Figure 13-3 Dixon's language-experience checklist.

ded sentences are found in the story? (For example, *The dog did not eat because he wanted to chase the cat.*)

Specific implications for instruction are apparent when you review a child's performance on the checklist. Low scores in the first category tend to suggest the need for more language-enrichment activities and exposure to stories before formal reading instruction. Low scores in the second category tend to indicate that language-enrichment and -development experiences should be an integral part of the formal reading instruction. Low scores in the third category tend to show a need for vocabulary-development and language-refinement activities as inherent parts of the formal reading program.

Look now at the total score on the checklist. Anything below 20 indicates that a child is not ready for formal reading instruction. A score between 20 and 30 suggests that a child can benefit from formal reading instruction; and a score of over 30 usually indicates that a child already possesses some reading skills.

REFERENCE NOTES

[1]Kenneth S. Goodman, ed. *Miscue Analysis.* Urbana, Ill.: Eric Clearinghouse on Reading and Communication Skills, 1973.

[2]Kenneth S. Goodman. "Effective Teachers of Reading Know Language and Children," *Elementary English,* vol. 51, September 1974, p. 824.

[3]Ibid., p. 835.

[4]Jean Piaget. *The Language and Thought of the Child.* New York: Harcourt Brace, 1926, p. 133.

[5]Goodman. "Effective Teachers of Reading Know Language and Children," p. 825.

[6]Mary Anne Hall. *Teaching Reading as a Language Experience.* Columbus, Ohio: Merrill, 1970, p. 1.

[7]Russell G. Stauffer and W. Dorsey Hammond. "The Effectiveness of Language Arts and Basic Reader Approaches to First Grade Reading Instruction—Extended into Second Grade," *Reading Teacher,* vol. 20, May 1967, pp. 740–746.

[8]Russell G. Stauffer and W. Dorsey Hammond. "The Effectiveness of Language Arts and Basic Reader Approaches to First Grade Reading Instruction—Extended into the Third Grade," *Reading Research Quarterly,* vol. 4, Summer 1969.

[9]Harry T. Hahn, "Three Approaches to Beginning Reading Instruction—ITA, Language Experience and Basic Readers—Extended into Second Grade," *Reading Teacher,* vol. 20, May 1967, pp. 711–715.

[10]William M. Kendrick and Clayton L. Bennett. "A Comparative Study of Two First Grade Language Arts Programs—Extended into Second Grade," *Reading Teacher,* vol. 20, May 1967, pp. 747–755.

[11]E. W. Dolch. *Teaching Primary Reading.* Champaign, Ill.: Gerrard Press, 1941, pp. 196–215.

[12]Wayne Otto and Robert Chester. "Sight Words for Beginning Readers," *The Journal of Educational Research,* vol. 65, no. 10, July–August 1972, pp. 435–443.

[13]Henry Kucera and W. Nelson Francis. *Computational Analysis of Present-Day American English.* Providence, R.I.: Brown University Press, 1967.

[14]Bernice E. Cullinan. *Literature and the Child.* New York: Harcourt Brace Jovanovich, 1981, p. 80.

[15]Robert Emans. "Children's Rhymes and Learning to Read," *Language Arts,* vol. 55, no. 8, November/December 1978, pp. 937–940.

[16]Carol Chomsky. "After Decoding: What?" *Language Arts,* no. 53, March 1976, pp. 288–296.

[17]A. D. Forester. "What Teachers Can Learn from Natural Readers," *The Reading Teacher,* vol. 31, November 1977, pp. 160–166.

[18]Kenneth Hoskisson. "Learning to Read Naturally," *Language Arts,* vol. 56, no. 5, May 1979, pp. 489–496.

[19]Ibid.

[20]Arthur N. Applebee. "Children's Narratives: New Directions," *The Reading Teacher,* vol. 34, no. 2, November 1980, pp. 137–142.

[21]Ibid.

[22]Helen Oxenbury. *Helen Oxenbury's ABC of Things.* New York: Franklin Watts, 1971.

[23]John Burningham. *John Burningham's ABC.* London: Jonathan Cape, 1964.

[24]Brian Wildsmith. *Brian Wildsmith's ABC.* New York: Franklin Watts, 1963.

[25]Robert Crowther. *The Most Amazing Hide-and-Seek Alphabet Book.* New York: Kestrel Books/Viking, 1977.

[26]Mildred Hart Bailey. "The Utility of Phonic Generalizations in Grades One through Six," *Reading Teacher,* vol. 20, February 1967, pp. 413–418.

[27]Theodore Clymer. "The Utility of Phonic Generalizations in the Primary Grades," *Reading Teacher,* vol. 16, January 1963, pp. 252–258.

[28]Robert Emans. "The Usefulness of Phonic Generalizations above the Primary Grades," *Reading Teacher,* vol. 20, February 1967, pp. 419–425.

[29]Carol N. Dixon. "Language Experience Stories as a Diagnostic Tool," *Language Arts,* vol. 54, no. 5, May 1977, pp. 501–505.

CHAPTER FOURTEEN

Integrating the Language Arts

PREVIEW QUESTIONS

1 What bases are there for planning a language arts program?

2 How can parents or other adults help the teacher to individualize and enrich language arts instruction for children?

3 How can a teacher extend one experience to include a variety of activities?

4 How can a teacher develop integrated language arts experiences?

Throughout this text we have emphasized the importance of considering what we know about how children acquire language and how they learn cognitively as a basis for planning classroom activities and structuring the classroom environment. The language arts involve certain skills that children need to learn and offer many possibilities for expressing individuality. The language arts also provide the basis for learning in a wide range of other content areas such as mathematics, social studies, and science. The ability to read, compose, and express ideas orally can be satisfying ends within themselves as well as means of acquiring and expressing knowledge in other areas.

The various aspects of the language arts are so interrelated that it is essential for teachers at each age level to plan a language arts program that is balanced. Overemphasizing one area at the expense of another often results in failing to accomplish one's first goal. We see this happening, for example, in reading programs which emphasize word-attack skills at the expense of language development. Children may learn to sound out words rather well, but their comprehension skills are restricted by their limited vocabulary and sentence structures. They do not become avid readers—readers who enjoy reading and good literature; rather, frequently they remain word callers. In a balanced program oral expression, written expression, and reading all have an important part. There is time for skills development and time for imaginative uses of language.

THE BASES FOR LANGUAGE ARTS

This text and the activities suggested in the various areas of the language arts are based on two areas of developmental theory: linguistic and cognitive. We have attempted to draw from these two theories implications for practice in the language arts. Thus, the language activities suggested are those that should help children further develop their language, and they should be appropriate to the children's levels of cognitive development.

Linguistic Bases

Research and study by psycholinguists suggest three implications that relate to planning language arts activities. One of these is the need for children to have a rich language environment throughout their elementary school experience. Although most basic language structures are known by children when they enter school, there are others still being acquired. The child's vocabulary is constantly increasing and becoming more and more refined. It is through exposure to rich and varied language that children acquire new structures and new vocabulary. The language of books and poetry is one rich source, but children also need to hear adults using language. Tapes, records, and personal interviews add to their contacts with mature adult language.

Another important implication from linguistic theory is the need for children to use language in a variety of ways. This suggests that children be given opportunities to compare and contrast things, to play with words and sounds, to categorize, describe, explain, and give directions. They must use language orally and in its written forms. Only through direct experiences with language can students learn about the changes one makes to fit certain situations. The teacher, knowledgeable about linguistic theory, helps children use language to express their own views to satisfy themselves and to communicate effectively with others. Situations in the classroom that call for using language in many different ways are very important and can influence all areas of learning.

The third important language concept is that language develops in a particular sequence although there may be great variations in the rate of development. Although differences in language ability are obvious in kindergarten and the early primary grades, they become even more obvious in the later grades. This suggests that teachers should provide a wide range of activities for children so that each child is challenged without being given tasks which are impossible to accomplish.

Cognitive Bases

The psychological bases for language arts activities are almost exclusively cognitive in nature. Our understanding of how children learn cognitively indicates three major needs for teachers to keep in mind when planning for language arts. The first is that children should be actively and physically involved in what they are learning, working with real, concrete, touchable materials. The more removed from direct firsthand experience the learning is, the more difficult or even impossible a task becomes. Children throughout most of the elementary grades do not learn well from reading about things secondhand. Their thinking and learning are best facilitated by direct, concrete experiences. Touching, observing, and active involvement are all components of this environment.

The second implication is for children to have a variety of experiences. These experiences should lead to divergent ends—not those that have some predetermined answer. These experiences should also present a real problem to be solved. Sometimes the teacher may ask a question or suggest, *What if . . .?* The classroom environment and the things that the teacher puts in this environment may structure the learning that goes on there. Children also should encounter experiences that are appropriate to their level of cognitive development. There will be many variations in the level of development within the same age group, and there must be experiences that will challenge each child at each level.

The third need is for children to make mistakes without feeling they have failed. Children, like adults, need to feel successful. This paradox presents a difficult but important problem for the teacher to handle. The key is that *trying* is the most important thing for children to do. Praise and encourage children for pursuing a reasonable approach, whether or not the approach works.

AN INTEGRATED EXPERIENCE IN LANGUAGE ARTS

A single experience often leads to many activities in the language arts reading area. Figure 14-1 shows a description or chart of what one class did after a visit to a historical home in their area. This chart may give you an idea of how interrelated the various aspects of language arts are and how one experience may be extended into oral and written language skills and imaginative work.

Some of the oral activities in this experience were specific speaking and

LANGUAGE ARTS EXPERIENCES AND THE FIELD TRIP

	Listening	Speaking	Writing	Reading
Visit to a Local Historical Home				
Making arrangements for the visit		✓	✓	
Previsit research and information with a discussion of highlights	✓	✓	✓	✓
Introducing the guide to the group	✓	✓		
Recording information in individual booklets—sketches and information and writings	✓		✓	
Expressing appreciation—to guide, parents, or others involved			✓	
Additional information—speaker and film	✓			
Follow-up activities				
Stories and poems about the house, the time period, the people, and so on			✓	
Making display model—of the home, of a single room, or of an interesting piece	✓	✓		
Mini-biographies of famous local people			✓	✓
Improvised dramatization of events in the home, town, or area	✓	✓		
Reading stories or events in that time period or of people from the area				✓
Choral readings	✓	✓		✓
Mock news reports of people or events in local area			✓	
Informational reports on objects, costumes, or events related to visit			✓	✓

Figure 14-1 What one class did after a field trip.

listening skill development, while others involved more imaginative uses of oral language. There were also many activities in written language—both reading and writing experiences. Some of these activities worked on skills such as letter writing and note-taking skills; others included more imaginative uses of the language such as writing mock news reports and reading stories of the time period.

The activities done in relation to this field trip show a variety of planning and follow-up work in a meaningful setting. Choices are provided so that children may pursue their own individual interests, and there are enough options so that each child may be challenged and still find activities that are manageable.

The table display shows the visible results of the learning that occurred through a variety of web activities about clocks.

Another method of organizing and integrating language arts experiences is through the process of *webbing*. This involves mapping a variety of activities that are related to one theme, topic, book, or concept. The final product, called a *web*, is a valuable resource for listening, speaking, reading, and writing activities.

Two webs,[1] one for primary grades and the other for the intermediate grades, are shown in Figures 14-2 and 14-3. If you were to consider either one for implementation in a class, you probably would want to select and initiate only some of the activities with your students. Conducting all the activities may cause students to tire of a particular subject rather than motivate and sustain an interest in it.

Also, as part of the selection process, you might think about the activities that are best suited for individual, small-group, or whole-group experiences. And when you are choosing activities, you cannot ignore what you know about students' interests, developmental levels, learning abilities, and backgrounds of experience.

READING EXPERIENCES

The Popcorn Book
Pancakes for Breakfast
Watch Out for the Chicken Feet in Your Soup
Peter Rabbit's Natural Foods Cookbook
Gustav the Gourmet Giant
The Gingerbread Boy
Bread and Jam for Frances
Stone Soup
Nail Soup
Smashed Potatoes
Munch
Kids' Cooking without a Stove: A Cookbook for Young Children
Kids Are Natural Cooks

FOODS
AND
COOKING

DEVELOPING THINKING SKILLS

Compare *Nail Soup* with *Stone Soup*
Brainstorm names of fruits and classify them by color, shape, or size

VOCABULARY DEVELOPMENT

Keep a word bank of food words
Record sensory words to describe fruits in the "grab bag" experience
Play the game "concentration" using names of foods

ART

Illustrate original recipes
Make designs with beans and seeds

WRITING EXPERIENCES

Write words for word banks
Individual dictation of original recipe
Cut out pictures of favorite foods and write captions for them
Write definition poems about food
Keep a daily record describing the progress of the sprouting seeds
Dictate a group experience story about the smells and sounds of popping popcorn
Each child names and writes a brief description of the "gingerbread boy" cookie

COOKING AND SCIENCE EXPERIMENTS

After reading *The Popcorn Book* pop popcorn
Using a sprouter jar and alfalfa seeds from a health food store, begin a sprout cultivation
Prepare and bake "gingerbread boy" cookies

LANGUAGE EXPERIENCES

Tell the story of the wordless book *Pancakes for Breakfast*
Retell the story of *The Gingerbread Boy*
Using a grab bag of fruit, share sensory experiences
Share original recipes

Figure 14-2
Web of possibilities for the topic "Foods and Cooking"
(adapted from a web by Debbie Swofford).
Books mentioned are listed as an appendix to this chapter.

LANGUAGE EXPERIENCES

Discussion of the topic:
  "Symbols: A Silent Language"
Discussion of the topic:
  "A World Without Symbols"
Sharing totem poles that represent
  chosen characters
Sharing a modern-day rebus story
Discussion of heraldry and the sig-
  nificance of a coat of arms

DEVELOPING THINKING SKILLS

Brainstorming new symbols to replace
  familiar symbols
Comparing Middle English and Modern
  English words
Brainstorming characters to be repre-
  sented on totem poles
Brainstorming the advantages and dis-
  advantages of picture writing
Brainstorming signs and symbols for
  the future

CREATIVITY

Develop symbolic name tags
Design a graphic symbol for the school
Depict a character on a totem pole
  using symbols that denote the chosen
  character
Develop personal cattle brands
Develop signs and symbols for the future
Create a family coat of arms

READING EXPERIENCES

Talking Hands
The Story of the Totem Pole
Heraldry: The Story of Armorial
  bearings
Handtalk
Signs and Symbols around the World
Indian Sign Language
Totem Poles and Tribes
Symbols and Their Meanings
Language and How to Use It
Sending Messages
Life in the Middle Ages

SYMBOLS:

A SILENT LANGUAGE

WRITING EXPERIENCES

Create a Middle English poem
Write a character description to accom-
  pany totem pole
Develop a modern-day rebus story
Write an advertisement that might sell
  your graphic symbol to the school
Write a description to accompany the
  signs and symbols of the future

Figure 14-3
Web of possibilities for the topic "Symbols: A Silent Language"
(adapted from a web by Nila Adair and Linda Shippey).
Books mentioned are listed as an appendix to this chapter.

TWENTY QUESTIONS TO ANSWER
ABOUT YOUR LANGUAGE ARTS PROGRAM

Considering how a language arts program should be planned and implemented if one understands the interrelatedness of reading, writing, speaking, and listening, what should one look for in evaluating a classroom program? And since language arts experiences should be developed on the basis of sound educational theory and a knowledge of students' cognitive and linguistic abilities, what questions are important to ask if one wishes to assess a program objectively?

Think of the following as a questionnaire that has been sent to you. How will you respond to each of the twenty questions with regard to your own language arts program?

1. Are students actively involved in their own learning?
2. Are the learning experiences designed to meet the students' individual needs?
3. Are the students' interests considered in the planning of learning experiences?
4. Is each student's level of cognitive development considered in planning learning experiences?
5. Are there many opportunities for students to develop facility with oral language?
6. Are there learning opportunities to help students become flexible users of language?
7. Are there planned experiences for concept development and vocabulary development?
8. Are there planned learning activities to develop and extend students' thinking skills?
9. Are grammar-based activities incorporated into the writing program?
10. Are listening experiences provided to improve students' listening skills?
11. Are discussions and sharing opportunities planned and conducted often in the classroom?
12. Are dramatic activities an integral part of the program?
13. Are spelling, punctuation, capitalization, and handwriting skills taught in relation to writing?
14. Are students given many opportunities to write, and are these opportunities accompanied by immediate feedback from the teacher to improve the quality of their writing?
15. Is the composing process considered an important component of the writing program?
16. Is there a proper balance between oral and written activities?
17. Are writing experiences purposeful and meaningful for students?
18. Do books and poetry play a significant role in the language arts program?
19. Are language experiences an integral part of the reading program?
20. Do you integrate the language arts whenever possible in your classroom?

INVOLVING PARENTS AND OTHER ADULTS
IN THE LANGUAGE ARTS PROGRAM

In a language arts program as highly individualized as the one we have suggested, it is often desirable to have additional help for the teacher. Parents, paid aides, volunteer adults in the community, and college and high school students may all help the teacher give more individualized attention to children. Such people may help in a very special way because of the unique skills they possess and the way each can relate to particular children.

Involvement of Parents

It is particularly important that parents become involved in their children's education—because of the effect on the children's attitude toward learning, because of the implied positive value of learning, and for the help provided the teacher. A child's learning is not restricted to five days a week or to the approximately six hours in school on each of those days. Children learn all year round and during all their waking hours. This learning may be enriched by the kinds of activities they do with their parents or older sisters and brothers, and the talk that accompanies such activities. Most parents are willing to help their children if they have some idea of what to do or how to do it. If you can give parents a choice of activities with which they are comfortable, they will work with their children. The following suggestions[2] should indicate the kinds of things you might ask of parents, depending upon the age and ability of their child.

Read to your child daily.
Help your child start a word collection of at least one unknown word daily.
Listen to your child read daily.
Take dictation (talk written down) of the stories, poems, and sayings your child creates.
Help your child pursue an interest and find five books to read on this topic.
Praise your child for at least one success daily.
Arrange for your child to use the library and visit bookstores or book counters to select his or her own books.
Help your child to find a listener to read to.
Allow your child to own books and educational games.
Listen to your child daily about his or her progress in school.
Let your child observe you reading.
Encourage your child to ask questions and help him or her find answers.
Broaden your child's experiences: take him or her to the zoo, park, museum, and so on.
Share newspaper and magazine articles with your child when appropriate.
Encourage your child to record his or her thoughts and feelings in a journal.
Watch special television programs with your child and talk about them afterward.

Parents can become involved in their children's education. This parent is assisting the teacher during a field trip.

Tasks Utilizing Parents and Other Adults

There are so many kinds of assistance that parents and other adults may give to help the classroom teacher in the language arts program that each volunteer should find something valuable to contribute. The following suggestions indicate some of the activities other adults may fulfill. As you develop your own ways of working with children, you may want to add to the lists or change items to correspond more closely to your needs and ways of working with your students.

Individualizing learning

Assist a student with some individual research.
Locate information books pertaining to topics that are being researched and studied.
Assist a student with mechanical corrections of a final draft of a composition.
Listen to a child read.
Read to a child or a small group.
Take dictation of children's compositions.
Read words or sentences for spelling practice or testing.
Help a child or small group of children with handwriting practice.

Assist children who are writing on their own with words they cannot spell, or provide other help as requested.

Go with a small group to an area on the school grounds for observations or experiments.

Work at a learning center.

Make books for children to use for their stories.

Make and play vocabulary games with children.

Special instruction or enrichment Numerous activities can be used as bases for listening, talking, writing, and reading. Almost everyone has some special ability or information they can share with elementary school children. Some possible enrichment activities might be woodworking and construction; arts and crafts activities; musical instruments; puppetry; film making; photography; knitting, crocheting, embroidery, appliqué, quilting; spinning and weaving; sharing special hobbies or collections; cooking; storytelling; bookbinding.

Clerical assistance Not all adults want to work directly with children; they may be more comfortable in lending assistance to the teacher in another capacity. There are numerous noninstructional jobs, and having someone else help with them frees the teacher to spend more time with students. Some require working at the school, but many can be done at home. The following are examples of possible clerical tasks: typing, printing or writing out materials, lists, and so on; collating and stapling; checking work and keeping records; preparing materials or supplies; making games and puzzles; mixing paint, clay, and so on; collecting scrap materials or picking up supplies; cutting out pictures or letters or mounting children's work to be displayed; and making booklets for writing.

Consider very carefully what kinds of additional adult help you may need and how you have organized your ways of working with your students. Then find out what parent or other adult assistance is available in your area and how it is arranged in your school. Plan how your students can best benefit from more individualization, an increased base of enrichment experiences, and help at home. Identify useful clerical tasks and how they might be efficiently done with someone's help. Make your plans with all these ideas in mind.

SUMMARY

A language arts program based on developmental theory provides for individualization and students' involvement in learning. A teacher will plan and implement a program that considers pupils' cognitive and linguistic development.

Because of the interrelatedness of the language arts, activities and experiences are planned to integrate reading, writing, listening, and speaking. How can one separate spelling from writing or listening from speaking? A planning chart or a web can be useful in developing and teaching integrated language arts experiences.

In a highly individualized language arts program, parents, aides, and volunteer adults can be of immeasurable help. Also, when the teacher works closely with adult volunteers, students' learning may be enriched.

APPENDIX TO CHAPTER 14: BOOKS IN THE SAMPLE TOPICAL WEBS

Books Mentioned in the Web for "Foods and Cooking"

Brown, Marcia. *Stone Soup*. New York: Scribner, 1947.

DePaola, Tomie. *Pancakes for Breakfast*. New York: Harcourt, 1978.

DePaola, Tomie. *The Popcorn Book*. New York: Holiday, 1978.

DePaola, Tomie. *Watch Out for the Chicken Feet in Your Soup*. Englewood Cliffs, N.J.: Prentice-Hall, 1974.

Djurklo, Nils. *Nail Soup,* adapted by Harve Zemach (Margo Zemach, illustr.). New York: Follett, 1964.

Dobrin, Arnold. *Peter Rabbit's Natural Foods Cookbook* (Beatrix Potter, illustr.). New York: Warne, 1977.

Gaeddert, LouAnn. *Gustav the Gourmet Giant* (Steven Kellogg, illustr.). New York: Dial, 1976.

Galdone, Paul. *The Gingerbread Boy*. New York: Seabury, 1975.

Hoban, Russell. *Bread and Jam for Frances* (Lillian Hoban, illustr.). New York: Harper, 1964.

Martel, Jane G. *Smashed Potatoes*. Boston: Houghton Mifflin, 1974.

Parents' Nursery School. *Kids Are Natural Cooks* (Lady McCrady, illustr.). Boston: Houghton Mifflin, 1974.

Paul, Aileen. *Kids Cooking without a Stove: A Cookbook for Young Children*. Garden City, N.Y.: Doubleday, 1975.

Wallner, Alexander. *Munch*. New York: Crown, 1976.

Books Mentioned in the Web for "Symbols: A Silent Language"

Amon, Aline. *Talking Hands*. Garden City, N.Y.: Doubleday, 1968.

Brindze, Ruth. *The Story of the Totem Pole*. (Yeffe Kimball, illustr.). New York: Vanguard, 1951.

Buehr, Walter. *Heraldry, The Story of Armorial Bearings*. New York: Putnam, 1964.

Charlip, Remy, and Mary Beth G. Ancona. *Handtalk*. New York: Nelson, 1961.

Helfman, Elizabeth S. *Signs and Symbols Around the World*. New York: Lothrop, 1967.

Hofsinde, Robert. *Indian Sign Language*. New York: Morrow, 1956.

Lyon, Nancy. *Totem Poles and Tribes*. New York: Raintree Children's Books, 1977.

Myller, Rolf. *Symbols and Their Meaning*. New York: Atheneum, 1978.

Schiller, Andrew. *Language and How to Use It*. Glenview, Ill.: Scott, Foresman, 1969.

Stewig, John W. *Sending Messages*. Boston: Houghton Mifflin, 1978.

Williams, Jay. *Life in the Middle Ages*. (Haig Shekerjian and Regina Shekerjian, illustrs.). New York: Random House, 1974.

REFERENCE NOTES

[1]The Web for "Foods and Cooking" was adapted from a web by Debbie Swofford. The web for "Symbols: A Silent Language" was adapted from a web by Nila Adair and Linda Shippey.

[2]Adapted from the Parent Committee of the Michigan Reading Association, "Parents: Help Your Child Read Better." Excerpted in *News for Parents from IRA,* vol. 2, no. 3, January 1981.

Acknowledgments

Harry Allard and James Marshall. *Miss Nelson Is Missing*. Copyright © 1977 by Harry Allard. Copyright 1977 by James Marshall. Reprinted by permission of Houghton Mifflin Company.

William Anderson and Patrick Groff. *A New Look at Children's Literature.* © 1972 by Wadsworth Publishing Company, Inc. Reprinted by permission of Wadsworth Publishing Company, Belmont, California 94002.

William H. Armstrong. *Sounder.* Excerpt from this Newbery Award Winner courtesy of Harper and Row, Publishers.

Natalie Babbitt. *The Eyes of the Amaryllis.* Reprinted by permission of Farrar, Straus and Giroux, Inc. Selection from *The Eyes of the Amaryllis* by Natalie Babbitt. Copyright © 1977 by Natalie Babbitt.

Harry Behn. "Far and Near," from *The Wizard in the Well.* © 1956 by Harry Behn. Reprinted by permission of Harcourt Brace Jovanovich, Inc.

Margery Williams Bianco. *The Velveteen Rabbit.* Excerpt from *The Velveteen Rabbit* by Margery Williams Bianco. Reprinted by permission of Doubleday and Company, Inc.

Ruth K. Carlson. "Carlson Analytical Originality Scale," *The Elementary Journal,* April 1965, pp. 366–374. By permission of the University of Chicago Press.

Carol Chomsky. "Stages in Language Development and Reading Exposure," *Harvard Educational Review,* vol. 42, February 1972. Copyright © 1972 by the President and Fellows of Harvard College.

John Ciardi. "Mummy Slept Late and Daddy Fixed Breakfast," from *You Read to Me, I'll Read to You* by John Ciardi. Copyright © 1962 by John Ciardi. By permission of J.B. Lippincott, Publishers.

John Ciardi. "Summer Song," from *The Man Who Sang the Sillies.* Copyright © 1961 by John Ciardi. By permission of J.B. Lippincott, Publishers.

Commission on English Curriculum of NCTE. *The English Language Arts.* With permission of the National Council of Teachers of English.

Roger T. Cunningham. "Developing Question-Asking Skills," in *Developing Teacher Competencies,* James Weigand, Ed. © 1971, p. 103. Adapted by permission of Prentice Hall, Inc. Englewood Cliffs, N.J.

Lee Deighton. *Vocabulary Development in the Classroom.* Copyright 1959 by Teachers College Press, Columbia University. By permission of the author.

Thomas G. Devine. "Listening: What Do We Know After Fifty Years of Research and Theorizing?" *Journal of Reading,* January 1978, pp. 302–303. By permission of the International Reading Association.

Wanda Gag. *Millions of Cats.* Reprinted by permission of Coward, McCann & Geoghegan, Inc., from *Millions of Cats* by Wanda Gag. Copyright 1928; renewed © 1956 by Wanda Gag.

Jack Hailey. *Teaching Writing K–8.* By permission of Berkeley California Instructional Lab, University of California—Berkeley.

William F. Herrnkind. "Strange March of the Spiny Lobster." Excerpt reprinted by permission of the *National Geographic Magazine.*

H. M. Hoover. *Return to Earth.* New York: The Viking Press, 1980. By permission of the Viking Press.

Leslie W. Johnson, "One Hundred Words Most Often Misspelled by Children in the Elementary Grades." Reprinted from the *Journal of Educational Research* (October 1950) courtesy of Heldref Publications, Washington, D.C. 20016.

Ezra Jack Keats. *Over in the Meadow.* Copyright © 1971, by permission of Four Winds Press.

Henry Kucera and W. Nelson Francis. List of 220 words most frequently used in English. Reprinted from *Computational Analysis of Present Day American English* by Henry Kucera and W. Nelson Francis by permission of University Press of New England. Copyright 1967 by Brown University Press.

Melvin Walker La Follette. "The Ballad of Red Fox," in *New Poets of England and America,* Donald Hall and Robert Pack, Eds. 1962. Reprinted by permission; © 1952, *The New Yorker Magazine, Inc.*

E. H. Lenneberg. "Motor and Language Development: Selected Milestones," in *Biological Functions of Language.* By permission of John Wiley & Sons, © 1967.

Myra Cohn Livingston. "Whispers," in *Whispers and Other Poems.* Copyright © 1958 by Myra Cohn Livingston. Reprinted by permission of Marian Reiner for the author.

Jean Malmstron and Constance Weaver. *Transgrammar.* Copyright © 1973 by Scott, Foresman and Company. Reprinted by permission.

David McCord. "Song of the Train." Copyright 1952 by David McCord. By permission of Little, Brown and Company.

David McNeill. *The Acquisition of Language.* Reprinted with permission of Harper and Row Publishers Inc.

Eve Merriam. "A Round," from *Finding a Poem.* Copyright © 1970 by Eve Merriam. Reprinted by permission of the author.

Eve Merriam. "Wake Up," from *The Birthday Cow.* Copyright © 1978 by Eve Merriam. Reprinted by permission of Alfred A. Knopf, Inc.

Lilian Moore. "Bedtime Stories," in *See My Lovely Poison Ivy.* Copyright © 1975 by Lilian Moore. New York: Atheneum, 1975. Reprinted with the permission of Atheneum Publishers.

Lilian Moore. "The Witch's Song." Reprinted by permission of Scholastic, Inc., from the book *Spooky Rhymes and Riddles* by Lilian Moore. Copyright © 1972 by Lilian Moore.

Robert C. Pooley. List of Elementary Speech Forms and Junior High Speech Forms Subject to Intensive Teaching. Reprinted from *The Teaching of English Usage* (1974) by permission of the National Council of Teachers of English.

Marjorie Kinnan Rawlings. *The Yearling.* Copyright 1938 by Marjorie Kinnan Rawlings; copyright renewed. Reprinted with the permission of Charles Scribner's Sons.

Henry D. Rinsland. List of 254 words of highest frequency from *A Basic Vocabulary of Elementary School Children.* By permission of the University of Oklahoma.

Marvin J. Roth. Teacher Competency Report of the American Association of School Administrators. By permission of the author, Dr. Marvin J. Roth, Selection Research, Inc., Reno, Nevada.

Sample of italic writing in manuscript and cursive from *D'Nealian™ Handwriting* by Donald N. Thurber. Copyright © 1978, Scott, Foresman and Company. Reprinted by permission.

Sample of traditional manuscript and cursive writing. Handwriting models are reproduced with permission of Zaner-Bloser, Inc., from the series *Creative Growth with Handwriting,* © 1975, 1979.

Clarice Short. "The Owl on the Aerial," *Western Humanities Review,* vol 28, no. 1, Winter 1974. By permission of *Western Humanities Review.*

Arthur Steckler. *101 Words and How They Began.* Excerpt from *101 Words and How They Began* by Arthur Steckler. Copyright © 1981 by Arthur Steckler. Reprinted by permission of Doubleday and Company, Inc.

Geoffrey Summerfield. "About Drama in England," *Elementary English,* vol. 47, no. 1. By permission of the National Council of Teachers of English.

Insup Taylor. *Introduction to Psycholinguistics.* Copyright © 1976 by Holt, Rinehart and Winston. Reprinted by permission of Holt, Rinehart and Winston.

Alvin Tresselt. *A Thousand Lights and Fireflies.* Four Winds Press, copyright 1965. By permission of Four Winds Press.

Alvin Tresselt. *White Snow Bright Snow.* Copyright 1947 by Lothrop, Lee and Shepard Company, Inc. By permission of the publisher.

Unknown. "One, Two," from *Poems for the Children's Hour.* Reprinted by permission of the Milton Bradley Company, Springfield, Massachusetts.

Andrew Wilkinson. "Oracy in English Teaching." Reprinted from *Elementary English* (October 1968) courtesy of the National Council of Teachers of English.

Evelyn Wright. "Wishes, Lies, and Dreams: A Pedagogical Prescription." Reprinted from *Elementary English* (April 1974) courtesy of the National Council of Teachers of English.

Index